Decline and Prosper!

Vegard Skirbekk

Decline and Prosper!

Changing Global Birth Rates and the Advantages of Fewer Children

Catherine E. Bowen, Editor

Vegard Skirbekk
Centre for Fertility and Health
Norwegian Institute of Public Health
Oslo, Norway

Mailman School of Public Health
Columbia University
New York City, USA

ISBN 978-3-030-91610-7 ISBN 978-3-030-91611-4 (eBook)
https://doi.org/10.1007/978-3-030-91611-4

This book was edited by Catherine E. Bowen

This Palgrave Macmillan imprint is published by the registered company Springer Nature Switzerland AG
The registered company address is: Gewerbestrasse 11, 6330 Cham, Switzerland

For Runa and Arvid
—of course!

Foreword

As I write in the summer of 2021, newspaper headlines are spreading worries about the looming crisis of shrinking population in high-income countries: Too few births will lead to empty schools and overflowing nursing homes, with no young people to care for the elderly. New census data from China and the United States shows falling birth rates; average birth rates have dropped below one child per woman in South Korea; and fertility in Southern Europe has been at "lowest-low" levels for decades. Prompted by these trends, journalists and pundits speculate about the dire consequences of "population stagnation." But the world's population is, in fact, still growing, and the United Nations projects that it will continue growing until at least 2100.

New worries about falling birth rates join ongoing concerns about the "population explosion" in low-income countries: Too many births will fuel rapid population growth rates, producing a wave of young people and overwhelming social systems and food sources. (Only rarely do policymakers or op-ed writers suggest jointly addressing these two crises by opening borders to migration; the unpopularity of this solution points to the continued centrality of national identities in the construction of demographic problems.)

Stories about population stagnation or population explosion are compelling because they show the connection between large-scale population processes and the most intimate of personal decisions, whether and when to have a child. Most of us are raised by parents and, despite falling birth rates, most people will eventually become parents. The parent-child relationship is the first emotional connection we make in childhood and, for many, the most intense relationship of adulthood. Parenthood as a social role carries cultural meaning that is reinforced by friends, families, and social structures; parenthood plays a key part in defining gender identity and is central to many religious, ethnic, and national identities. Like all social behaviors, childbearing is shaped by social influences and constrained by social boundaries. And, conversely, our individual decisions about childbearing add up to produce social patterns and alter social systems.

The demographic study of fertility links individual and population-level approaches to study childbearing. The demographic approach begins with description of the basic biological determinants of childbearing; proceeds to the measurement and definition of fertility at the individual and population levels; and quantifies the relationship between birth rates and the size, growth, and structure of populations. Demographers use these tools to study why fertility varies across different population subgroups and to predict how birth rates evolve over time.

Demographic methods confirm the intuition that birth rates are a core determinant of population "stagnation" and "explosion." But, somewhat less intuitively, death rates are equally consequential for both. Take, for example, population aging, a key concern associated with stagnation. A population is described as "aging" when the older-age population is growing faster than the working-age population, which can mean that there are too few young people to economically support or provide care for older people who need it. But population aging is caused as much (if not more) by improved mortality at older ages as by falling birth rates. Similarly, improvements in child health and the resulting precipitous decline in child mortality, not just birth rates, are a main driver of rapid population growth.

Yet concerns about population stagnation or population explosion rarely focus on the role of reduced mortality. Instead, authors and policymakers worry about births: how to get women to control their childbearing or how to get them to prioritize childbearing over other competing demands on their time and resources. The focus on birth rates, and the corresponding lack of attention to death rates, is in part because improved mortality is an unequivocal good—we all want to live a longer and healthier life, and governments want it for their citizens. Motivations for childbearing, in contrast, are more mixed. For parents, children bring joy (at least some of the time), connections to friends and family, and, potentially, support in old age. But children also demand time, energy, and money. These demands on parents have increased as growing economic inequality in much of the world makes the pressure to invest in children's education and training more intense. For governments, children mean larger populations, which can increase military might, economic production, and innovation, but also aggravate demand for social services, infrastructure, and environmental resources. The childbearing goals of (potential) parents may be out of alignment with the population goals of national governments, and national population goals may conflict with international consensus. As a result, birth rates are contested terrain.

In *Decline and Prosper*, Vegard Skirbekk brings reason and data to bear in this contested terrain. Skirbekk provides a comprehensive, thoughtful, and readable overview of the broad scope of demographic research on fertility, with the goal of explaining why lower birth rates, at the population level, are not harmful and may be beneficial. He begins with the nuts and bolts—how demographers define and measure birth rates, the sources of data they draw on, and the demographic accounting that links birth rates with population size and structure. Skirbekk touches on the biology of human fertility and biological limits on the maximum number of children. He then describes how actual birth rates have fluctuated over the course of human history, from the early hunter-gatherers to what demographers call the "First Demographic Transition," the beginning of deliberate family planning in the nineteenth century. Skirbekk discusses the two most prominent population "problems" of the past century, rapid population growth in low-income countries, and the current turn toward potentially shrinking populations. He cogently explains both the demographic phenomena and the social and geopolitical contexts that frame them as "problems," highlighting the ways that social structures and government policies can mitigate the potential negative consequences associated with particular levels of fertility.

Decline and Prosper spotlights the individual-level impacts of demographic phenomena and the human motivations that drive them. Skirbekk addresses the persistent relationship between education and fertility, especially how children are connected to social and economic status; the close connection between stable partnerships and childbearing; the role of religion in promoting higher birth rates; and the consequences of increased childlessness for individuals and societies. In so doing, he makes clear that high or low birth rates are not, in themselves, good or bad. Rather, the impact of fertility, both for populations and for individuals, is determined by the way childbearing intersects with education, work, family structure, health care, and social safety nets.

Skirbekk emphasizes the active role that governments can take in addressing the *impacts* of fertility. He also illustrates the limitations of governmental attempts to control the *level* of fertility. Policies to raise birth rates have had at most small and short-term effects. Policies to reduce birth rates have been somewhat more successful, especially when they work by meeting existing demand for contraception, but substantial declines in fertility have rarely taken place without sustained and substantial social and economic change. Top-down efforts to change fertility levels can veer into coercion or enforce racist hierarchies. Skirbekk's argument that governments can best address demographic challenges by enacting policies that help individuals have and raise the number of children they want is a needed counterpoint to the sometimes hyperbolic discourse on population stagnation and population explosion. *Decline and Prosper* is both a balanced, inviting, and reliable introduction for the lay reader and a useful summary for the expert.

Sarah Hayford
Professor, Director of the Institute
for Population Research and
Director of Graduate Studies
Department of Sociology
Ohio State University
Columbus, USA

Preface

Globally, women are having about half the number of children they had just fifty years ago. The decline in global fertility is expected to continue and there is no reason to believe that fertility will rebound in countries where it is already low. Discourse surrounding the new normal of low fertility is often dramatic, if not alarmist. While the discourse used to be centered around the negative consequences of "population explosion" just a few decades ago, now the discourse in many countries revolves around the threat of the "baby bust" as a "time bomb" which will lead to a "grey tsunami" of older people in the population and even "population collapse." At the time of writing, Elon Musk and Jack Ma had recently proclaimed that low fertility was in fact the worst problem of our time. Existing books on fertility, such as *Empty Planet: The Shock of Global Population Decline* by Darrel Bricker and John Ibbitson, have likewise tended to catastrophize low fertility. The drivers of fertility are often misunderstood and misrepresented. In many settings, postponing or foregoing childbearing is seen as a personal failure or selfishness, as opposed to the result of informed choice or systemic constraints.

Politicians in the low fertility countries are quick to take credit whenever fertility increases, even though the increase probably would have happened anyway. Egg freezing and other forms of assisted reproductive technology have been promoted as ways women can postpone fertility without foregoing a career, but the high failure rates—particularly after age 40—are often undiscussed.

In light of the passionate, yet often unscientific discussion about fertility and its importance for the future of our planet and our species, a comprehensive and evidence-based examination of fertility is needed now more than ever before. There is a need to view current fertility within a greater biological, sociocultural, and historical context, and more thoroughly consider its causes and its consequences. Doomsday prophecies about low fertility as the harbinger of economic and societal collapse need to be tempered by adequate recognition of its benefits, and false assumptions must be corrected. The spread of low fertility is largely the product of what most people would consider improvements in the human condition: the expansion of education, greater gender equality, lower child mortality, better social safety nets, and vastly increased reproductive autonomy and control. Yet, low fertility is seldom celebrated as the accomplishment that it really is. Fertility decline has certainly come along with new challenges, such as the increasing prevalence of involuntary childlessness in the world's richer countries and a need to re-think the structure of social security systems due to population aging. But it has also come along with greater gender equality and the possibility to invest more resources in children's health and education, and likely contributes to less violence and crime. Given human's enormous impact on the environment, relatively low human fertility may well be essential for the continuation of life on Earth. Population aging—one of the most feared negative consequences of low fertility—is not nearly as disastrous as many people presume.

This book reflects my attempt to provide such a comprehensive and evidence-based overview of global fertility. I aim to introduce readers to scientific research on fertility in all its breadth and complexity. This includes providing readers with a basic understanding of how fertility is studied and how research results can be (mis)interpreted. Fertility is a very broad field, including topics as varied as the childbearing patterns of early humans, the biology of reproduction, human evolution, gender roles, the effect of family planning programs, the environmental consequences of population growth, public health, and government policy. Scientists interested in fertility, however, are often highly specialized. They typically focus on concepts and models specific to their own particular discipline with the aim of publishing their results in an academic journal that is read, primarily, by researchers working in the same field. Real-life fertility is, however, both caused by and affects factors that overlap disciplinary boundaries. Drivers of fertility include, for instance, sociocultural factors such as education, religion, and gender roles; economic factors such as recessions, job opportunities for young people, and the costs of housing and raising a family; biological factors such as age, semen quality, and the age of menarche; and, of course, contraception and assisted reproductive technologies. These different factors act simultaneously, evolve over time, and constantly interact with one another. I therefore believe there is much to be gained by taking a more holistic view. This book brings together key results from many different disciplines and covers a diverse array of subtopics studied within the field of fertility. Some readers will no doubt find my attempt to integrate everything we know about fertility into just one book overly ambitious, and lament that in attempting to cover everything I can only pay lip service to the nuances and complexities of each topic and perspective. I maintain that the breadth of this book is, in fact, its unique strength.

Fertility is a highly emotional and politicized subject. I therefore wish to clarify that this book concerns fertility *on the population level*, that is, average fertility behavior. Lower fertility on the population level does not preclude some individuals from having a lot of children, just as higher fertility on the population level does not preclude some individuals from remaining childless or having just one child. Thus, while I argue that low—but not too low—fertility is generally best for societies and for the globe as a whole, it is not my intention to make prescriptive statements about how many children each individual person "should" have. I strongly believe that people should be empowered to realize their own personal fertility preferences, and that societies should not only accept but also work hard to make life meaningful and pleasurable for people regardless of their family size. I also think that people should be empowered to make *informed* reproductive choices. To this end, I hope that this book might make some small contribution. In particular, I hope that this book will draw attention to the importance of education, contraception, and reproductive autonomy for our collective future. It is in our own best interest to ensure that every person, everywhere in the world, has access to quality education, affordable and effective contraception, the right and confidence to decide whether and when to have a(nother) child, and fully understand the consequences of their decisions.

Oslo, Norway Vegard Skirbekk

Acknowledgments

Writing a comprehensive book about fertility is a daunting task, even for a seasoned demographer. It has been an extremely long process which often tried my infamously limited patience. Delving into new fields of research, navigating dead-ends, and revising the manuscript literally hundreds of times often exhausted my batteries, but it has also given me great joy and pleasure. In the end, it has been the single most rewarding academic exercise I have ever had.

This book would never have been possible on my own, and I am extremely grateful for all of the support I have received. I am hugely grateful to my editor Catherine Bowen for working with me through landslides and earthquakes, and for finding a way forward on many occasions. Katie polished, reorganized, and worked through all text, graphs, and logic. The materials she received from me were anything but complete, yet she was able to make the text accessible, structured, and fluent thanks to her brilliant, hard-working, and perfectionist character. Without Katie, there would be no book.

A number of individuals provided support on particular topics or aspects of this book. I thank Guido Alfani at Bocconi University for historical insights and publishing advice—a book provides much more freedom than a journal article. I thank Martin Dribe at Lund University for his support and Neil Cummins at the London School of Economics for excellent insights and advice. I am grateful to Bernardo Queiroz at Belo Horizonte University for his work on Latin America, Martin Kolk at the Stockholm University Demography Unit for his understanding of Scandinavian fertility patterns, and K. S. James at the International Institute for Population Sciences in Mumbai for his insights on South Asia. I am thankful to Hiro Ogawa and Riki Matsukura at Nihon University for their insights on Japan (Japan now has more dogs than babies!). I thank the Frisch Centre and Bernt Bratsberg and Ole Røgeberg in particular for helping me to better understand the relationships between fertility and labor markets. I am indebted to Brian Grim at the Religious Forum and Business Foundation and Gina Zurlo at the Gordon-Conwell Theological Seminary for helping me better understand the relationships between global fertility dynamics and religion, and also for our collaboration regarding global religious change. I thank Muhammed Asif Wazir at the United Nations for helping me understand the impact of religion on fertility in Pakistan. A big thank you also goes to Susana Adamo and Alex De Sherbenin at Columbia University's Earth Institute for helping me understand the links between climate change and demography (I thought I had it all figured out—before I met you!). I thank Wenke Apt at the Institute for Innovation and Technology Berlin for motivation and for policy insights—the modern world needs your type of broad skills. I thank Matthew Cantele at the University of Melbourne, and Kåre Bævre and Fredrik Swift at the Centre for Fertility and Health in Oslo for their help with this book. I thank Krystian Fejkel at the Cracow School of Economics for creating neat figures.

I would also like to acknowledge a number of people who have inspired and supported me over the course of my career. Thank you in particular to Ursula Staudinger, now President of the Technical University Dresden, who has long been a pillar in my life, always with new insights, global ambitions, and grounded encouragement for my many ideas. I thank Michaela Potančoková at the International Institute for Applied Systems Analysis for her blunt (and usually correct) criticism and insight on what is possible—and not possible—with global demographic data. Thanks to Marcin Stonawski at Statistics Denmark for his reliable support and for structuring my work—he is the most organized and patient research leader I have ever met. I am grateful to Stein Emil Vollset from the Institute of Health Metrics Evaluation for always providing a global perspective and for appreciating the need to present data in an understandable way. I thank Conrad Hackett at PEW Research Center for being such a great communicator and for always answering my e-mails within a few hours (any time of the night). I am also grateful to Anne Goujon at the European Union's Joint Research Centre for providing support and clarity through our many conversations. I also thank Melissa Hardy from Pennsylvania State University—quite possibly the best research writer I have ever known—for her support and for countless discussions over the many years. I am grateful to Ron Lee for writing some of the most inspiring papers in demography—and for lending me his office at the University of California Berkeley filled with inspirational books and materials. I thank the late Nobel Laurate Paul Crutzen who inspired me to work on the implications of human behavior for the world around us. His work on human-environment interaction and ozone layer degradation led to one of the most important environmental agreements ever made, and hope for the next generations. I had the unique pleasure of sharing my office with Paul, a kind and down-to-earth man who even cheered me on during my triathlon.

This book is largely the product of the incredible opportunities I have had to pursue my own research and engage with some of the best minds in academia and policy. I am grateful for my position at Columbia University and the support of the Robert Butler Fund. My position at Columbia University has allowed me to meet and interact with a myriad of experts outside my own field, ranging from Nobel laureates in literature, top geneticists, law professors, and global business leaders. Many thanks to Columbia public relations expert Caitlin Hawke for helping me communicate and keep my head above water, and to administrator Rosine Moussa for keeping me focused and for answering far too many e-mails. I am also grateful for my position at the Norwegian Institute of Public Health, a friendly institute with the flattest hierarchy ever in existence. I thank the Norwegian Institute of Public Health and Else Karin Grøholt, Camilla Stoltenberg and Bjørn Heine Strand, and the Norwegian Research Council for providing us with a generous "Centre of Excellence" grant in Oslo to understand the links between fertility and health using some of the the world's largest datasets. I thank all of the funding bodies that have supported my research and allowed me to attend countless meetings all around the world. I am grateful for their trust and mindful of the privileges I have been awarded. I have really profited from participating in conferences such as those organized by the International Union for the Scientific Study of Populations and the Population Association of America. I thank the policy world for inviting me to give presentations and keynotes, and participate in discussions with global leaders many times over the last two decades.

Last but not least, I thank my family whose support has helped make this book possible. This book is for you.

Vegard Skirbekk

Contents

About the Author

Vegard Skirbekk is a social scientist currently based in Oslo and New York City. His research focuses on the global implications of demographic change for health, sustainability, culture, and economic productivity. He is co-founder of the Centre for Fertility and Health at the Norwegian Institute of Public Health in Oslo. He additionally holds professorships at Columbia University, the University of Oslo, and the Cracow School of Economics. He has published more than 250 scientific articles and he has presented for policymakers in Europe, Asia, North America, and Latin America. His work is frequently cited by mass media outlets around the world, including CNN, *The New York Times*, *The Economist*, BBC, *Times of India*, *Die Welt* and *Mainichi Daily Japan*.

List of Figures

1

Introduction

At the time of writing in 2021, the average global woman could expect to have around two and a half children. By 2100, she is expected to have just 1.9 or even just 1.5 children [1]. Such low levels of fertility are not entirely unprecedented. European nobles in the Middle Ages sometimes limited their fertility to just two children to avoid diluting the family's resources, and human fertility occasionally temporarily declined to such low levels during famines and other periods of distress at various times throughout our history. Contemporary low fertility is, however, no longer restricted to selected social groups or to some transient period. For the first time in our history, low fertility is now the norm for the majority of the world's population. Why has human fertility declined? How have the experiences of different countries and population groups been similar, and how have they been different? What are the benefits and challenges of low fertility? How will fertility change in the future, and how can societies best adapt to a world with fewer children? Research can help us answer many of these questions.

For most of human existence, fertility has been determined primarily by biological factors such as the age of menarche and menopause, nutrition and disease. But many social and cultural factors have long played

V. Skirbekk, *Decline and Prosper!*,
https://doi.org/10.1007/978-3-030-91611-4_1

critical roles in determining when and how many children are born. The "European marriage pattern" observed in post-medieval Europe (relatively late marriage, low extra- and pre-marital sex) is one decisive example and a key reason why fertility was historically lower in Europe than in other world regions.

> *"To secure our future, we must make our own babies, enough of them. Because if all of the next generation are not our own, then where do they come from and what is the point of this?"*
> *-Lee Hsien Loong, Prime Minister of Singapore [2]*

Sociocultural factors have become even more important since the advent of modern contraception. Although the (potentially changing) biological capacity to reproduce remains a vital determinant of contemporary fertility, factors such as whether one has a partner (which in many countries is no longer something to be taken for granted), the costs of housing and raising children, gender roles, and personal preferences now play a much greater role. Many government policies have also effectively influenced fertility in one way or another (sometimes by infringing on human rights, but often through empowerment).

Education and religion stand out as two powerful sociocultural "meta-determinants" of fertility. Both education and religion affect more proximate determinants of fertility, such as people's contraceptive use, their ideas about marriage, family and gender roles, as well as their experiences with the labor market. Global education has increased dramatically over the last decades: While just 40% of the world's population was literate in 1960, over 80% was literate in 2010 [3]. The increase in education is probably the main reason why global fertility has decreased, and increasing educational participation and attainment appears to be the most effective way to reduce fertility without resorting to coercion. Despite ongoing secularization in many Western countries, religion also remains a highly influential driver of fertility. Fertility continues to vary between the world's biggest religious groups, and most dramatically between the secular and the highly religious. The relatively low fertility of highly educated and secular people may be resulting in an evolutionary process by which the share of religious and more family-oriented people will increase over time.

What about similarities and differences between societies? In many ways, contemporary fertility is a story of global *convergence*. Starting with France, the Western countries were the first to transition from high to low fertility. Fertility in the Western countries was already relatively low due to the European pattern of marriage. Beginning in the latter half of the nineteenth century, fertility in the Western countries gradually decreased over the course of a century. After around 1950, the pace of fertility decline in the Western countries tapered off, eventually stagnating around or just below two children per woman. Many scholars argue that the early onset of fertility decline and the comparatively low number of surviving children are key reasons for the West's political and economic success and high living standards.

Due in great part to the expansion of education, fertility decline has since occurred all over the world. Countries which began fertility decline later have often experienced much more rapid declines. Fertility in what used to be some of the highest fertility countries in the world such as South Korea, Iran, Kuwait, Brazil, India, and China dropped from above six to below two children per woman within just a few decades. In 1950, an average woman in North America or Europe had fewer than three children, while an average woman in Latin America or Eastern Asia had around six. Today, the average woman in each region has either just below (North America and Europe, Eastern Asia) or just above (Latin America) two children. Even in countries with relatively high fertility such as Ethiopia, fertility tends to be very low in urban centers. In recent years, many of the highest fertility countries have experienced fertility declines at the same time that many low fertility countries have experienced slight rebounds—thereby reducing differences between countries. Other aspects of fertility appear to be converging across populations, too. The proportion of mothers under 25 years old is shrinking and the proportion of unplanned pregnancies is also falling over time all around the globe [1, 4].

> *"I did my part, but we need to have higher birth rates in this country."*
>
> *-Paul Ryan, former United States Speaker in the House of Representatives. Ryan called on Americans to have more children as a way to sustain public transfers to older people. He "did his part" by having three children. [5]*

As much as fertility decline has, on the whole, been a shared experience for societies around the globe, there have been and continue to be remarkable differences between countries and world regions. Compared to the West, countries which began fertility decline later typically experienced periods of rapid population growth due to longer periods of high fertility combined with low mortality. Today, the countries of sub-Saharan Africa stand out as high-fertility outliers more than ever before: Whereas contemporary women in South Korea and Taiwan have on average just one child, women in Niger have nearly seven children (2021 estimates) [6]. Adolescent pregnancies are also about twice as common in developing than in richer countries. While women in many of the world's poorest countries often have their first child in their late teens or early twenties, women in the world's richest countries are starting families much later, often not until well into their thirties. The proportion of women who are childless at age 40 is often below 5% in developing countries [7, 8], but commonly around 10% (and often much higher and rising) in developed countries. An important reason for the high childlessness in developed countries is that many people do not try to have a child until their late 30s or 40s. Many people overestimate the likelihood of successfully conceiving at older ages and are also overly optimistic about the effectiveness of assisted reproductive technologies (ART).

Is low fertility good or bad for society? Many public figures have voiced very strong—and unfortunately often rather simplistic—opinions. I contend that whether low fertility is "good" or "bad" always depends on the context and the particular outcome considered. In high mortality contexts where many infants and children die before reaching adulthood, having many children ensures the survival of the family and the population as a whole. In poorer contexts, having more children can protect against some of the challenges of illness, old age, and unemployment. In settings of intergroup conflict and in the aftermath of natural disasters, high fertility might be perceived as important for "replenishing" those who have died, ensuring the longevity of one's culture, or increasing the power of the social group. Many people have also argued that having a certain number of babies is necessary for economic growth and stability and for ensuring that there will be an adequate tax base for supporting the older population.

Today, most global citizens live relatively long lives and most babies born survive to adulthood. In such a low mortality context, I argue that low—but not too low—fertility is generally best when one considers the impact of childbearing on the environment, public health, living standards, and women's empowerment. Fears about population aging and population collapse due to low fertility are overblown. Countries that have invested in education, health, and productivity can to a large extent "compensate" for population aging because their citizens—particularly their older citizens—have comparatively high cognitive capacity and good health. Investing in education and health across the life span can enable more people to be more productive for longer, permitting later retirement while also reducing healthcare costs and the number of people in need of care. Decreasing population size is also likely to be less of a threat to economic growth as new technologies are able to take over more tasks. Meanwhile, many high fertility countries experience problems with congestion, resource erosion, and lower economic growth—and getting stuck in a sort of "poverty trap." Even though the environmental impact of contemporary population growth is often exaggerated (given that most population growth takes place in countries with the lowest levels of consumption), high fertility is ultimately unsustainable. We will not be able to establish colonies on Mars (or anywhere else) to offset the impact of global population growth. There really is no alternative to low global fertility. Not only governments, but also other institutions may need to re-think their pro-natalist messages. Perhaps religious authorities should re-consider encouraging (married, heterosexual) people to have more children and instead switch their focus toward helping people to build intimate, supportive, and meaningful networks (with or without biological children).

Low fertility does come with a new set of challenges. There is a growing incidence of "coincidental" childlessness—that is, people who wind up childless without ever purposefully deciding not to have children. Childlessness has also become a disproportionally male phenomenon with, for example, about *one in four* American men and almost *one in three* Norwegian men childless as they turn 40 years old [9, 10]. The low fertility countries will therefore need to address a growing risk group of low-educated men that do not marry and do not have children. Childlessness is also particularly high among highly educated women. Even the richest and most gender egalitarian countries in the world still have a lot of work to do when it comes to enabling women to exploit their talents *and* establish and nurture a family. Another challenge is how societies should manage the contrasting needs and interests of people with low and people with high fertility. In particular, the fertility differential between highly religious and secular populations may exacerbate tensions between the two groups. Finally, low fertility means that populations will get older. The consequences of population aging do not necessarily have to be negative. "Social families" can compensate for biological families, and much can be done to optimize life in old age. Low fertility societies will nevertheless have to adjust by, for instance, extending working life, restructuring welfare systems, and adapting formal and informal systems of care.

"[Yichang] city has been entering a period of low fertility, with every woman giving birth to less than one child on average. If this situation continues, it will ... lead to population aging, a shortage of labor and reverse urbanization, therefore affecting the city's competitive power."

-The Health and Family Planning Commission in the Chinese city Yichang in an open letter to all Communist Party members in the district. The letter encouraged all party members to have a second child [11].

What about the future of fertility? Although research does not provide us with a crystal ball, it does help us make some informed predictions. There is unanimous agreement that fertility will continue to decline in countries where it is currently three or more children per woman. Fertility projections have traditionally assumed that fertility in all countries will eventually converge around two children per woman. That would imply that fertility in the countries where it is already below two or 1.5 children (mostly countries in North America, Europe, and East Asia) would substantially increase. I contend, however, that fertility is unlikely to rebound once it has dropped below two children per woman, and even less likely to rebound once it has dropped below 1.5 children per woman. My colleagues and I developed the *low fertility trap hypothesis* to explain why [12, 13]. First, fewer births in one generation imply that there will be fewer potential parents in the next generation. Second, people formulate their fertility preferences based upon their own experiences. When people grow up with fewer siblings, when their peers also have fewer siblings, and smaller families are simply the norm, they too will likely prefer to have small families. They will also experience less social pressure from their parents, peers, and community to have bigger families. Third, most people want to establish themselves on the labor market and reach a certain standard of living before they have children. Due in part to changes in labor demand, it is taking each generation longer and longer to complete their education, earn a steady and sufficient income, and establish their own household. This means that each new generation will tend to wait longer to have children than the previous generation. The consequence is that fewer children will be born. The spread of more female-controlled, long-acting contraceptives will also likely contribute to fewer unplanned births.

Given that fertility will most likely continue to decline where it is high and unlikely to substantially rebound where it is already low, countries need to start adapting to a world with fewer children. Policies should focus on helping people make informed fertility choices and achieve their own fertility preferences, as opposed to encouraging people to have more or fewer children per se. High fertility countries need to expand access to modern contraception and invest much more in improving women's educational and labor market opportunities. In the low fertility countries, measures that help young people establish a partnership, a career, and their own household, and improve work-life balance (and not just once people have already become parents) would be more effective than a one-time "baby bonus" cash payment. Governments in the low fertility countries need to acknowledge that neither more babies nor more young immigrants are solutions to population aging. Population aging is primarily driven by declining mortality as opposed to declining fertility, and it is unrealistic to expect that an influx of young immigrants could keep the population as young as it is now. (Migrants tend to move from higher to lower fertility societies and then adopt the fertility patterns of the host country—migration may therefore actually accelerate the aging of the global population.) Instead of encouraging people to have more children, low fertility societies need to respond to population aging by investing in education and health across the entire adult life span, and creating new opportunities for productive engagement and meaningful social connections in the second half of life.

After it was announced that China's birth rate had dropped to 1.3 children per woman in 2021, a hashtag with "How to get China out of a low fertility trap" on Weibo (the Chinese version of Twitter) was viewed more than 120 million times. One user wrote: "Instead of encouraging multiple births, it would be better to work hard on lifting the 'quality' of the new population." Another user wrote: "…declining fertility actually reflects progress in the thinking of Chinese people - women are no longer a fertility tool." I completely agree. Low—but not too low—global fertility is good for all of us. We need to disavow the assumption that a younger, bigger, and growing population is automatically more innovative, more productive, or more powerful. The cultural and economic influence of the West and China has, for instance, increased strongly at the same time that their populations make up ever smaller proportions of the global population. A coordinated, global effort to strive toward and maintain low fertility would help to reduce fears that one's own culture will die out and other cultures will take over. It is time for the global community to more seriously invest in women's empowerment, education, family planning, and quality work opportunities. Such investments would not only enable more people to exercise autonomy over their reproduction, but also enable longer, more productive working lives and reduce healthcare costs—as well as help more people to lead happy, satisfying lives. Fertility is a decisive determinant of human's social, economic, environmental, and biological future. With a larger number of women in reproductive age than any other time in history, even minor changes in fertility now will have profound effects on the future global population.

> *"Norway needs more children. I do not think I need to explain how this is done."*
> *-Erna Solberg, Prime Minister of Norway [14]*

This introduction has foreshadowed many of the topics I address in this book. After first describing some of the methods used in fertility research, I devote several chapters to describing fertility at different phases of human history. I start with humans' biological capacity to reproduce and how it has changed over the course of human history. Fertility was primarily determined by biological factors from the dawn of humanity all the way up until the nineteenth century. Mortality then began to fall in Europe, and fertility eventually began to decline as well. This sequence of events—mortality decline eventually followed by fertility decline—has eventually spread around the world. I then devote several chapters to contemporary fertility, including overall trends as well as regional differences, the increasing prevalence of childlessness, and fertility delay. I describe many important drivers of contemporary fertility: contraception, fertility preferences, education, economics, catastrophes and disasters, and religion. I devote approximately the last third of the book to the future of fertility. I discuss what fertility will probably look like in the future, considering contemporary fertility from an evolutionary perspective, and the consequences of fertility and population growth on the environment, human welfare, and shifts in the (future) characteristics of the global population. I describe how governments have tried to influence fertility in the past and present, and what I think countries *should* be doing: in a nutshell, accepting and also recognizing the benefits of low fertility. The increasing importance of sociocultural versus biological determinants of fertility in general and education and religion in particular, convergence and polarization, and the benefits *and* challenges associated with any given level of fertility are three recurrent themes that bind the chapters together.

References

1. United Nations (2019). World Population Prospects 2019. https://population.un.org/wpp/. Accessed 25 May 2021.
2. Yong, N. (2019, October 17). We must make enough of our own babies to secure Singapore's future: Lee Hsien Loong. *Yahoo News Singapore*. Retrieved from https://sg.news.yahoo.com/we-must-make-enough-of-our-own-babies-to-secure-our-future-lee-hsien-loong-083432783.html?guccounter=1.
3. Van Zanden, J. L., Baten, J., Mira d'Ercole, M., Rijpma, A., Smith, C., & Timmer, M. (Eds.) (2014). *How was life?: Global well-being since 1820*. Paris: OECD Publishing.
4. Sobotka, T. (2017). Post-transitional fertility: The role of childbearing postponement in fuelling the shift to low and unstable fertility levels. *Journal of Biosocial Science*, 49(S1), S20–S45. https://doi.org/10.1017/S0021932017000323.
5. Thomas, L. (2017, December 15). Paul Ryan wants you to have more kids. *Newsweek*. Retrieved from https://www.newsweek.com/paul-ryan-wants-you-have-more-kids-749328.
6. Central Intelligence Agency Total fertility rate. https://www.cia.gov/the-world-factbook/field/total-fertility-rate/. Accessed 2 June 2021.
7. Sarkar, K. (2017). Fertility transition in India: Emerging significance of infertility and childlessness. In A. Ranjan, & B. K. Singh (Eds.), *India 2016: Population. Transition Selected Papers of Bhopal Seminar 2016* (pp. 87–100). Bhopal: MLC Foundation and Shyam Institute. http://www.shyaminstitute.in/monograph_16.pdf.
8. Rutstein, S. O., & Shah, I. H. (2004). Infecundity, infertility, and childlessness in developing countries. Demographic and Health Surveys (DHS) Comparative reports No. 9. Calverton, MD: ORC Macro, & World Health Organization. https://www.who.int/reproductivehealth/publications/infertility/DHS_9/en/. Accessed 1 June 2021.

9. Statistics Norway (2019). Population statistics. Statistics Norway. www.ssb.no/befolkning.
10. Martinez, G., Daniels, K., & Chandra, A. (2012). Fertility of men and women aged 15–44 years in the United States: National Survey of Family Growth, 2006–2010. National health statistics reports no. 51. https://stacks.cdc.gov/view/cdc/12356. Accessed 2 June 2021.
11. City govt urges workers to have a second child (2016, September 22). *Global Times*. Retrieved from https://www.globaltimes.cn/content/1007610.shtml.
12. Lutz, W., Skirbekk, V., & Testa, M. R. (2006). The low-fertility trap hypothesis: Forces that may lead to further postponement and fewer births in Europe. *Vienna Yearbook of Population Research*, 167–192. http://www.iiasa.ac.at/Admin/PUB/Documents/RP-07-001.pdf.
13. Lutz, W., & Skirbekk, V. (2005). Policies addressing the tempo effect in low-fertility countries. *Population and Development Review*, 31(4), 699–720. https://doi.org/10.1111/j.1728-4457.2005.00094.x.
14. Lag flere barn, ber statsministeren i sin nyttårstale [Have more children, says the Prime Minister in her New Year's address] (2019, January 1). *NRK Nyheter*. Retrieved from https://www.nrk.no/norge/statsministeren-bekymret-over-lave-fodselstall-1.14362212.

2

Measuring Fertility

How is fertility studied, and why is it important to understand how it is measured? Spontaneously, it might seem like all one would have to do to measure fertility would be to count up all of the babies born. Counting births may sound easy enough, but in fact it is not always a straightforward process, especially when one wants to know about the number of babies born in the distant past, or in countries where just a minority of births are officially registered. Moreover, the number of newborns in a certain time period would not provide any information about how many people remain childless or average family size. Interpreting whether the number of births is "high" or "low" also depends on how many women and men of reproductive age there are in the population. There are therefore many different ways to measure fertility. The optimal measure depends on what one wants to know, along with the availability and quality of the underlying data. In this chapter, I describe sources of fertility data, some of the most common fertility metrics, and how fertility data can be interpreted wisely.

V. Skirbekk, *Decline and Prosper!*,
https://doi.org/10.1007/978-3-030-91611-4_2

Reliable Fertility Data Is Widely Available

Governments have long been interested in monitoring births for tax purposes and for estimating their own future political, military, and societal power. Today, countries monitor births in order to plan and provide the population with adequate health care, education, housing, and infrastructure. Countries thus have plenty of incentive to do a good job recording and monitoring births. By now, people in most countries are legally required to officially register births along with other major life events (marriage, death, change of address). The first country to establish a nationwide population register (in collaboration with religious authorities) was France in 1539, followed by Sweden in 1631. In other countries, birth registration did not become compulsory until much later: in 1874 in England and Wales, in 1969 in India, and in 1992 in Nigeria, as a few examples. As a result, we know much more about how fertility has developed in some countries than in others.

In some world regions, population registry data is a highly reliable source of fertility data because it covers everyone or nearly everyone in the population. According to the United Nations Children Fund (UNICEF), all children under 5 are registered in Western Europe and North America, and nearly all children under 5 are registered in Eastern Europe and Central Asia (99%), and Latin America and the Caribbean (94%). Birth registration is generally much lower in sub-Saharan Africa (44%) and South Asia (39%) [1]. Registry data in these world regions thus tends to be less reliable, though there are examples of countries in both sub-Saharan Africa and South Asia with very high rates of registration (e.g., 95.9% of all births in the Democratic Republic of the Congo are registered [2]).

There are many reasons why people might not register a birth. Conflict and war can make it more difficult to register, and fees and the time needed to travel to distant registration facilities might prevent people in more rural and/or poor areas from registering. Legal particularities may make it impossible to register some births. For example, birth registration generally requires a marriage certificate in Indonesia, and children in Bhutan cannot be registered if their paternity is unknown. Minority groups may have less access to registration services and may also distrust that their data will be handled confidentially [1]. Registration data may thus be more reliable for particular groups than for others.

11

Child Date	Parents	Witnesses
Jan June 13, 1750	Gerret Noorstrant, Marya Vanderbilt.	Jan Vanderbilt.
Gerret	Joost Durye, Sara Fillit	Hendrick Durye and wife Marya Brenkelhof.
Jan	Nicklas Van Kats. Jannetje Woertman	Jan Woertman and wife Jannetje Letten.
Barnadus	Johannis Van Sant.	Barnadus Van Sant and wife Beletje Letten.
Sara Annatje	Peter Van Velsen, Femmden	Willem Van Velsen and wife Jannetje Lose. Frederick and his wife Marya Van Velsen.
Daniel Oct. 3	Jan Luyster.	Daniel Voorhees and wife Femmetje Bennet.
Henderikus.	Frederick Kousson, Maragrite Hardenbergh	Henderikus Hardenbergh and wife Jannetje Dorbant.
Leena	Lukus Koevert, Cornelia Lefferson.	
Jannetje March 17, 1751.	Frederick Rynhart. Marya Van Velsen	Willem Van Velsen and wife Jannetje Lose.
Jacop	Jacop Kossou, Lena Stockholm.	
Mehittibal	David Karseboom, Sara Van Velsen	

Much of what we know about fertility prior to the eighteenth century is based on church records like the one pictured here. The record shown is from the United States Dutch Reformed Church Records. The record documents the baptism of three children in 1750 and 1751. Image: U.S. Dutch Reformed Church Records in Selected States, 1639–1989. Public domain, https://commons.wikimedia.org/w/index.php?curid=94400975.

National censuses, tax registers, and household surveys are other important sources of fertility data, especially when registry data is not available or when one is interested in something other than how many children were born in a particular period of time. Sometimes researchers have to rely on data from smaller, rather selective samples of people due to budget or logistical constraints. Sometimes it would simply not be feasible to interview a representative, random sample of people from the population of interest (e.g., infertile couples). When it comes to fertility of the more distant past, researchers often have no choice but to rely on whatever data is available. Most of what is known about fertility before the eighteenth century is based exclusively on data from Western European countries, because they have the oldest registry systems and because, prior to the existence of national registry systems, churches tended to keep detailed records of births, deaths, marriage, and sometimes also migration.

In general, there is reliable fertility data covering at least the last few decades for most of the world's countries. Many international organizations like the World Bank, the United Nations, and the Organisation of Economic Co-operation and Development (OECD) publish and regularly update fertility data by country on their websites. There are also ongoing efforts to compile and harmonize different fertility datasets from around the world. IPUMS provides individual-level fertility data from 82 countries since 1960 based on national censuses (ipums.org), and the Human Fertility Database provides detailed and reliable fertility data from more than 30 countries covering more than 100 years (www.humanfertility.org). The quality of the data must be evaluated on a case-by-case basis and depends in part on the size and representativeness of the sample. It is also important to consider whether individuals or reporting bodies might be motivated to over- or under-report births. The sanctions associated with having an unplanned and/or additional child during the period of China's One Child Policy from 1980 to 2016 are widely assumed to have resulted in the underreporting of births.

Common Measures of Fertility

To understand fertility statistics, it is critically important to understand the distinction between period and cohort measures of fertility. *Period fertility* measures inform us about births that take place within a particular time interval, usually a calendar year. One period measure of fertility is the *crude birth rate*, which refers to the number of live births per 1000 individuals in a population in a given calendar year. The crude birth rate is relatively easy to calculate. It provides information about population growth (or decline) and could therefore be useful for societal planning, such as preparing health and education systems. However, the crude birth rate does not provide reliable information about family size (i.e., how many children an average person has at the end of their reproductive window). It can also be misleading to use the crude birth rate to compare fertility across different populations. This is because the proportion of women who could potentially have a child in the first place (namely women between roughly 15 and 49 years of age) differs across populations. All else held equal, populations with a lower proportion of women of childbearing age will also have a lower birth rate.

The *net reproduction rate* (NRR) is another useful period measure of fertility [3–5]. The NRR is the average number of surviving daughters a cohort of women would have at the end of their reproductive life span if they were subject to the prevailing fertility and mortality rates for their entire reproductive lives. If all women would survive to the oldest possible age for that population, the NRR is simply the sum of the average number of daughters that one would produce at each age (i.e., the age-specific fertility rates). However, some women will die before reaching the end of their reproductive window. The number of women who will die before reaching the end of their reproductive window is captured by age-specific mortality rates. Hence, higher mortality rates reduce the NRR. Assuming that migration does not affect population size, a NRR above 1 (i.e., each woman has more than one surviving daughter) implies that the population will grow over the long term, while a NRR below 1 implies that the population will shrink.

Because the NRR (like many other fertility indicators) typically considers only the number of daughters born to women, it describes only the growth of the female part of the population. The traditional NRR will therefore lead to inaccurate predictions about population growth whenever the *sex ratio*—that is, the proportion of men to women in the population—is unbalanced. There is no intrinsic reason why the NRR should be based only on women's fertility. Theoretically, the NRR could also be calculated for the male part of the population, but this is seldom done in practice because data on men's fertility is relatively rare. It is also possible to calculate the *two-sex net reproduction rate* (2SNRR) as a measure of how many children in total (and not just daughters) survive to mid-reproductive age [6], taking into account the fertility of both women *and* men in a single indicator.

If one is interested in comparing reproduction across populations, the *total fertility rate* (TFR) is a more informative period measure than the crude birth rate. The TFR is the number of children a woman would have if she were to live through her entire reproductive period—again, typically defined as 15 to 49 years—and the age-specific birth rates currently observed in a given calendar year (e.g., how many babies per 1000 women aged 15–19, 20–24, 25–29, and so on were born in a particular year) would remain stable. The TFR is useful because it accounts for differences or changes in the age and sex composition of the population. It is also intuitively easy to understand: A TFR of, say, 2.2 implies that an average woman is expected to have a total of 2.2 children in her lifetime, assuming that the fertility rates from a particular year do not change. However, it should be kept in mind that the TFR is a period measure of fertility and only describes completed fertility *if* fertility rates remain stable over time. Age-specific fertility rates might change, for example, due to increases in educational attainment which might decrease the fertility rates of younger women, or changes in access to or success rates of assisted reproductive technology (ART) which might increase the fertility rates of older women.

Unlike period measures which indicate how many children were born within a particular time interval, *cohort fertility* indicates how many children people (through generally just women) born in a particular time period have actually had when they have reached the end of their reproductive window, typically set at 40, 45, or 50 years of age. Although cohort fertility is the "gold standard" measure of family size, it nevertheless has its downsides. First, cohort fertility cannot be computed until the cohort has reached the end of their childbearing years. It may therefore not be very useful for tracking, for instance, the effects of an economic downturn or policy measure on fertility. Authors also often use slightly different cut-off ages to demark the end of the reproductive window (e.g., age 40, 45, or 50), which can make it somewhat difficult to compare results across different studies and datasets. Calculating cohort fertility also requires either detailed longitudinal data (i.e., individuals are observed at multiple time points covering their entire reproductive window) which may not be available, or retrospective survey data (i.e., people at the end of their reproductive window report how many children they ever had). It might seem reasonable to assume that people accurately recall and report how many children they ever had, and hence that retrospective data would be a reliable and efficient way of measuring cohort fertility whenever longitudinal data is not available. However, retrospective data can be uncertain because there is no information about the fertility of cohort members who did not participate in the study (e.g., because they died or emigrated), or cohort members who participated in the study but did not answer the question. There are also a number of reasons why people might mis-report their fertility. Sometimes people report only children still living as opposed to children ever born, or report only children born within the context of their current marriage or partnership.

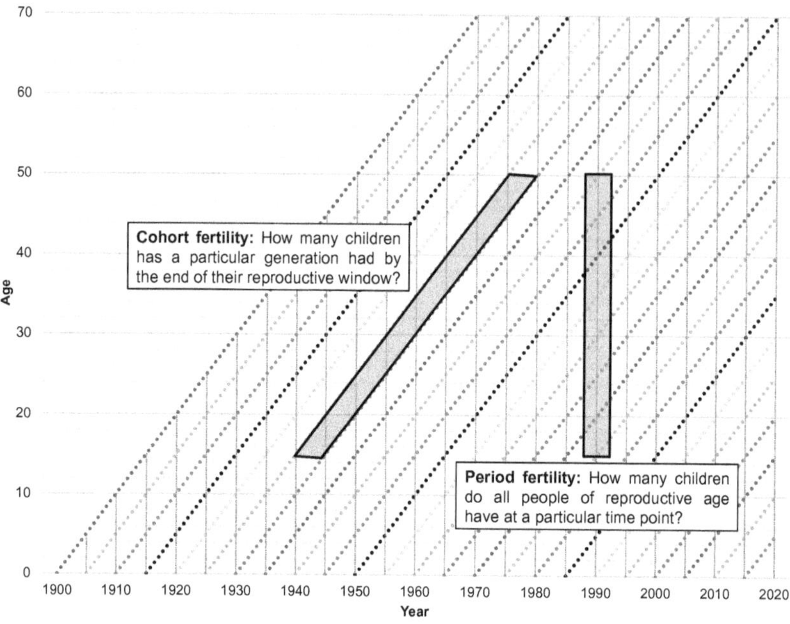

Fig. 2.1 Schematic representation of cohort versus period measures of fertility. Shown are the cohort fertility of people born between 1925 and 1930 (left) and period fertility in 1990 (right)

Figure 2.1 illustrates the difference between period and cohort measures of fertility. Period fertility describes how many children are born during a certain time period, while cohort fertility describes how many children were born to a particular cohort. Both types of measures have their advantages and disadvantages and provide different kinds of information.

Cohort and Period Fertility in Sweden

Period measures of fertility like the crude birth rate or TFR tend to fluctuate quite a bit from year to year. Demographers sometimes discuss the phenomenon of increases and decreases in period fertility as "roller-coaster fertility" [7]. Fluctuations in period fertility may occur because people tend to delay childbearing when conditions are adverse or uncertain, and have more children when the conditions seem more suitable. Period measures are thus best for studying the impact of transient conditions or a specific event such as an economic boom or crisis, political unrest, natural disaster, or new family policy. In some countries, fluctuations in people's access to family planning resources may be reflected in the fertility rate. In East Asia, many people try to avoid having children in inauspicious years, such as the unlucky year of the Fire Horse in 1966 when there was a strong decrease in the number of births [8]. Fluctuations in period fertility are largely due to differences in *when* women have children, as opposed to differences in how many children women have at the end of their reproductive years. Relative to period fertility, cohort fertility tends to change much more gradually. Because it can only be calculated with a significant delay, it is difficult to use cohort fertility to evaluate the effect of a specific event.

Figure 2.2 compares historical trends in the TFR and cohort fertility in Sweden between 1930 and 2015. Cohort fertility in each year is based

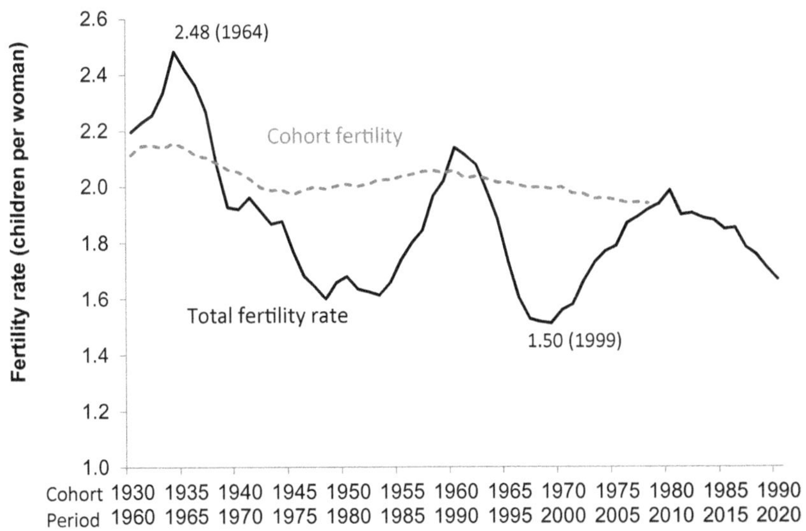

Fig. 2.2 Period fertility, 1930 to 2015 and cohort fertility, mothers born 1930 to 1974 in Sweden. Adapted from [9]

on the number of children born to women aged 30 or below. The figure shows that the TFR varies much more year to year than cohort fertility. It is easy to imagine how people analyzing data on TFR in 1980 or 2000 might have jumped to the conclusion that the population was going to drastically decrease. In actuality, the Swedish TFR "caught up" shortly thereafter, resulting in relatively stable cohort fertility.

As in the Swedish example, fertility decline in one period is often at least partially offset by a fertility increase in a subsequent period as many couples postpone but then eventually realize their childbearing plans. Hence, relative to the ups and downs of period fertility, changes in cohort fertility tend to be more modest [10]. Other examples of fertility decline followed by a period of "catch-up" were observed during the oil crisis of 1973 [11], and in Eastern Europe between the late 1990s and 2010s, where, after years of low period fertility in the aftermath of the collapse of the communist regime, period fertility once again increased. In the Czech Republic, for example, the TFR rose from 1.1 children per woman in 1999 to 1.6 children per woman in 2010 [9]. Although period fertility often rebounds once conditions improve, people can only postpone fertility for so long. People who wait too long are likely to wind up with fewer children or no children at all. Long-term declines in period fertility therefore imply a decline in cohort fertility [12].

What About the Dads?

An important caveat of most fertility indicators is that they are based only on the number of children per *woman*. There are many reasons why fertility measures have tended to ignore male fertility [13]. For one, women have a more defined reproductive life span than men, so it is easier to determine when they could potentially have children and when they have had all of the children they will ever have. It is also often assumed that data on men's fertility is less reliable because men may not always be aware that they have a child, or because they are more apt to lie about children born out of wedlock.

Most fertility data is based only on women. We thus know very little about men's fertility. Image: Statue by Gustav Vigeland in the Vigeland Park, Oslo, Norway—Vegard Skirbekk.

Due to a lack of data, much less is known about men's fertility than about women's fertility. It is not always reasonable to assume that men's fertility is the same as women's fertility. In some populations, there are strong imbalances between the number of men and women in their reproductive ages. Such imbalances may be caused by selective migration (as in the Gulf States which have large male surpluses), by unbalanced sex ratios at birth (as in China with a large male surplus), or by excess mortality of one sex (as in France during World War I, when many male soldiers died). In France at the beginning of 1921, there were just 82 men aged 20 to 39 for every 100 women in the same age range. As a result of the unbalanced sex ratio, the NRR in France between 1920 and 1923 was 0.98 for women but 1.19 for men [14]. Men and women's fertility may also differ because, depending on the cultural context, mothers may be more or less likely than fathers to have children with multiple partners.

To be able to track gender-specific trends and make more accurate predictions about population growth, it would be ideal to have and use data on *both* men and women's fertility. Instead of the traditional NRR which considers only the number of surviving daughters born to women, one might consider the mean number of surviving children of *both* sexes per woman [3], or better yet, the 2SNRR (the mean number of surviving children per person), or the two-sex TFR, which likewise takes both the fertility of men and women into account [6]. Two-sex measures are more intuitive because they indicate the extent to which adults in the population are expected to be replaced by children. Two-sex measures also lead to more accurate predictions about population growth whenever men and women's fertility differs. For example, when there are more men than women aged 20 to 39 in a population, the two-sex TFR is lower than the traditional TFR based only on women's fertility [6].

Interpreting Fertility Data Wisely

Reliable and often quite detailed fertility data covering the last several decades is widely available for much of the world. There are nevertheless a number of issues that should be considered when interpreting and evaluating different fertility statistics, research findings, or discussions of fertility in the media or political realm. The first thing to consider is the quality of the data source. In general, data from representative and large samples is more reliable than data from smaller and selective samples. Registry data tends to be highly reliable, but low rates of birth registration in some countries may increase uncertainty. What we know about fertility before the eighteenth century is based on data from just a few countries or archaeological sites and often highly selective samples.

The second, and probably most critical thing to consider, is the meaning of the specific fertility indicator. Both period and cohort measures can be useful; it depends what one wants to know. Although cohort measures are theoretically better for tracking changes in family size over time, in practice most discussions of fertility are based on period indicators. This is because period fertility is more relevant for tracking recent societal changes. It is important to keep in mind that reports based on period measures of fertility are likely to draw exaggerated conclusions about how family size has changed or is changing, and how population size will change in the future. It is also important to be aware that declines in period fertility tend to be temporary. In countries where low fertility is seen as a problem, politicians can be quick to take credit for increases in period fertility, arguing that the increase is due to their policies. However, much of the increase is probably because people are "catching up" after delaying fertility as opposed to having more children because of the new policy [15].

References

1. United Nations Children's Fund (2013). Every child's birth right: Inequities and trends in birth registration. New York: UNICEF. https://www.unicef.org/documents/every-childs-birth-right. Accessed 2 June 2021.
2. World Health Organization (2018). Birth registration coverage, data by country. https://apps.who.int/gho/data/view.main.HS09v?lang=en. Accessed 2 June 2021.
3. Kuczynski, R. R. (1932). *Fertility and reproduction: Methods of measuring the balance of births and deaths*. New York: Falcon Press.
4. Lewes, F. M. M. (1984). A note on the origin of the net reproduction ratio. *Population Studies*, 38(2), 321–324. https://doi.org/10.2307/2174080.
5. De Gans, H. A. (1999). *Population forecasting 1895–1945: The transition to modernity*. Dordrecht: Kluwer Academic Publishers.
6. Keilman, N., Tymicki, K., & Skirbekk, V. (2014). Measures for human reproduction should be linked to both men and women. *International*

Journal of Population Research, 2014(908385). https://doi.org/10.1155/2014/908385.
7. Hoem, B., & Hoem, J. M. (1996). Sweden's family policies and roller-coaster fertility. *Journal of Population Problems*, 52(3–4), 1–22.
8. Kim, Y. S. (1979). Fertility of the Korean population in Japan influenced by a folk superstition in 1966. *Journal of Biosocial Science*, 11(4), 457–464. https://doi.org/10.1017/s0021932000012530.
9. Sobotka, T. (2017). Post-transitional fertility: The role of childbearing postponement in fuelling the shift to low and unstable fertility levels. *Journal of Biosocial Science*, 49(S1), S20–S45. https://doi.org/10.1017/S0021932017000323.
10. Yoo, S. H., & Sobotka, T. (2018). Ultra-low fertility in South Korea: The role of the tempo effect. *Demographic Research*, 38, 549–576. https://doi.org/10.4054/DemRes.2018.38.22.
11. Sobotka, T., Skirbekk, V., & Philipov, D. (2011). Economic recession and fertility in the developed world. *Population and Development Review*, 37(2), 267–306. https://doi.org/10.1111/j.1728-4457.2011.00411.x.
12. Lutz, W., & Skirbekk, V. (2005). Policies addressing the tempo effect in low-fertility countries. *Population and Development Review*, 31(4), 699–720. https://doi.org/10.1111/j.1728-4457.2005.00094.x.
13. Zhang, L. (2011). *Male fertility patterns and determinants*. New York: Springer.
14. Kuczinsky, R. R. (1928). *The balance of births and deaths. Vol. 1: Western and Northern Europe*. New York: Macmillan.
15. Sobotka, T., & Lutz, W. (2011). Misleading policy messages derived from the period TFR: Should we stop using it? *Comparative Population Studies*, 35(3). https://doi.org/10.12765/CPoS-2010-15.

3

How Many Children Can Humans Have Biologically?

Reproduction is fundamentally a biological process. The biological capacity to reproduce therefore provides an important frame of reference for understanding the significance of historical changes in fertility. In this chapter, I discuss the upper limits of human reproduction and how the biological capacity to reproduce has changed over time.

Female, Male, and Couple Fecundity

Fecundity refers to the biological capacity to have a child, and it can refer to either an individual or to a couple. Women are generally fecund between menarche and menopause. The average female reproductive life span differs somewhat across world regions. In Western countries, women typically experience menarche around age 13 and menopause in their late 40s. In South Asia, women tend to experience menarche a few years later (around age 14 or 15) [1, 2] and menopause a few years earlier (in the mid-40s) [3–6]. Men generally have a longer reproductive window, although they also experience declines in fertility as they get older (e.g., semen quality declines with age [7]). One study based on a

V. Skirbekk, *Decline and Prosper!*,
https://doi.org/10.1007/978-3-030-91611-4_3

sample of pregnant couples found that men over 45 were 4.6 and 12.5 times more likely than men under 25 to need at least one or two years, respectively, to get their partners pregnant, independent of the mother's age [8].

While fecundity is obviously related to fertility, it is perhaps less obvious that fecundity is also related to health and longevity. Men and women with reduced fecundity have an increased risk for many different kinds of cancers and tend to die sooner than their peers [9], making fecundity an important indicator of population health. Given its relationships with fertility and health, it would certainly seem important to monitor and understand population fecundity and how it might be changing over time. It is, however, difficult to assess the fecundity of an entire population. While newborns provide a clear-cut and quantifiable indicator of fertility, there is no direct way to measure a population's *potential* to reproduce. Researchers therefore have to rely on a number of proxy and somewhat ambiguous measures. Common measures of female fecundity include hormonal profiles, menstruation, and ovulation. Common measures of male fecundity include different indicators of semen quality (e.g., sperm count and motility), testicular volume, and hormonal profiles [9]. The fecundity of heterosexual couples can be measured by counting the number of months or menstrual cycles it takes for the woman to become pregnant, with shorter time-to-pregnancy indicating higher fecundity. Measures of fecundity are often expensive and/or invasive to implement. As a result, studies on fecundity are often based on data from relatively small and select samples (e.g., women and men who visit fertility clinics), which may differ in relevant ways from the full population.

Natural Fertility: Seven to Ten Children Per Woman

While measuring fecundity remains rather elusive, measuring the upper limits of childbearing is more clear-cut. *Natural fertility* refers to the number of children an average woman would have if she were to have regular, unprotected sex across her entire reproductive life span. Scientific estimates of natural fertility are based on data from populations in which women marry at a young age and do not typically use contraception (i.e., *natural fertility populations*). Some studies have estimated that natural fertility is around seven or eight children [10–12]. Evidence from some religious populations suggests that natural fertility may be even higher [13, 14]. Up until the 1950s, cohorts of Hutterites—an Anabaptist religious group based primarily in the Western Plains of Canada and the United States—had an average of about ten children per woman [15]. According to survey data, very few women (often just 1 to 3%) in natural fertility populations remain childless [16–18]. About half of women in natural fertility populations have their last child before age 41, and about half have their last child between the ages of 41 and 50 [19].

> According to Guinness World Records, the greatest officially recorded number of children born to one mother is 69. The wife of Feodor Vassilyev (1707–1782) from Shuya, Russia, was pregnant 27 times and gave birth to 16 pairs of twins, seven sets of triplets and four sets of quadruplets [20].

Data from natural fertility populations has been used as the basis for drawing conclusions about the reproductive potential of humans in general: seven to ten children per woman across her reproductive life span, depending on factors such as the duration of breastfeeding, diet, and stress levels. Very few women are probably biologically unable to reproduce for reasons unrelated to menopause, and about half appear to remain fecund well throughout their 40s.

For the Most Part, Fecundity Has Likely Improved

Contemporary fertility is much lower and childlessness is much higher than in natural fertility populations. The vast divergence between contemporary fertility and estimates of natural fertility has prompted many to question whether human fecundity has decreased in the general population. There is not enough solid historical data to be able to empirically assess how exactly fecundity has changed over time, but the available evidence nonetheless supports the hypothesis that fecundity has probably *improved* as opposed to declined. There are two main reasons why it is safe to assume that fecundity has improved. First, the prevalence of several fecundity-reducing health conditions (e.g., infectious diseases such as tuberculosis, syphilis, and pelvic inflammatory disease, being underweight) has decreased over time [21], resulting in higher fecundity [22] and also a lower proportion of people who are biologically unable to reproduce due to disease. Furthermore, in many populations, the age of menarche has decreased while the age of menopause has remained relatively stable [23, 24] or even increased [25, 26], suggesting that the potential female reproductive life span has been extended by about one to three years or so over the past 150 years [27–29]. In Norway, for instance, the age of menarche (based on retrospective assessment) declined from an average of just above 16 years for women born around 1830 to just above 13 years for women born around 1960 [30]. Several of the relatively few studies of couple fecundity likewise suggest that couple fecundity has generally improved over time [31, 32]. Some investigations estimate that around 2% of people in contemporary populations are infecund for reasons unrelated to menopause [33, 34], similar to the percentage observed in natural fertility populations. In sum, there is no reason to believe that contemporary patterns of relatively low fertility reflect changes in the biological capacity to reproduce. Instead, sociocultural as opposed to biological factors appear to be responsible for the historical decrease in fertility observed in most areas of the world.

Save the Sperm?

Although fecundity *on the whole* is probably improving over time, several recent studies suggest that semen quality has in fact declined rather dramatically over the past few decades. Research on sperm quality suffers from many of the same limitations as other fecundity research: It is very difficult to get data on semen quality from representative samples of men, and hence, most studies are based on data from small and selective samples (e.g., men who go to fertility clinics due to problems conceiving, semen donors). The data may therefore not always truly reflect what is happening in the full population. Recently, however, a number of studies have provided more conclusive evidence about semen quality at the population level. One highly cited analysis integrated data from 185 existing studies on sperm quality. Together, the studies involved a total of 42,935 men who provided semen samples between 1973 and 2011 [35]. The analysis found that sperm concentration and total sperm count had declined more than 50% over the last four decades in North America, Europe, Australia, and New Zealand, and there was no indication that the decline in sperm quality was "leveling off" (see Fig. 3.1). Other studies based on samples of men in Madrid, Spain [36], China [37], and northern Norway [38] have reached similar conclusions. The decline in sperm quality is thought to be related to a number of different occupational, environmental, and lifestyle factors. One popular hypothesis is that the decline in semen quality is due to increased exposure to endocrine-disrupting chemicals. There is also some evidence that lifestyle factors such as maternal smoking and mobile telephone use are related to lower sperm quality [39]. It should be noted, however, that the sperm density levels observed in the studies cited earlier are still well above the cut-off level for low sperm quality as defined by the World Health Organization (WHO) [40].

> *"I think that sperm counts are really low in many places in the world, and people should be very concerned. Yes, I take it seriously. Am I panicking? No."*
>
> *-Dr. Shanna Swan, epidemiologist and author of the book,* Count Down: How Our Modern World Is Threatening Sperm Counts, Altering Male and Female Reproductive Development, and Imperiling the Future of the Human Race *[41]*

Evidence of decreasing semen quality has found a lot of resonance in the media, as exemplified by articles such as "Sperm Count Zero" in *GQ* [42] or "Sperm Count Continues to Fall" in *The Atlantic* [43]. While it is certainly remarkable that many studies conducted in different areas of

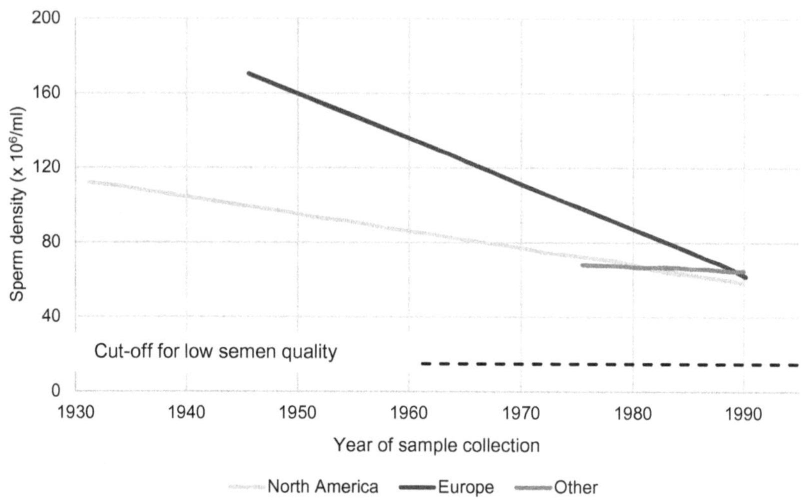

Fig. 3.1 Sperm density over time. Higher density indicates higher fecundity. Adapted from [35]. Cut-off for low semen quality according to the WHO [40]

the world have yielded similar results, it is important to consider some of the limitations of the data and to view the results with a bit of perspective. Considering the available research, it is not yet possible to conclude whether or not male fecundity is declining or not. Other recent studies have found no evidence of a decline in semen quality, or even found evidence that semen quality is improving [44–46]; however, studies that reach less cataclysmic conclusions about semen quality tend to attract less media attention. Furthermore, the relationship between semen quality and fecundity is not straightforward. Lower sperm count, for instance, does not necessarily mean that a man is less fecund. Most men still have sufficient semen quality to reproduce, and there is no evidence that *couple* fertility is decreasing (and in fact it seems to be increasing over time). Moreover, assisted reproductive technology has made it possible for less fecund men to have their own biological children. In sum, it is unlikely that current low levels of fertility are driven by historical declines in semen quality, and there is also no current cause for alarm. There is, however, definitely a need to monitor population fecundity (including semen quality) more closely [47].

Interpreting Contemporary Fertility Against the Backdrop of Fecundity and Natural Fertility

Despite its caveats, research on human fecundity offers helpful reference points for interpreting historical and contemporary fertility patterns. Women are probably biologically able to have an average of somewhere between seven and ten children, and probably just a few percent are biologically unable to have their own children during their reproductive window. On the whole, fecundity generally seems to be improving due to declines in infectious diseases and other improvements in health [21], though research is still limited and some studies suggest that male's fecundity may be declining.

Two things become clear when fertility patterns are considered against the backdrop of what is known about human fecundity. First, women rarely have as many children as they theoretically could. This has been the case for several decades and, in some world regions, even centuries—and hence, well before the advent of modern contraception. Second, the decline in fertility has not been driven by changes in human fecundity. In fact, contemporary women could probably produce more children than their early human ancestors. Contemporary fertility is primarily driven by *sociocultural* factors such as education, religion, contraception, and the labor market. The next two chapters take a closer look at historical changes in human fertility, when the determinants of fertility began to shift from predominantly biological to predominantly sociocultural factors.

References

1. Thomas, F., Renaud, F., Benefice, E., de Meeus, T., & Guegan, J. F. (2001). International variability of ages at menarche and menopause: Patterns and main determinants. *Human Biology*, 73(2), 271–290. https://doi.org/10.1353/hub.2001.0029.

2. InterLACE Study Team (2019). Variations in reproductive events across life: A pooled analysis of data from 505 147 women across 10 countries. *Human Reproduction*, 34(5), 881–893. https://doi.org/10.1093/humrep/dez015.
3. Broekmans, F. J., Knauff, E. A., te Velde, E. R., Macklon, N. S., & Fauser, B. C. (2007). Female reproductive ageing: Current knowledge and future trends. *Trends in Endocrinology & Metabolism*, 18(2), 58–65. https://doi.org/10.1016/j.tem.2007.01.004.
4. Yamaguchi, K., & Ferguson, L. R. (1995). The stopping and spacing of childbirths and their birth-history predictors: Rational-choice theory and event-history analysis. *American Sociological Review*, 60(2), 272–298. https://doi.org/10.2307/2096387.
5. Bengtsson, T., & Dribe, M. (2006). Deliberate control in a natural fertility population: Southern Sweden, 1766–1864. *Demography*, 43(4), 727–746. https://doi.org/10.1353/dem.2006.0030.
6. Sardon, J.-P., & Robertson, G. D. (2004). Recent demographic trends in the developed countries. *Population*, 59(2), 263–314. https://doi.org/10.2307/3654905.
7. Johnson, S. L., Dunleavy, J., Gemmell, N. J., & Nakagawa, S. (2015). Consistent age-dependent declines in human semen quality: A systematic review and meta-analysis. *Ageing Research Reviews*, 19, 22–33. https://doi.org/10.1016/j.arr.2014.10.007.
8. Hassan, M. A., & Killick, S. R. (2003). Effect of male age on fertility: Evidence for the decline in male fertility with increasing age. *Fertility and Sterility*, 79, 1520–1527. https://doi.org/10.1016/s0015-0282(03)00366-2.
9. Smarr, M. M., Sapra, K. J., Gemmill, A., Kahn, L. G., Wise, L. A., Lynch, C. D., et al. (2017). Is human fecundity changing? A discussion of research and data gaps precluding us from having an answer. *Human Reproduction*, 32(3), 499–504. https://doi.org/10.1093/humrep/dew361.
10. Garenne, M. (2017). Record high fertility in sub-Saharan Africa in a comparative perspective. *African Population Studies*, 31(2). https://doi.org/10.11564/31-2-1043.
11. Wilson, C. (1984). Natural fertility in pre-industrial England, 1600–1799. *Population Studies*, 38(2), 225–240. https://doi.org/10.2307/2174074.
12. Romaniuk, A. (1980). Increase in natural fertility during the early stages of modernization: Evidence from an African case study, Zaire. *Population Studies*, 34(2), 293–310. https://doi.org/10.2307/2175188.

13. Jarvis, G. K., & Northcott, H. C. (1987). Religion and differences in morbidity and mortality. *Social Science & Medicine*, 25(7), 813–824. https://doi.org/10.1016/0277-9536(87)90039-6.
14. Robinson, W. C. (1986). Another look at the Hutterites and natural fertility. *Social Biology*, 33(1–2), 65–76. https://doi.org/10.1080/19485565.1986.9988623.
15. Eaton, J. W., & Mayer, A. J. (1953). The social biology of very high fertility among the Hutterites; The demography of a unique population. *Human Biology*, 25(3), 206–264. https://www.jstor.org/stable/41449079.
16. Nahar, P. (2015). Childlessness in Bangladesh: Women's experiences of access to biomedical infertility services. In K. Hampshire, & B. Simpson (Eds.), *Assisted reproductive technologies in the third phase: Global encounters and emerging moral worlds* (pp. 119–134). New York and Oxford: Berghahn.
17. Sarkar, K. (2017). Fertility transition in India: Emerging significance of infertility and childlessness. In A. Ranjan, & B. K. Singh (Eds.), *India 2016: Population. Transition Selected Papers of Bhopal Seminar 2016* (pp. 87–100). Bhopal: MLC Foundation and Shyam Institute. http://www.shyaminstitute.in/monograph_16.pdf.
18. Poston, D. L. J., & Trent, K. (1982). International variability in childlessness: A descriptive and analytical study. *Journal of Family Issues*, 3(4), 473–491. https://doi.org/10.1177/019251382003004004.
19. Eijkemans, M. J. C., van Poppel, F., Habbema, D. F., Smith, K. R., Leridon, H., & te Velde, E. R. (2014). Too old to have children? Lessons from natural fertility populations. *Human Reproduction*, 29(6), 1304–1312. https://doi.org/10.1093/humrep/deu056.
20. Guinness World Records (2020). Most prolific mother ever. https://www.guinnessworldrecords.com/world-records/most-prolific-mother-ever. Accessed 2 June 2021.
21. Murray, C. J., Barber, R. M., Foreman, K. J., Ozgoren, A. A., Abd-Allah, F., Abera, S. F., et al. (2015). Global, regional, and national disability-adjusted life years (DALYs) for 306 diseases and injuries and healthy life expectancy (HALE) for 188 countries, 1990–2013: Quantifying the epidemiological transition. *The Lancet*, 386(10009), 2145–2191. https://doi.org/10.1016/S0140-6736(15)61340-X.
22. Inhorn, M. C., & Patrizio, P. (2015). Infertility around the globe: New thinking on gender, reproductive technologies and global movements in the 21st century. *Human Reproduction Update*, 21(4), 411–426. https://doi.org/10.1093/humupd/dmv016.

23. Ramakuela, N. J., Akinsola, H. A., Khoza, L. B., Lebese, R. T., & Tugli, A. (2014). Perceptions of menopause and aging in rural villages of Limpopo province, South Africa. *Health SA Gesondheid*, 19(1), 01–08. https://doi.org/10.4102/hsag.v19i1.771.
24. Towner, M. C., Nenko, I., & Walton, S. E. (2016). Why do women stop reproducing before menopause? A life-history approach to age at last birth. *Philosophical Transactions of the Royal Society of London. Series B, Biological sciences*, 371(1692), 20150147. https://doi.org/10.1098/rstb.2015.0147.
25. Rodstrom, K., Bengtsson, C., Milsom, I., Lissner, L., Sundh, V., & Bjourkelund, C. (2003). Evidence for a secular trend in menopausal age: A population study of women in Gothenburg. *Menopause*, 10(6), 538–543. https://doi.org/10.1097/01.Gme.0000094395.59028.0f.
26. Nichols, H. B., Trentham-Dietz, A., Hampton, J. M., Titus-Ernstoff, L., Egan, K. M., Willett, W. C., et al. (2006). From menarche to menopause: Trends among us women born from 1912 to 1969. *American Journal of Epidemiology*, 164(10), 1003–1011. https://doi.org/10.1093/aje/kwj282.
27. Song, Y., Ma, J., Agardh, A., Lau, P. W., Hu, P., & Zhang, B. (2015). Secular trends in age at menarche among Chinese girls from 24 ethnic minorities, 1985 to 2010. *Global Health Action*, 8(1), 26929. https://doi.org/10.3402/gha.v8.26929.
28. Talma, H., Schönbeck, Y., van Dommelen, P., Bakker, B., van Buuren, S., & HiraSing, R. A. (2013). Trends in menarcheal age between 1955 and 2009 in The Netherlands. *PLoS One*, 8(4), e60056. https://doi.org/10.1371/journal.pone.0060056.
29. Wyshak, G., & Frisch, R. E. (1982). Evidence for a secular trend in age of menarche. *New England Journal of Medicine*, 306(17), 1033–1035. https://doi.org/10.1056/NEJM198204293061707.
30. Rosenberg, M. (1991). Menarcheal age for Norwegian women born 1830–1960. *Annals of Human Biology*, 18(3), 207–219. https://doi.org/10.1080/03014469100001532.
31. Joffe, M. (2000). Time trends in biological fertility in Britain. *The Lancet*, 355(9219), 1961–1965. https://doi.org/10.1016/S0140-6736(00)02328-X.
32. Scheike, T. H., Rylander, L., Carstensen, L., Keiding, N., Jensen, T. K., Stromberg, U., et al. (2008). Time trends in human fecundability in Sweden. *Epidemiology*, 19(2), 191–196. https://doi.org/10.1097/EDE.0b013e31816334ad.
33. Bongaarts, J., & Potter, R. E. (2013). *Fertility, biology, and behavior: An analysis of the proximate determinants*. Cambridge: Academic Press.

34. Frank, O. (1983). Infertility in sub-Saharan africa: Estimates and implications. *Population and Development Review*, 9(1), 137–144. https://doi.org/10.2307/1972901.
35. Levine, H., Jørgensen, N., Martino-Andrade, A., Mendiola, J., Weksler-Derri, D., Mindlis, I., et al. (2017). Temporal trends in sperm count: A systematic review and meta-regression analysis. *Human Reproduction Update*, 23(6), 646–659. https://doi.org/10.1093/humupd/dmx022.
36. Romero-Otero, J., Medina-Polo, J., García-Gómez, B., Lora-Pablos, D., Duarte-Ojeda, J. M., García-González, L., et al. (2015). Semen quality assessment in fertile men in Madrid during the last 3 decades. *Urology*, 85(6), 1333–1338. https://doi.org/10.1016/j.urology.2015.02.001.
37. Huang, C., Li, B., Xu, K., Liu, D., Hu, J., Yang, Y., et al. (2017). Decline in semen quality among 30,636 young Chinese men from 2001 to 2015. *Fertility and Sterility*, 107(1), 83–88. e2. https://doi.org/10.1016/j.fertnstert.2016.09.035.
38. Basnet, P., Hansen, S. A., Olaussen, I. K., Hentemann, M. A., & Acharya, G. (2016). Changes in the semen quality among 5739 men seeking infertility treatment in northern Norway over past 20 years (1993–2012). *Journal of Reproductive Biotechnology and Fertility*, 5. https://doi.org/10.1177/2058915816633539.
39. Virtanen, H. E., Jørgensen, N., & Toppari, J. (2017). Semen quality in the 21st century. *Nature Reviews Urology*, 14(2), 120–130. https://doi.org/10.1038/nrurol.2016.261.
40. World Health Organization Department of Reproductive Health and Research (2010). WHO laboratory manual for the examination and processing of human semen. Geneva: World Health Organization. https://www.who.int/reproductivehealth/publications/infertility/9789241547789/en/. Accessed 2 June 2021.
41. Zaleski, A. (2021, March 22). An alarming decline in sperm quality could threaten the future of the human race, and the chemicals likely responsible are everywhere. *GQ*. Retrieved from https://www.gq.com/story/shanna-swan-interview.
42. Halpern, D. N. (2018, September 4). Sperm count zero. *GQ*. Retrieved from https://www.gq.com/story/sperm-count-zero.
43. Fetters, A. (2018, October 12). Sperm counts continue to fall, Magazine. *The Atlantic*. Retrieved from https://www.theatlantic.com/family/archive/2018/10/sperm-counts-continue-to-fall/572794/.

44. te Velde, E., Habbema, D., Nieschlag, E., Sobotka, T., & Burdorf, A. (2017). Ever growing demand for in vitro fertilization despite stable biological fertility—A European paradox. *European Journal of Obstetrics and Gynecology and Reproductive Biology*, 214, 204–208. https://doi.org/10.1016/j.ejogrb.2017.04.030.
45. Priskorn, L., Nordkap, L., Bang, A., Krause, M., Holmboe, S., Egeberg Palme, D., et al. (2018). Average sperm count remains unchanged despite reduction in maternal smoking: Results from a large cross-sectional study with annual investigations over 21 years. *Human Reproduction*, 33(6), 998–1008. https://doi.org/10.1093/humrep/dey090.
46. Fisch, H., Goluboff, E. T., Olson, J. H., Feldshuh, J., Broder, S. J., & Barad, D. H. (1996). Semen analyses in 1,283 men from the United States over a 25-year period: No decline in quality. *Fertility and Sterility*, 65(5), 1009–1014. https://doi.org/10.1016/s0015-0282(16)58278-8.
47. te Velde, E., Burdorf, A., Nieschlag, E., Eijkemans, R., Kremer, J. A. M., Roeleveld, N., et al. (2010). Is human fecundity declining in Western countries? *Human Reproduction*, 25(6), 1348–1353. https://doi.org/10.1093/humrep/deq085.

4

Fertility from the Dawn of Humanity Through the Nineteenth Century

To understand the significance of more recent historical shifts in fertility, it is important to have some knowledge of fertility in the distant past. In this chapter, I therefore very briefly describe what is known about fertility from the onset of human existence through the end of the eighteenth century. I focus on the intertwined relationships between fertility, mortality, and population growth and some of the biological and later sociocultural reasons why fertility was often below natural fertility.

The Other Determinant of the Number of Surviving Offspring: Mortality

Demographers studying fertility are interested in births *and* deaths. This is because the consequences of fertility largely depend on the risk of dying at different ages—which determines how long adults live, and how many children survive. Together, births and deaths drive population growth and decline. Migration also plays a role, but it is typically much less important for population growth than either fertility or mortality.

V. Skirbekk, *Decline and Prosper!*,
https://doi.org/10.1007/978-3-030-91611-4_4

Furthermore, for individuals and their families, the benefits of having a certain number of children depend to a great extent on how many children are likely to survive to adulthood. The benefits and challenges of a particular level of fertility for society and for individuals therefore greatly depend on mortality patterns and how they are changing over time.

Researchers measure mortality in different ways. Common indicators include the *crude death rate* (i.e., the number of deaths occurring in the population within a given period of time, typically a calendar year) and *age-specific mortality rates* (i.e., the number of deaths within specific age groups). Death rates are commonly expressed as the number of deaths per 1,000 or 100,000 people. Demographers are often particularly interested in *infant mortality* and *child mortality*, which are usually defined as the number of deaths among children under 1 and 5 years old, respectively. Infant mortality and child mortality are often used to compare the general health of different populations. Other common indicators of mortality refer specifically to *longevity*, or how long people live. One of the most well-known indicators of longevity is *life expectancy at birth* (or some other age). Life expectancy refers to the number of years a person at birth (or of a certain age) can expect to live given specified mortality rates. When a high proportion of infants and children die, estimates of life expectancy at birth tend to be quite low and hence may create the mistaken impression that adults in the population tend to live rather short lives. When infant mortality and child mortality are high—as they have been for most of human existence [1]—the *median* or *mode* age of death (i.e., the age at which 50% of the population has died and the most common age of death, respectively) and/or age-specific mortality rates provide better indications of how long most people actually lived.

Prehistoric Mortality and Fertility

Modern humans likely evolved sometime between 350,000 and 100,000 years ago [2–5], long before the advent of writing and careful record keeping. Crude estimates of how long early humans lived, why they died, and how many children they had can, however, be derived from archaeological evidence (e.g., size of early settlements, skeletal remains used to estimate the age at death, facilities for food production and storage). More recently, satellite imagery [6, 7] and DNA libraries [8–10] have helped researchers to better assess the size, growth rate, and distributions of prehistoric human settlements. Advances in population genetics have helped scientists identify periods of mass human extinction, sometimes called "genetic bottlenecks," when only a few individuals were able to successfully pass on their genes to the next generation. Evidence about population size and dynamics provides some indication of the prevailing mortality and fertility patterns, as population dynamics largely depend on how many members of the population were dying and how many were being born. After the emergence of written language, burial inscriptions and records of selective groups (e.g., nobles, members of religious orders) provide important additional clues. Finally, given that humans have lived as hunter-gathers for the vast majority of their existence, inferences about prehistoric human fertility and mortality are also sometimes based on anthropological observations of more recent or contemporary hunter-gatherer societies (e.g., the ! Kung or Ju/'hoansi people of Southern Africa, the Aché people of Paraguay). However, it is difficult to determine the extent to which the patterns observed in more modern hunter-gatherer societies truly reflect the demographic patterns of the distant past. All in all, estimates of prehistoric fertility, mortality, and population size are highly uncertain and become less and less certain the further one goes back in time [11–14].

Limitations aside, it is likely that prehistoric mortality was often cataclysmic, with many people suddenly dying due to pandemics, food shortages, and natural catastrophes. Based on an integration of archaeological, anthropological, and historical data, one study estimated that 27% of newborns in pre-modern societies probably died within their first year of life, and almost half (47.5%) probably died before reaching puberty [15]. Crude estimates based on archaeologic findings put life expectancy at birth of the earliest humans at around 20 years [16]. Children who survived the first years of life, however, were likely to survive to adulthood and many lived into old age. One study based on observations of more recent hunter-gatherer societies concluded that more than two-thirds of early hunter-gatherers probably survived to age 30 (i.e., potential grandparental age, assuming that sexual maturity is reached at age 15), and that just 1% of the population probably died per year between the ages of 15–40. After age 40, mortality probably increased exponentially. Of the people who survived to adulthood, many were probably in their 60s and 70s when they died [17].

Climatic conditions generally improved for humankind over the last millennia, and the spread of agriculture and animal husbandry provided more stable access to food which could have lowered mortality risks [18–20]. Advancements in housing, clothing (and hence temperature regulation), food conservation, sanitation and hygiene, infrastructure, along with work specialization, and the spread of basic literacy improved health [21–25]. However, infectious diseases became even more prevalent as people began to live in denser communities and in closer proximity to animals [26, 27]. Closer proximity to other humans and animals together with higher temperatures likely contributed to the spread of infectious diseases [28–31]. Administrative records indicate, for instance, that between one- and two-thirds of the European population probably died as a result of the bubonic plague in the fourteenth century [32, 33], and more than half and as many as 90% of several Native American populations probably died as a result of contracting infectious diseases from European settlers for which they lacked immunity [34–36]. In Oceania, outbreaks of measles, whooping cough, influenza, and smallpox periodically led to mortality peaks and limited population size [37–39]. Meanwhile, violent conflicts, wars, and slavery, indentured work, and dismal working conditions for lower classes slowed the growth of populations around the world [40–43]. The increase in infectious disease essentially "cancelled out" much of the positive effects of improvements in nutrition, hygiene, and other social advancements on mortality. As a result, improvements in mortality and longevity from the dawn of humanity through the 1800s were on the whole rather modest. Studies based on archaeological evidence, gravestone inscriptions, and written records put the average life expectancy at birth somewhere within the range of 20–30 years up until about the 1400s [20]. While estimates vary somewhat depending on the sample, time point, and population, all in all the evidence suggests that, up until the 1800s, life expectancy at birth improved only moderately and only in some regions, rarely exceeding 40 years and fluctuating substantially due to wars, famines, and epidemics [24]. Around 1800, global life expectancy at birth has been estimated to be around 28.5 years [44].

With regard to fertility, many early human settlements were probably natural fertility populations who initiated childbearing early and had regular sexual intercourse across the entire reproductive life span. Fertility and the spacing between children therefore largely depended on women's fecundity, which fluctuated along with access to food and other essential resources, energy expenditure, and how long mothers breastfed (a lack of food and breastfeeding both suppress fertility [45]). Although higher levels of fertility have been observed among more recent natural fertility populations (e.g., the Hutterites with around 10 children per woman [46]), the earliest humans likely had worse health and nutrition, and often experienced famine. Hence, the fertility of early humans was likely significantly lower than that of the Hutterites. Women probably had up to an average of seven to eight births, but often fewer, and many newborns probably died in infancy and childhood [47–49].

The gradual transition from nomadic to agricultural livelihood (circa 10,000–15,000 years ago) probably helped to make access to food more reliable. In turn, greater food security probably increased fecundity and lengthened the reproductive life span (with an earlier onset of puberty), as diet determines reproductive capacity [50]. Women may have been able to recover better and faster from each childbirth, allowing them to have more children. Nevertheless, considering the tens of thousands of years that humans have existed, historical increases in human fertility up until the 1800s were probably on the whole rather modest, just like historical decreases in mortality.

Traditional Mechanisms and Methods of Limiting Family Size

For most of human existence, reproduction has been primarily regulated by biological factors such as access to nutrition and exposure to disease. Nevertheless, mechanisms and methods to limit pregnancy have likely existed as long as humans have. The most important social mechanism for regulating fertility has probably been the institution of marriage. While the precise meaning of "marriage" has varied, cultures around the world have traditionally frowned upon fertility outside of wedlock. Elites may have practiced polygamy, but monogamy was the rule for common people [51, 52]. Polygamy was, for instance, illegal in the Roman Empire. In the Western countries following the spread of Christianity, religious institutions promoted and enforced monogamous marriages, and monogamy gradually replaced polygamy [53]. Both the Protestant and Catholic churches strongly penalized pre-marital and extra-marital sex [54]. Men and women who had pre-marital sex or children out of wedlock faced harsh penalties, including the holy notion of sin, fines, and imprisonment [55]. In Iceland, pre-marital sexual relations were punishable by death, even when both partners consented, and only people who could financially support themselves were allowed to marry [56]. Control of extramarital fertility appears to have been very effective: In eighteenth-century Europe, only about 1% of births in France, Italy, and Spain, 3% of births in Sweden and Finland, and 2–4% of births in England were to an unmarried mother. However, many women were already pregnant at the time of marriage [57]. One study estimated that, in the latter half of the eighteenth century, three out of ten brides in England gave birth within eight months of marrying [58].

The active use of contraception may have also at least partially contributed to historical fertility levels [59, 60]. Demographers sometimes use the term "traditional contraception" to denote methods of reducing the risk of pregnancy that pre-date the advent of modern contraceptives. Evidence from historical texts, archaeological findings, instructional drawings, laws, and other sources provides at least a partial picture of which contraceptive methods were available and how commonly they were used. Calendar methods in which sexual activity is restricted to days of the month when the risk of conception is lower may have been partially effective in limiting fertility [61, 62]. A number of herbs, balms, and plants such as acacia, pomegranate, Queen Anne's lace, and artemisia were used to prevent pregnancy. Some were at least partially effective; others were likely to have had only a very limited or no effect at all [60, 63, 64]. Other historical contraceptive techniques included vaginal plugs to stop semen from reaching the egg, applying cedar oil to the womb, or using pessaries from wool or other organic materials drenched in oil to block the cervix. Several methods were dangerous, including some based on the use of quicksilver and copper [60, 65, 66]. Indian sources refer to a range of birth control methods, such as the twelfth-century *Ratirahasya* ("Love Secrets") which describes potions made of red chalk and pessaries made of leaves and ghee (clarified butter) [67]. Mechanical methods, discussed in the book of Genesis, included *coitus interruptus* (withdrawal before ejaculation) and also coitus obstructus (pressing hard on a spot between the scrotum and anus in order to divert semen from the penis to the bladder) [65]. Breastfeeding depresses fertility [68], and cultural practices with regard to breastfeeding may also have contributed to historical and regional differences in fertility prior to the 1800s. Babies in pre-industrialized societies were often breastfed for two to three years and likely for a shorter duration in agricultural societies [69–71].

Thirteenth-century drawing of from Pseudo-Apuleius's *Herbarium*. The woman on the right is holding pennyroyal, historically used as an herbal abortifacient. Image: Public domain, https://commons.wikimedia.org/w/index.php?curid=2855459.

Unsurprisingly, there is little data about the prevalence of abortion in historical periods (as an exception, abortion rates were recorded in the Japanese Edo era, possibly due to famines and greater taxation [72]). Hence, how abortion has historically affected birth rates is largely unknown [60]. Written accounts and records of people who performed abortions—such as the "wise women" in Western societies [60, 73]—suggest that abortion has been a relatively common practice throughout history. An early written record of induced abortion is found in the Egyptian Ebers papyrus from 1550 BC [74]. Techniques included the intake of herbs, the use of tight girdles, jumping up and down, squeezing the belly, diuretics, fasting, and bloodletting. Surgical abortion is seldom mentioned [60, 72, 75]. In the Indian Ramayana (written as early as 700 BC), abortion is described as being carried out by surgeons or barbers (Ramayana; 5.28.6). The Bible refers to using a "bitter water to bring on the curse" (i.e., menstruation) (Numbers 5:18), which some infer as referring to a means of inducing an abortion. The Roman naturalist Pliny the Elder (circa 23/24–79 AD) documented many effective plant-based contraceptives and abortifacients used in the Mediterranean, including pomegranate, pennyroyal, rue, and myrrh [76]. Tools designed to dilate the cervix to provoke abortion have also been described [77]. Some of the interventions were effective, some less so, and many highly dangerous to the woman's health. Pre-modern abortion techniques are often associated with very high health risks and continue to be widespread in some parts of Asia, Latin America, and Africa [78–82].

Infanticide of newborn babies to limit the number of surviving offspring has been practiced in cultures all over the world. Infanticide took different forms, entailing either killing the newborn child directly or by withholding resources and nourishment [83–85]. Infanticide may have been more common in societies with high fertility including in parts of Asia [86–93]. Some have argued that infanticide was so common that it reduced overall population growth [92, 94]. Others, however, have argued that infanticide took place seldomly and would not have affected past demographic developments [95]. Legal and cultural regulations against infanticide were gradually introduced, not least following the spread of religions advocating the sanctity of human life [96, 97].

Low Fertility in Pre-industrial Europe

While fertility for humanity *as a whole* may have changed only modestly, historical evidence suggests that, by the 1700–1800s, there were already large differences in fertility across populations. Namely, fertility is thought to have been around 7–8 children in some hunter-gatherer societies [49, 98, 99] but just 4–5 children in other, predominantly European societies [100–102]. The depressed fertility of Western Europeans was to a large extent caused by the fact that Europeans tended to marry relatively late (in some cases not until the late 20s), foregoing at least a quarter of their reproductive life span [103, 104]. Remaining unmarried (and hence celibate) throughout reproductive years was also rather common in many European societies [105, 106]. It has been estimated that up to 25% of the population in seventeenth-century England [107] and 15–22% in urban France prior to the French revolution [108] never married. Clearly, there were exceptions to the overall European pattern of late marriage and low fertility. European descendants in French Quebec, for example, experienced rapid population growth due to high fertility in the eighteenth and nineteenth centuries [34, 100, 109, 110].

Religious institutions were to a large degree responsible for the European pattern of late marriage [111, 112]. In addition to encouraging late marriage and limiting extra- and pre-marital sex, religious authorities also encouraged married couples to abstain from sex for substantial periods of the year. Medieval penitential handbooks (guidelines for religious clerics) discouraged sex on fast days and religious holidays such as Sundays, Christmas, Good Friday, Easter, and during Lent—together comprising at least 25% of the year and often more [107]. To varying degrees, all of the major world religions espouse the belief that sex impedes spirituality [113]. Religiously devout men and women thus often abstain from sex (either temporarily or permanently) to enhance their inner spirituality, and religious authorities are often required to remain celibate (e.g., Christian monks, nuns, and Catholic clergy [114, 115]). Relatively high proportions of European women and men in the eighteenth and nineteenth centuries, many of them highly devout, exhibited low fertility [102, 116].

Relative to other regional populations, Europeans have historically tended to place a greater emphasis on nuclear family structures and hence postpone childbearing until they have the resources to form a new household [117, 118]. Hence, another key reason why many Europeans married late is that they simply could not afford to form a family in their teens. Large shares of the population in the Western European countries (where data is available) spent their teens and twenties serving as apprentices or working as servants (e.g., 30–55% of people aged 15–24 in North-western Europe, and 5–20% in Southern Europe) [112, 119]. Cultural and technological innovation drove increases in pastoralism, which brought about a rise in female employment (partly because female labor was less costly than male labor) and in turn depressed female fertility [120]. Work as a servant generally ended once a person married; two-thirds of servants married immediately before or after the end of their contracts. There was thus an economic incentive to postpone marriage, and the incidence of service was inversely related to age of marriage and fertility [112]. Often, Europeans only married after first working for several years, and relatively large proportions never married at all [121, 122].

Comparatively high levels of education may have also contributed to the relatively low fertility in pre-industrial Europe compared to other world regions [123]. By 1650, studies estimate that already about half of Dutch and British, and about a quarter of Italians could read and write. In most of the rest of the world, the spread of literacy was much slower. As examples, 20% of Bolivians were literate in 1910, 11% of Haitians were literate in 1950, 18% of Afghanis were literate in 1979, and 19% of Nigeriens (people from Niger) were literate in 2015—at which point 86% of the world's population was literate [124–126].

Higher Status, Higher Fertility

When mortality is high, having many children often comes along with many benefits. For much of human existence, children represented "helping hands" that increased the probability of survival for the whole family and community [127]. Children provided a net benefit to the family and community very early on in life. In more modern hunter-gatherer societies, young children take care of themselves and contribute to the family by taking care of younger siblings and helping with food acquisition. A meta-ethnography based on 58 studies of modern hunter-gatherer societies found that most children are able to efficiently collect food by the end of middle childhood and can manufacture tools by adolescence. Later, children contribute to the family's welfare by farming, taking care of animals, producing textiles, and preparing food [128]. Evidence from Mayan communities suggests that children produce more than they consume by their early to mid-teens [129]. In early industrial societies, child labor was common in regions all over the world and it was normal for pre-teen children to earn a salary through work that was often physically and mentally demanding as well as dangerous [127, 130–132]. Historically, having children could also be a way of ensuring support in old age. In ancient Rome, for instance, children were legally obliged to take care of their aging parents [133].

Given the benefits of having more children in high mortality contexts, it is not surprising that people with a higher *social status*—that is, people who had better access to important resources relative to other members of their social group—in pre-industrial societies generally tended to have more children [134–136]. Historically, wealthy and powerful men have had extraordinary numbers of children. Genghis Khan, the founder of the Mongol Empire who lived in the late twelfth century, is thought to be the direct ancestor of up to 8% of the entire Asian population [137]. Another well-researched example is Giocanggai, born in the sixteenth century, who is thought to be a direct ancestor of 1.5 million living Chinese men (his grandchild also founded the Qing Dynasty) [138]. In Europe, the founder of the Irish *Uí Néill* royal lineage might be the ancestor of up to one in five contemporary Irish men [139, 140].

Before 1750, people with high social status had **+35.8%** more children than their low status peers [141].

In several societies, cultural systems linked status with sexual access as a means of regulating overall fertility levels and population growth [142, 143]. In more modern hunter-gatherer societies, men who successfully hunt and provide the group with more meat tend to have more sexual partners and also more children [144, 145]. Rank and social position were also closely aligned with sexual access to women also among the Aztecs in Mexico, the Ngungi in Kenya, and in the Chinese empires [146, 147]. Gaining access to sexual relationships may have acted as an incentive for community members to carry out particular duties [141, 148]. For example, by working hard indentured servants in many regions of the world could earn their freedom, which in turn gave them the right to marry and have children.

The dependency of marriage on a couple's financial resources served to perpetuate the relationship between status and fertility. Societies have often required either a dowry (where the bride's family pays the groom's family) or bride price (where the man pays the bride's family) as means of ensuring that only couples with adequate financial resources could marry. Women or men whose families could not afford to pay often did not get married. In Western societies, churches were responsible for sanctioning marriages (and hence sexual relations and childbearing) and often discouraged those who lacked sufficient wealth to enter holy matrimony [56]. Men with fewer resources were therefore unable to marry early in adulthood [56, 149]. Wealthier men, in contrast, were able to marry earlier and also tended to marry younger wives, and were hence more likely to become parents and have more children as they spent more of their reproductive years being married [57]. In polygamous societies, wealthier men could marry more women and hence have more children. Even in monogamous societies, wealthier men probably had more extramarital relationships and were more likely to re-marry in the case of widowhood or divorce, all contributing to higher fertility. Like their male counterparts, wealthier women tended to marry younger, while poorer married women may have tried to restrict their fertility [150]. Wealthier women probably also had better access to professional healthcare, reducing post-partum mortality and extending their reproductive life [151–153].

The higher status, higher fertility relationship can be observed in most pre-industrial populations. There have, of course, been some exceptions: In Europe, some aristocratic families appeared to have purposefully restrained their fertility in order to reduce the number of heirs and avoid diluting the family's resources [154]. In modern developed societies, social status (as indicated by education or wealth) tends to be unrelated or even negatively related to fertility [141]—an important trend reversal that I discuss at length later on in this book.

Slow Population Growth and Modest Changes in Mortality and Fertility Until the 1800s

For most of human history, fertility but also especially infant and child mortality were high. Fertility was primarily influenced by resource availability and access to food, though marriage, religious beliefs and rules about sex, traditional methods of contraception and abortion also played meaningful roles. Societies tended to incentivize having many children, as children contributed to the family welfare from a very early age and were also the primary source of security in old age. High mortality essentially "cancelled out" the effect of high fertility. As a result, population growth was generally slow. From 10,000 BCE to 1700, the world population grew by just 0.04% annually [155]. Cultural differences in sexual practices, ideas about family, contraceptives, and abortion may have contributed to different levels of fertility in different populations, but any differences in fertility tended to be matched by corresponding differences in mortality. Where fertility was higher, mortality also tended to be higher, leading to negligible differences in net fertility across populations.

For the entire span of time between the dawn of humanity up until 1800 or so, mortality and fertility changed only moderately when considering the global population as a whole, and the determinants and concomitants of fertility changed to only a small degree. Nevertheless, due to relatively late marriage, along with low extra- and pre-marital sex, by the eighteenth century, fertility in Europe was already substantially lower than in many other world regions. Its low fertility put Europe in a very unique position to profit immensely from the dramatic drop in mortality observed in the ensuing centuries.

References

1. Lee, R. B. (2012). *The Dobe Ju/'hoansi*. Belmont, CA: Cengage Learning.
2. Henn, B. M., Gignoux, C. R., Jobin, M., Granka, J. M., Macpherson, J., Kidd, J. M., et al. (2011). Hunter-gatherer genomic diversity suggests a southern African origin for modern humans. *Proceedings of the National Academy of Sciences*, 108(13), 5154–5162. https://doi.org/10.1073/pnas.1017511108.
3. Mayr, E. (2001). *What evolution is*. New York: Basic Books.
4. Leakey, R. (2008). *The origin of humankind*. New York: Basic Books.
5. Richter, D., Grün, R., Joannes-Boyau, R., Steele, T. E., Amani, F., Rué, M., et al. (2017). The age of the hominin fossils from Jebel Irhoud, Morocco, and the origins of the Middle Stone Age. *Nature*, 546, 293–296. https://doi.org/10.1038/nature22335.
6. Pérez González, M. E., & Gallego Revilla, J. I. (2020). A new environmental and spatial approach to the Tiwanaku World Heritage site (Bolivia) using remote sensing (UAV and satellite images). *Geoarchaeology*, 35(3), 416–429. https://doi.org/10.1002/gea.21778.
7. Feurdean, A., Munteanu, C., Kuemmerle, T., Nielsen, A. B., Hutchinson, S. M., Ruprecht, E., et al. (2017). Long-term land-cover/use change in a traditional farming landscape in Romania inferred from pollen data, historical maps and satellite images. *Regional Environmental Change*, 17(8), 2193–2207. https://doi.org/10.1007/s10113-016-1063-7.
8. Freeman, J., Byers, D. A., Robinson, E., & Kelly, R. L. (2018). Culture process and the interpretation of radiocarbon data. *Radiocarbon*, 60(2), 453–467. https://doi.org/10.1017/RDC.2017.124.
9. Poznik, G. D., Xue, Y., Mendez, F. L., Willems, T. F., Massaia, A., Sayres, M. A. W., et al. (2016). Punctuated bursts in human male demography inferred from 1,244 worldwide Y-chromosome sequences. *Nature Genetics*, 48(6), 593–599. https://doi.org/10.1038/ng.3559.
10. Kavanagh, P. H., Vilela, B., Haynie, H. J., Tuff, T., Lima-Ribeiro, M., Gray, R. D., et al. (2018). Hindcasting global population densities reveals forces enabling the origin of agriculture. *Nature Human Behaviour*, 2, 478–484. https://doi.org/10.1038/s41562-018-0358-8.
11. Fagan, B. M., & Durrani, N. (2018). *People of the Earth: An introduction to world prehistory*. New York: Routledge.

12. Bowen, W. M., & Gleeson, R. E. (2018). *The evolution of human settlements: From Pleistocene origins to Anthropocene prospects*. Cham: Palgrave Macmillan.
13. Klein Goldewijk, K., Beusen, A., & Janssen, P. (2010). Long-term dynamic modeling of global population and built-up area in a spatially explicit way: HYDE 3.1. *The Holocene*, 20(4), 565–573. https://doi.org/10.1177/0959683609356587.
14. McEvedy, C. (1978). *Atlas of world population history*. Harmondsworth: Penguin Books.
15. Volk, A. A., & Atkinson, J. A. (2013). Infant and child death in the human environment of evolutionary adaptation. *Evolution and Human Behavior*, 34(3), 182–192. https://doi.org/10.1016/j.evolhumbehav.2012.11.007.
16. Gage, T. B., Dewitte, S. N., & Wood, J. W. (2012). Demography part 1: Mortality and migration. In S. Stinson, B. Bogin, & D. H. O'Rourke (Eds.), *Human biology: An evolutionary and biocultural perspective* (pp. 693–755). Hoboken, NJ: Wiley. https://doi.org/10.1002/9781118108062.ch14.
17. Gurven, M., & Kaplan, H. (2007). Longevity among hunter-gatherers: A cross-cultural examination. *Population and Development Review*, 33(2), 321–365. https://doi.org/10.1111/j.1728-4457.2007.00171.x.
18. Knapp, A. B. (1993). Social complexity: Incipience, emergence, and development on prehistoric Cyprus. *Bulletin of the American Schools of Oriental Research*, 292(1), 85–106. https://doi.org/10.2307/1357250.
19. Cohen, J. E. (1995). *How many people can the Earth support?* New York: Rockefeller University.
20. Preston, S. H. (1995). Human mortality throughout history and prehistory. In J. L. Simon (Ed.), *The state of humanity* (pp. 30–36). Malden, MA and Oxford: Wiley-Blackwell.
21. Cipolla, C. M. (2017). Four centuries of Italian demographic development. In D. V. Glass, & D. E. C. Eversley (Eds.), *Population in history: Essays in historical demography, volume II: Europe and United States* (pp. 570–587). New York: Routledge.
22. Lee, R. D. (2003). The demographic transition: Three centuries of fundamental change. *Journal of Economic Perspectives*, 17(4), 167–190. https://doi.org/10.1257/089533003772034943.
23. Murtin, F. (2012). Long-term determinants of the demographic transition, 1870–2000. *Review of Economics and Statistics*, 95(2), 617–631. https://doi.org/10.1162/REST_a_00302.

24. Riley, J. C. (2001). *Rising life expectancy: A global history*. Cambridge: Cambridge University Press.
25. Van Poppel, F., Jennissen, R., & Mandemakers, K. (2009). Time trends in social class mortality differentials in The Netherlands, 1820–1920: An assessment based on indirect estimation techniques. *Social Science History*, 33(2), 119–153. https://doi.org/10.1017/S0145553200010932.
26. Wolfe, N. D., Dunavan, C. P., & Diamond, J. (2007). Origins of major human infectious diseases. *Nature*, 447(7142), 279–283. https://doi.org/10.1038/nature05775.
27. Dobson, A. P., & Carper, E. R. (1996). Infectious diseases and human population history. *BioScience*, 46(2), 115–126. https://doi.org/10.2307/1312814.
28. Epstein, P. R. (2001). Climate change and emerging infectious diseases. *Microbes and Infection*, 3(9), 747–754. https://doi.org/10.1016/S1286-4579(01)01429-0.
29. Burney, D. A., & Flannery, T. F. (2005). Fifty millennia of catastrophic extinctions after human contact. *Trends in Ecology & Evolution*, 20(7), 395–401. https://doi.org/10.1016/j.tree.2005.04.022.
30. Guhl, F. (2017). Chagas disease in pre-Colombian civilizations. In J. Telleria, & M. Tibayrenc (Eds.), *American Trypanosomiasis Chagas Disease (Second Edition)* (pp. 23–46). Amsterdam, Oxford and Cambridge, MA: Elsevier. https://doi.org/10.1016/B978-0-12-801029-7.00002-2.
31. Dantas-Torres, F. (2015). Climate change, biodiversity, ticks and tick-borne diseases: The butterfly effect. *International Journal for Parasitology: Parasites and Wildlife*, 4(3), 452–461. https://doi.org/10.1016/j.ijppaw.2015.07.001.
32. Alfani, G., & Murphy, T. E. (2017). Plague and lethal epidemics in the pre-industrial world. *The Journal of Economic History*, 77(1), 314–343. https://doi.org/10.1017/S0022050717000092.
33. Schmid, B. V., Büntgen, U., Easterday, W. R., Ginzler, C., Walløe, L., Bramanti, B., et al. (2015). Climate-driven introduction of the Black Death and successive plague reintroductions into Europe. *Proceedings of the National Academy of Sciences*, 112(10), 3020–3025. https://doi.org/10.1073/pnas.1412887112.
34. Haines, M. R., & Steckel, R. H. (Eds.) (2000). *A population history of North America*. Cambridge: Cambridge University Press.

35. Snow, D. R. (1995). Microchronology and demographic evidence relating to the size of pre-Columbian North American Indian populations. *Science*, 268(5217), 1601–1604. https://doi.org/10.1126/science.268.5217.1601.
36. Stannard, D. E. (1993). *American holocaust: The conquest of the new world*. New York: Oxford University Press.
37. Patterson, K. B., & Runge, T. (2002). Smallpox and the Native American. *The American Journal of the Medical Sciences*, 323(4), 216–222. https://doi.org/10.1097/00000441-200204000-00009.
38. Byrne, J. P. (Ed.) (2008). *Encyclopedia of pestilence, pandemics, and plagues*. Westport, CT and London: Greenwood Press.
39. Crosby, A. W. (2015). *Germs, seeds and animals: Studies in ecological history*. London and New York: Routledge.
40. Kiernan, B. (2007). *Blood and soil: A world history of genocide and extermination from Sparta to Darfur*. New Haven, CT and London: Yale University Press.
41. Chalk, F. R., & Jonassohn, K. (1990). *The history and sociology of genocide: Analyses and case studies*. New Haven, CT and London: Yale University Press.
42. Gluckman, M. (2013). *Order and rebellion in tribal Africa*. London: Routledge.
43. Marsh, B. (2011, November 11). 100 worst atrocities over the last millenia. *The New York Times*. Retrieved from https://archive.nytimes.com/www.nytimes.com/imagepages/2011/11/06/opinion/06atrocities_timeline.html.
44. Riley, J. C. (2005). Estimates of regional and global life expectancy, 1800–2001. *Population and Development Review*, 31(3), 537–543. https://doi.org/10.1111/j.1728-4457.2005.00083.x.
45. Tietze, S. L., & Lincoln, R. (1987). The effect of breastfeeding on the rate of conception. In S. L. Tietze, & R. Lincoln (Eds.), *Fertility regulation and the public health: Selected papers of Christopher Tietze* (pp. 333–338). New York: Springer. https://doi.org/10.1007/978-1-4612-4702-9_37.
46. Jarvis, G. K., & Northcott, H. C. (1987). Religion and differences in morbidity and mortality. *Social Science & Medicine*, 25(7), 813–824. https://doi.org/10.1016/0277-9536(87)90039-6.
47. Bongaarts, J. (1986). The transition in reproductive behavior in the Third World. In J. Menken (Ed.), *World population and U.S. policy: The choices ahead* (pp. 105–132). New York: W. W. Norton.

48. Kelly, R. L. (2013). *The lifeways of hunter-gatherers: The foraging spectrum*. Cambridge: Cambridge University Press.
49. Pennington, R. (2001). Hunter-gatherer demography. In C. Panter-Brick, R. H. Layton, & P. Rowley-Conwy (Eds.), *Hunter-gatherers: An interdisciplinary perspective* (pp. 170–204). Cambridge: Cambridge University Press.
50. Spielmann, K. A. (1989). A review: Dietary restrictions on hunter-gatherer women and the implications for fertility and infant mortality. *Human Ecology*, 17(3), 321–345. https://www.jstor.org/stable/4602928.
51. Betzig, L. (1993). Sex, succession, and stratification in the first six civilizations: How powerful men reproduced, passed power on to their sons, and used power to defend their wealth, women, and children. In L. Ellis (Ed.), *Social stratification and socioeconomic inequality: Vol. 1. A comparative biosocial analysis* (pp. 37–74). New York: Praeger Publishers/Greenwood Publishing Group.
52. Murdock, G. P. (1981). *Atlas of world cultures*. Pittsburgh: University of Pittsburgh Press.
53. White, D. R., Betzig, L., Mulder, M. B., Chick, G., Hartung, J., Irons, W., et al. (1988). Rethinking polygyny: Co-wives, codes, and cultural systems [and comments and reply]. *Current Anthropology*, 29(4), 529–572. https://doi.org/10.1086/203674.
54. Goody, J. (2000). *The European family*. Oxford: Wiley-Blackwell.
55. Lombardi, D. (2008). *Storia del matrimonio. Dal Medioevo a oggi [History of marriage. From the Middle Ages to today]*. Bologna: Il mulino.
56. Gunnarson, G. (1980). Fertility and nuptiality in Icelandic's demographic history. PhD Thesis, Lund University.
57. Livi Bacci, M. (1999). *The population of Europe*. Oxford: Blackwell.
58. Wrigley, E. A., & Schofield, R. (1989). *The population history of England 1541–1871: A reconstruction*. Cambridge: Cambridge University Press.
59. Van De Walle, E. (1997). Flowers and fruits: Two thousand years of menstrual regulation. *The Journal of Interdisciplinary History*, 28(2), 183–203. https://doi.org/10.2307/206401.
60. Riddle, J. M. (1997). *Eve's herbs: A history of contraception and abortion in the West*. Cambridge, MA and London: Harvard University Press.
61. Sheon, A. R., & Stanton, C. (1989). Use of periodic abstinence and knowledge of the fertile period in 12 developing countries. *International Family Planning Perspectives*, 29–34. https://doi.org/10.2307/2133276.

62. Wright, K., Iqteit, H., & Hardee, K. (2015). Standard Days Method of contraception: Evidence on use, implementation and scale-up. Washington, DC: Population Council (The Evidence Project). https://pdf.usaid.gov/pdf_docs/PA00MGJM.pdf. Accessed 3 June 2021.
63. Connell, E. B. (1999). Contraception in the prepill era. *Contraception*, 59(1), 7S–10S. https://doi.org/10.1016/s0010-7824(98)00130-9.
64. Abou-Gamrah, H. (1982). Fertility levels and differentials by mother's education in some countries of the ECWA region. *Determinants of fertility in some African and Asian countries* (pp. 191–211). Cairo: Cairo Demographic Centre.
65. Bullough, V. L. (2001). *Encyclopedia of birth control*. Santa Barbara, CA: ABC-CLIO.
66. Lipsey, R. G., Carlaw, K., & Bekar, C. (2005). Appendix 9.1 Historical record on the control of family size. *Economic transformations: General purpose technologies and long-term economic growth* (pp. 335–340). Oxford and New York: Oxford University Press.
67. Middleberg, M. I. (2006). *Promoting reproductive security in developing countries*. New York: Springer US.
68. Finlay, J. E., Mejía-Guevara, I., & Akachi, Y. (2016). Delayed marriage, contraceptive use, and breastfeeding: Fertility patterns over time and wealth quintiles in sub-Saharan Africa. WIDER working paper 2016/43. Helsinki: UNU-WIDER. https://www.wider.unu.edu/publication/delayed-marriage-contraceptive-use-and-breastfeeding. Accessed 3 June 2021.
69. Ellison, P. T. (1995). Breastfeeding, fertility, and maternal condition. In P. Stuart-Macadam, & K. A. Dettwyler (Eds.), *Breastfeeding: Bicultural perspectives* (pp. 305–345). New York: Aldine De Gruyter.
70. Veile, A., & Miller, V. (2021). Duration of breast feeding in ancestral environments. In T. K. Shackelford, & V. A. Weekes-Shackelford (Eds.), *Encyclopedia of evolutionary psychological science*. Cham: Springer. https://doi.org/10.1007/978-3-319-19650-3_818.
71. Sellen, D. W. (2001). Comparison of infant feeding patterns reported for nonindustrial populations with current recommendations. *The Journal of Nutrition*, 131(10), 2707–2715. https://doi.org/10.1093/jn/131.10.2707.
72. Obayashi, M. (1982). [Historical background of the acceptance of induced abortion]. *Josanpu zasshi = The Japanese Journal for Midwife*, 36(12), 1011–1016.

73. Green, M. H. (1990). Female sexuality in the medieval West. *Trends in History*, 4(4), 127–158. https://doi.org/10.1300/J265V04N04_06.
74. Potts, M., & Campbell, M. (2009). History of contraception. *The Global Library of Women's Medicine*. https://doi.org/10.3843/GLOWM.10376.
75. Dickison, S. K. (1973). Abortion in antiquity. *Arethusa*, 6(1), 159–166. https://www.jstor.org/stable/26307468.
76. Heilmeyer, M. (2007). *Ancient herbs*. Los Angeles: J. Paul Getty Museum.
77. Riddle, J. M. (1992). *Contraception and abortion from the ancient world to the Renaissance*. Cambridge, MA: Harvard University Press.
78. Huss, S., & Dwight, L. (2018). Planned Parenthood: 100 years of leadership and controversy. In J. K. Beggan, & S. T. Allison (Eds.), *Leadership and sexuality: Power, principles and processes* (pp. 37–53). Cheltenham and Northampton, MA: Edward Elgar. https://doi.org/10.4337/9781786438652.00008.
79. Antadze, N., & Blacklock, J. (2017). The legalization of birth control in North America. In F. Westley, K. McGowan, & O. Tjörnbo (Eds.), *The evolution of social innovation: Building resilience through transitions* (pp. 73–87). Cheltenham and Northampton, MA: Edward Elgar. https://doi.org/10.4337/9781786431158.00010.
80. Briozzo, L. (2016). From risk and harm reduction to decriminalizing abortion: The Uruguayan model for women's rights. *International Journal of Gynecology & Obstetrics*, 134(S1), S3–S6. https://doi.org/10.1016/j.ijgo.2016.06.003.
81. Murray, C. (2016). The Protection of Life during Pregnancy Act 2013: Suicide, dignity and the Irish discourse on abortion. *Social & Legal Studies*, 25(6), 667–698. https://doi.org/10.1177/0964663916668246.
82. Devereux, G. (1954). A typological study of abortion in 350 primitive, ancient and pre-industrial societies. In H. Rosen (Ed.), *Abortion in America* (pp. 97–152). Boston: Beacon.
83. United Nations (1973). The determinants and consequences of population trends: New summary of findings on interaction of demographic, economic and social factors. Population studies no. 50. New York: United Nations.
84. Heer, D. M. (1968). The demographic transition in the Russian Empire and the Soviet Union. *Journal of Social History*, 193–240. https://www.jstor.org/stable/378645.
85. Gráda, C. Ó. (2011). Famines past, famine's future. *Development and Change*, 42(1), 49–69. https://doi.org/10.1111/j.1467-7660.2010.01677.x.

86. Ryan, W. B. (1862). *Infanticide: Its law, prevalence, prevention, and history*. London: J. Churchill.
87. Langer, W. L. (1974). Infanticide: A historical survey. *The Journal of Psychohistory*, 1(3), 353–365.
88. Lee, B. J. (1981). Female infanticide in China. *Historical Reflections/Réflexions Historiques*, 8(3), 163–177. http://www.jstor.org/stable/41298766.
89. Dalby, J. (1995). Women and infanticide in nineteenth-century rural France. In V. Shepherd, B. Brereton, & B. Bailey (Eds.), *Engendering history* (pp. 337–368). New York: Palgrave Macmillan. https://doi.org/10.1007/978-1-137-07302-0_18.
90. Michelle Oberman, J. (2003). A brief history of infanticide and the law. In M. G. Spinelli (Ed.), *Infanticide: Psychosocial and legal perspectives on mothers who kill* (pp. 3–18). Washington, DC: American Psychiatric Publishing Inc.
91. Mungello, D. E. (2008). *Drowning girls in China: Female infanticide in China since 1650*. Lanham, MD: Rowman & Littlefield Publishers.
92. Drixler, F. F. (2013). *Infanticide and fertility in Eastern Japan: Discourse and demography, 1660–1880*. Berkeley: University of California Press.
93. Rose, L. (2015). *Massacre of the innocents: Infanticide in Great Britain 1800–1939*. London: Routledge.
94. Hausfater, G., & Hrdy, S. B. (Eds.) (2017). *Infanticide: Comparative and evolutionary perspectives*. London and New York: Routledge.
95. Caldwell, B. K. (2006). Family size control by infanticide in the great agrarian societies of Asia. *Demographic transition theory* (pp. 131–153). Dordrecht: Springer. https://doi.org/10.1007/978-1-4020-4498-4_7.
96. Banda, F., & Joffe, L. F. (Eds.) (2016). *Women's rights and religious law: Domestic and international perspectives*. London: Routledge.
97. Garlati, L. (2016). Honour and guilt. A comparative study on regulations on infanticide between the nineteenth and twentieth century. In M. di Renzo Villata (Ed.), *Family law and society in Europe from the Middle Ages to the contemporary era* (pp. 257–281). Cham: Springer. https://doi.org/10.1007/978-3-319-42289-3_11.
98. Howell, N. (1979). *Demography of the Dobe Kung*. New York: Academic Press.
99. Teper, S. (1984). Birth intervals—Demographic factors. In R. F. Harrison, J. Bonnar, & W. Thompson (Eds.), *Fertility and sterility* (pp. 351–355). Dordrecht: Springer. https://doi.org/10.1007/978-94-015-1308-1_33.

100. Sánchez-Barricarte, J. J. (2018). Historical reproductive patterns in developed countries: Aggregate-level perspective. *Demographic Research*, 38, 37–94. https://doi.org/10.4054/DemRes.2018.38.2.
101. Coale, A. J. (2017). *The decline of fertility in Europe*. Princeton: Princeton University Press.
102. Rothenbacher, F. (2002). *The European population 1850–1945*. Basingstoke: Palgrave Macmillan.
103. Wrigley, E. A., Davies, R. S., Oeppen, J. E., & Schofield, R. S. (1997). *English population history from family reconstitution 1580–1837*. New York: Cambridge University Press.
104. Wachter, K. W. (2014). *Essential demographic methods*. Cambridge, MA: Harvard University Press.
105. Abbott, E. (2000). *A history of celibacy*. New York: Simon and Schuster.
106. Cusack, C. M. (2017). Wagner's Parsifal: Christianity, celibacy, and medieval brotherhood as ideal in modernity. In S. C. Marshall, & C. M. Cusack (Eds.), *The medieval presence in the modernist aesthetic: Unattended moments* (pp. 10–26). Brill. https://doi.org/10.1163/9789004357020_003.
107. Brundage, J. A. (2009). *Law, sex, and Christian society in medieval Europe*. Chicago: University of Chicago Press.
108. Bennett, J. M., & Froide, A. M. (Eds.) (1999). *Singlewomen in the European past, 1250–1800*. Philadelphia: University of Pennsylvania Press.
109. Thornton, P. A., & Gauvreau, D. (2002). Reconciling cross-sectional and longitudinal measures of fertility, Quebec 1890–1900. *History and Computing*, 14(1–2), 129–152. https://doi.org/10.3366/hac.2002.14.1-2.129.
110. Charbonneau, H., Desjardins, B., Légaré, J., & Denis, H. (2000). The population of the St-Lawrence Valley, 1608–1760. In M. R. Haines, & R. H. Steckel (Eds.), *A population history of North America* (pp. 99–142). Cambridge: Cambridge University Press.
111. Henrich, J., Boyd, R., & Richerson, P. J. (2012). The puzzle of monogamous marriage. *Philosophical Transactions of the Royal Society B: Biological Sciences*, 367(1589), 657–669. https://doi.org/10.1098/rstb.2011.0290.
112. Hajnal, J. (1982). Two kinds of preindustrial household formation system. *Population and Development Review*, 8(3), 449–494. https://doi.org/10.2307/1972376.
113. Sobo, E. J., & Bell, S. (Eds.) (2001). *Celibacy, culture, and society: The anthropology of sexual abstinence*. Madison: University of Wisconsin Press.

114. Nelson, J. L. (2015). Monks, secular men and masculinity, c. 900. In D. Hadley (Ed.), *Masculinity in medieval Europe* (pp. 131–152). London: Routledge. https://doi.org/10.4324/9781315840475.
115. Höfert, A., Mesley, M., & Tolino, S. (Eds.) (2017). *Celibate and childless men in power: Ruling eunuchs and bishops in the pre-modern world*. London: Routledge.
116. Watkins, S. C. (1984). Spinsters. *Journal of Family History*, 9(4), 310–325. https://doi.org/10.1177/036319908400900401.
117. Laslett, P., & Harrison, J. (1963). Clayworth and Cogenhoe. In H. E. Bell, & R. L. Ollard (Eds.), *Historical Essays, 1600–1750* (pp. 157–184). London: A. & C. Black.
118. Smith, T. M. F. (1993). Populations and selection: Limitations of statistics. *Journal of the Royal Statistical Society. Series A. Statistics in Society*, 156(2), 145–166. https://doi.org/10.2307/2982726.
119. Reher, D. S. (1998). Family ties in Western Europe: Persistent contrasts. *Population and Development Review*, 24(2), 203–234. https://doi.org/10.2307/2807972.
120. Voigtländer, N., & Voth, H.-J. (2013). How the West "invented" fertility restriction. *American Economic Review*, 103(6), 2227–2264. https://doi.org/10.1257/aer.103.6.2227.
121. Hajnal, J. (1965). European marriage patterns in perspective. In D. V. Glass, & D. E. C. Eversley (Eds.), *Population in history. Essays in historical demography, Volume I: General and Great Britain* (pp. 101–143). New York: Routledge. https://doi.org/10.4324/9781315127019.
122. Goody, J. (1983). *The development of the family and marriage in Europe*. Cambridge and New York: Cambridge University Press.
123. Vleuten, L. (2016). Empowerment and education. A historical study into the determinants of global educational participation of women, ca. 1850–2010. PhD thesis, Radboud University. https://repository.ubn.ru.nl/handle/2066/162181.
124. Buringh, E., & Van Zanden, J. L. (2009). Charting the "rise of the West": Manuscripts and printed books in Europe, a long-term perspective from the sixth through eighteenth centuries. *The Journal of Economic History*, 69(2), 409–445. https://doi.org/10.1017/S0022050709000837.
125. Van Zanden, J. L., Baten, J., Mira d'Ercole, M., Rijpma, A., Smith, C., & Timmer, M. (Eds.) (2014). *How was life? Global well-being since 1820*. Paris: OECD Publishing.
126. Roser, M., & Ortiz-Ospina, E. (2018). Literacy. Our World in Data. https://ourworldindata.org/literacy. Accessed 3 June 2021.

127. Rahikainen, M. (2017). *Centuries of child labour: European experiences from the seventeenth to the twentieth century*. London and New York: Routledge.
128. Lew-Levy, S., Reckin, R., Lavi, N., Cristóbal-Azkarate, J., & Ellis-Davies, K. (2017). How do hunter-gatherer children learn subsistence skills? *Human Nature*, 28(4), 367–394. https://doi.org/10.1007/s12110-017-9302-2.
129. Kramer, K. (2005). *Maya children*. Cambridge, MA: Harvard University Press.
130. Basu, K. (1999). Child labor: Cause, consequence, and cure, with remarks on international labor standards. *Journal of Economic Literature*, 37(3), 1083–1119. https://doi.org/10.1257/jel.37.3.1083.
131. Burra, N. (1997). *Born to work: Child labour in India*. Dehli: Oxford University Press.
132. Grootaert, C., & Kanbur, R. (1995). Child labour: An economic perspective. *International Labour Review*, 134(2), 187–203.
133. Parkin, T. G. (2003). *Old age in the Roman World: A cultural and social history*. Baltimore: Johns Hopkins University Press.
134. Livi-Bacci, M. (2017). Social-group forerunners of fertility control in Europe. In S. Watkins (Ed.), *The decline of fertility in Europe* (pp. 182–200). Princeton: Princeton University Press. https://doi.org/10.1515/978 1400886692-008.
135. Dribe, M., Hacker, J. D., & Scalone, F. (2014). The impact of socio-economic status on net fertility during the historical fertility decline: A comparative analysis of Canada, Iceland, Sweden, Norway, and the USA. *Population Studies*, 68(2), 135–149. https://doi.org/10.1080/00324728. 2014.889741.
136. Scalone, F., & Dribe, M. (2010). Socioeconomic status and net fertility in the demographic transition: Sweden in 1900—A preliminary analysis. *Popolazione e storia*, 11(2), 111–132.
137. Zerjal, T., Xue, Y., Bertorelle, G., Wells, R. S., Bao, W., Zhu, S., et al. (2003). The genetic legacy of the Mongols. *American Journal of Human Genetics*, 72(3), 717–721. https://doi.org/10.1086/367774.
138. Callaway, E. (2015, January 29). Genghis Khan's genetic legacy has competition. *Scientific American*. Retrieved from https://www.scientificam erican.com/article/genghis-khan-s-genetic-legacy-has-competition1/.
139. Xue, Y., Zerjal, T., Bao, W., Zhu, S., Lim, S.-K., Shu, Q., et al. (2005). Recent spread of a y-chromosomal lineage in Northern China

and Mongolia. *American Journal of Human Genetics*, 77(6), 1112–1116. https://doi.org/10.1086/498583.
140. Moore, L. T., McEvoy, B., Cape, E., Simms, K., & Bradley, D. G. (2006). A y-chromosome signature of hegemony in Gaelic Ireland. *The American Journal of Human Genetics*, 78(2), 334–338. https://doi.org/10.1086/500055.
141. Skirbekk, V. (2008). Fertility trends by social status. *Demographic Research*, 18(5), 145–180. https://doi.org/10.4054/DemRes.2008.18.5.
142. Puleston, C. O., & Tuljapurkar, S. (2008). Population and prehistory II: Space-limited human populations in constant environments. *Theoretical Population Biology*, 74(2), 147–160. https://doi.org/10.1016/j.tpb.2008.05.007.
143. Petersen, W., Braidwood, R. J., Dobyns, H. F., Eberhard, W., Kennedy Jr, R. E., Kurth, G., et al. (1975). A demographer's view of prehistoric demography [and comments and replies]. *Current Anthropology*, 16(2), 227–245. https://doi.org/10.1086/201542.
144. Keeley, L. H. (1988). Hunter-gatherer economic complexity and "population pressure": A cross-cultural analysis. *Journal of Anthropological Archaeology*, 7(4), 373–411. https://doi.org/10.1016/0278-4165(88)90003-7.
145. Smith, E. A. (2004). Why do good hunters have higher reproductive success? *Human Nature*, 15(4), 343–364. https://doi.org/10.1007/s12110-004-1013-9.
146. Scheidel, W. (2000). *Ancient empires and sexual exploitation: A Darwinian perspective*. Stanford: Stanford University Press.
147. Vining, D. R. (1986). Social versus reproductive success: The central theoretical problem of human sociobiology. *Behavioral and Brain Sciences*, 9(01), 167–187. https://doi.org/10.1017/S0140525X00021968.
148. Rueden, C. v., Gurven, M., & Kaplan, H. (2010). Why do men seek status? Fitness payoffs to dominance and prestige. *Proceedings of the Royal Society B: Biological Sciences*, 278(1715), 2223–2232. https://doi.org/10.1098/rspb.2010.2145.
149. Lesthaeghe, C., & Wilson, C. (1983). Modes of production, secularization and the pace of the fertility decline in western Europe, 1870–1930. In A. J. Coale, & S. C. Watkins (Eds.), *The decline of fertility in Europe* (pp. 261–292). Princeton, NJ: Princeton University Press.
150. Skjærvø, G. R., Bongard, T., Viken, Å., Stokke, B. G., & Røskaft, E. (2011). Wealth, status, and fitness: A historical study of Norwegians in

variable environments. *Evolution and Human Behavior*, 32(5), 305–314. https://doi.org/10.1016/j.evolhumbehav.2010.11.006.

151. Dribe, M. (2004). Long-term effects of childbearing on mortality: Evidence from pre-industrial Sweden. *Population Studies*, 58(3), 297–310. https://doi.org/10.1080/0032472042000272357.
152. Hurt, L. S., Ronsmans, C., & Thomas, S. L. (2006). The effect of number of births on women's mortality: Systematic review of the evidence for women who have completed their childbearing. *Population Studies*, 60(1), 55–71. https://doi.org/10.1080/00324720500436011.
153. Gagnon, A., Smith, K. R., Tremblay, M., Vézina, H., Paré, P. P., & Desjardins, B. (2009). Is there a trade-off between fertility and longevity? A comparative study of women from three large historical databases accounting for mortality selection. *American Journal of Human Biology*, 21(4), 533–540. https://doi.org/10.1002/ajhb.20893.
154. Johansson, S. R. (1987). Status anxiety and demographic contraction of privileged populations. *Population and Development Review*, 13(3), 439–470. https://doi.org/10.2307/1973134.
155. Roser, M., Ritchie, H., & Dadonaite, B. (2013). Child and infant mortality. https://ourworldindata.org/child-mortality. Accessed 2 June 2021.

5

The Demographic Transition: Fewer Deaths and Eventually Fewer Births

At some point during the nineteenth century, most Western societies experienced a profound decline in mortality. More children survived their first years of life, and more people began to reach mid-life and older ages. As a result, populations grew dramatically. Eventually, the decline in mortality was followed by a decline in fertility. Demographers refer to this sequence of events as the *demographic transition*. In this chapter, I discuss the demographic transition in Western Europe and its eventual spread around the world, its drivers, and regional variations in its onset, duration, and consequences.

Mortality Declines in Western Europe

After millennia of only modest decline, mortality in Europe suddenly declined very radically between approximately 1850 and 1950. The drops in infant and child mortality were particularly dramatic. Some assessments suggest that before 1800, around a quarter of children died before reaching adulthood [1]. Infant mortality was still quite high in

V. Skirbekk, *Decline and Prosper!*,
https://doi.org/10.1007/978-3-030-91611-4_5

the late nineteenth century but also varied substantially between countries (e.g., circa 100 per 1000 live births in Norway and Sweden versus 200 or 250 per 1000 live births in Germany, Austria, and Russia [2]). Around the turn of the twentieth century, infant mortality began to fall in almost every European country and eventually converged at a much lower level. By the 1950s, national rates of infant mortality ranged between just 20 and 50 per 1000 live births [2]. In 2019, for comparison, infant mortality was 3.4 per 1000 live births in the EU-27 countries [3].

Mortality dropped at older ages as well, albeit to a lesser extent. In Europe up until about 1750 or 1800, average life expectancy at birth tended to fluctuate within the range of 20–40 years and death rates varied a lot from year to year. During the nineteenth century, average life expectancy at birth in Europe increased steadily from just over 30 to just over 40 years mainly due to reductions in infant and child mortality [4]. The primary causes of death gradually shifted from infection and malnutrition to degenerative and lifestyle-related diseases. Researchers often refer this shift as the *epidemiological transition.* Famine nevertheless continued to occasionally pose a major threat, for example in Ireland where the potato plague in the middle of the nineteenth century led to catastrophic undernourishment and starvation [5]. The epidemiological transition went along with a rapid decline in infant, child, and maternal mortality, and later also a decline in old-age mortality. As a result, the increase in life expectancy in Europe accelerated between 1900 and 1950. By 1950, an average European newborn could expect to live over 60 years [4]—more than twice as long as at the start of the nineteenth century.

Human mortality had always fluctuated along with resource availability, conflicts, and disease outbreaks, but the sustained mortality decline experienced in nineteenth-century Europe was revolutionary. In fact, mortality decline has been experienced by only very few of the roughly 8,000 human generations that have ever lived over the last hundred millennia [6]. The reasons for the sustained drop in mortality are not completely understood. Improved personal hygiene, housing conditions, fewer violent deaths, better nutrition, public health measures, sewer and water systems, and better care for children jointly contributed to the sustained decline in mortality observed in many European countries [7–11]. These changes were driven by better economic standards; scientific, industrial, and technological progress; as well as increased literacy and education.

France: The Birth Place of Lower Birth Rates

At the beginning of the 1800s and simultaneous with declines in mortality, France experienced a steady and sustained decrease in fertility. By 1870, the TFR in France was 20% lower than it had been in 1800 [12]. France hence became the first country to experience what demographers call the *demographic transition*: the shift from high mortality and high fertility to sustained low mortality and low fertility.

As with mortality, temporary periods of fertility decline had occurred in the past. However, for the first time in history, the fertility decline in eighteenth-century France was permanent and *on purpose*. The decrease in French fertility was not because fewer people were marrying, or because people were marrying later. In fact, marriage in France *increased* during the 1800s. Rather, declines in the *marital fertility rate* (i.e., how many children an average married couple had) indicate that the observed fertility decline was due to married people purposefully limiting the size of their families [12, 13]. Before 1800, marital fertility in France was similar to that of other European countries, but after 1800 it dropped rapidly. By 1840, marital fertility in France was just two-thirds of the 1800 level, and by 1900, it was just half of the 1800 level [13].

Except among special subpopulations, fertility in most of the rest of Europe did not fall until about 1870 or even later [14], beginning roughly between 1880 and 1920 in the other European countries [12] (e.g., in the 1890s in Germany, England/Wales, and The Netherlands; in the 1920s in Ireland [14]). Most European countries experienced a period of gradual fertility decline for about 50 to 100 years. Gross fertility in most European countries had converged to about two children per woman by the 1970s. With the exception of France, mortality decline in most European countries preceded fertility decline by many decades. As a result, populations grew.

Why Did the Demographic Transition Take Place in Europe First?

The demographic transition took place in Europe before spreading to other world regions [7, 8, 15, 16]. Why did it take place in France and in Europe first? The causes of fertility decline in nineteenth-century France are widely debated. Improved living standards, lower mortality, better education and literacy, the Enlightenment, the French Revolution, widespread critique of religion and authorities, changing social structures, and new attitudes toward fatalism have all been implicated as factors leading to the purposeful drop in fertility [17, 18]. Strong restrictions to sexual freedom in Europe in the mid- and late nineteenth century (sometimes called the Victorian era) may have lowered fertility [19–21]. Fertility-limiting behaviors like *coitus interruptus* (withdrawal) may have spread across Europe due to the spread of information via printed pamphlets, political organizations including those propagating women's rights, and increased schooling [18, 22]. Still, it remains somewhat of a mystery why fertility decline began in Europe and not, for instance, in Asia. Some researchers have suggested that living standards in Asia up through the late eighteenth century were on par with or only slightly lower than the living standards in Western Europe [23, 24]. China also has a long tradition of using natural techniques to limit fertility [25]—yet fertility limitation was less widespread there than in Europe.

One reason why the demographic transition may have started in Europe is related to industrialization, which first took place in The Netherlands and England. Increasingly efficient modes of production took over the type of work tasks previously done by children, reducing the financial incentive to have (more) children. However, one cannot conclude that industrialization "caused" the demographic transition [26, 27]. France was a mostly agrarian society when fertility began to decline, while England, one of the first industrialized countries, experienced fertility decline relatively late compared to its European neighbors [8]. The many cultural, institutional, and social transformations that took place around the same time as industrialization undoubtedly played a role in stimulating the demographic transition, not least changing work opportunities for women, better contraception, new reproductive ideals, and religious change [15, 16, 28]. Mortality improvements might have contributed to the early onset of European fertility decline, as people needed to have fewer children in order to ensure that they would have a particular number of surviving offspring. However, researchers have also identified a number of regions where fertility decline *preceded* mortality decline, such as in regions of France [12]. Hence, it seems unlikely that people adjusted their fertility *only* as part of a rational reaction to mortality decline.

Education as the Driving Force of Fertility Decline

While the demographic transition was and is likely caused by many different, interacting factors, most experts agree that increased education was and continues to be one of the key drivers of fertility decline [29, 30]. The Enlightenment, belief in the value of education, and religious teachings that encouraged self-study of religious texts all led to relatively high levels of education in Europe—earlier than in any other world region [31–33]. The establishment of the Protestant church in sixteenth-century Germany was particularly influential in encouraging mass literacy across Europe. In the seventeenth and eighteenth centuries, German Pietists (early Protestants) persuaded authorities to mandate Bible reading in primary schools, which was a major impetus for the spread of mass literacy [34]. The Protestant church also encouraged girls' education. Before the Protestant County Palatine of Zweibrücken in Germany mandated compulsory schooling for boys *and* girls in 1592 [35], girls had only had access to cloister education. Neighboring countries who also adopted national language versions of the Bible, including Great Britain, The Netherlands, and the Scandinavian countries, likewise developed relatively high levels of schooling early on [36]. A law passed in Norway in 1736 required people to pass the Protestant confirmation—essentially a literacy test—in order to get married, be a godparent, or to witness in court, which provided a strong incentive to invest in education [37, 38].

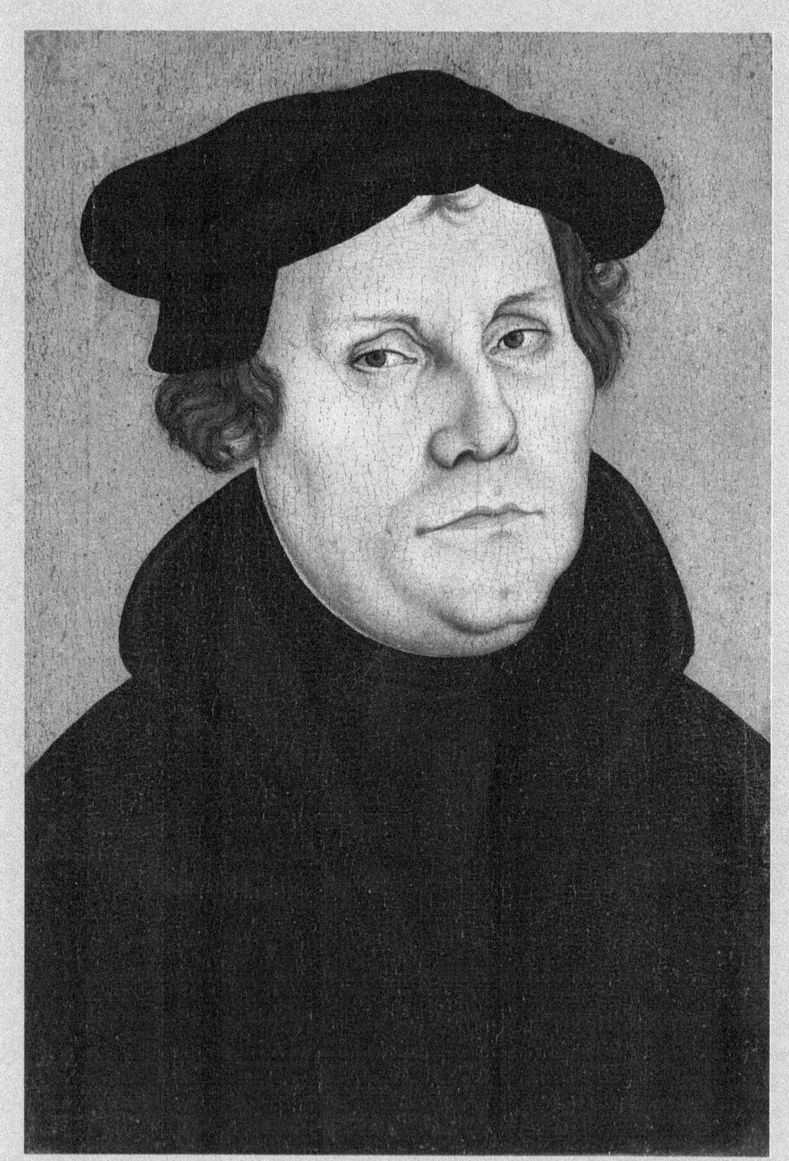

"We are living in a new world today and things are being done differently. My idea is to let boys go to such a school for one or two hours a day, and spend the remainder of the time working at home, learning a trade or doing whatever their parents desired; so that both study and work might go hand in hand while they were young and able to do both. They spend at least ten times as much time with their peashooters or playing ball or racing and tussling. In like manner, a girl can surely find time enough to go to school one hour a day and still attend to all her duties at home; she sleeps, dances and plays away more time than that."

-Martin Luther, German Professor of Theology and seminal figure in the Christian Reformation, in 1524 [47]. Luther's views helped to lay the foundation of the German public school system. Image: Portrait of Martin Luther from the workshop of Lucas Cranach the Elder, The Bridgeman Art Library, Object 308462. Public domain, https://commons.wikimedia.org/w/index.php?curid=24973472.

The high level of education of the nineteenth-century European population clearly set it apart from the populations in other world regions. In fact, the educational level of the German, English, and French populations in the early nineteenth century was already as high as the educational level observed in many countries in other world regions at the turn of the twenty-first century [36, 39, 40]. Some sources suggest that, by 1700, about 35–45% of the population in Protestant Europe could read [41]. In 1750, about 85% of the Dutch population was literate, and by 1870, 80% of the US population was literate. The average length of education in United Kingdom rose from around 4.1 years in 1870 to 6.8 years in 1920; during the same time period, fertility in the United Kingdom fell from around 5 to 2.5 children [36, 42, 43]. For comparison, in Burkina Faso, 28.7% of the population was literate in 2007 (the most recent data available) [44], and fertility first fell below 6 children per woman in 2010–2015 [45, 46]. Education affects fertility via a number of different mechanisms, which I will discuss in detail later on.

The Timing and Pace of the Demographic Transition in Asia, Africa, and South America

The demographic transition has gradually spread to other parts of the world, though there are still some places where it has not yet started. Different world regions have begun the demographic transition (defined as the year that mortality decline is thought to have begun) at different time points [48]. Often the declines in mortality and fertility have taken place at a much faster pace than in Europe. In Japan, for example, life expectancy at birth (both sexes) did not rise above 50 years until after World War II. Within just a few decades, however, Japan had the highest period life expectancy in the world. Similarly, life expectancy in South Korea in 1950–1955 was just 47.9 years, but it rose to 81.3 years for the 2010–2015 period, having experienced one of the most rapid mortality declines in recorded history [46]. Life expectancy did not exceed 40 years in any African country until the early 1960s, and life expectancy in some countries like Sierra Leon, Niger, and Guinea was still in the early to mid-30s at this point. The Latin American and Caribbean countries had already begun sustained mortality decline by the early 1950s, and life expectancy at birth was 51.3 years by the early 1950s. However, large differences between countries persisted (e.g., life expectancy of 37.5 years in Haiti versus 63.5 years in Puerto Rico) [46].

In some parts of the world, fertility decline has occurred only recently. In Africa as a whole, fertility fluctuated between six and seven children per woman until the early 1990s when it fell to 5.7 children [46]. There have been, however, large differences between the African countries. For example, fertility in the 1970–1975 period was already below 3.5 children per woman in Mauritius but 7.6 children in Algeria. By the early 2010s, the TFR in Mauritius had declined to 1.5 children per woman, while the TFR in Somalia was 6.6. In Latin America, fertility fell from between five and six children per woman to below five children per woman in the mid-1970s, and then rapidly decreased to around 2.1 children by the mid-2010s. There were large differences between the Latin American countries as well: In the early 1950s, fertility in the Central American countries (including Mexico and El Salvador) was 6.8 children per woman and only declined below six children in the late 1970s. Meanwhile, fertility in Argentina was below 3.2 children per woman already in the early 1950s [46].

It is important to understand that different countries and world regions have begun the transition from different "starting points" and have also experienced the demographic transition at very different paces. Based on mortality estimates from about 700 sources, one study [49] estimated that life expectancy at birth in Europe just before the demographic transition (in the 1770s) was 34.4 years. In comparison, pre-transition life expectancy at birth was 22.5 years in Oceania (indigenous populations; 1860s–1870s), 34.8 years in the Americas (1820s–1830s), 27.5 in Asia (1870s–1890s), 29 years in the former Soviet Union (1890s–1900s), and 26.4 years in Africa (1920). Thus, relative to Western Europe, other world regions typically had lower average life expectancies before entering a phase of sustained mortality decline. Relative to Western countries, mortality decline has also tended to happen at a much faster pace. While in France the increase in life expectancy from about 40 to 70 years occurred over a period of more than 100 years [46, 50, 51], the same increase in life expectancy took place in just about fifty years in China [46, 52]. Figure 5.1 displays how life expectancy changed between 1850 and 1950 in a number of other

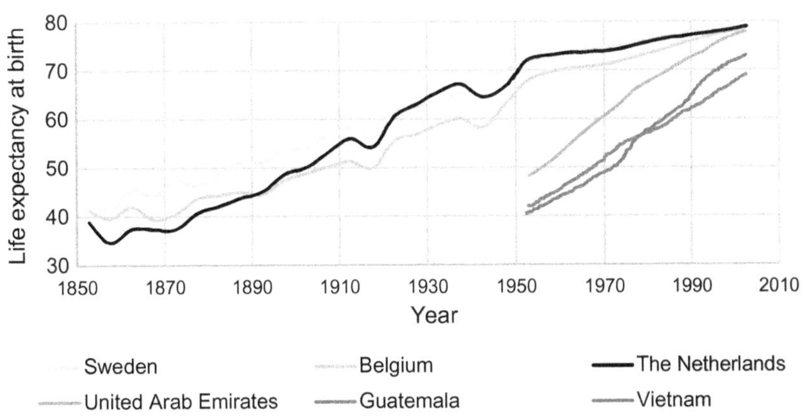

Fig. 5.1 Pace of mortality decline in selected countries. Years on the X-axis refer to the start of a five-year period. Based on data from [46, 50, 51]

selected countries. In Sweden, for example, it took about 90 years for life expectancy at birth to increase from 40 to 70 years (from 1860 to 1950). In Vietnam, a similar increase in life expectancy took place in just about 45 years (from 1950 to 1995). The rapid pace in mortality decline in non-Western regions implies that countries have had much less time to plan for and adjust to the new low mortality context.

There have also been huge differences in the starting point and pace of fertility decline in different regions. Before the demographic transition, fertility was already well below natural fertility in Europe (around four to five children per woman) but seven to eight children per woman in most non-European societies. While it took almost 100 years for fertility to fall from 6 to 3 children per woman in the European countries like the United Kingdom or Poland, the same decline took place in just 20 years or even less in countries such as South Korea, Bangladesh, China, and Iran [53]. The pace of fertility decline has varied strongly depending on countries' level of development (see Fig. 5.2). Since the 1950s, global fertility has fallen from around five children to around two and a half children. In more developed regions, fertility has fallen from slightly below three to below two children. In less developed regions, fertility has fallen from around six to below three children, while in the least developed regions it has fallen from over six to around four children.

The Demographic Transition Causes Rapid Population Growth

The demographic transition can be roughly divided into four stages: (1) an equilibrium of relatively high mortality and high fertility, (2) sustained mortality decline, (3) gradual fertility decline, and finally, (4) a new equilibrium of low mortality and low fertility [11, 16]. The time spent in the second and third stages—when mortality is low but fertility is still high—results in population growth, as births outnumber deaths and more children survive through infancy and reproduce. As fertility declines, population growth slows down and the population gets older.

The rapid population growth observed during the demographic transition is unique to humans and has never been observed for any other

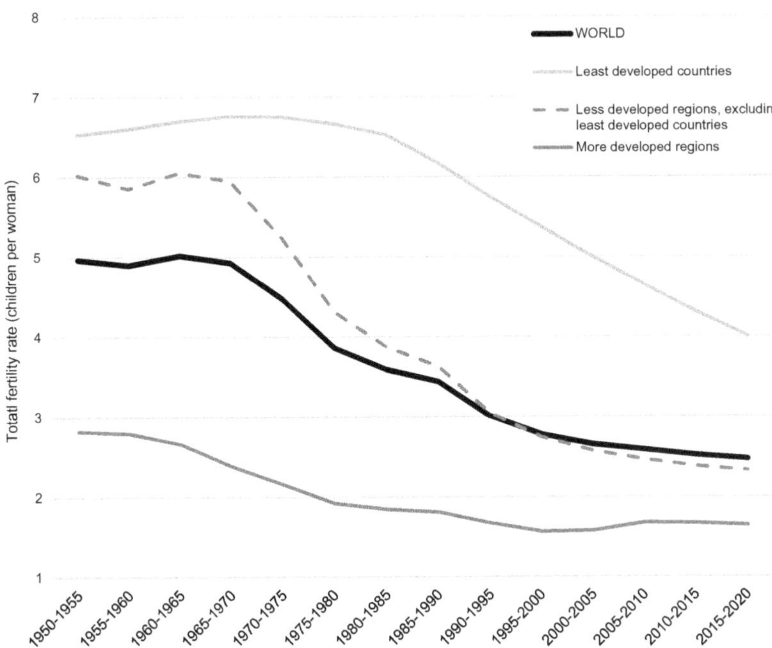

Fig. 5.2 Change in the total fertility rate by level of development, 1950–2020. Based on data from [46]

large mammal [54, 55]. Due to higher pre-transition fertility and faster mortality decline, the demographic transition has resulted in even higher population growth in most non-Western regions [7, 16]. Figure 5.3 compares the population growth observed during the demographic transition in different world regions. The figure displays historical and projected population growth between the years 1820 and 2100 in Africa, Asia, and Europe combined with North America. Europe and North America are considered together due to large-scale migration from Europe to North America during the demographic transition. The numbers on the vertical axis represent the *demographic transition multiplier* (DTM), that is, the factor by which the population size increased or is expected to increase relative to the population size in 1820. For example, a DTM of 2 indicates that the population size has doubled, 3 indicates that the population size has tripled. The West-European fertility

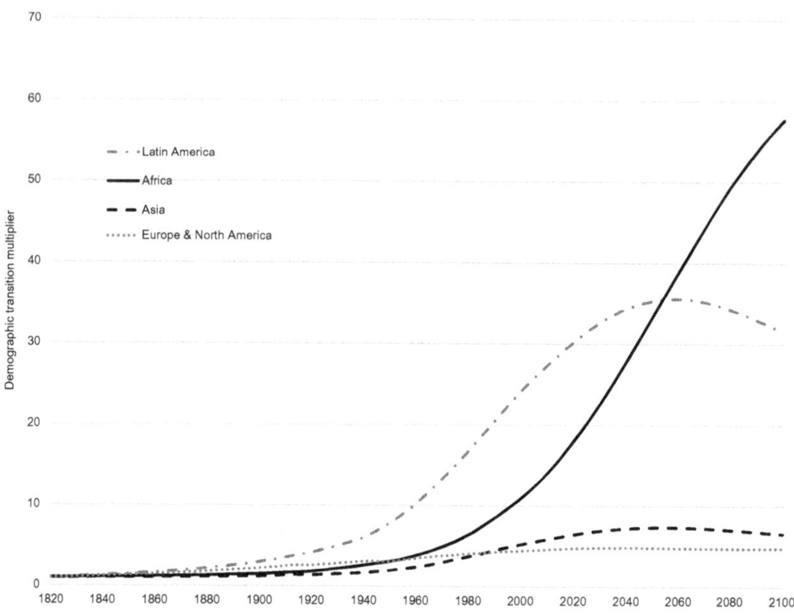

Fig. 5.3 Population increase (observed and projected) as indicated by the demographic transition multiplier in Asia, Africa, Latin America, and Europe/North America, 1820–2100. A demographic transition multiplier of 1 indicates that the population size is the same as in 1820. Based on [3, 5–46, 46, 48–58], United Nations medium variant assumptions

pattern has led to a relatively low population growth [56]. Although the demographic transition took place over a longer time period, the DTM has generally been lower in Europe than in most other world regions. Between 1820 and 2020, the population of Europe/North America increased by slightly less than a factor of five, while the population of Asia has increased by a factor of six. The biggest changes in population size are observed in regions that initially had relatively small populations: namely the Latin America population, which increased 27-fold, and the African population, which has increased 12-fold. Until 2100, the populations of Asia and Europe/North America are projected (UN medium scenario) to remain relatively stable, while the Asian and Latin American population is projected to slightly decrease. Meanwhile, by 2100, the population in Africa is expected to be *more than 40 times* larger than it was in 1820 [56].

Another way of examining the consequences of the demographic transition on population growth is to consider changes in net fertility, that is, the average number of *surviving* children. Recall that the 2SNRR is the average number of surviving sons and daughters per person; a higher 2SNRR implies greater population growth. Before the demographic transition, European couples had on average four to five children and just about half survived until adulthood [12, 16]. For the European countries, the gradual increase in longevity was more or less matched by declines in gross fertility. Net fertility therefore remained relatively stable. In France, people had on average two surviving children throughout the demographic transition from 1801 until the present. The 2SNRR never rose above 2.3 children before the baby boom in the post-war period. For England, data from the late sixteenth century suggests that net fertility never exceeded three surviving children [59]. Similar observations have been made in other European countries: For all the European countries for which we have data, the highest 2SNRR observed was around 3 children. One study [60] found that 11 of 15 European countries with available data had below replacement net fertility already for the generations born 1901–1906. Some European "offshoots" also had low net fertility very early on. For example, urban white women born 1846–1855 in the northeastern part of the United States had only 1.8 surviving children at age 45–54 in the year 1900 [61]. Hence, the demographic transition has not had as drastic effects on net fertility in Europe and its offshoots as elsewhere. This makes the European situation unique compared to other world regions for which we have data, where, prior to the demographic transition, women generally bore seven or eight children of which just slightly more than two children survived [57, 62] and population growth rates were often less than 0.02% [57]. In other world regions, mortality decline happened so fast that the TFR and the 2SNRR were essentially the same for many years before fertility eventually began to decline—with huge consequences for population growth. Figure 5.4 compares gross and net fertility in a number of selected European (panel a) and other countries (panel b) between 1800 and 2000 [16, 46, 60]. The figures show that European countries had much lower net fertility

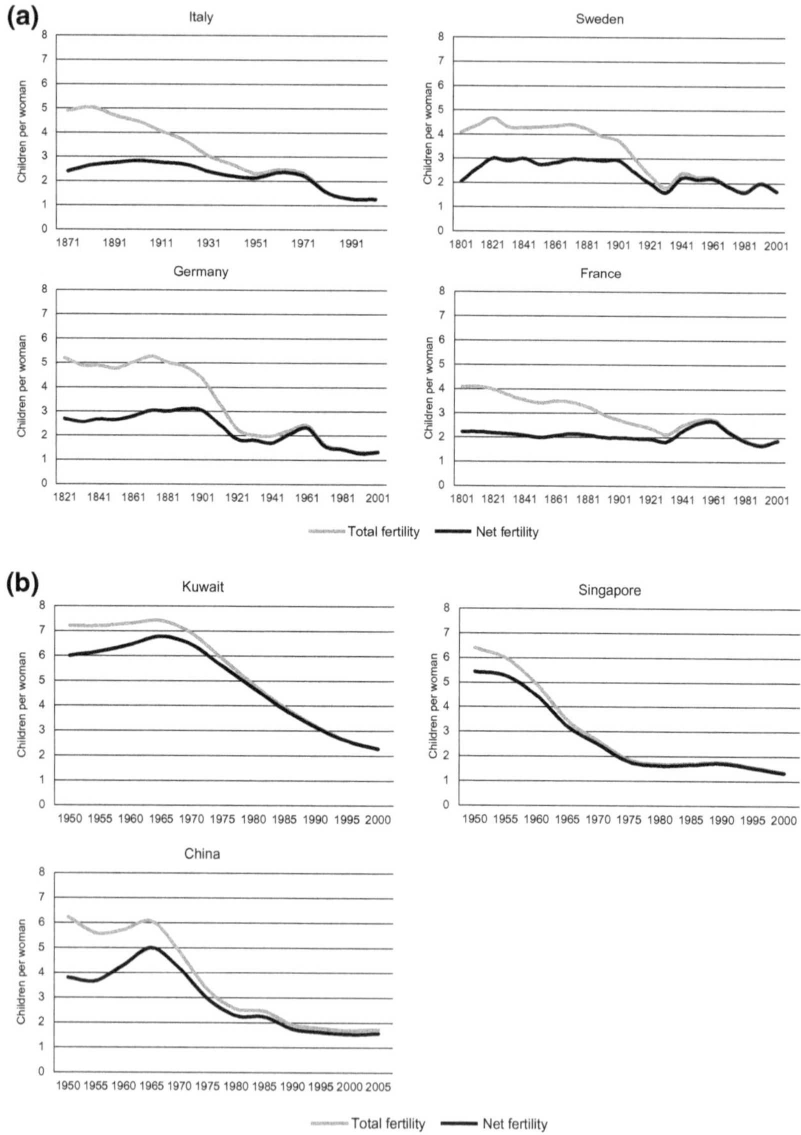

Fig. 5.4 Gross and net fertility in selected European (panel a) and other countries (panel b). Net fertility is based on the two-sex net reproduction rate. Based on data from [46]

throughout recorded history; net fertility never exceeded three children per woman. In other countries, net fertility exceeded four children per woman for multiple decades.

Comparison of the Guatemalan and Danish experiences can illuminate just how profoundly the pace of the demographic transition can affect the population. The demographic transition began around 1820 in Denmark and around 1920 in Guatemala. At the onset of the transition, the two countries were roughly comparable with regard to population size (about 1 million) and population density (about 20 individuals per square kilometer). They were also similar with regard to the level of economic development: GDP per capita (measured in 2005 USD) was $1870 in Denmark in 1820 and $1869 in Guatemala in 1920 [58]. The TFR at the onset of the transition was, however, much higher in Guatemala (around 7 children per woman) than in Denmark (around 4–5 children per woman). Mortality decline thus had a drastically different impact on population growth in the two countries, with population growth during the demographic transition in Guatemala expected to be five times greater than the population growth experienced in Denmark. Guatemala is also projected to have about five times higher population density than Denmark; it is estimated that population sizes will stabilize at slightly above 31 million in Guatemala compared with slightly above 6 million in Denmark [46]. Meanwhile, in 2019, the World Bank estimated that GDP per capita (purchasing power parity adjusted) was more than six times greater in Denmark than in Guatemala [63]. The relatively low population growth during the demographic transition may be a key reason why Western countries like Denmark prospered. Lower net fertility meant that societies were relatively stable, there were more resources per capita, and more could be invested in the health and education of subsequent generations. World regions with higher pre- and mid-transition fertility (such as large parts of Africa, regions within South Asia) may have been negatively affected by rapid and high population growth. I discuss some of the consequences of fertility and population growth in more detail later on in this book.

Reversal in the Status–Fertility Relationship

Another important change that has typically accompanied the demographic transition is the reversal in the relationship between social status and fertility. With few exceptions, higher status generally tended to go along with higher fertility prior to the demographic transition. In Europe, the relationship between social status and fertility reversed early on in the demographic transition [64]. People with higher income and wealth, more education and higher-level occupations are likely to have initiated fertility decline [65, 66]. People higher up on the social hierarchy began to have fewer children, while poorer families continued to have larger families. Eventually, poorer families began to have fewer children, too. The reversal in the status-fertility relationship appears to be driven at least in part by the spread of education as a new measure of status. Unlike other measures of social status, education has consistently been related to later and lower fertility [65]. People who *attain* status (through, for instance, education) rather than *maintain* or inherit status (through, for instance, inheritance of wealth) may have especially low fertility, as demonstrated by a study based on an urban Belgian population in the nineteenth and twentieth centuries [67].

In 1990–2006, people with higher social status had **-19.1%** fewer children than their lower status peers [65].

Figure 5.5 displays the relationship between fertility and different indicators of social status—namely income/wealth, occupational status, and education—between the years 1300 and 2000. The data points indicate the observed percentage-point difference in fertility between people with the highest relative to people with the lowest status (i.e., wealthiest/poorest, highest/lowest occupational class, most/lowest educated). Positive values (between 0 and 100) indicate that fertility was higher among people with higher status. For example, a value of 10 indicates that fertility was 10% higher among people with higher status. As can be seen in the figure, higher wealth and higher occupational

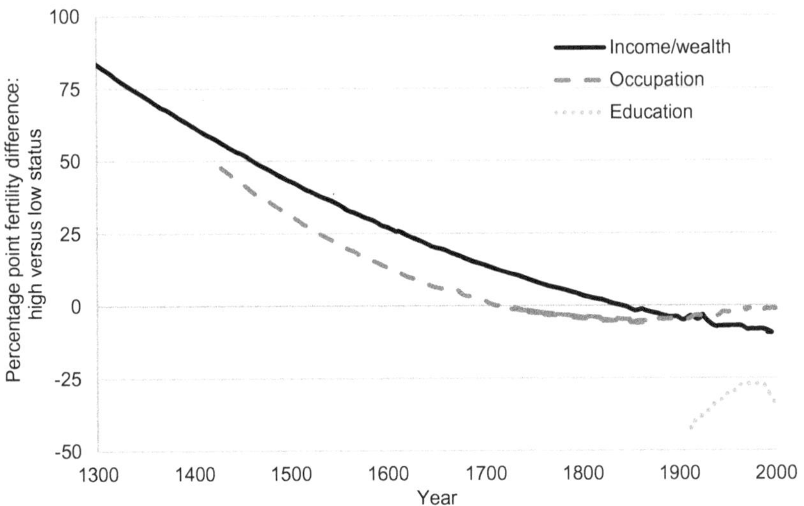

Fig. 5.5 Differences in fertility between people with higher and lower social status, 1300 and 2000. Data points indicate the percentage-point fertility difference of an individual study. Based on [65]

status were both associated with higher fertility until sometime between 1800 and 1900, when the relationships flattened out and eventually turned negative. The relationship between education and fertility has been consistently negative, with the difference between the most and least educated groups becoming somewhat less dramatic over time. The convergence between high and low educated groups is probably because fertility patterns tend to spread from high to low status groups [65].

Lessons Learned from the Demographic Transition

The shift from high mortality/high fertility to low mortality/low fertility is one of the most profound changes known to mankind. The lag between mortality and fertility decline has resulted in unprecedented population growth for the world as a whole, and the different starting points and pace of the demographic transition have resulted in unequal population growth in different world regions. The Western countries—which had the lowest pre-transition fertility and the slowest decreases in mortality—experienced the lowest increases in population size. Limited population growth is probably the main reason why the Western world prospered in the twentieth century. At the other end of the spectrum, Africa had the highest pre-transition fertility, experienced a rapid increase in life expectancy and has been experiencing the highest population growth. When comparing the demographic transition in different world regions, it is important to keep in mind that many non-Western countries began the transition with initially higher fertility and also experienced faster mortality decline than in Europe. In other words, Western countries generally took longer to make less dramatic changes in fertility compared with the rest of the world. Thus, high population growth in some countries due to lag between mortality and fertility decline should not be interpreted as reflecting an inferior ability to adapt.

The demographic transition has taken place in a wide variety of socioeconomic and cultural contexts, and it is difficult to pinpoint one decisive factor that "caused" it. Education is one very important factor, though—and one of the first markers of high social status that was related to low fertility. Thus, one of the most important lessons of the demographic transition is thus that investing in education can accelerate fertility decline and reduce population growth.

References

1. Roser, M., Ritchie, H., & Dadonaite, B. (2013). Child and infant mortality. https://ourworldindata.org/child-mortality. Accessed 2 June 2021.
2. Corsini, C. A., & Viazzo, P. P. (1993). The historical decline of infant mortality: An overview. In P. P. Viazzo, & C. A. Corsini (Eds.), *The decline of infant mortality in Europe, 1800–1950: Four case studies* (pp. 9–18). Florence: UNICEF. https://www.unicef-irc.org/publications/pdf/hisper_decline_infantmortality.pdf.
3. Eurostat. (2021). Infant mortality rate. https://ec.europa.eu/eurostat/databrowser/view/tps00027/default/table?lang=en. Accessed 2 June 2021.

4. Roser, M., Ortiz-Ospina, E., & Ritchie, H. (2013). Life expectancy. https://ourworldindata.org/life-expectancy. Accessed 2 June 2021.
5. O'grada, C. (1995). *The great Irish famine*. Cambridge: Cambridge University Press.
6. Burger, O., Baudisch, A., & Vaupel, J. W. (2012). Human mortality improvement in evolutionary context. *Proceedings of the National Academy of Sciences*, 109(44), 18210–18214. https://doi.org/10.1073/pnas.1215627109.
7. Lee, R. D. (2003). The demographic transition: Three centuries of fundamental change. *Journal of Economic Perspectives*, 17(4), 167–190. https://doi.org/10.1257/089533003772034943.
8. Livi-Bacci, M. (2017). *A concise history of world population (sixth edition)*. Chichester: Wiley.
9. Reher, D. S. (2004). The demographic transition revisited as a global process. *Population, Space and Place*, 10(1), 19–41. https://doi.org/10.1002/psp.313.
10. Livi-Bacci, M. (1991). *Population and nutrition: An essay on European demographic history*. Cambridge: Cambridge University Press.
11. Davis, K. (1945). The world demographic transition. *The Annals of the American Academy of Political and Social Science*, 237(1), 1–11. https://doi.org/10.1177/000271624523700102.
12. Coale, A. J. (2017). *The decline of fertility in Europe*. Princeton: Princeton University Press.
13. Wrigley, E. A. (1985). The fall of marital fertility in nineteenth-century France: Exemplar or exception? (Part I). *European Journal of Population*, 1(1), 31–60. https://doi.org/10.1007/bf01796917.
14. Knodel, J., & van de Walle, E. (1979). Lessons from the past: Policy implications of historical fertility studies. *Population and Development Review*, 5(2), 217–245. https://doi.org/10.2307/1971824.
15. Coale, A. J. (1989). Demographic transition. In J. Eatwell, M. Milgate, & P. Newman (Eds.), *Social economics* (pp. 16–23). London: Palgrave Macmillan. https://doi.org/10.1007/978-1-349-19806-1_4.
16. Chesnais, J. C. (1992). *The demographic transition: Stages, patterns, and economic implications*. Oxford: Oxford University Press.
17. Shorter, E. (1981). L'âge des premières règles en France, 1750–1950. *Annales. Histoire, Sciences Sociales*, 36(3), 495–511. https://doi.org/10.3406/ahess.1981.282759.

18. Weir, D. R. (1984). Life under pressure: France and England, 1670–1870. *The Journal of Economic History*, 44(1), 27–47. https://doi.org/10.1017/S0022050700031351.
19. Banks, J. A., & Banks, O. (1964). *Feminism and family planning in Victorian England*. New York: Schocken.
20. Smith, D. S. (1973). Family limitation, sexual control, and domestic feminism in Victorian America. *Feminist Studies*, 1(3/4), 40–57. https://www.jstor.org/stable/1566479.
21. Woods, R. (2000). *The demography of Victorian England and Wales*. Cambridge: Cambridge University Press.
22. González-Bailón, S., & Murphy, T. E. (2013). The effects of social interactions on fertility decline in nineteenth-century France: An agent-based simulation experiment. *Population Studies*, 67(2), 135–155. https://doi.org/10.1080/00324728.2013.774435.
23. Broadberry, S., & Gupta, B. (2006). The early modern great divergence: Wages, prices and economic development in Europe and Asia, 1500–1800. *The Economic History Review*, 59(1), 2–31. https://doi.org/10.1111/j.1468-0289.2005.00331.x.
24. Pomeranz, K. (2000). *The great divergence: China, Europe, and the making of the modern world economy*. Princeton and Oxford: Princeton University Press.
25. Zhao, Z. (2006). Towards a better understanding of past fertility regimes: The ideas and practice of controlling family size in Chinese history. *Continuity and Change*, 21(01), 9–35. https://doi.org/10.1017/S0268416006005777.
26. Livi Bacci, M. (1999). *The population of Europe*. Oxford: Blackwell.
27. Livi-Bacci, M. (2017). Social-group forerunners of fertility control in Europe. In S. Watkins (Ed.), *The decline of fertility in Europe* (pp. 182–200). Princeton: Princeton University Press. https://doi.org/10.1515/9781400886692-008.
28. Cervellati, M., & Sunde, U. (2005). Human capital formation, life expectancy, and the process of development. *The American Economic Review*, 95(5), 1653–1672. https://www.jstor.org/stable/4132770.
29. Basu, A. M. (2002). Why does education lead to lower fertility? A critical review of some of the possibilities. *World Development*, 30(10), 1779–1790. https://doi.org/10.1016/S0305-750X(02)00072-4.
30. Martin, T. C., & Juarez, F. (1995). The impact of women's education on fertility in Latin America: Searching for explanations. *International Family Planning Perspectives*, 21(2), 52–80. https://doi.org/10.2307/2133523.

31. Green, L. (1979). The education of women in the Reformation. *History of Education Quarterly*, 19(1), 93–116. https://doi.org/10.2307/367811.
32. Ramirez, F. O., & Boli, J. (1987). The political construction of mass schooling: European origins and worldwide institutionalization. *Sociology of Education*, 60(1), 2–17. https://doi.org/10.2307/2112615.
33. Maynes, M. J. (1985). *Schooling in Western Europe: A social history*. Albany: State University of New York Press.
34. Gawthrop, R., & Strauss, G. (1984). Protestantism and literacy in early modern Germany. *Past & Present*, 104(1), 31–55. https://doi.org/10.1093/past/104.1.31.
35. Sehling, E. (2006). Dorfschulmandat. *Die evangelischen Kirchenordnungen des XVI. Jahrhunderts (18. Band = Rheinland-Pfalz, 1)* (pp. 406–407). Tübingen: Mohr Siebeck. https://digi.hadw-bw.de/view/eko18/0010.
36. Murtin, F. (2012). Long-term determinants of the demographic transition, 1870–2000. *Review of Economics and Statistics*, 95(2), 617–631. https://doi.org/10.1162/REST_a_00302.
37. Rasmussen, T. (2007). Fra reformasjon til 1814. In B. T. Oftestad, T. Rasmussen, & J. Schumacher (Eds.), *Norske kirkehistorie* (pp. 85–177). Oslo: Universitetsforlaget.
38. Hope, N. (1999). *German and Scandinavian Protestantism 1700–1918*. Oxford: Clarendon Press.
39. Morrisson, C., & Murtin, F. (2009). The century of education. *Journal of Human Capital*, 3(1), 1–42. https://doi.org/10.1086/600102.
40. Barro, R. J., & Lee, J.-W. (2015). *Education matters: Global schooling gains from the 19th to the 21st century*. New York: Oxford University Press.
41. Cipolla, C. M. (1969). *Literacy and development in the West*. Baltimore: Penguin.
42. Vallin, J. (2006). Europe's demographic transition 1740–1940. In G. Caselli, J. Vallin, & G. Wunsch (Eds.), *Demography: Analysis and synthesis, four volume set (Vol. III)* (pp. 41–66). Burlington, MA, San Diego, London: Academic Press.
43. Buringh, E., & Van Zanden, J. L. (2009). Charting the "rise of the West": Manuscripts and printed books in Europe, a long-term perspective from the sixth through eighteenth centuries. *The Journal of Economic History*, 69(2), 409–445. https://doi.org/10.1017/S0022050709000837.
44. UNESCO Institute for Statistics (2013). *Adult and youth literacy: National, regional and global trends, 1985–2015*. Montreal: UNESCO Institute for Statistics.

45. Barro, R. J., & Lee, J. W. (2013). A new data set of educational attainment in the world, 1950–2010. *Journal of Development Economics*, 104, 184–198. https://doi.org/10.1016/j.jdeveco.2012.10.001.
46. United Nations (2019). World Population Prospects 2019. https://population.un.org/wpp/. Accessed 25 May 2021.
47. Luther, M. (1524). An die Ratsherrn aller Städte deutschen Landes, dass sie christliche Schulen aufrichten und halten sollen [To the councilmen of all cities in Germany that they establish and maintain Christian schools]. https://www.checkluther.com/wp-content/uploads/1524-To-the-Councilmen-of-All-Cities-in-Germany-that-they-Establish-and-Maintain-Christian-Schools.pdf.
48. Dyson, T., & Murphy, M. (1985). The onset of fertility transition. *Population and Development Review*, 11(3), 399–440. https://doi.org/10.2307/1973246.
49. Riley, J. C. (2005). Estimates of regional and global life expectancy, 1800–2001. *Population and Development Review*, 31(3), 537–543. https://doi.org/10.1111/j.1728-4457.2005.00083.x.
50. Davis, K. (1963). The theory of change and response in modern demographic history. *Population Index*, 29(4), 345–366. https://doi.org/10.2307/2732014.
51. Notestein, F. W. (1953). Economic problems of population change. *Proceedings of the Eighth International Conference of Agricultural Economists* (pp. 13–31). London: Oxford University Press.
52. Zimmer, Z., & McDaniel, S. (2016). Global ageing in the twenty-first century: An introduction. In S. McDaniel, & Z. Zimmer (Eds.), *Global ageing in the twenty-first century* (pp. 21–32). London: Routledge.
53. Roser, M. Fertility rate. https://ourworldindata.org/fertility-rate. Accessed 26 May 2021.
54. Keinan, A., & Clark, A. G. (2012). Recent explosive human population growth has resulted in an excess of rare genetic variants. *Science*, 336(6082), 740–743. https://doi.org/10.1126/science.1217283.
55. Davidson, A. D., Shoemaker, K. T., Weinstein, B., Costa, G. C., Brooks, T. M., Ceballos, G., et al. (2017). Geography of current and future global mammal extinction risk. *PLoS ONE*, 12(11), e0186934. https://doi.org/10.1371/journal.pone.0186934.
56. Skirbekk, V., Stonawski, M., & Alfani, G. (2015). Consequences of a universal European demographic transition on regional and global population distributions. *Technological Forecasting and Social Change*, 98, 271–289. https://doi.org/10.1016/j.techfore.2015.05.003.

57. United Nations (1973). The determinants and consequences of population trends: New summary of findings on interaction of demographic, economic and social factors. Population studies no. 50. New York: United Nations.
58. Maddison, A. (2010). Statistics on world population, GDP, and per capita GDP 1-2008 AD. Groningen: Groningen Growth and Development Centre, University of Groningen. http://ghdx.healthdata.org/record/statistics-world-population-gdp-and-capita-gdp-1-2008-ad. Accessed 26 May 2021.
59. Wrigley, E. A., Davies, R. S., Oeppen, J. E., & Schofield, R. S. (1997). *English population history from family reconstitution 1580–1837*. New York: Cambridge University Press.
60. Sardon, J.-P. (1991). Generation replacement in Europe since 1900. *Population: An English Selection*, 3, 15–32. https://doi.org/10.2307/2949130.
61. Sanderson, W. C. (1987). Below-replacement fertility in nineteenth century America. *Population and Development Review*, 13(2), 305–313. https://doi.org/10.2307/1973195.
62. Cleland, J. (2001). The effects of improved survival on fertility: A reassessment. *Population and Development Review*, 27, 60–92. https://doi.org/10.2307/3115250.
63. The World Bank (2020). World Bank Open Data. https://data.worldbank.org/. Accessed 25 May 2021.
64. Bardet, J.-P. (1983). *Rouen au XVIIe et XVIIIe siecles. Les mutations d'un espace social [Rouen in the XVIIth and XVIIIth centuries. changes of a social environment]*. Paris: Societe D'Edition D'Ensieignement Superieur.
65. Skirbekk, V. (2008). Fertility trends by social status. *Demographic Research*, 18(5), 145–180. https://doi.org/10.4054/DemRes.2008.18.5.
66. Jejeebhoy, S. (1995). *Women's education, autonomy and reproductive behaviour: Experience from developing countries*. Oxford: Clarendon Press.
67. Van Bavel, J. (2006). The effect of fertility limitation on intergenerational social mobility: The quality-quantity trade-off during the demographic transition. *Journal of Biosocial Science*, 38(4), 553–569. https://doi.org/10.1017/S0021932005026994.

6
Contemporary Global Fertility

Fertility has declined all over the world, but there is still enormous variation between countries and world regions. In the 2015–2020 period, for instance, the TFR was nearly three times as high in sub-Saharan Africa as in Europe [1]. Even within regions and countries, some subpopulations display very different fertility behavior than their peers. Prior to the demographic transition, higher fertility tended to be offset by higher mortality. Today, however, fertility variation almost always translates directly into variations in population size and growth. In this chapter, I describe contemporary fertility around the globe in relation to the "replacement level" and population growth.

Replacement Level: How Many Births Does It Take to Sustain a Population?

The *replacement level* is the level of fertility at which a population would exactly "replace" itself from one generation to the next, disregarding migration and any changes in mortality. In other words, it is the level of

V. Skirbekk, *Decline and Prosper!*,
https://doi.org/10.1007/978-3-030-91611-4_6

fertility at which population size would remain stable over the long term if there were no migration and constant mortality rates. Fertility above the replacement level implies that the population will grow, while fertility below the replacement level implies that the population will shrink.

The replacement level depends on mortality through the reproductive years: Higher mortality means that fertility also needs to be higher in order to have two surviving children who survive long enough to reproduce themselves. Figure 6.1 illustrates the relationship between the replacement level and life expectancy at birth. Here, the replacement level is defined specifically as the average number of children women must have for two children to survive to their mid-reproductive years [2]. As can be seen in the figure, when life expectancy at birth is in the early 20s, the replacement level is six to seven children. When life expectancy at birth is around 50 years, the replacement level is around three children per woman. When life expectancy at birth is 70 or higher (as it is in most countries today), the replacement level is just over two children per woman [2]. Average life expectancy for the 2015–2020 period was just under 71 years in less developed countries and just over 79 years in

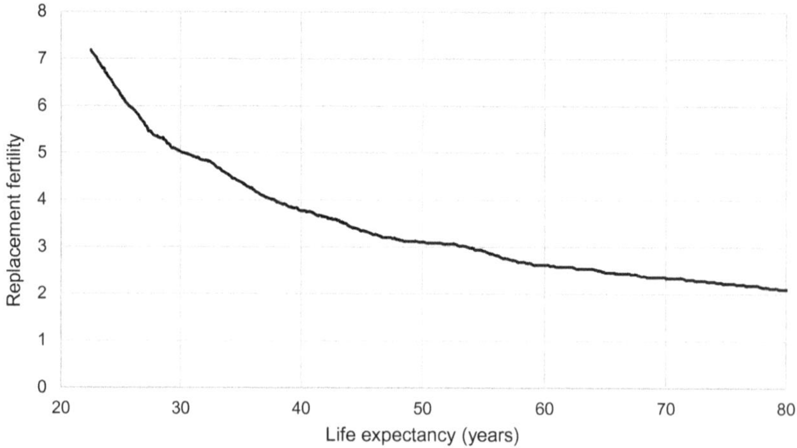

Fig. 6.1 Replacement fertility by life expectancy at birth. When life expectancy is lower, the replacement level is higher. Here, replacement fertility is defined as the number of children per woman required to for two children to survive to their mid-reproductive years. Own estimates based on [2]

more developed countries [1]. Accordingly, the United Nations currently defines global replacement fertility as slightly above two children per woman, declining over time as mortality falls [3].

The replacement level is a common cut-off for categorizing countries; countries with fertility above the replacement level are often said to have high fertility, while countries with fertility below the replacement level are said to have low fertility. Another common cut-off is a TFR of 1.3 children per woman. A TFR below 1.3 children per woman implies that each subsequent generation will be less than two-thirds the size of the preceding generation. Scholars sometimes refer to a TFR below 1.3 as the "lowest-low" fertility level [4, 5]. Lowest-low fertility implies that the median age of the population will increase, independent of migration and changes in mortality. Assuming there is no migration and without dramatic increases in life expectancy, in the longer term a TFR of 1.3 or less implies that the population will dwindle toward extinction.

It is important to note that a population with replacement fertility will experience zero population growth *only* if mortality rates remain constant and net migration is zero (i.e., the number of immigrants equals the number of immigrants) [6]. In contexts where life expectancy is increasing over time, fertility can be substantially below two children per woman, and one can nevertheless still observe population stability. Notably, the optimal level of fertility for maximizing per capita income over the longer term has been estimated to be somewhere in the range from 1.48 to 1.78 children per woman—much lower than the replacement level [7].

Global Fertility Has Declined Radically, but Remains Above the Replacement Level

Average global fertility in the 2010s (around 2.5 children per woman) was about half of global average fertility just 50 years ago (around 5 children per woman from 1960 to 1965), and by now most of the world's population live in countries with low fertility. In 2017, almost half of the world's countries had below replacement fertility [8], and by the 2010s, the majority of the world's population lived in countries with below replacement fertility [9, 10]. Low fertility is not exclusively a modern phenomenon; low and even very low fertility was observed among elite groups in Japan already among those born 1910–1919 [11], among European nobility and aristocrats well before the first quarter of the twentieth century [12], and in certain regions of the United States already in the nineteenth century [13]. However, the global preponderance of low fertility represents a new and truly dramatic historical change.

World total fertility rate [14]
1950: 5.05 children per woman
2020: 2.44 children per woman

Figure 6.2 makes it clear just how dramatically global fertility has declined within the last fifty years [14]. The figure displays the proportion of the world population living in countries with high and low fertility in 1950–1955, 1975–1980, and 2005–2010. Countries are

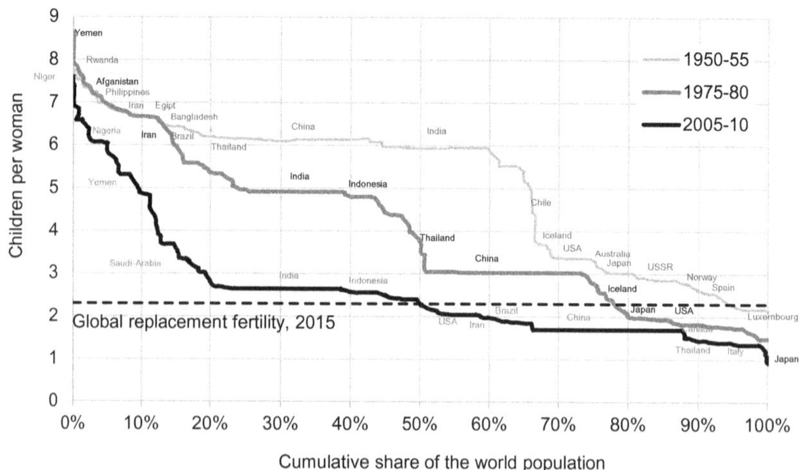

Fig. 6.2 Share of the world population living in countries with high and low fertility, 1950/1955, 1975/1980, and 2005/2010. Adapted from [14]

displayed according to their TFR in descending order; the country with the highest fertility rate in each time period is visible in the upper left corner. In 1950/1955, about two-thirds of the world's population lived in countries with very high fertility (i.e., an average of more than five children per woman), and almost the entire world population lived in countries with a TFR well above the current global replacement level. By the 2000s, more than half of the world's population lived in countries with a TFR *below* the current global replacement level, and just about 10% lived in countries with a TFR above five children per woman. Many countries with high fertility in the 1950s (e.g., Brazil, Thailand, China) had fertility below the global replacement level by 2000/2005. Figure 6.2 also shows that the highest TFR and lowest TFR in the world have both fallen somewhat over the past fifty years.

The United Nations estimates that average global fertility between 2010 and 2015 was 2.5 children per woman; another estimate put average global fertility at 2.4 children per woman in 2017 [3]. Thus, despite dramatic decline, global fertility is still greater than the replacement level and hence implies that the global population will grow. Absolute declines in fertility have been larger for countries with initially high fertility. This implies that, overall, fertility is converging over time at a lower level, but also that the gap between countries early on in the fertility transition and the rest of the world has widened [15]. Returning to Fig. 6.2, the current global range of fertility levels is not very different from the global range observed in 1950/1955 or 1975/1980, as the highest and lowest observed fertility rates have changed only moderately. However, there are far fewer countries "in the middle" than before; in other words, there is increased polarization between countries with high fertility and countries with low fertility.

Fertility Still Varies Widely Across World Regions

Although fertility is declining in all regions of the world, considerable differences between world regions and countries remain. In the 2015–2020 period, for example, the TFR was 1.61 children per woman in

Europe, 1.65 in Eastern Asia, 1.75 in North America, 2.04 in Latin America, 3.25 in Northern Africa, 3.46 in Oceania (excluding New Zealand and Australia), and 4.72 in sub-Saharan Africa [1]. The TFR in sub-Saharan Africa was thus nearly three times that of Europe. In the same time period, country-level fertility ranged from 1.11 in South Korea to 6.95 children per woman in Niger [1].

Figure 6.3 displays the world map with countries shaded according to their TFR in 2015. Looking at the map, it becomes readily apparent that fertility varies widely across countries, ranging from 7–8 children per woman in Niger to just 1–2 children per woman in most European and North American countries, several Asian and Latin American countries, as well as Australia and New Zealand.

Figure 6.3 shows that most of the high fertility countries are concentrated in sub-Saharan Africa, including Nigeria, Africa's most populous country [3]. The only exceptions are Afghanistan, Iraq, and East Timor. Compared with the rest of the world, sub-Saharan Africa has relatively high levels of illiteracy (34% in 2018 [16]) and low education. There are fewer economic opportunities and often restricted access to contraception. People in this world region are generally more religious, tend to have more traditional family values and fatalistic attitudes toward

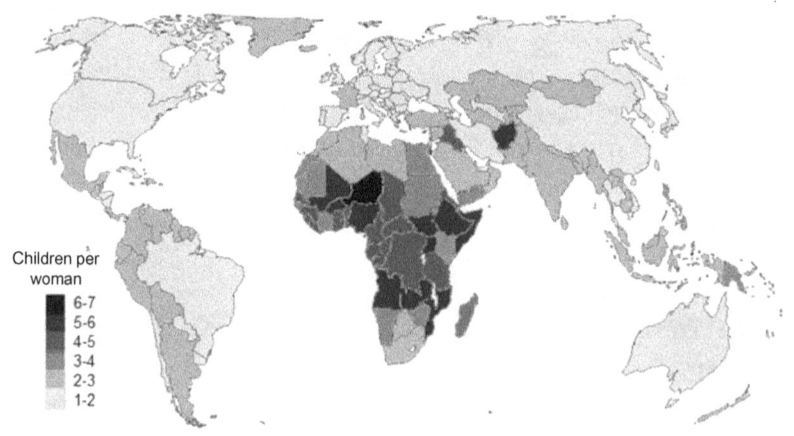

Fig. 6.3 Total fertility rate by country, 2015. Based on [14]

childbearing are widespread [17, 18]. Childbearing and marriage remain close to universal, and majorities marry at a relatively young age. Within marriages, childbearing is often expected and is the basis for legal, social, and cultural systems [19]. Fertility preferences (i.e., how many children people say they want to have) also remain higher in sub-Saharan Africa than in other world regions [20].

Figure 6.3 also makes it clear, however, that fertility across the African countries also varies widely, much more so than across the countries in any other world region. Fertility rates in several sub-Saharan African countries have declined significantly over the past two decades. Ethiopia, Malawi, and Rwanda have reduced average fertility partly through educational expansion and successful family planning programs. Between 1990 and 2010, for instance, the fertility rate in Ethiopia decreased by almost two children per woman [21]. Tunisia has a TFR below 2 children per woman, and South Africa has a TFR between 2 and 3 children per woman. Other data indicates that the TFR in Mauritius had fallen to just 1.4 children per woman in the 2010s [22]. There are also examples of subpopulations or areas within countries with very low fertility, such as in the Ethiopian capital Addis Ababa, where in the 2010s the TFR was below 1.7 children per woman [23].

Compared to sub-Saharan Africa, fertility in North America, Latin America, Oceania, Western, and Northern Europe is generally low (i.e., around the replacement level in most countries) [24–26]. In these world regions, increasing proportions of the population do not marry and people have children later in life. Once again, it is important to keep in mind that fertility in pre-transition Europe was already lower than in the rest of world (four to six versus six to eight children on average). In Europe, fertility thus only had to be reduced by a bit more than half in order reach the replacement level. A much more dramatic reduction was and is needed to attain replacement fertility under low mortality conditions in other world regions. Iran has witnessed an especially dramatic decline. Iranian fertility fell from 5.62 in 1985–1990 to below two children per woman in 2000–2005 [1], due in large part to government policies aimed at reducing fertility, rapid increases in education, and better access to contraception [27].

In the last decades, the lowest fertility in the world has been observed in East Asia and in Southern and Eastern Europe. At some point in the 1990s and the 2010s, the TFR in the East Asian "Tiger" economies of Taiwan, Singapore, Macau, Hong Kong, and South Korea fell to 1.3 or fewer children per woman [4]. Fertility is similarly low in several countries in Southern and Eastern Europe (Bosnia and Herzegovina, Greece, Italy, Moldova, Portugal, Spain), as well as in Cyprus and Puerto Rico [1]. Notably, in some low fertility countries, including in Eastern Europe, fertility has slightly rebounded in recent years—but this likely largely reflects a "tempo effect," whereby cohorts who postponed childbearing in an earlier period are "catching up" as they near the end of their reproductive window [28, 29].

In many of the lowest-low fertility countries/territories, fertility is close to around one birth per woman [8]. In Puerto Rico, for example, fertility was just 1.2 children per woman in the 2015–2020 period [1]. The very high costs of childbearing and fear that having children will deteriorate one's living standards have been cited as reasons for very low fertility in some countries. Other factors include difficulties finding a partner and difficulties combining work with childbearing and traditional gender norms [30]. The One Child Policy is a major reason why China had very low fertility from the 1970s onwards [31]. The One Child Policy has contributed to the internalization of low fertility norms even in the generations born after fertility decline [32, 33]. Many of the very low fertility countries have had below replacement fertility for more than four decades, suggesting that fertility will not easily rebound and is likely to remain below the replacement level in the years to come [22, 34, 35].

Differences *Within* Countries Can Be as Dramatic as Differences *Between* Countries

Fertility differences within countries can be just as dramatic as differences between countries. India serves as an excellent example. Overall, the TFR in India was 2.24 children per woman in the 2015–2020 period [1], yet there are major differences between the northern and southern Indian states. Fertility in the southern states such as Tamil Nadu, Kerala, and

Karnataka was below replacement fertility in 2016. In fact, Kerala had below replacement fertility already in the late decades of the twentieth century [36] and much of the central and southern regions of India had low fertility by the early twenty-first century [37, 38]. In contrast, large proportions of the population in the northern Indian states (including Bihar and Uttar Pradesh) have relatively high fertility—around three children per woman in 2016 [39].

Fertility in the Indian state of Kerala reached replacement level already in the late 1980s. Interestingly, Kerala's fertility decline occurred in the absence of significant economic development. Instead, high education, high female empowerment due to a matrilineal cultural system, and successful family planning campaigns are thought to be the main catalysts of Kerala's fertility decline [40].

Fertility generally tends to be higher in areas where the population is less educated, where more people are illiterate, and where there is more poverty and fewer economic opportunities. Regional variation in religion and culture also plays a role. In Finland, fertility rates are substantially higher in regions with a higher share of Laestadians (a traditional religious group) [41]. Fertility also tends to be higher in rural than in urban regions. The urban/rural difference has been observed in higher fertility countries such as Brazil [42], Afghanistan [43], and Egypt [44], but also in low fertility countries such as Russia [45], The Netherlands [46], Finland [47, 48], and the United States [49]. Some of the largest urban/rural differences are observed in sub-Saharan Africa [50, 51], where women in the capital cities typically have three fewer children than their peers in rural areas [52].

Contemporary Fertility: A Polarized World

Global fertility has declined dramatically over the past fifty years, and most people now live in countries where fertility is below the replacement level. The key take-home message of this chapter is, however, one of diversity. Huge differences between world regions, countries, and even between different subpopulations within countries remain. Fertility is by far the highest in sub-Saharan Africa and lowest in parts of Eastern Asia and the Western world. Due to lower mortality, differences in fertility translate more or less directly into differences in the rate of population growth. Fertility tends to be higher in regions where the population is less educated, more religious, poorer, and more rural. I discuss how education, religion, and costs of childbearing are related to fertility at length in subsequent chapters.

References

1. United Nations (2019). World Population Prospects 2019. https://population.un.org/wpp/. Accessed 25 May 2021.
2. Coale, A. J., Demeny, P. G., & Vaughan, B. (1983). *Regional model life tables and stable populations*. Princeton: Princeton University Press.
3. Population Reference Bureau (2018). World Population Data Sheet. https://www.prb.org/2018-world-population-data-sheet-with-focus-on-changing-age-structures/.
4. Jones, G., Straughan, P. T., & Chan, A. (2009). *Ultra-low fertility in Pacific Asia: Trends, causes and policy issues*. New York: Routledge.
5. Anderson, T., & Kohler, H. P. (2015). Low fertility, socioeconomic development, and gender equity. *Population and Development Review*, 41(3), 381–407. https://doi.org/10.1111/j.1728-4457.2015.00065.x.
6. Craig, J. (1994). Replacement level fertility and future population growth. *Population Trends*, 78, 20–22.
7. Lee, R., Mason, A., Amporfu, E., An, C.-B., Bixby, L. R., Bravo, J., et al. (2014). Is low fertility really a problem? Population aging, dependency, and consumption. *Science*, 346(6206), 229–234. https://doi.org/10.1126/science.1250542.
8. Billari, F. C. (2018). A "great divergence" in fertility? In D. J. Poston (Ed.), *Low fertility regimes and demographic and societal change* (pp. 15–35). Cham: Springer. https://doi.org/10.1007/978-3-319-64061-7_2.
9. United Nations (2019). World Population Prospects 2019: Highlights. New York: U. Nations. https://www.un-ilibrary.org/content/publication/13bf5476-en. Accessed 26 May 2021.

10. Wilson, C., & Pison, G. (2004). More than half of the global population lives where fertility is below replacement level. *Population and Societies*, 405, 1–4.
11. Müller, U. (1991). The reproductive success of the elites in Germany, Great Britain Japan and the USA during the 19th and 20th century. ZUMA-Arbeitsbericht Nr. 91/22. Mannheim: Zentrum für Umfragen Methoden und Analysen.
12. Johansson, S. R. (1987). Status anxiety and demographic contraction of privileged populations. *Population and Development Review*, 13(3), 439–470. https://doi.org/10.2307/1973134.
13. Sanderson, W. C. (1987). Below-replacement fertility in nineteenth century America. *Population and Development Review*, 13(2), 305–313. https://doi.org/10.2307/1973195.
14. Roser, M. Fertility rate. https://ourworldindata.org/fertility-rate. Accessed 26 May 2021.
15. Strulik, H., & Vollmer, S. (2015). The fertility transition around the world. *Journal of Population Economics*, 28(1), 31–44. https://doi.org/10.1007/s00148-013-0496-2.
16. The World Bank (2020). Literacy rate, adult total (% of people ages 15 and above). https://data.worldbank.org/indicator/SE.ADT.LITR.ZS?end=2018&start=2018&view=map. Accessed 1 June 2021.
17. May, J. F. (2017). The politics of family planning policies and programs in sub-Saharan Africa. *Population and Development Review*, 43(S1), 308–329. https://doi.org/10.1111/j.1728-4457.2016.00165.x.
18. Howse, K. (2015). What is fertility stalling and why does it matter? *Population Horizons*, 12(1), 13–23. https://doi.org/10.1515/pophzn-2015-0003.
19. OECD (2011). The future of families to 2030. Paris: OECD. https://www.oecd.org/futures/49093502.pdf. Accessed 1 June 2021.
20. Bongaarts, J., & Casterline, J. (2013). Fertility transition: Is sub-Saharan Africa different? *Population and Development Review*, 38, 153–168. https://doi.org/10.1111/j.1728-4457.2013.00557.x.
21. May, J. F. (2017). The politics of family planning policies and programs in sub-Saharan Africa. *Population and Development Review*, 43, 308–329. https://doi.org/10.1111/j.1728-4457.2016.00165.x.
22. United Nations (2017). World Population Prospects 2017. United Nations. https://population.un.org/wpp/Download/Archive/Standard/. Accessed 26 May 2021.

23. Hailemariam, A. (2017). The second biggest African country undergoing rapid change: Ethiopia. In H. Groth, & J. F. May (Eds.), *Africa's population: In search of a demographic dividend* (pp. 53–69). Cham: Springer International.
24. Sobotka, T. (2017). Post-transitional fertility: The role of childbearing postponement in fuelling the shift to low and unstable fertility levels. *Journal of Biosocial Science*, 49(S1), S20–S45. https://doi.org/10.1017/S0021932017000323.
25. Jones, G. (2018). What is driving marriage and cohabitation in low fertility countries? In D. J. Poston (Ed.), *Low fertility regimes and demographic and societal change* (pp. 149–166). Cham: Springer.
26. Raymo, J. M., Park, H., Xie, Y., & Yeung, W.-j. J. (2015). Marriage and family in East Asia: Continuity and change. *Annual Review of Sociology*, 41, 471–492. https://doi.org/10.1146/annurev-soc-073014-112428.
27. Vahidnia, F. (2007). Case study: Fertility decline in Iran. *Population and Environment*, 28(4–5), 259–266. https://doi.org/10.1007/s11111-007-0050-9.
28. Lutz, W., & Skirbekk, V. (2005). Policies addressing the tempo effect in low-fertility countries. *Population and Development Review*, 31(4), 699–720. https://doi.org/10.1111/j.1728-4457.2005.00094.x.
29. Sobotka, T., Skirbekk, V., & Philipov, D. (2011). Economic recession and fertility in the developed world. *Population and Development Review*, 37(2), 267–306. https://doi.org/10.1111/j.1728-4457.2011.00411.x.
30. Yoon, S.-Y. (2016). Is gender inequality a barrier to realizing fertility intentions? Fertility aspirations and realizations in South Korea. *Asian Population Studies*, 12(2), 203–219. https://doi.org/10.1080/17441730.2016.1163873.
31. Feng, W., Gu, B., & Cai, Y. (2016). The end of China's One-Child Policy. *Studies in Family Planning*, 47(1), 83–86. https://doi.org/10.1111/j.1728-4465.2016.00052.x.
32. Guo, Z. (2016). Understanding fertility trends in China. In C. Z. Guilmoto, & G. W. Jones (Eds.), *Contemporary demographic transformations in China, India and Indonesia* (pp. 97–111). Cham: Springer.
33. Zhao, Z. C. (2011). China's far below-replacement fertility and its long-term impact: Comments on the preliminary results of the 2010 census. *Demographic Research*, 25(26), 819–836. https://doi.org/10.4054/DemRes.2011.25.26.
34. McDonald, P. (2006). An assessment of policies that support having children from the perspectives of equity, efficiency and efficacy. *Vienna*

Yearbook of Population Research, 213–234. https://www.jstor.org/stable/23025484.

35. Lutz, W., Skirbekk, V., & Testa, M. R. (2006). The low-fertility trap hypothesis: Forces that may lead to further postponement and fewer births in Europe. *Vienna Yearbook of Population Research*, 167–192. http://www.iiasa.ac.at/Admin/PUB/Documents/RP-07-001.pdf.
36. George, M. V. (2010). The fertility decline in India's Kerala state: A unique example of below replacement fertility in a high fertility country. *Canadian Studies in Population*, 37(3–4), 563–600. https://doi.org/10.25336/P6X89J.
37. Sarkar, K. (2017). Fertility transition in India: Emerging significance of infertility and childlessness. In A. Ranjan, & B. K. Singh (Eds.), *India 2016: Population. Transition Selected Papers of Bhopal Seminar 2016* (pp. 87–100). Bhopal: MLC Foundation and Shyam Institute. http://www.shyaminstitute.in/monograph_16.pdf.
38. Driver, E. D. (2015). *Differential fertility in central India*. Princeton, NJ: Princeton University Press.
39. International Institute for Population Sciences (2017). Fourth National Family Health Survey, India. http://rchiips.org/nfhs/nfhs4.shtml. Accessed 1 June 2021.
40. Nair, P. S. (2010). Understanding below-replacement fertility in Kerala, India. *Journal of Health, Population, and Nutrition*, 28(4), 405–412. https://doi.org/10.3329/jhpn.v28i4.6048.
41. Terämä, E. (2010). Regional demographic differences: The effect of Laestadians. *Finnish Yearbook of Population Research*, 45, 123–141.
42. Coutinho, R. (2016). The transition to low fertility in Brazil. PhD thesis, University of North Carolina at Chapel Hill. https://core.ac.uk/reader/210597355.
43. Fernández, R., Rodríguez Wong, L. L., & Tia, M. (2017). The reproductive behaviour in Afghanistan—Signals of the onset of the fertility transition in Kabul and selected provinces at the 2nd decade of the XXI century (Paper presented at the 18th International Population Conference of the IUSSP, Cape Town). https://iussp.confex.com/iussp/ipc2017/mediafile/Presentation/Paper7525/IPC2017-Fertility%20in%20Afghanistan%20%28full%20paper%29.pdf.
44. Ambrosetti, E., Angeli, A., & Novelli, M. (2019). Ideal family size and fertility in Egypt: An overview of recent trends. *Statistica*, 79(2), 223–244. https://doi.org/10.6092/issn.1973-2201/8811.

45. Zakharov, S. V., & Ivanova, E. I. (1996). Regional fertility differentiation in Russia: 1959–1994. *Studies on Russian Economic Development*, 7(4), 354–368.
46. Mulder, C. H., & Wagner, M. (2001). The connections between family formation and first-time home ownership in the context of West Germany and The Netherlands. *European Journal of Population/Revue europeenne de demographie*, 17(2), 137–164. https://doi.org/10.1023/A:1010706308868.
47. Kulu, H. (2013). Why do fertility levels vary between urban and rural areas? *Regional Studies*, 47(6), 895–912. https://doi.org/10.1080/00343404.2011.581276.
48. Lainiala, L., & Berg, V. (2016). Spatial trends of fertility rates in Finland between 1980 and 2014. *Finnish Yearbook of Population Research*, 51, 89–95.
49. Glusker, A. I., Dobie, S. A., Madigan, D., Rosenblatt, R. A., & Larson, E. H. (2000). Differences in fertility patterns between urban and rural women in Washington State, 1983–1984 to 1993–1994. *Women & Health*, 31(1), 55–70. https://doi.org/10.1300/J013v31n01_04.
50. Desta, C. G. (2019). Rural-urban differential in fertility and maternal work participation: A study in Northwestern Ethiopia. *African Population Studies*, 33(2), 4861–4875. https://doi.org/10.11564/33-2-1389.
51. Lerch, M. (2017). Urban and rural fertility transitions in the developing world: A cohort perspective. MPIDR Working Paper WP 2017-011. Rostock: Max Planck Institute for Demographic Research. https://www.demogr.mpg.de/papers/working/wp-2017-011.pdf. Accessed 1 June 2021.
52. Lesthaeghe, R. (2014). The fertility transition in sub-Saharan Africa into the 21st century. Population Studies Center Research Reports 14-823. Ann Arbor: University of Michigan Institute for Social Research. https://www.vub.be/demography/wp-content/uploads/2016/02/rr14-823_SS_Afric.pdf. Accessed 1 June 2021.

7

The New Have-Nots: Childlessness in the Twenty-First Century

Around the world, both the number and the proportion of people without their own biological children have increased. In some countries, the increase has been quite dramatic. The increase in childlessness partly reflects increases in both the number of people with fertility problems (primarily due to people postponing when they first try to have a baby) and the number of people who purposefully choose to remain "child free" (and their ability to remain childfree thanks to contraception and the liberalization of family norms). More often than not, contemporary childlessness is "coincidental;" that is, people often end up childless without explicitly intending to do so. Another key trend in childlessness has been the diverging gender pattern—in many countries, childlessness is increasingly becoming more of a male than a female phenomenon. In this chapter, I discuss recent trends in childlessness around the world, their causes and some implications—including societal polarization between those who have children (the haves) and those who do not (the have nots).

V. Skirbekk, *Decline and Prosper!*,
https://doi.org/10.1007/978-3-030-91611-4_7

Childlessness Is Increasing Globally

Childlessness has increased all over the world, particularly in richer countries [1–5]. The increase in childlessness has been associated with many different factors, including improving education and economic opportunities (particularly for women), the delay and decline in marriage, increases in the use of reliable contraception, higher costs of housing, the stubborn incompatibility of many professional careers with childbearing, many alternatives for time use, and the increased social acceptance of choosing not to have children. In more developed countries, typically more than one in 10 women in their late 40s does not have children [3]. In some countries, the proportion is much higher. Approximately one in five women in their late 40s is childless in England, Germany, The Netherlands, and the United States, and one in four women in their late 40s is childless in Italy, Switzerland, and Singapore [6]; moreover, the proportion of women who are childless in their late 40s is increasing [7]. In most less developed countries, the proportion of women who are childless at the end of their reproductive window is generally much lower, often below 5% [4, 8]. Liberia and Congo report that less than 2% of women remain childless, although the United Nations has suggested that childlessness typically does not dip below 3% [9]. Nevertheless, childlessness is also on the increase in many lower income countries as well, increasing, for instance, among married women aged 40–44 in India from 4% in 1981 to 7% in 2011 [4]. When considering these statistics, it is important to keep in mind that statistics about childlessness (a measure of cohort fertility typically assessed at age 40, 45, or 49) can only be collected with considerable delay, as the fertility of women in their 40s mainly reflects behaviors and decisions carried out during their peak reproductive years one or two decades earlier.

Notably, low fertility does not always correspond with high childlessness. To illustrate this point, Fig. 7.1 displays the proportion of women born in 1972 who were childless at the end of their reproductive windows in a number of low fertility countries (i.e., where fertility is substantially below the replacement level). Although fertility is low in

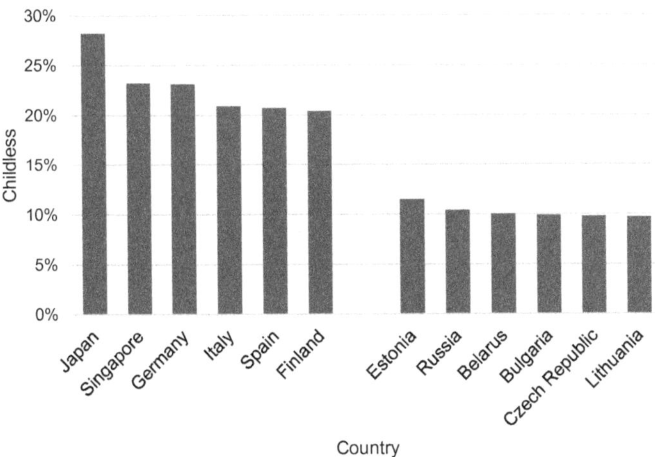

Fig. 7.1 Percent of women born in 1972 who were childless in their 40s (observed in 2013–2014) in selected low fertility countries. Based on [3, 10]

all of the selected countries, childlessness was about twice as common in the low fertility countries in East Asia and Western Europe than in the low fertility Eastern European countries. In Japan, for instance, more than one out of four (28.2%) women in this birth cohort were childless; similarly, childlessness ranged between 20.4 and 23.2% for women in Spain, Italy, Finland, Germany, and Singapore. In contrast, childlessness was much less common in the selected low fertility Eastern European countries (around one out of ten women), where low fertility is due to the high share of women who have just one child as opposed to a high proportion of childless women.

Childlessness Has Become a Male Phenomenon

Not only is childlessness increasing, in a number of industrialized countries it is also becoming more of a male as opposed to a female phenomenon. In several industrialized countries, childlessness is now more common among men than it is among women [11]. In the United

Kingdom, for instance, 22% of men born in 1958 were childless at the age of 46, compared with just 16% of women. In the period between 2006 and 2010, one in four men in the United States was childless at age 40, compared to around one in seven women [2]. In Finland, an astonishing *one in three* men was childless at age 40 in 2015; in some Finnish regions, the proportion was as high as 40% [12]. The observed differences in statistics on male and female childlessness reflect a real and increasing gender divergence in reproduction as opposed to just gender differences in reporting (e.g., men failing to report that they have children) [13, 14].

Overall, there is far less data on male than on female childlessness. The Nordic countries are an anomaly in that they have excellent historical data on *both* male and female fertility. Nordic data provides an indication of how male and female childlessness has changed over time. The data provides an indication not only of how childlessness has changed in the Nordic countries specifically, but also in other industrialized countries more generally.

"I expected to be a dad, I wanted to be a dad and at times, I have been desperate to be a dad. How did I not become a dad? I did not become a dad through a whole constellation of circumstances....Now there are times when I am very sad not to have been a dad. I am surprised to be revisiting my jealousy, envy, and difference because, unlike my peers, I am not going to be a grandad either."

-Dr. Robin Hadley on his personal experience of involuntarily childlessness [15]. Dr. Hadley's research on male childlessness dispels the myth that men do not care about having children.

According to Norwegian data, childlessness among Norwegian women aged 40 increased from 9% for women born in 1940 to 16% for women born in 1979. In comparison, the increase in childlessness for the same birth cohorts among men aged 40 has been much more dramatic—rising from 14 to 30%, see Fig. 7.2 [16]. Although the precise numbers shown

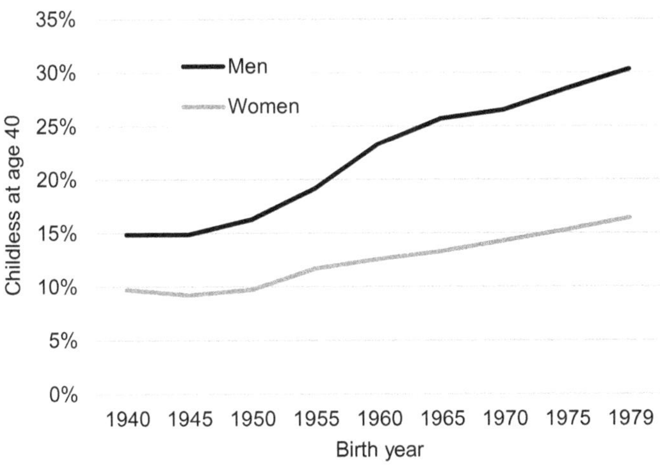

Fig. 7.2 Percent of birth cohort childless at age 40, Norway. Based on [16]

in Fig. 7.2 are particular to Norway, the general pattern is thought to hold true for many other high-income countries. Similarly, a Danish study indicated a recent and rapid rise in male, but not female, childlessness [17]. The high and increasing childlessness among men in several industrialized countries is a public health concern because men without children tend, on average, to be less socially integrated and have smaller social networks. They also tend to have less education, lower income and less stable jobs, worse health, and shorter lives.

From a Lack of Surviving Men to a Lack of "Suitable" Men

With rates of childlessness upwards of 20% and overall fertility rates well below the replacement level, childlessness has become a concern for many European countries. High childlessness is, however, not a new phenomenon in Europe. About 20–30% of European women born at the beginning of the twentieth century remained childless, making childlessness early in the twentieth century just as common, if not more common, than it is today. For the cohorts of women born in the mid-twentieth century, in most European countries only about 15% remained childless. The proportion was as low as 5% in the Czech Republic and Bulgaria. Female childlessness began to gradually rise again among the cohorts of women born in 1950 onwards. For the 1968 female cohort, childlessness ranged from a high of 23% in Germany to a low of about 8% in Bulgaria [18]. For cohorts born in the 1970s, childlessness in some countries reached levels between 20 and 30%, although some may still have children [3].

Although childlessness in several European countries was just as (or even more) prevalent at the start than at the end of the twentieth century, the gender pattern in childlessness has reversed [19, 20] and the reasons for remaining childlessness have changed. The high childlessness for women born in the early 1900s arose mainly because their peak reproductive years coincided with a period of deep economic recession, improvements in contraception, large political upheavals, social and economic uncertainties, and two world wars [21]. High male mortality during World War I [22] was a key reason why so many European women born at the beginning of the twentieth century remained childless: Because so many of their male peers had died, many women were simply unable to find a mate. Although there is a lack of representative data on male childlessness in the same time period, it is safe to assume that fewer men than women remained childless.

Unlike at the start of the twentieth century, nowadays there is no shortage of men in Europe. In most countries around the world, the sex ratio of men and women in their reproductive ages is close to unity, except for some countries in which migration and/or sex-selective abortion have (at least temporarily) altered the balance [23]. Contemporary childlessness thus has less to do with a lack of men, and much more to do with a lack of "suitable" men, as women have become increasingly selective. Even in the world's most gender-egalitarian countries, women tend to prefer men with relatively high income and education, as well as specific personal characteristics (e.g., low neuroticism) [16, 24]. More men than women have mental health problems, drink excessively, are prone to violence, or have drug problems [25–27] which might make some men less attractive as potential co-parents. Men with "undesirable" characteristics do not tend to fare well in the marriage and parenting market. Now, many women form families with men who already have children from a previous relationship. As a result, there is increasing polarization between men with relatively high fertility and men with no children at all.

Social Inequalities in Childlessness: Highest Among Highly Educated, Professional Women and Low-Educated Men

The growing divergence between male and female childlessness is just one way in which childlessness is unequally distributed within society. In many industrialized countries, childlessness is also particularly common among highly educated, professional women and among low-educated men. Recent data from Taiwan nicely illustrates some of the social inequalities in childlessness observed in many industrialized countries. Figure 7.3 displays the proportion of men and women of nine birth cohorts who were childless at age 40, split by educational level (less than secondary education, secondary degree, or tertiary degree). The figure illustrates three key patterns in contemporary childlessness. The

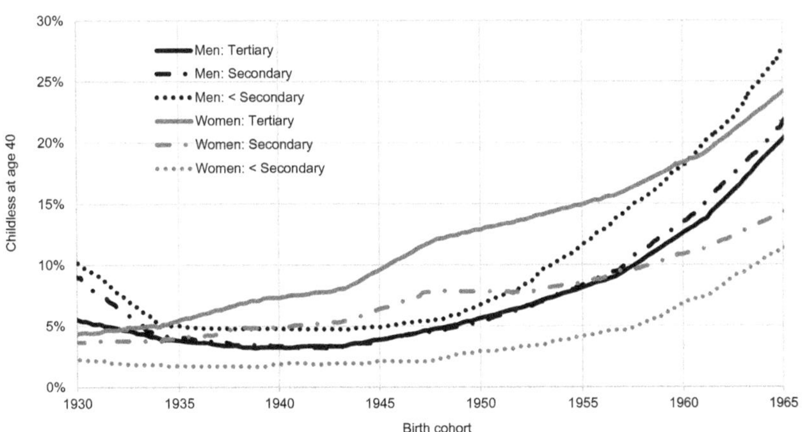

Fig. 7.3 Childlessness in Taiwan by gender, education, and birth cohort. Five-year birth cohorts; last year is displayed. Adapted from [28]

first important pattern is the inverse relationship between education and childlessness across genders. For women, childlessness is highest among the most highly educated and lowest among the least educated across all birth cohorts. For men, the relationship between education and childlessness is reversed: Childlessness is highest among the least educated men, and lowest among the most highly educated men. The second key trend is that childlessness has increased across historical time for all gender and educational groups. Finally—and perhaps most intriguingly—Fig. 7.3 shows how dramatically the disparity between educational groups has increased over time for both men and women. Whereas rates of female childlessness differed by just a few percentage points across educational groups for the oldest cohorts, more contemporary cohorts of highly educated women are now more than twice as likely to remain childless than their less-educated peers. Likewise, childlessness has increased most strongly among the least educated men. Among the most recent birth cohorts for which data are available, in Taiwan 29% of men with less than secondary education were childless compared to 22% of more highly educated men. Among women, just 12% of those with less than secondary education were childless, compared to 25% among those with a tertiary degree [28]. The disparity between men with high and low levels of education has been observed in many other low fertility countries. For example, among men born in the early 1970s in the former West Germany, 36% of men without a university degree versus 28% of their peers with a degree were childless [29]. The gendered relationship between childlessness and education is quite similar to the gendered relationship between childlessness on the one hand and income and/or occupational status on the other hand. Namely, childlessness is particularly high among men with low income and among women in high-status professional occupations. French men who never worked are about twice as likely to be childless as French men with higher status white-collar jobs [30]. In Australia, childlessness is higher among female professionals (doctors, lawyers, dentists, and veterinarians) than among women working in lower-status occupations [31].

Interestingly, the gendered relationship between education and childlessness does not seem to reflect differences in fertility preferences. That is, it is does not appear to be the case that women with high education and men with low education *prefer* to remain childless to a greater extent than their peers. To illustrate this point, Fig. 7.4 compares the proportion of childless women (bars) as well as the proportion of women/people intending to remain childless (squares) split by level of education in a number of selected countries. The proportion of women who are involuntarily childless has been estimated by subtracting the proportion of people who intend to remain childless from the proportion who are in fact childless (which gives a proxy of the share of people with an unrealized preference for children). The figure shows that, in every country, the proportion of women who intend to remain childless is far lower than the proportion of women who are in fact childless. There are, however, meaningful differences across countries with respect to how many women are actually childlessness, how many women intend to remain childless, and how actual childlessness and the intention to remain childless are each related to education. In Norway, the Czech Republic, and Hungary, the proportion of women who are childless is more or less similar among women with higher and lower levels of education (about 10%), and few women say that they intend to remain childless. In other countries, childlessness is substantially higher among women with more education. In some countries, the proportion of women who are childless is remarkably high among the highly educated, for instance in Great Britain, Spain, Austria, Switzerland, and Italy where at least one out of four women with a tertiary degree is childless. In these same countries, the intention to remain childless is generally unrelated or only weakly related to educational attainment.

Modern Childlessness: Biological, Intentional, or Coincidental?

There are many different reasons why individuals remain childless, and it is often difficult to pinpoint just one reason why someone does not have children. Nevertheless, to understand why childlessness has increased in recent years (particularly among men), it is helpful to distinguish between three different pathways to childlessness: (1) people who are biologically unable to have children, (2) people who intentionally do not

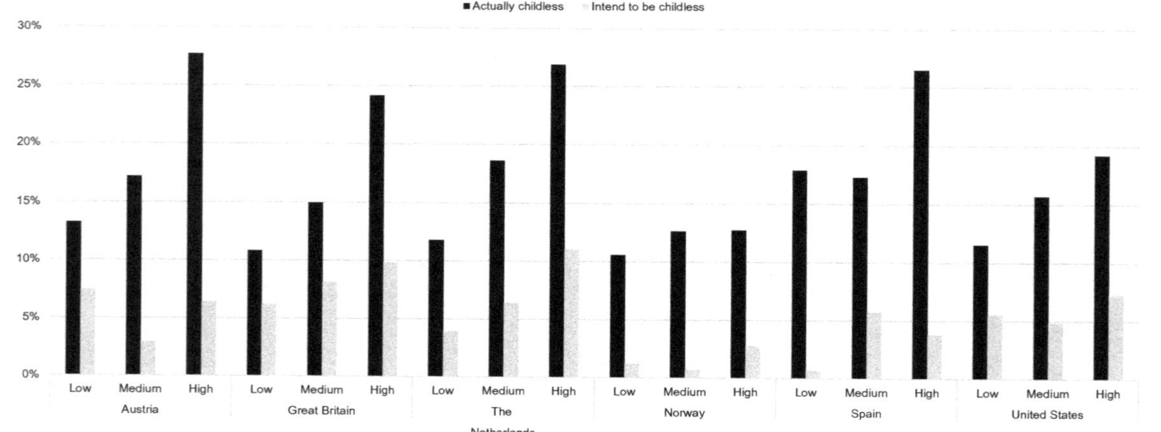

Fig. 7.4 Percent of women with low, medium, and high education who are childless (black) and intend to remain childless (gray) in selected countries. Based on [32]

want children, and (3) people who end up childless without explicitly wanting to do so ("coincidental childlessness").

What does the available data tell us about the prevalence of each of the three pathways? Although the prevalence of biological infecundity is unknown, research has shown that typically around 3% (or less) of married couples in countries where marriage is close to universal remain childless [33]. Data also suggests that, despite evidence of recent declines in sperm quality, fecundity is probably *improving* over time, and just a minority of people state that they prefer to remain "child free" (details provided in the following section). It hence seems plausible that the recent rise in childlessness has little to do with fundamental changes in either the ability or desire or to have children. That leaves the coincidentally childless. It seems that, more often than not, in the modern era people wind up childlessness not because they are biologically unable to reproduce nor because they have made a single, purposeful decision never to have children [20, 34], but rather because the "right" constellation of circumstances did not occur at all or occurred too late.

People perceive a number of different factors as inconducive to parenthood. Some people feel that they do not have enough time, money, or energy to raise children, feel uncertain about the future, have career goals that they perceive as incompatible with childbearing, or lack a partner who also desires children. It is therefore often difficult to dichotomize childlessness as either "voluntary" or "involuntary," as life priorities and fertility preferences may change as people proceed through adulthood [35, 36]. Some people who initially wanted to have children may decide that they do not want to have children after all given their life circumstances [37–39]. It is also difficult—if not impossible—to determine the extent to which a person's life circumstances reflect voluntary and conscious choices to increase and/or decrease the probability of having children (e.g., actively seeking a partner or not; enrolling in a specific educational track or choosing a professional career that one later realizes is at odds with childbearing; prioritizing career over relationships).

Many People Are Childless Because They Do Not Find the "Right" Partner

One key reason for contemporary coincidental childlessness is that many men and women lack a partner with whom they share a mutual desire to have children during their reproductive years [12, 40]. In many low fertility countries, many women are now postponing marriage to their 30s, which has implications for their fertility. Lacking a partner appears to be a particular problem in the lowest fertility East Asian countries, where the average age of maternity has increased most rapidly.

Figure 7.5 displays the proportion of women aged 30–34 who had never been married in 1970 and 2010 in some of the Asian countries. As easily seen in the graph, the proportion of never married women aged 30–34 has increased dramatically in Hong Kong, South Korea, Japan, Taiwan, and Singapore: In 1970, just 1–10% of 30- to 34-year-old women had never been married in these countries. In 2010, the proportion had increased to 25–40% [41]. In high fertility countries, marriage remains close to universal, and people also marry much earlier.

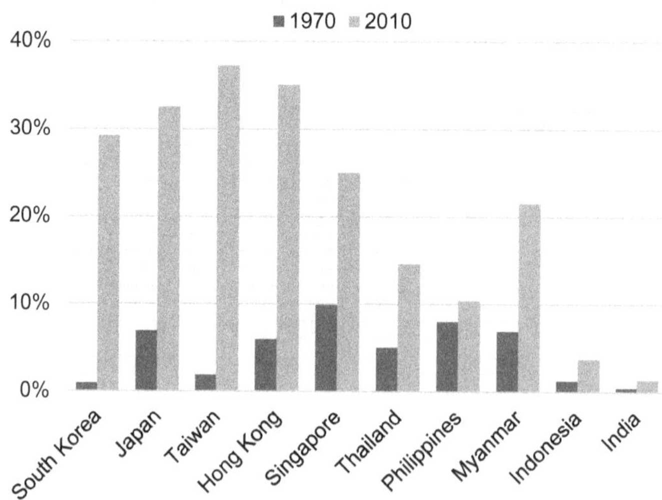

Fig. 7.5 Percent of women aged 30–34 who have never married in selected Asian countries, 1970 and 2010. Based on [41]

In Nigeria, for instance, nearly half of women marry by the time they are 18 (43% of women aged 25–49 in 2018) [33]. Between the 1980s and the 2000s, the share of women aged 25–49 who had ever married fell in most higher fertility countries, but nevertheless remained above 75%.

Sex-selective abortion has led to a surplus of men in some East and South Asian (sub)populations. In Korea, for example, there were 115 men for every 100 women for the cohorts born in the mid-1990s. Very skewed sex ratios are also found in the urban northern states of India [42, 43]. The unbalanced sex ratios imply that current generations of young men will face serious problems finding a female partner, and many will remain unmarried and childless [44, 45]. Even according to the most conservative projections, by 2050, more than 10% of Chinese men aged 25 and older will be unable to find a wife and may thus end up involuntarily single and childless [46].

One might wonder why finding a partner of the opposite sex continues to be so important for fertility and childlessness in particular, given that having children as a single parent or as part of a homosexual couple has become much more socially acceptable (at least in some, mostly Western countries), and the possibilities to conceive with the help of assisted reproductive technologies (ART) and donor gametes have increased. Theoretically at least, women without a male partner can become biological mothers relatively easily. However, it is still relatively rare for women to have their own biological child in the absence of a male partner. Among American women using ART between 2010 and 2014, less than 5% used donor sperm [47]. Men without a female partner could theoretically have their own biological children through surrogacy. However, few women are prepared to donate their eggs, surrogacy is often very expensive and legally restricted, and there is often strong social resistance to the idea of having a child without a mother/female partner [48–50]. One study based on a small sample of men who chose to become single fathers through surrogacy found that most had high incomes. Most (61%) were satisfied with their decision to "go it alone," although a majority would have preferred to have the child within the context of a relationship [51]. In sum, few people currently

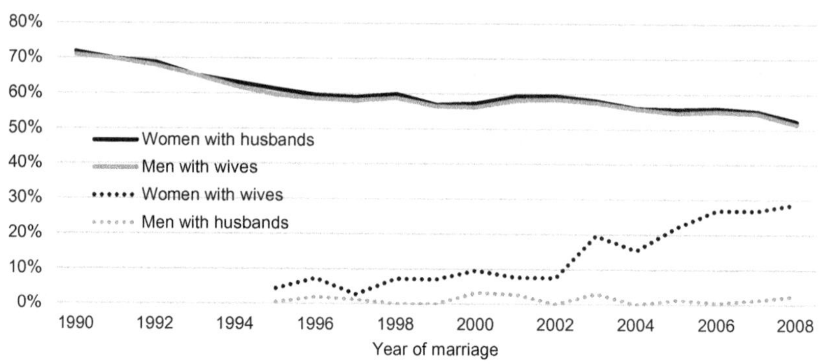

Fig. 7.6 Percent of Swedish married couples who have a child within five years of marriage. Based on [54]

make use of the relatively new opportunities to have biological children without a partner of the opposite sex, and even those who do appear to see it only as a last resort.

Statistics about the fertility of same-sex couples further substantiate the importance of having a partner of the opposite sex for fertility. Despite increasing social acceptance of homosexuality, the fertility of homosexual couples tends to be low and childlessness tends to be very high [52, 53]. Figure 7.6 compares the proportion of Swedish-born women and men who married a partner of the same or opposite sex between 1990 and 2008 and had a child within five years of getting married. As displayed in the figure, the proportion of people who were still childless after five years of marriage is much higher among men and women in homosexual than in heterosexual marriages. In 2008, about 70% of women and about 95% of men in homosexual marriages were childless after five years, compared with about 50% of women and men in heterosexual marriages. Notably, the proportion of childless lesbian married couples has decreased somewhat in recent years, at least in Sweden [54]. While certainly important in own right, changes in the fertility of same-sex couples—who tend to represent less than 5% of the population according to surveys from various countries [55–57]—have little impact on the overall fertility of a population.

The Incompatibility of Work and Family: The Example of University Research Careers

Concern about people's ability to reconcile their career and family goals is widespread, not least for highly educated individuals (particularly women) pursuing careers in science at universities and research institutions. Working as a research scientist typically demands long hours, frequent travel, limited off-time, and a need to relocate. There are limited financial rewards particularly in the early years of a research career and jobs are often insecure, as competition is high and permanent positions are scarce. Research scientists seldom acquire a full professorship (i.e., permanent position) before age 40, and commonly not before reaching their 50s [58]. Moreover, given their skills, research scientists often earn less than what they would in other professions [59].

The demands of a science career appear to make it particularly difficult for women to achieve their family goals. One survey found that female scientists in Austria aged 40–45 had an average of just 0.9 children; 44% were childless [60]. Female scientists may see the very long working hours as difficult to combine with childbearing [60, 61]. Fertility and family conflicts with work are key reasons why many women choose to end a research career—surveys indicate that 42% of women (versus 16% of men) cite "issues related to children" and 32% of women (versus 19% of men) cite "issues related to spouse/partner" as very important factors in their decision to stop pursing the goal of becoming a research professor [62]. The low fertility and high childlessness among (particularly female) scientists could have further societal consequences, as other social groups may in time emulate the childbearing patterns of academic elites. More support for women to combine work and fertility may affect childbearing patterns among women with active research careers [63, 64].

> *"Don't do it! Just don't get a PhD: there are so many other things in life that you can do for a living that are as intellectually challenging, pay more, and where women having children is not a big deal. Academia is stuck at best in the 1970s on this issue."*

-female PhD student at the University of California [62].

Childlessness Due to (Age-Related) Infertility

The recent rise in childlessness does not appear to reflect major changes in infertility. The World Health Organization (WHO) defines *infertility* as a disease of the reproductive system, defined by failure to achieve clinical pregnancy after 12 months or more of regular unprotected sexual intercourse. It is important to note that infertility can be defined and measured in different ways (e.g., based on the ability to become pregnant versus have a live birth; observational time periods varying from one year or up to five years). *Primary infertility*—that is, people who are unable to have their first live birth; most relevant for childlessness—can also be distinguished from *secondary infertility*, parents who are unable to have an additional child. The results of studies that try to assess the prevalence of infertility depend on how infertility is defined in each particular study. Statistics based on shorter periods of "exposure to the risk for pregnancy" (i.e., how long people been having regular unprotected sex) generally indicate that more people are infertile than statistics based on longer periods of "exposure."

Infertility (according to the WHO definition) is thought to affect around one in ten couples worldwide, although no globally representative data exists [65, 66]. Based on a five- as opposed to a one-year period of exposure, another study integrated data from 277 different surveys. The study estimated that, between 1990 and 2010, globally 1.9% of women aged 20–44 years who wanted to have children were unable to have their first live birth; 10.5% of mothers were unable to have an additional live birth [65]. Although conditions which caused infertility in earlier decades are being more successfully treated than in the past [5, 67, 68], the prevalence of infertility was more or less the same in 1990 and 2010, with only a slight overall decrease in primary infertility (0.1%, but with a more pronounced drop in sub-Saharan Africa and South Asia; secondary infertility increased by 0.4%) [65]. In the United

States, relatively good data [69] is available on both the proportion of married women who are infertile (here defined as women who have not been surgically sterilized and have had at least 12 consecutive months of unprotected sexual intercourse without becoming pregnant) and the proportion of women with impaired fecundity (i.e., women who have not been surgically sterilized and for whom it is difficult or impossible to get pregnant or carry a pregnancy to term). In the period 2011–2015, it was estimated that 6.7% of all married women aged 15–44 were infertile and 12.1% of all women aged 15–44 had impaired fecundity.

Based on these statistics, it might not seem like infertility and impaired fecundity are hugely problematic for the population as a whole, nor that infertility would be a major driver of lower fertility. However, the proportion of women with impaired fecundity and infertility increases dramatically with age. Based on the United States data cited above [69], the proportion of women trying to have their first child who faced problems getting pregnant or carrying a pregnancy to term was 15% among women aged 15–29 years, 18% among women 30–34 years, 40% among women 35–39 years, and 39% of women aged 40–44 years. Hence, *four out of ten* married women 35+ in the United States who were trying to have their first child were affected by impaired fecundity, putting them at high risk for unwanted childlessness. Given the postponement of childbearing observed in the United States and many other more developed countries, age-related decline in fecundity has become an important driver of modern-day childlessness in industrialized countries. According to statistics from 2017, on average women were over age 30 when they had their first child in eight OECD countries: Ireland, Greece, Spain, Luxembourg, Italy, Switzerland, South Korea, and Japan [70].

Infertility is hardly just a female problem. Among couples that are not able to conceive, about half are infertile due exclusively to female factors, about 30% are infertile exclusively due to male factors, and about 20% are infertile due to a combination of both male and female factors. Thus, male factor infertility plays a significant role in about 50% of all infertile couples [71–73]. While it is well known that women's fecundity decreases with age, it is less well known that men's fecundity also declines as they grow older [74, 75]. Relatively common diseases and risk factors that depress women's ability to conceive include polycystic ovary syndrome, endometriosis, hormonal disorders, diabetes, and irregular menstrual cycles [65, 66]. Obesity, which has been increasing in countries all over the world [76], can also reduce women's fecundity [77]. Male infertility can be caused by low sperm count due to certain infections, endocrine problems, drug use, or radiation exposure, as well as testicular malformations and hormone imbalances [71, 78]. Infectious diseases, including sexually transmitted diseases, are relatively common in some world regions and therefore important for male fecundity in parts of Africa and Latin America [66, 79]. As previously discussed, there is some concern that the decline in sperm quality—if it continues—may put more couples at risk for infertility.

Only a Minority Prefer to Remain "Childfree"

With the publication of popular books like Corinne Maier's *No Kids: 40 Good Reasons Not to Have Children* and the multi-authored *Selfish, Shallow and Self-Absorbed* [80], the Childfree Movement—that is, people who actively decide to abstain from parenthood—has gained visibility in a number of industrialized countries. In the last five years, the Childfree Movement has been featured in just about every major news source in the English-speaking world. For instance, a newspaper article in *The Guardian* June 2019 with the title "Childfree by choice: Stop telling me I'll change my mind later" recently discussed how many women are exasperated by the social pressure to have children [81]. Countless social media forums now facilitate exchange between people interested in being childfree and discussion of childfree issues.

According to a 2018 survey from the PEW Research Center, more than one out of three (37%) United States adults aged 18–49 who did not currently have children said it was "not at all likely" or "not too likely" that they would have a child in the future. Of these, 63% said it was because they just don't want children. This group of adults who are "childfree by choice" represents just over 10% of the adults surveyed [82].

Despite the increasing visibility of the Childfree Movement, data suggests that people who purposefully want to remain childfree represent just a small minority of the population. Figure 7.7 displays the proportion of men and women aged 18–40 who say that they would prefer to remain childless in a selection of European countries. The proportion of people who would prefer to remain childless is relatively high in Western European countries as compared to Eastern and Southern European countries. Nevertheless, the proportion of people who say that they would prefer to be childless is still very low across all of the countries, and also generally far lower than the proportion of people who in fact end up childless [83, 84]. The proportion of women who state that they prefer to remain childless is below 10% in all of the countries in the figure, and even below 5% in most of the countries. More men than women would generally prefer to remain childless, but the proportion is still under 10% in most countries. Data from the Demographic and Health Surveys suggests that less than 5% of men and women in most developing countries prefer to remain childless [33].

People cite a number of different reasons for wanting to remain childfree. Having children is commonly perceived as costly, time-demanding,

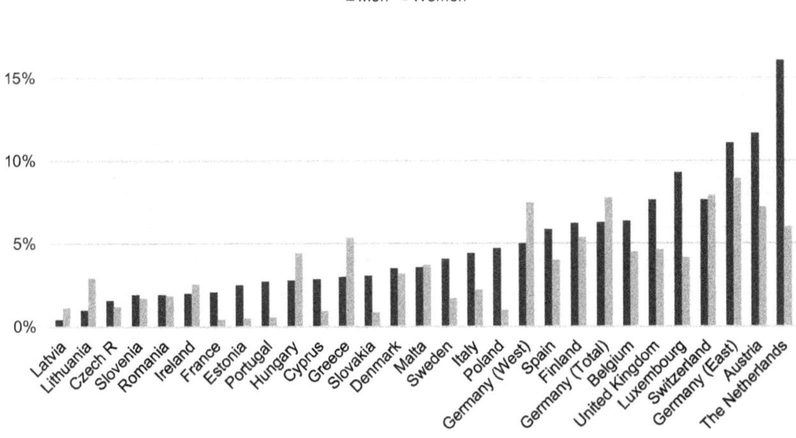

Fig. 7.7 Percent of men and women aged 18–40 who do not want to have children, European countries, 2011. Based on [37]

and at odds with other life goals, and some people decide that they do not want to compromise their own freedom. Other people are concerned with the effects of childbearing on their own physical and mental health. Some people do not want to have children due to the risk of passing on a medical condition or predisposition for violence. As a celebrity example, United States comedian Sarah Silverman (born 1970) said she did not want to become a mother because she did not want to pass on her depression [85]. Some childfree people cite ethical reasons, such as the belief that reproducing is an egocentric act, particularly in a world with many orphans, or a belief that it is immoral to reproduce because an unborn child cannot provide consent. Some childfree people do not see the sense in having children on a dying planet, while others abstain from childbearing in order to reduce humans' negative impact on the planet [86, 87]. In rare cases, some people choose to be childless due to their religious beliefs (e.g., Catholic priests, monks, and nuns), though most religions tend to be pro-natal.

"It's a moral movement"

Raphael Samuel, a businessman in his late 20s from Mumbai, India, began the Stop Making Babies group to create awareness that it's okay to not to have a child.

For Samuel, anti-natalism is a "moral movement." Other participants of India's Voluntary Human Extinction Movement cite different reasons for remaining child free. Some say that India is already overpopulated, others argue that having a child means that the new person will be forced to endure a life of suffering [88]. "Also, let's be honest, there are some people who don't want to clean kid shit," says Samuel [89].

Samuel recently made headlines for suing his parents—both lawyers—for having him without his consent [90].

Early in adulthood and well before most people have initiated childbearing, only very small proportions of men and women state that they would prefer to remain childless, even in countries where childlessness is common, such as in Finland [37]. It is, however, important to recognize that young adults may change their mind about wanting children as they gradually begin to comprehend the different costs and benefits of childbearing. In environments where childbearing is the norm, men and women who felt negatively about parenthood as young adults may come to see childbearing as an attractive ideal [91, 92]. Other young adults may decide that they do not want children after more fully realizing the sacrifices involved.

The Consequences of Childlessness for Individuals

Although traditionally higher in Western countries, the social acceptance of childlessness has increased over time all around the world [93, 94]. Moreover, what people perceive as the ideal number of children for society has fallen in many countries. In Nepal, for instance, the perceived ideal number of children fell from 2.9 children per woman in 1996 to 2.1 children per woman in 2016 [33]. Shrinking ideal family size implies that many people now see low (and even no) fertility as acceptable or even advantageous. Nevertheless, people without children still face negative social attitudes in many countries—particularly in high fertility contexts where having (many) children is seen as a critical part of life. Qualitative interviews suggest that childless people often feel that they are treated negatively and perceived as having "less value" within their families and communities [95]. Many people continue to see choosing to remain childfree as selfish with grave personal, economic, and societal consequences, and some even argue that people who choose to remain childfree will never know the true meaning of life [96, 97]. Some assume childless individuals care less about long-term social investments, long-term environmental challenges, kindergartens, schools, and family benefits [98]. Other data suggests that childless people are perceived as being less satisfied, having a lower quality of life, and less moral [99]. European data from 2005/2006 indicates that while childlessness is highly accepted in some countries, it continues to carry a strong social stigma in others: The proportion of people who disapproved of women remaining childless by choice ranged from 4% in Sweden to 86% in Ukraine. The proportion of people who disapproved of men remaining childless by choice similarly varied from 6% in Denmark to

85% in Ukraine. Generally, social opposition to remaining childfree by choice appears to be higher in Eastern relative to Western European countries [100], which may be related to their low fertility and fear of depopulation, or because several former socialist countries had pronatal policy programs [101, 102]. Interestingly, public attitudes in several countries (specifically Estonia, Romania, Latvia, France, Portugal, Spain, The Netherlands, Finland, and Sweden) were more negative toward childfree men than toward childfree women.

> *"It's an African thing. If you don't have a child, you are like, not complete. That's an evidence of womanhood. ...If you have girls and you don't have a boy, you are still not a woman."*
> *-Anonymous woman on being childless in Nigeria in an interview for the BBC's "Focus on Africa" [103]*

In addition to the difficulty of social stigmatization, being childless (or childfree) has a number of additional psychological, economic, and health consequences. For couples who want to have children, infertility can result in stress, relationship problems, and even trauma [104]. Danish findings suggest that unsuccessful attempts to have children are associated with an increased risk of suicide [105]. Some couples who have problems conceiving may turn to ART, which can also be costly and stressful. Nordic data suggests that being childless and without a partner is strongly related to health and mortality: Childless men and women without a partner have much higher morbidity and mortality compared to people with children and a partner [106]. In a Norwegian population-based study, the mortality rates of childless and never married men and women were *three times* higher than married men or women with two or more children [107]. The effects of family constellations on health have been identified in different world regions. For example, in Jordan, not being able to have children is related to reduced physical and emotional well-being [108]. Childlessness may be particularly difficult for people with traditional family values and/or for people in communities which promote family formation [109], and childless adults often have worse health-related outcomes particularly if they live in countries with high fertility and lower tolerance for childlessness [94, 110, 111]. Studies from Bangladesh and Ghana suggest that childless women in societies with higher stigma of childlessness may face a greater disease burden [112, 113].

In light of the research findings on the negative effects of childlessness on health and well-being, it is important to keep in mind that the effects of childlessness are neither all bad nor all good, and also depend on gender, country, and the each person's particular circumstances. In contrast to studies indicating *worse* health among childless individuals, one Australian study found that never-married, 65-year-old women without children were in fact healthier and had higher levels of well-being compared with mothers of the same age [114]. Some people experience childlessness as freedom: One can travel, take time off work, and have more freedom to pursue whatever one wants, whenever one wants. Childless men may feel that they can work less, as securing income is not as important, while women may feel more freedom to pursue a career [115].

Is Modern Childlessness a Problem?

To sum up, childlessness is increasing in many developed countries, particularly among men. In some countries, there is also increasing polarization between men who are childless and men who have multiple partnerships and a relatively high number of children (often 3–4) [116, 117]. Social inequality with regard to childlessness is also increasing; highly educated women and low-educated men are at higher risk of remaining childless. The overall increase in childlessness does not appear to reflect fundamental changes in human fecundity, nor major changes in people's desire to become a parent. Instead, it seems likely that the majority of childless individuals in the modern era wind up childless because they feel that their life circumstances simply did not line up at the right time.

To assess the extent to which contemporary childlessness represents a problem, one can consider whether people in the modern era are generally able to realize their fertility ideals. We cannot conclude that modern-day childlessness is a “problem” simply because it is higher than it was before. It is unreasonable to assume that people in the past universally wanted to get married and have as many children as they did. Historical rates of childlessness thus do not offer an informative baseline for comparison. Nevertheless, data suggests that far fewer people want to remain childless than actually do. Hence, modern-day childlessness does indeed appear to be problematic because many people appear to be involuntarily childless and because certain social groups (highly educated women and low-educated men) appear to be more at risk than others. Furthermore, the lingering stigma of (voluntary) childlessness in many countries certainly presents a problem from a human rights perspective.

Another relevant question is whether current levels of childlessness have negative consequences for societies as a whole. Childlessness does not necessarily correspond perfectly with fertility; fertility can be low without childlessness being high. The societal consequences of childlessness thus need to be considered separately from the societal consequences of higher and lower fertility. In industrialized societies, contemporary childlessness is problematic in at least two ways. The first is with regard to the growing risk group of childless and low-educated men. Until relatively recently, in many higher income countries men with lower socioeconomic status (e.g., less education, lower income) tended to have relatively high fertility; as previously discussed, however, the relationship between fertility and men’s status has in many countries reversed [118, 119]. The reversal of the relationship between men’s status and fertility implies that increasing proportions of men will not only lack both financial and/or educational resources, but also have less family support as they grow older. Second, fairly reconciling the needs of people with (many) children and people without children presents a major societal challenge. It seems highly unlikely that childlessness will decrease in the future. Societies therefore urgently need to begin considering how they can fairly maximize the well-being of both parents and non-parents given their potentially conflicting interests, needs, and resources.

References

1. Kaklamanidou, B.-D. (2018). The voluntarily childless heroine: A post-feminist television oddity. *Television & New Media*, 20(3), 275–293. https://doi.org/10.1177/1527476417749743.
2. Frejka, T. (2017). Childlessness in the United States. In M. Kreyenfeld, & D. Konietzka (Eds.), *Childlessness in Europe: Contexts, causes, and consequences* (pp. 159–179). Cham: Springer.
3. Sobotka, T. (2017). Childlessness in Europe: Reconstructing long-term trends among women born in 1900–1972. In M. Kreyenfeld, & D. Konietzka (Eds.), *Childlessness in Europe: Contexts, causes, and consequences* (pp. 17–53). Cham: Springer.
4. Sarkar, K. (2017). Fertility transition in India: Emerging significance of infertility and childlessness. In A. Ranjan, & B. K. Singh (Eds.), *India 2016: Population. Transition Selected Papers of Bhopal Seminar 2016* (pp. 87–100). Bhopal: MLC Foundation and Shyam Institute. http://www.shyaminstitute.in/monograph_16.pdf.
5. Ombelet, W., & Goossens, J. (2017). Global reproductive health—Why do we persist in neglecting the undeniable problem of childlessness in resource-poor countries? *Facts, Views & Vision in ObGyn*, 9(1), 1–3.
6. Sobotka, T., & Beaujouan, É. (2017). Late motherhood in low-fertility countries: Reproductive intentions, trends and consequences. In D. Stoop (Ed.), *Preventing age related fertility loss* (pp. 11–29). Cham: Springer. https://doi.org/10.1007/978-3-319-14857-1_2.
7. Zeman, K., Beaujouan, É., Brzozowska, Z., & Sobotka, T. (2018). Cohort fertility decline in low fertility countries: Decomposition using parity progression ratios. *Demographic Research*, 38(25), 651–690. https://doi.org/10.4054/DemRes.2018.38.25.
8. Rutstein, S. O., & Shah, I. H. (2004). Infecundity, infertility, and childlessness in developing countries. Demographic and Health Surveys (DHS) Comparative reports No. 9. Calverton, MD: ORC Macro, & World Health Organization. https://www.who.int/reproductivehealth/publications/infertility/DHS_9/en/. Accessed 1 June 2021.
9. United Nations (2013). World fertility report 2012. New York: United Nations. https://www.un.org/development/desa/pd/content/world-fertility-report-2012. Accessed 26 May 2021.
10. Sobotka, T. (2017). Post-transitional fertility: The role of childbearing postponement in fuelling the shift to low and unstable fertility levels.

Journal of Biosocial Science, 49(S1), S20–S45. https://doi.org/10.1017/S0021932017000323.
11. Kneale, D., & Joshi, H. (2008). Postponement and childlessness: Evidence from two British cohorts. *Demographic Research*, 19, 1935–1968. https://doi.org/10.4054/DemRes.2008.19.58.
12. Rotkirch, A., & Miettinen, A. (2017). Childlessness in Finland. In M. Kreyenfeld, & D. Konietzka (Eds.), *Childlessness in Europe: Contexts, causes, and consequences* (pp. 139–158). Cham: Springer. https://doi.org/10.1007/978-3-319-44667-7.
13. Rendall, M. S., Clarke, L., Peters, H. E., Ranjit, N., & Verropoulou, G. (1999). Incomplete reporting of men's fertility in the United States and Britain: A research note. *Demography*, 36(1), 135–144. https://doi.org/10.2307/2648139.
14. Joyner, K., Peters, H. E., Hynes, K., Sikora, A., Taber, J. R., & Rendall, M. S. (2012). The quality of male fertility data in major US surveys. *Demography*, 49(1), 101–124. https://doi.org/10.1007/s13524-011-0073-9.
15. Hadley, R. 2021 (2018). Coping with Father's Day as a childless man. A guest blog by Dr. Robin Hadley. *Gateway Women* [Blog]. June 13, 2018. Gateway Women June 13. https://gateway-women.com/coping-with-fathers-day-as-a-childless-man-a-guest-blog-by-dr-robin-hadley/.
16. Skirbekk, V., & Blekesaune, M. (2013). Personality traits increasingly important for male fertility: Evidence from Norway. *European Journal of Personality*, 28(6), 521–552. https://doi.org/10.1002/per.1936.
17. Priskorn, L., Holmboe, S. A., Jacobsen, R., Jensen, T. K., Lassen, T. H., & Skakkebaek, N. E. (2012). Increasing trends in childlessness in recent birth cohorts—A registry-based study of the total Danish male population born from 1945 to 1980. *International Journal of Andrology*, 35(3), 449–455. https://doi.org/10.1111/j.1365-2605.2012.01265.x.
18. Beaujouan, É., Sobotka, T., Brzozowska, Z., & Zeman, K. (2017). Has childlessness peaked in Europe? *Population & Societies*, 540(1), 1–4. https://doi.org/10.3917/popsoc.540.0001.
19. Dykstra, P. A., & Hagestad, G. O. (2007). Childlessness and parenthood in two centuries: Different roads-different maps? *Journal of Family Issues*, 28(11), 1518–1532. https://doi.org/10.1177/0192513X07303881.
20. Morgan, S. P. (1991). Late nineteenth-and early twentieth-century childlessness. *American Journal of Sociology*, 97(3), 779–807. https://doi.org/10.1086/229820.

21. Rowland, D. T. (2007). Historical trends in childlessness. *Journal of Family Issues*, 28(10), 1311–1337. https://doi.org/10.1177/0192513X07303823.
22. Onnen-Isemann, C. (2003). Familienpolitik und Fertilitätsunterschiede in Europa: Frankreich und Deutschland [Family politics and fertility differences in Europe: France and Germany]. *Aus Politik und Zeitgeschichte: Beilage zur Wochenzeitung das Parlament* 44, 31–38. https://www.bpb.de/apuz/27312/erwerbstaetigkeit-von-frauen-und-kinderbetreuungskultur-in-europa.
23. United Nations (2019). World Population Prospects 2019. https://population.un.org/wpp/. Accessed 25 May 2021.
24. Fieder, M., Huber, S., & Bookstein, F. L. (2011). Socioeconomic status, marital status and childlessness in men and women: An analysis of census data from six countries. *Journal of Biosocial Science*, 43(5), 619–635. https://doi.org/10.1017/S002193201100023X.
25. Björkenstam, E., Björkenstam, C., Vinnerljung, B., Hallqvist, J., & Ljung, R. (2011). Juvenile delinquency, social background and suicide—A Swedish national cohort study of 992 881 young adults. *International Journal of Epidemiology*, 40(6), 1585–1592. https://doi.org/10.1093/ije/dyr127.
26. Lee, K., Hutton, H. E., Lesko, C. R., Monroe, A. K., Alvanzo, A., McCaul, M. E., et al. (2018). Associations of drug use, violence, and depressive symptoms with sexual risk behaviors among women with alcohol misuse. *Women's Health Issues*, 28(4), 367–374. https://doi.org/10.1016/j.whi.2018.04.004.
27. Muhuri, P. K., & Gfroerer, J. C. (2011). Mortality associated with illegal drug use among adults in the United States. *The American Journal of Drug and Alcohol Abuse*, 37(3), 155–164. https://doi.org/10.3109/00952990.2011.553977.
28. Cheng, Y.-h. A. (2017, April 26–28). Educational and sex differences in period and cohort fertility patterns: The case of Taiwan (Paper presented at the Population Association of America 2018 Annual Meeting, Denver, CO). https://paa.confex.com/paa/2018/mediafile/ExtendedAbstract/Paper21758/PAA%202018_Educational%20and%20Sex%20Differences%20in%20Fertility_long.pdf.
29. The rise of childlessness (2017, July 29). *The Economist*. Retrieved from https://www.economist.com/international/2017/07/27/the-rise-of-childlessness.

30. Köppen K., Mazuy M., Toulemon L. (2017). Childlessness in France. In M. Kreyenfeld, & D. Konietzka (Eds.), *Childlessness in Europe: Contexts, Causes, and Consequences. Demographic Research Monographs*. Cham: Springer. https://doi.org/10.1007/978-3-319-44667-7_4.
31. Miranti, R., McNamara, J., Tanton, R., & Yap, M. (2009). A narrowing gap? Trends in the childlessness of professional women in Australia 1986–2006. *Journal of Population Research*, 26(4), 359–379. https://doi.org/10.1007/s12546-009-9022-5.
32. Beaujouan, E., & Berghammer, C. (2019). The gap between lifetime fertility intentions and completed fertility in Europe and the United States: A cohort approach. *Population Research and Policy Review*, 38, 1–29. https://doi.org/10.1007/s11113-019-09516-3.
33. The Demographic and Health Surveys Program (2020). Demographic and Health Surveys. ICF International. https://www.dhsprogram.com/. Accessed 31 May 2021.
34. Poston, D. L. J., & Trent, K. (1982). International variability in childlessness: A descriptive and analytical study. *Journal of Family Issues*, 3(4), 473–491. https://doi.org/10.1177/019251382003004004.
35. Kodzi, I. A., Johnson, D. R., & Casterline, J. B. (2010). Examining the predictive value of fertility preferences among Ghanaian women. *Demographic Research*, 22, 965. https://doi.org/10.4054/DemRes.2010.22.30.
36. Edmonston, B., Lee, S. M., & Wu, Z. (2010). Fertility intentions in Canada: Change or no change? *Canadian Studies in Population*, 37(3–4), 297–337. https://doi.org/10.25336/P6B037.
37. Miettinen, A., & Szalma, I. (2014). Childlessness intentions and ideals in Europe. *Finnish Yearbook of Population Research*, 49, 31–55.
38. Miettinen, A., Gietel-Basten, S., & Rotkirch, A. (2011). Gender equality and fertility intentions revisited: Evidence from Finland. *Demographic Research*, 24, 469–496. https://doi.org/10.4054/DemRes.2011.24.20.
39. Dey, I., & Wasoff, F. (2010). Another child? Fertility ideals, resources and opportunities. *Population Research and Policy Review*, 29(6), 921–940. https://doi.org/10.1007/s11113-009-9174-1.
40. Burkimsher, M., & Zeman, K. (2017). Childlessness in Switzerland and Austria. In M. Kreyenfeld, & D. Konietzka (Eds.), *Childlessness in Europe: Contexts, causes, and consequences* (pp. 115–137). Cham: Springer. https://doi.org/10.1007/978-3-319-44667-7_6.

41. Jones, G. (2018). What is driving marriage and cohabitation in low fertility countries? In D. J. Poston (Ed.), *Low fertility regimes and demographic and societal change* (pp. 149–166). Cham: Springer.
42. Hesketh, T. (2011). Selecting sex: The effect of preferring sons. *Early Human Development*, 87(11), 759–761. https://doi.org/10.1016/j.earlhumdev.2011.08.016.
43. Wahlberg, A., & Gammeltoft, T. M. (Eds.) (2018). *Selective reproduction in the 21st century*. Cham: Palgrave Macmillan.
44. Das Gupta, M., Ebenstein, A., & Sharygin, E. J. (2010). China's marriage market and upcoming challenges for elderly men. Policy Research Working Paper 5351. The World Bank. https://documents.worldbank.org/curated/en/948771468212988136/pdf/WPS5351.pdf.
45. Jiang, Q., Li, S., & Feldman, M. W. (2012). China's missing girls in the three decades from 1980 to 2010. *Asian Women*, 28(3), 53–73.
46. Guilmoto, C. Z. (2012). Skewed sex ratios at birth and future marriage squeeze in China and India, 2005–2100. *Demography*, 49(1), 77–100. https://doi.org/10.1007/s13524-011-0083-7.
47. Gerkowicz, S. A., Crawford, S. B., Hipp, H. S., Boulet, S. L., Kissin, D. M., & Kawwass, J. F. (2018). Assisted reproductive technology with donor sperm: National trends and perinatal outcomes. *American Journal of Obstetrics and Gynecology*, 218(4), 421.e1–421.e10. https://doi.org/10.1016/j.ajog.2017.12.224.
48. Whittaker, A. (2011). Cross-border assisted reproduction care in Asia: Implications for access, equity and regulations. *Reproductive Health Matters*, 19(37), 107–116. https://doi.org/10.1016/S0968-8080(11)37575-1.
49. Homanen, R. (2018). Reproducing whiteness and enacting kin in the Nordic context of transnational egg donation: Matching donors with cross-border traveller recipients in Finland. *Social Science & Medicine*, 203, 28–34. https://doi.org/10.1016/j.socscimed.2018.03.012.
50. Stark, B. (2012). Transnational surrogacy and international human rights law. *ILSA Journal of International & Comparative Law*, 18(2), 1–16.
51. Carone, N., Baiocco, R., & Lingiardi, V. (2017). Single fathers by choice using surrogacy: Why men decide to have a child as a single parent. *Human Reproduction*, 32(9), 1871–1879. https://doi.org/10.1093/humrep/dex245.
52. Patterson, C. J., & Riskind, R. G. (2010). To be a parent: Issues in family formation among gay and lesbian adults. *Journal of GLBT Family Studies*, 6(3), 326–340. https://doi.org/10.1080/1550428X.2010.490902.

53. Kurdek, L. A. (2004). Are gay and lesbian cohabiting couples really different from heterosexual married couples? *Journal of Marriage and Family*, 66(4), 880–900. https://doi.org/10.1111/j.0022-2445.2004.00060.x.
54. Kolk, M., & Andersson, G. (2018). Two decades of same-sex marriage in Sweden. A demographic account of developments in marriage, childbearing and divorce. *Demography*, 57(1), 147–169. https://doi.org/10.1007/s13524-019-00847-6.
55. Statistics Canada (2015). Same-sex couples and sexual orientation... by the numbers. https://www.statcan.gc.ca/eng/dai/smr08/2015/smr08_203_2015. Accessed 29 May 2021.
56. Trandafir, M. (2014). The effect of same-sex marriage laws on different-sex marriage: Evidence from The Netherlands. *Demography*, 51(1), 317–340. https://doi.org/10.1007/s13524-013-0248-7.
57. Hoover, K. W., Tao, K. L., & Peters, P. J. (2017). Nationally representative prevalence estimates of gay, bisexual, and other men who have sex with men who have served in the US military. *PloS One*, 12(8), e0182222.
58. The disposable academic (2010, December 16). *The Economist*. Retrieved from https://www.economist.com/node/17723223.
59. Balsmeier, B., & Pellens, M. (2016). How much does it cost to be a scientist? *The Journal of Technology Transfer*, 41(3), 469–505. https://doi.org/10.1007/s10961-014-9388-1.
60. Buber, I., Berghammer, C., & Prskawetz, A. (2011). Doing science, forgoing childbearing? Evidence from a sample of female scientists in Austria. VID Working Papers, No. 1/2011. Vienna: Austrian Academy of Sciences/Vienna Institute of Demography. http://hdl.handle.net/10419/96965. Accessed 1 June 2021.
61. Weisgram, E., & Diekman, A. (2015). Family friendly STEM: Perspectives on recruiting and retaining women in STEM fields. *International Journal of Gender, Science and Technology*, 8(1), 38–45. https://doi.org/10.3390/socsci6020061.
62. Mason, M. A., Wolfinger, N. H., & Goulden, M. (2013). *Do babies matter? Gender and family in the ivory tower*. New Brunswick, NJ and London: Rutgers University Press.
63. Mills, M., Mencarini, L., Tanturri, M. L., & Begall, K. (2008). Gender equity and fertility intentions in Italy and The Netherlands. *Demographic Research*, 18, 1. https://doi.org/10.4054/DemRes.2008.18.1.

64. McDonald, P. (2000). Gender equity in theories of fertility transition. *Population and Development Review*, 26(3), 427–439. https://doi.org/10.1111/j.1728-4457.2000.00427.x.
65. Mascarenhas, M. N., Flaxman, S. R., Boerma, T., Vanderpoel, S., & Stevens, G. A. (2012). National, regional, and global trends in infertility prevalence since 1990: A systematic analysis of 277 health surveys. *PLoS Med*, 9(12), e1001356. https://doi.org/10.1371/journal.pmed.1001356.
66. Inhorn, M. C., & Patrizio, P. (2015). Infertility around the globe: New thinking on gender, reproductive technologies and global movements in the 21st century. *Human Reproduction Update*, 21(4), 411–426. https://doi.org/10.1093/humupd/dmv016.
67. Starrs, A. M., Ezeh, A. C., Barker, G., Basu, A., Bertrand, J. T., Blum, R., et al. (2018). Accelerate progress—Sexual and reproductive health and rights for all: Report of the Guttmacher–Lancet Commission. *The Lancet*, 391(10140), 2642–2692. https://doi.org/10.1016/S0140-6736(18)30293-9.
68. Boerma, T., Requejo, J., Victora, C. G., Amouzou, A., George, A., Agyepong, I., et al. (2018). Countdown to 2030: Tracking progress towards universal coverage for reproductive, maternal, newborn, and child health. *The Lancet*, 391(10129), 1538–1548. https://doi.org/10.1016/S0140-6736(18)30104-1.
69. Center for Disease Control and Prevention (2019). Key statistics from the National Survey of Family Growth. https://www.cdc.gov/nchs/nsfg/key_statistics/i.htm#infertility. Accessed 1 June 2021.
70. OECD Family Database (2019). SF2.3: Age of mothers at childbirth and age-specific fertility. Paris. https://www.oecd.org/els/soc/SF_2_3_Age_mothers_childbirth.pdf. Accessed 28 May 2021.
71. Kumar, N., & Singh, A. K. (2015). Trends of male factor infertility, an important cause of infertility: A review of literature. *Journal of Human Reproductive Sciences*, 8(4), 191–196. https://doi.org/10.4103/0974-1208.170370.
72. Jungwirth, A., Diemer, T., Kopa, Z., Krausz, C., Minhas, S., & Tournaye, H. (2018). EAU Guidelines on male infertility. European Association of Urology. https://uroweb.org/wp-content/uploads/EAU-Guidelines-on-Male-Infertility-2018-large-text.pdf. Accessed 1 June 2021.
73. Kovac, J. R., Pastuszak, A. W., & Lamb, D. J. (2013). The use of genomics, proteomics, and metabolomics in identifying biomarkers of male infertility. *Fertility and Sterility*, 99(4), 998–1007. https://doi.org/10.1016/j.fertnstert.2013.01.111.

74. Lemoine, M.-E., & Ravitsky, V. (2015). Sleepwalking into infertility: The need for a public health approach toward advanced maternal age. *The American Journal of Bioethics*, 15(11), 37–48. https://doi.org/10.1080/15265161.2015.1088973.
75. Kühnert, B., & Nieschlag, E. (2004). Reproductive functions of the ageing male. *Human Reproduction Update*, 10(4), 327–339. https://doi.org/10.1093/humupd/dmh030.
76. Ng, M., Fleming, T., Robinson, M., Thomson, B., Graetz, N., Margono, C., et al. (2014). Global, regional, and national prevalence of overweight and obesity in children and adults during 1980–2013: A systematic analysis for the Global Burden of Disease Study 2013. *The Lancet*, 384(9945), 766–781. https://doi.org/10.1016/S0140-6736(14)60460-8.
77. Yilmaz, N., Kilic, S., Kanat-Pektas, M., Gulerman, C., & Mollamahmutoglu, L. (2009). The relationship between obesity and fecundity. *Journal of Women's Health*, 18(5), 633–636. https://doi.org/10.1089/jwh.2008.1057.
78. Ventimiglia, E., Capogrosso, P., Boeri, L., Serino, A., Colicchia, M., Ippolito, S., et al. (2015). Infertility as a proxy of general male health: Results of a cross-sectional survey. *Fertility and Sterility*, 104(1), 48–55. https://doi.org/10.1016/j.fertnstert.2015.04.020.
79. Agarwal, A., Mulgund, A., Hamada, A., & Chyatte, M. R. (2015). A unique view on male infertility around the globe. *Reproductive Biology and Endocrinology*, 13(1), 37. https://doi.org/10.1186/s12958-015-0032-1.
80. Daum, M. (2015). *Selfish, shallow, and self-absorbed: Sixteen writers on the decision not to have kids*. New York: Picador.
81. Shephard, T. (2019, June 1). Childfree by choice: stop telling me I'll change my mind later. *The Guardian*. Retrieved from https://www.theguardian.com/lifeandstyle/2019/jun/02/childfree-by-choice-stop-telling-me-ill-change-my-mind-later.
82. Pew Research Center (2018). 2018 Pew Research Center's American Trends Panel. https://www.pewresearch.org/wp-content/uploads/2018/12/FT_18.12.12_WantingChildren_Topline.pdf. Accessed 1 June 2021.
83. Coleman, D. (1996). New patterns and trends in European fertility: International and sub-national comparisons. In D. Coleman (Ed.), *Europe's population in the 1990s* (pp. 1–61). Oxford: Oxford University Press.
84. Miettinen, A. (2010). Voluntary or involuntary childlessness? Socio-demographic factors and childlessness intentions among childless Finnish

men and women aged 25–44. *Finnish Yearbook of Population Research*, 45, 5–24.
85. The Week Staff (2012, January 10). Is it irresponsible for the depressed to have children? *The Week*. Retrieved from https://theweek.com/articles/474974/irresponsible-depressed-have-children.
86. Speidel, J. J. (2017). Dysfunctional population growth: The links to human suffering. In A. R. (Ed.), *Alleviating world suffering* (pp. 249–265). Cham: Springer. https://doi.org/10.1007/978-3-319-51391-1_15.
87. Baus, D. (2017) Overpopulation and the impact on the environment. MA thesis, City University of New York.
88. Menezes, N. (2019, February 11). Stop making babies: Group from Bengaluru says it is okay to not have children. *The Economic Times*. Retrieved from https://economictimes.indiatimes.com/magazines/panache/stop-making-babies-group-from-bengaluru-says-it-is-okay-to-not-have-children/articleshow/67937835.cms.
89. Ghosh, P. (2019, March 18). The tribe of Samuel: Joining forces with child-free and anti-natalist evangelists. *Hindustan Times*. Retrieved from https://www.hindustantimes.com/india-news/the-tribe-of-samuel/story-5fhD0UUQ5O6T3t9OUJz3cI.html.
90. Pandey, G. (2019, February 7). Indian man to sue parents for giving birth to him. *BBC Dehli*. Retrieved from https://www.bbc.com/news/world-asia-india-47154287.
91. Kulu, H. (2013). Why do fertility levels vary between urban and rural areas? *Regional Studies*, 47(6), 895–912. https://doi.org/10.1080/00343404.2011.581276.
92. Berghammer, C. (2009). Religious socialisation and fertility: Transition to third birth in The Netherlands. *European Journal of Population/Revue européenne de Démographie*, 25(3), 297–324. https://doi.org/10.1007/s10680-009-9185-y.
93. Koropeckyj-Cox, T., & Pendell, G. (2007). Attitudes about childlessness in the United States: Correlates of positive, neutral, and negative responses. *Journal of Family Issues*, 28(8), 1054–1082. https://doi.org/10.1177/0192513X07301940.
94. Noordhuizen, S., de Graaf, P., & Sieben, I. (2010). The public acceptance of voluntary childlessness in The Netherlands: From 20 to 90 per cent in 30 years. *Social Indicators Research*, 99(1), 163–181. https://doi.org/10.1007/s11205-010-9574-y.
95. O'Driscoll, R. (2016). 'I was looking for something different and I found it': A constructivist grounded theory study with women who choose not

to have children. PhD thesis, Cardiff Metropolitan University. https://repository.cardiffmet.ac.uk/handle/10369/8475.

96. Vartan, S. (2017, May 31). Parents are 'morally outraged' about those who go childless, study finds. *Treehugger*. Retrieved from https://www.treehugger.com/parents-morally-outraged-about-childless-adults-study-finds-4868413.
97. Smith, I., Knight, T., Fletcher, R., & Macdonald, J. A. (2020). When men choose to be childless: An interpretative phenomenological analysis. *Journal of Social and Personal Relationships*, 37(1). https://doi.org/10.1177/0265407519864444.
98. Mulligan, C. B., & Sala-i-Martin, X. (1999). Gerontocracy, retirement, and social security. NBER Working Paper 7117. Cambridge, MA: N. B. o. E. Research. https://www.nber.org/papers/w7117. Accessed 1 June 2021.
99. Koropeckyj-Cox, T., & Pendell, G. (2007). The gender gap in attitudes about childlessness in the United States. *Journal of Marriage and Family*, 69(4), 899–915.
100. Liefbroer, A. C., Merz, E.-M., & Testa, M. R. (2015). Fertility-related norms across Europe: A multi-level analysis. In D. Philipov, A. Liefbroer, & J. Klobas (Eds.), *Reproductive decision-making in a macro-micro perspective* (pp. 141–163). Dordrecht: Springer. https://doi.org/10.1007/978-94-017-9401-5_6.
101. Pop-Eleches, C. (2010). The supply of birth control methods, education, and fertility evidence from Romania. *Journal of Human Resources*, 45(4), 971–997. https://doi.org/10.3368/jhr.45.4.971.
102. Drezgić, R. (2010). Policies and practices of fertility control under the state socialism. *The History of the Family*, 15(2), 191–205. https://doi.org/10.1016/j.hisfam.2009.11.001.
103. Mosuro, B. (2016). Is being childless a taboo in Africa? *Focus on Africa*. BBC. https://www.bbc.co.uk/programmes/p04hcfzf. Accessed 1 June 2021.
104. Hansen, T., Slagsvold, B., & Moum, T. (2009). Childlessness and psychological well-being in midlife and old age: An examination of parental status effects across a range of outcomes. *Social Indicators Research*, 94(2), 343–362. https://doi.org/10.1007/s11205-008-9426-1.
105. Kjaer, T. K., Jensen, A., Dalton, S. O., Johansen, C., Schmiedel, S., & Kjaer, S. K. (2011). Suicide in Danish women evaluated for fertility problems. *Human reproduction (Oxford, England)*, 26(9), 2401–2407. https://doi.org/10.1093/humrep/der188.

106. Agerbo, E., Mortensen, P. B., & Munk-Olsen, T. (2012). Childlessness, parental mortality and psychiatric illness: A natural experiment based on in vitro fertility treatment and adoption. *Journal of Epidemiology and Community Health*, 67, 374–376. https://doi.org/10.1136/jech-2012-201387.
107. Kravdal, Ø., Grundy, E., Lyngstad, T. H., & Wiik, K. A. (2012). Family life history and late mid-life mortality in Norway. *Population and Development Review*, 38(2), 237–257. https://doi.org/10.1111/j.1728-4457.2012.00491.x.
108. Obeidat, H. M., Hamlan, A. M., & Callister, L. C. (2014). Missing motherhood: Jordanian women's experiences with infertility. *Advances in Psychiatry*, 2014. https://doi.org/10.1155/2014/241075.
109. Moss, C. R., & Baden, J. S. (2015). *Reconceiving infertility: Biblical perspectives on procreation and childlessness*. Princeton, NJ: Princeton University Press.
110. Tanaka, K., & Johnson, N. E. (2014). Childlessness and mental well-being in a global context. *Journal of Family Issues*. https://doi.org/10.1177/0192513X14526393.
111. Ibisomi, L., & Mudege, N. N. (2014). Childlessness in Nigeria: Perceptions and acceptability. *Culture, Health & Sexuality*, 16(1), 61–75. https://doi.org/10.1080/13691058.2013.839828.
112. Alhassan, A., Ziblim, A. R., & Muntaka, S. (2014). A survey on depression among infertile women in Ghana. *BMC Women's Health*, 14(1). https://doi.org/10.1186/1472-6874-14-42.
113. Nahar, P., & Geest, S. (2014). How women in Bangladesh confront the stigma of childlessness: Agency, resilience, and resistance. *Medical Anthropology Quarterly*, 28(3), 381–398. https://doi.org/10.1111/maq.12094.
114. Graham, M. (2015). Is being childless detrimental to a woman's health and well-being across her life course? *Women's Health Issues*, 25(2), 176–184. https://doi.org/10.1016/j.whi.2014.12.002.
115. Agrillo, C., & Nelini, C. (2008). Childfree by choice: A review. *Journal of Cultural Geography*, 25(3), 347–363. https://doi.org/10.1080/08873630802476292.
116. Rostgaard, T., & Møberg, R. J. (2014). Fathering: The influence of ideational factors for male fertility behaviour. In G. B. Eydal, & T. Rostgaard (Eds.), *Fatherhood in the Nordic welfare states: Comparing care policies and practice* (p. 23). Bristol and Chicago: Policy Press/Bristol University Press. https://doi.org/10.1332/policypress/9781447310471.003.0002.

117. Statistics Norway (2019). Population statistics. Statistics Norway. www.ssb.no/befolkning. Accessed 10 July 2020.
118. Skirbekk, V. (2008). Fertility trends by social status. *Demographic Research*, 18(5), 145–180. https://doi.org/10.4054/DemRes.2008.18.5.
119. Dribe, M., Hacker, J. D., & Scalone, F. (2014). The impact of socio-economic status on net fertility during the historical fertility decline: A comparative analysis of Canada, Iceland, Sweden, Norway, and the USA. *Population Studies*, 68(2), 135–149. https://doi.org/10.1080/00324728.2014.889741.

8

More Education, Fewer Children

In response to value changes and changes in the demands of the labor market, the global population is much more educated today than it was 100, 50 or even 20 years ago. Scholars widely agree that global educational expansion is one of the key reasons why global fertility has declined. In countries where people are more educated, average fertility is lower; within countries, people who have more education also tend to have fewer children than their less-educated peers. In this chapter, I describe the global rise in education along with how and why education affects fertility.

The Global Rise in Education

Once a privilege for the few, basic education is now regarded as a fundamental human right similar to health [1]. Structural changes in the labor market have also increased the demand for educated workers [2–4]. According to the *skill-biased technological change* hypothesis, technological advances during industrialization have increased the demand for

V. Skirbekk, *Decline and Prosper!*,
https://doi.org/10.1007/978-3-030-91611-4_8

skilled workers who are able to use the new technologies. Technological advances also tend to decrease the demand for low-skilled and child labor, as technology can take over the kind of routine tasks formerly performed by minors and low-skilled employees [5].

As a result of value shifts and skill-based technological change, the world has experienced a huge educational expansion over the past two hundred years. The most dramatic growth has been in primary education. Whereas two hundred years ago less than 20% of the population even in the world's richest countries had any schooling, today even the poorest countries such as Niger the majority of the population has at least some schooling [6]. In wealthier world regions, large shares of the young adult population complete a university education and average educational levels exceed the secondary school level in several countries [4, 7]. Educational differences between countries have shrunk, with a greater share of the world's population having secondary or higher education while fewer people are illiterate [6, 8]. Education nevertheless remains low in many of the sub-Saharan African countries, where substantial proportions of young adults—and particularly adolescent mothers—are illiterate [9, 10].

Figure 8.1 illustrates the increase in the average number of years of schooling in different countries and world regions. As can be seen in the graph, the average length of education has increased in every world region. In developing countries, the increase in education began to accelerate around the middle of the twentieth century, primarily due to the expansion of primary schooling [4, 7]. The average length of education in sub-Saharan Africa was about four years in 2000, similar to the average length of education of Western countries in mid-nineteenth century.

Higher Education Tends to Go Along with Lower Fertility, but the Relationship is Weaker in Low Fertility Contexts

The global rise in education has gone hand in hand with decreasing fertility. Research has robustly demonstrated that increases in education

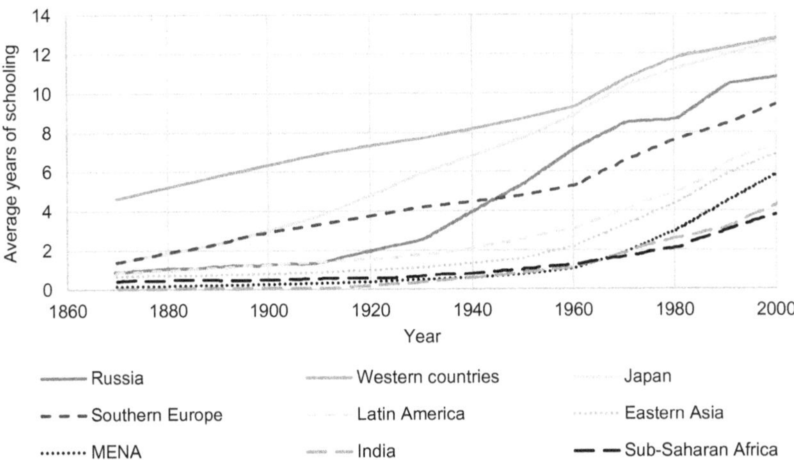

Fig. 8.1 Rise in education across the globe, 1950 through 2010. MENA = Middle East and Northern Africa. Based on [4, 7]

are related to a delay in childbearing to older ages as well as declines in overall fertility [11–13]. Within countries, education has similar effects on fertility across different demographic groups. More schooling relates to *later* fertility among both men and women, and also *lower* fertility for women and much lower fertility for men [14, 15]. The fertility of more educated women in many poorer countries is often comparable to the fertility of more educated women in richer nations [16, 17].

Variation in the pace and extent of educational expansion is one of the key reasons why fertility has declined more and faster in some countries than in others [18–20]. However, the relationship between education and fertility tends to weaken after the initial stages of the demographic transition, that is, after fertility has already declined to the replacement level or below [4, 21, 22]. At such low fertility levels, the relationship between education and female fertility is close to neutral [16, 23, 24]. For instance, in Denmark, Sweden, and Norway, women with high education born in the 1940s tended to have around 0.3 fewer children than women with low education; this difference had almost disappearedby the time those born in the 1970s had their first child [24].

The Effect of Education on Fertility Is Causal, Not Just Coincidental

The fact that increases in education tend to go along with decreases in fertility does not necessarily mean that more education *causes* lower fertility. There might, for instance, be other factors that change at the same time as education increases (e.g., increases in income, better access to contraception). There might also be selection effects, whereby the people who would have fewer children anyway (e.g., due to a preference for fewer children) might also be more likely to attain higher levels of education. The relationship between education and fertility could also potentially go in both directions: not only could education cause lower fertility, it might also be the case that fertility causes education (e.g., having a child might cause someone to drop out of school or prevent them from pursuing an advanced degree). Thus, results from cross-sectional studies (i.e., studies that examine how education and fertility are related based on indicators of education and fertility measured at the same, single-point in time) are insufficient for determining whether education has a causal impact on fertility.

Several "natural-" or "quasi-experiments," however, provide strong evidence that education indeed causes lower fertility. In a number of countries, educational regulations and policy changes make it possible to compare fertility between groups of people who differ only with regard to their educational attainment. In such cases, selection effects are unlikely to play a role because the length of their education is unrelated to individual characteristics or choice. Several quasi-experimental studies in diverse contexts such as England [25], Sweden [26], Norway [27], Ethiopia [28], Kenya [29], Turkey [30], and Israel [31] have demonstrated that longer education causes a delay in the age at which people have their first child and, in high fertility settings, reduce overall fertility. As one example, in 1985, a change in policy extended the length of primary education in Kenya by one year. The extension increased women's schooling by 0.74 years, increased the use of birth control, and reduced women's fertility at age 25 by an average of 0.3 children [29].

Extending the length of compulsory education appears to be especially effective for reducing teenage fertility. A study on education reform in

Norway found that one additional year of compulsory schooling reduced the chance of teenage pregnancy by 8%. The reform essentially delayed first births but had no effect on completed family size [27]. Similarly, extending compulsory schooling in Turkey from five to eight years led to significantly lower marriage and fertility among teenagers. The proportion of women who were married at age 16 dropped by 44%, and the proportion of women who have given birth by age 17 fell by 36% [30]. In Israel, removing the travel restrictions placed on Israeli-based Arabs resulted in a one year increase in Arab girls' schooling and reduced their fertility by an average of 0.6 children [31].

Education Affects Fertility Through Different Mechanisms

Education is thought to affect fertility via several mechanisms. First, attending school is associated with fewer opportunities to have children, a so-called incarceration effect. There is a relatively rigid sequencing of demographic events in early adulthood, and the age at graduation from school appears to be an important determinant of when people have their first child. Evidence from Sweden convincingly demonstrates the causal impact of graduation age on the timing of parenthood [26]. In Sweden, all children born between January and December within a single calendar year start and finish school at the same time. Children born just one month apart (December and the following January) are, however, split into different grades. Compared to people born in December, people born in the following January are 11 months older when they begin and finish compulsory education. Because birth month is random, people born in December are unlikely to differ from their peers born the following January in any meaningful way other than their age at graduation. The Swedish study found that women born in January had their first child 4.9 months later than their similarly aged peers born in December; that is, graduating at an older age meaningfully delayed their childbearing [26]. The incarceration effect of online educational settings or distance learning may be somewhat weaker than the incarceration effect of onsite schooling. One study found that students enrolled in onsite education were 70% less likely to have a first child than non-students, whereas students enrolled in a distance program were just 43% less likely to have a first child than non-students [32], though it is unclear how much of the difference is driven by selection (e.g., people may enroll in distance programs because they anticipate having a child).

"If you look at the body language of young people in the villages, and especially girls who have gone to school, they look more confident; when you talk to them they have more determination, and many of them are convincing their families not to get them married early, to allow them to study...There are still young girls who have no control over their lives: they get married early, go through violence. But I am looking at girls who are stepping out. And also young boys who relate more to the values of their peers and not necessarily the family values of tradition and patriarchy."

—Poonam Muttreja, Executive Director of the Delhi-based Population Foundation of India, in 2020 [33]

A second—and more long-lasting—mechanism by which education can affect fertility is by changing people's beliefs, values, and preferences. More educated people tend to see fertility as a manageable matter of personal choice as opposed to something unpredictable and unavoidable [34]. Education may also change one's concept of what constitutes a "good" or "successful" life, where having (many) children becomes less of a priority vis-à-vis other life goals (e.g., individual well-being, achievement, occupational prestige, autonomy) [35–37]. Childbearing decisions may therefore increasingly be based on rational consideration of the costs and benefits of having (more) children at a particular moment in time, including the impact of childbearing on one's education and career, material well-being, capacity for self-actualization, and one's capacity to nurture and invest in (an additional) child. Given that people with more education tend to earn more than people with less education, education also raises the financial *opportunity costs* of having children (i.e., how much income one must forego in order to have children) and hence tends to postpone childbearing and reduce early childbearing [17, 38]. On the whole, education has been found to depress fertility preferences in high fertility countries [39, 40] and also increase contraceptive use [41, 42] and hence reduce unplanned pregnancies [43, 44].

There are also some mechanisms by which education might *increase* fertility. Women with more education tend to be healthier than women with less education; they are, for instance, less likely to be obese [43] and hence more fecund [46]. Because they tend to earn more, more highly educated people may be more able to afford (more) children. For men, greater education may also increase the likelihood of finding a partner. Still, the negative effects of education on fertility tend to outweigh its potential positive effects. All in all, people with more education may be better able to realize their own fertility preferences due to their better knowledge, sense of control over own reproduction, more contraceptive use, fewer unintended pregnancies, and fewer abortions [47, 48]. In other words, education may narrow the gap between preferences and behavior. Further educational expansion might in fact result in higher fertility in richer countries where people tend to have fewer children than they would ideally want, but lower fertility in high fertility settings where people tend to have more children than they would ideally want [49].

Education Increases Women's Childbearing Autonomy

Another important effect of education is that it empowers women to exercise more control over their own reproduction [50]. The empowering effect of education would seem to be particularly important for fertility in many developing countries where many women have less autonomy in reproductive matters. In addition to being better informed about reproduction and contraception, more educated women have more confidence to act on their knowledge. Their education may improve their "bargaining power" with their husbands and male partners, giving them a greater say in fertility decisions. Increasing women's education is thus often cited as an effective mechanism for reducing unintended pregnancies in developing countries [51, 52].

A number of studies substantiate the effect of women's education on fertility in developing countries. One Ethiopian study found that women without any formal education had more than six children on average. In comparison, women with secondary or higher education had only two children, a key reason why the TFR in Addis Abbeba (the capital) has fallen to 1.8 children per woman [53]. An Indonesian study based on a school construction program that took place between 1973 and 1978 found that increasing women's education by one year reduced women's average fertility at age 25 by 0.1 children [54]. A Nigerian study on a universal primary education program that took place between 1976 and 1981 found that women with an additional year of schooling had, on average, 0.26 fewer children before age 25 compared with other students from the same region [55]. One Cochrane review concluded that interventions involving a combination of education and contraception promotion significantly reduced unintended pregnancy over the medium and long term [56].

Figure 8.2 shows how fertility differs by education in developing countries based on data from 2017 to 2019. For the selected countries, fertility was 3.3 children per woman among women with secondary or higher education, compared with 4.8 children per woman among women with primary or no education.

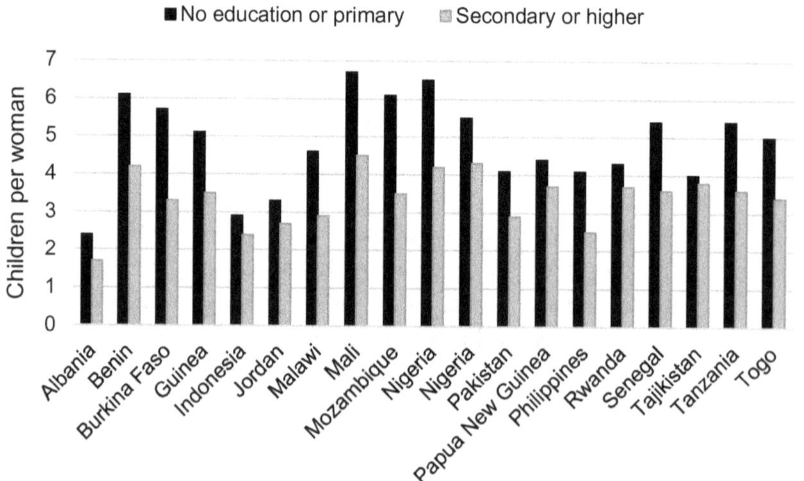

Fig. 8.2 Total fertility rate by education in selected developing countries, 2017–2019. Based on [57]

Children Are Getting More Expensive

Contemporary children now often represent a net monetary *cost* as opposed to benefit for the family [58, 59]. An increasing number of regulations limit child labor, and countries all over the world have banned children from working in industries such as mining and textiles [60, 61]. At the same time, skill-biased technological change and educational expansion have meant that children now tend to spend a longer time in school [8], and enter the labor market at increasingly older ages [7, 62–65]. Prior to the twentieth century, children often began full-time work around age 10 [66]. While the same continues to be true in some countries (e.g., in Venezuela, many children without education begin working around age 10 [67]), in richer countries most people are in their 20s when they begin working [68] (also in Venezuela, people with university education typically enter the workforce in the mid-20s [69]). As a result, children have become much more expensive and the period that a child is financially dependent on his or her parents has been dramatically extended [60, 69–73].

The extension in the period of children's financial dependence also means that it takes longer for young people to accumulate the necessary financial resources for forming their own family. In response to ongoing skill-biased technological changes, individuals need to invest more time and effort in acquiring formal education, skills, and experience before entering the workforce [74]. In the United States, for example, labor force participation among 16- to 19-year-olds fell from slightly above 50% in 1992 to less than a third in 2012, with labor force participation declining also among those in their 20s [75]. Later labor market entry causes a delay in family formation [76]. As members of successive generations need more and more schooling in order to be "on par" with or exceed their peers, fertility may be delayed more and more [76].

Technology may be able to take over many of the tasks performed by today's workforce, particularly routine and repetitive tasks currently performed by employees with less education. It has been estimated that the automation of production processes could perform large proportions of all jobs in developed economies in the next decades [77, 78], particularly jobs requiring few skills, which tend to be low paid [79–81].

Many foresee that these ongoing developments will lead to large-scale unemployment, with more jobs disappearing than new ones being created [82]. Thus, skill-biased technological change is likely to continue to depress fertility via two pathways: first, by requiring that successive generations pursue even longer periods of education and training; second, by making it much more difficult for people with low education to acquire the necessary financial resources and economic stability to have children.

More Education Is a Good Thing

Education is a key driver of skills and cognitive competencies. It has a range of positive effects for individuals as well as for society. Education is related to better health, well-being, and a greater capacity to function well in modern societies. Education also empowers men and particularly women to control their reproduction, and improves their ability to make childbearing decisions that lead to better outcomes for both children and parents over the long term. Ongoing labor market changes imply a greater need for education in order to be able to get a decent job.

However, education also increases the costs of childbearing: for individuals with high education who face higher opportunity costs, but also for all prospective parents who need to be able to provide for a child for 20 years or even more. Many societies have underinvested in education for long periods and could benefit tremendously from incentivizing and mandating longer schooling. However, governments must consider how they might offset the increase in childbearing costs that tend to come along with educational expansion so that people are better able to realize their own fertility preferences.

References

1. World Health Organization (2015). *Health in 2015: From MDGs, millennium development goals to SDGs, sustainable development goals*. Geneva: World Health Organization.
2. Manning, A. (2004). We can work it out: The impact of technological change on the demand for low-skill workers. *Scottish Journal of Political Economy*, 51(5), 581–608. https://doi.org/10.1111/j.0036-9292.2004.00322.x.
3. Machin, S., & Reenen, J. V. (1998). Technology and changes in skill structure: Evidence from seven OECD countries. *The Quarterly Journal of Economics*, 113(4), 1215–1244. https://doi.org/10.1162/003355398555883.
4. Murtin, F. (2012). Long-term determinants of the demographic transition, 1870–2000. *Review of Economics and Statistics*, 95(2), 617–631. https://doi.org/10.1162/REST_a_00302.
5. Goldin, C., & Katz, L. F. (1998). The origins of technology-skill complementarity. *The Quarterly Journal of Economics*, 113(3), 693–732. https://doi.org/10.1162/003355398555720.
6. Lee, J.-W., & Lee, H. (2016). Human capital in the long run. *Journal of Development Economics*, 122, 147–169. https://doi.org/10.1016/j.jdeveco.2016.05.006.
7. Morrisson, C., & Murtin, F. (2009). The century of education. *Journal of Human Capital*, 3(1), 1–42. https://doi.org/10.1086/600102.
8. Barro, R. J., & Lee, J. W. (2013). A new data set of educational attainment in the world, 1950–2010. *Journal of Development Economics*, 104, 184–198. https://doi.org/10.1016/j.jdeveco.2012.10.001.
9. Barro, R. J., & Lee, J.-W. (2015). *Education matters: Global schooling gains from the 19th to the 21st century*. New York: Oxford University Press.
10. Psaki, S. R., Soler-Hampejsek, E., Saha, J., Mensch, B. S., & Amin, S. J. D. (2019). The effects of adolescent childbearing on literacy and numeracy in Bangladesh, Malawi, and Zambia. *Demography*, 56(5), 1899–1929. https://doi.org/10.1007/s13524-019-00816-z.
11. Bongaarts, J., & Watkins, S. C. (1996). Social interactions and contemporary fertility transitions. *Population and Development Review*, 22(4), 639–682. https://doi.org/10.2307/2137804.
12. Chesnais, J. C. (1992). *The demographic transition: Stages, patterns, and economic implications*. Oxford: Oxford University Press.

13. Cochrane, S. (1979). *Fertility and education. What do we really know?* Baltimore and London: Johns Hopkins University Press.
14. Myrskylä, M., Kohler, H., & Billari, F. (2009). Advances in development reverse fertility declines. *Nature*, 460(7256), 741–743. https://doi.org/10.1038/nature08230.
15. Kravdal, Ø., & Rindfuss, R. R. (2008). Changing Relationships between education and fertility: A study of women and men born 1940 to 1964. *American Sociological Review*, 73(5), 854–873. https://doi.org/10.2307/25472561.
16. Skirbekk, V. (2008). Fertility trends by social status. *Demographic Research*, 18(5), 145–180. https://doi.org/10.4054/DemRes.2008.18.5.
17. Jejeebhoy, S. (1995). *Women's education, autonomy and reproductive behaviour: Experience from developing countries*. Oxford: Clarendon Press.
18. Basu, A. M. (2002). Why does education lead to lower fertility? A critical review of some of the possibilities. *World Development*, 30(10), 1779–1790. https://doi.org/10.1016/S0305-750X(02)00072-4.
19. Martin, T. C., & Juarez, F. (1995). The impact of women's education on fertility in Latin America: Searching for explanations. *International Family Planning Perspectives*, 21(2), 52–80. https://doi.org/10.2307/2133523.
20. Cleland, J. (2009). Education and future fertility trends, with special reference to mid-transitional countries. *Population bulletin of the United Nations: Completing the fertility transition* (pp. 183–194). New York: United Nations, Population Division, Department of Economic and Social Affairs. http://www.un.org/esa/population/publications/completingfertility/bulletin-english.pdf#page=196.
21. Bongaarts, J. (2003). Completing the fertility transition in the developing world: The role of educational differences and fertility preferences. *Population Studies*, 57(3), 321–335. https://doi.org/10.1080/0032472032000137835.
22. United Nations (2019). World Population Prospects 2019. https://population.un.org/wpp/. Accessed 25 May 2021.
23. Bratsberg, B., & Rogeberg, O. (2018). Flynn effect and its reversal are both environmentally caused. *Proceedings of the National Academy of Sciences*, 115(26), 6674–6678. https://doi.org/10.1073/pnas.1718793115.
24. Jalovaara, M., Neyer, G., Andersson, G., Dahlberg, J., Dommermuth, L., Fallesen, P., et al. (2019). Education, gender, and cohort fertility in the Nordic countries. *European Journal of Population*, 35(3), 563–586. https://doi.org/10.1007/s10680-018-9492-2.

25. Breen, R., & Ermisch, J. (2017). Educational reproduction in Great Britain: A prospective approach. *European Sociological Review*, 33(4), 590–603. https://doi.org/10.1093/esr/jcx061.
26. Skirbekk, V., Kohler, H.-P., & Prskawetz, A. (2004). Birth month, school graduation, and the timing of births and marriages. *Demography*, 41(3), 547–568. https://doi.org/10.1353/dem.2004.0028.
27. Monstad, K., Propper, C., & Salvanes, K. G. (2008). Education and fertility: Evidence from a natural experiment. *Scandinavian Journal of Economics*, 110(4), 827–852. https://doi.org/10.1111/j.1467-9442.2008.00563.x.
28. Tequame, M., & Tirivayi, N. (2015). Higher education and fertility: Evidence from a natural experiment in Ethiopia. UNU-MERIT Working Papers; No. 019. Maastricht: Maastricht Economic and Social Research Institute on Innovation and Technology. https://core.ac.uk/download/pdf/231371129.pdf. Accessed 31 May 2021.
29. Chicoine, L. (2012). Education and fertility: Evidence from a policy change in Kenya. IZA Discussion Paper No. 6778. https://ssrn.com/abstract=2157920. Accessed 31 May 2021.
30. Kirdar, M. G., Tayfur, M. D., & Koç, Ī. (2018). The effect of compulsory schooling laws on teenage marriage and births in Turkey. *Journal of Human Capital*, 12(4). https://doi.org/10.1086/700076.
31. Lavy, V., & Zablotsky, A. (2015). Women's schooling and fertility under low female labor force participation: Evidence from mobility restrictions in Israel. *Journal of Public Economics*, 124, 105–121. https://doi.org/10.1016/j.jpubeco.2015.02.009.
32. Andersson, L. (2018). Online distance education and transition to parenthood among female university students in Sweden. *European Journal of Population*, 35(4), 795–823. https://doi.org/10.1007/s10680-018-9503-3.
33. Safi, M. (2020, July 25). All the people: What happens if humanity's ranks start to shrink? *The Guardian*. Retrieved from https://www.theguardian.com/world/2020/jul/25/all-the-people-what-happens-if-humanitys-ranks-start-to-shrink.
34. Söderberg, M., Christensson, K., Lundgren, I., & Hildingsson, I. (2015). Women's attitudes towards fertility and childbearing—A study based on a national sample of Swedish women validating the Attitudes to Fertility and Childbearing Scale (AFCS). *Sexual & Reproductive Healthcare*, 6(2), 54–58. https://doi.org/10.1016/j.srhc.2015.01.002.
35. Sobotka, T. (2017). Post-transitional fertility: The role of childbearing postponement in fuelling the shift to low and unstable fertility levels.

Journal of Biosocial Science, 49(S1), S20–S45. https://doi.org/10.1017/S0021932017000323.

36. Sobotka, T., & Beaujouan, É. (2017). Late motherhood in low-fertility countries: Reproductive intentions, trends and consequences. In D. Stoop (Ed.), *Preventing age related fertility loss* (pp. 11–29). Cham: Springer. https://doi.org/10.1007/978-3-319-14857-1_2.
37. Balbo, N., Billari, F. C., & Mills, M. (2013). Fertility in advanced societies: A review of research. *European Journal of Population/Revue Européenne de Démographie*, 29, 1–38. https://doi.org/10.1007/s10680-012-9277-y.
38. Gustafsson, S. (2001). Optimal age at motherhood: Theoretical and empirical considerations on postponement of maternity in Europe. *Journal of Population Economics*, 14(2), 225–247. https://doi.org/10.1007/s001480000051.
39. Poelker, K. E., & Gibbons, J. L. (2018). Guatemalan women achieve ideal family size: Empowerment through education and decision-making. *Health Care for Women International*, 39(2), 170–185. https://doi.org/10.1080/07399332.2017.1395028.
40. Mocan, N. H., & Cannonier, C. (2012). Empowering women through education: Evidence from Sierra Leone. NBER Working Paper Series No. 18016. Cambridge, MA: National Bureau of Economic Research. http://www.nber.org/papers/w18016. Accessed 31 May 2021.
41. Lopez, L. M., Grey, T. W., Tolley, E. E., Chen, M., Oringanje, C., Meremikwu, M. M., et al. (2016). Brief educational strategies for improving contraception use in young people. *The Cochrane Database of Systematic Reviews*, 3(3), CD012025. https://doi.org/10.1002/14651858.CD012025.pub2.
42. Alabi, O., Odimegwu, C. O., De-Wet, N., & Akinyemi, J. O. (2019). Does female autonomy affect contraceptive use among women in northern Nigeria? *African Journal of Reproductive Health*, 23(2), 92–100. https://doi.org/10.29063/ajrh2019/v23i2.9.
43. Alkema, L., Kantorova, V., Menozzi, C., & Biddlecom, A. (2013). National, regional, and global rates and trends in contraceptive prevalence and unmet need for family planning between 1990 and 2015: A systematic and comprehensive analysis. *The Lancet*, 381(9878), 1642–1652. https://doi.org/10.1016/S0140-6736(12)62204-1.
44. Islam, M. M., Dorvlo, A. S. S., & Al-Qasmi, A. M. (2012). Proximate determinants of declining fertility in Oman in the 1990s. *Canadian Studies in Population*, 38(3–4), 133–152. https://doi.org/10.25336/P6731K.

45. Kinge, J. M., Strand, B. H., Vollset, S. E., & Skirbekk, V. (2015). Educational inequalities in obesity and gross domestic product: Evidence from 70 countries. *Journal of Epidemiology and Community Health*, 69(12), 1141–1146. https://doi.org/10.1136/jech-2014-205353.
46. Viner, R. M., Hargreaves, D. S., Ward, J., Bonell, C., Mokdad, A. H., & Patton, G. (2017). The health benefits of secondary education in adolescents and young adults: An international analysis in 186 low-, middle-and high-income countries from 1990 to 2013. *SSM-Population Health*, 3, 162–171. https://doi.org/10.1016/j.ssmph.2016.12.004.
47. Wusu, O. (2015). Religious influence on non-use of modern contraceptives among women in Nigeria: Comparative analysis of 1990 and 2008 NDHS. *Journal of Biosocial Science*, 47(05), 593–612. https://doi.org/10.1017/S0021932014000352.
48. Ananat, E. O., & Hungerman, D. M. (2012). The power of the pill for the next generation: Oral contraception's effects on fertility, abortion, and maternal and child characteristics. *Review of Economics and Statistics*, 94(1), 37–51. https://doi.org/10.1162/rest_a_00230.
49. Fort, M., Schneeweis, N., & Winter-Ebmer, R. (2011). More schooling, more children: Compulsory schooling reforms and fertility in Europe. NRN working papers 2011-11. Linz. http://ideas.repec.org/p/jku/nrnwps/2011_11.html. Accessed 1 June 2021.
50. Phan, L. Y. (2013). Women's empowerment and fertility changes. *International Journal of Sociology of the Family*, 39(1/2), 49–75. www.jstor.org/stable/43488406.
51. Alkema, L., Kantorova, V., Menozzi, C., & Biddlecom, A. J. S.-. (2013). National, regional, and global rates and trends in contraceptive prevalence and unmet need for family planning between 1990 and 2015: A systematic and comprehensive analysis. *The Lancet*, 381(9878), 1642–1652. https://doi.org/10.1016/S0140-6736(12)62204-1.
52. Bellizzi, S., Palestra, F., & Pichierri, G. (2019). Adolescent women with unintended pregnancy in low-and middle-income countries: Reasons for discontinuation of contraception. *Journal of Pediatric and Adolescent Gynecology*, 33(2), 144–148. https://doi.org/10.1016/j.jpag.2019.11.004.
53. Hailemariam, A. (2017). The second biggest African country undergoing rapid change: Ethiopia. In H. Groth, & J. F. May (Eds.), *Africa's population: In search of a demographic dividend* (pp. 53–69). Cham: Springer International.
54. Breierova, L., & Duflo, E. (2004). The impact of education on fertility and child mortality: Do fathers really matter less than mothers? NBER

Working Paper Series, Working Paper 10513. Cambridge, MA: N. B. o. E. Research. http://www.nber.org/papers/w10513. Accessed 1 June 2021.

55. Osili, U. O., & Long, B. T. (2008). Does female schooling reduce fertility? Evidence from Nigeria. *Journal of Development Economics*, 87(1), 57–75. https://doi.org/10.1016/j.jdeveco.2007.10.003.
56. Oringanje, C., Meremikwu, M. M., Eko, H., Esu, E., Meremikwu, A., & Ehiri, J. E. (2016). Interventions for preventing unintended pregnancies among adolescents. *Cochrane Database of Systematic Reviews*, 2(CD005215). https://doi.org/10.1002/14651858.CD005215.pub3.
57. The Demographic and Health Surveys Program (2020). Demographic and Health Surveys. ICF International. https://www.dhsprogram.com/. Accessed 31 May 2021.
58. Willis, R. J. (1982). The direction of intergenerational transfers and demographic transition: The Caldwell hypothesis reexamined. *Population and Development Review*, 8, 207–234. https://doi.org/10.2307/2808116.
59. Turra, C. M., Queiroz, B. L., & Rios-Neto, E. L. G. (2011). Idiosyncrasies of intergenerational transfers in Brazil. In R. Lee, & A. Mason (Eds.), *Population aging and the generational economy: A global perspective* (pp. 394–407). Cheltenham, UK and Northampton, MA: Edward Elgar. https://doi.org/10.4337/9780857930583.00032.
60. Rahikainen, M. (2017). *Centuries of child labour: European experiences from the seventeenth to the twentieth century*. London and New York: Routledge.
61. Grootaert, C., & Kanbur, R. (1995). Child labour: An economic perspective. *International Labour Review*, 134(2), 187–203.
62. Burnette, J. (2006). How skilled were English agricultural labourers in the early nineteenth century? *The Economic History Review*, 59(4), 688–716. https://doi.org/10.1111/j.1468-0289.2006.00363.x.
63. Acemoglu, D. (2002). Technical change, inequality, and the labor market. *Journal of Economic Literature*, 40(1), 7–72. https://doi.org/10.2307/2698593.
64. Gangl, M. (2002). Changing labour markets and early career outcomes: Labour market entry in Europe over the past decade. *Work, Employment and Society*, 16(1), 67–90.
65. Becker, R., & Blossfeld, H.-P. (2017). Entry of men into the labour market in West Germany and their career mobility (1945–2008). *Journal for Labour Market Research*, 50(1), 113–130. https://doi.org/10.1007/s12651-017-0224-6.

66. Boot, H. M. (1995). How skilled were Lancashire cotton factory workers in 1833? *The Economic History Review*, 48(2), 283–303. https://doi.org/10.1111/j.1468-0289.1995.tb01419.x.
67. Psacharopoulos, G. (1995). The profitability of investment in education: Concepts and methods. Human capital development and operations policy working papers, no. HCO 63. Washington, DC: W. B. Group. http://documents.worldbank.org/curated/en/909711468761947964/The-profitability-of-investment-in-education-concepts-and-methods. Accessed 1 June 2021.
68. OECD (2012). OECD Employment Outlook 2012. Paris: OECD. http://www.oecd-ilibrary.org/employment/oecd-employment-outlook-2012_empl_outlook-2012-en. Accessed 1 June 2021.
69. Nesi, G., Nogler, L., & Pertile, M. (Eds.) (2016). *Child labour in a globalized world: A legal analysis of ILO action*. London: Routledge.
70. Tsogas, G. (2015). *Labor regulation in a global economy*. New York: Routledge.
71. D'Alessandro, S., & Fioroni, T. (2016). Child labour and inequality. *The Journal of Economic Inequality*, 14(1), 63–79. https://doi.org/10.1007/s10888-015-9319-x.
72. Åslund, O., & Grönqvist, H. (2010). Family size and child outcomes: Is there really no trade-off? *Labour Economics*, 17(1), 130–139. https://doi.org/10.1016/j.labeco.2009.05.003.
73. Angrist, J., Lavy, V., & Schlosser, A. (2006). New evidence on the causal link between the quantity and quality of children. IZA Discussion Paper Series No. 2075. Bonn: I. f. t. S. o. L. (IZA). http://ftp.iza.org/dp2075.pdf. Accessed 1 June 2021.
74. Skirbekk, V. (2008). Age and productivity potential: A new approach based on ability levels and industry-wide task demand. *Population and Development Review*, 34, 191–207. https://doi.org/10.2307/25434764.
75. Toossi, M. (2013, December). Labor force projections to 2022: The labor force participation rate continues to fall. *Monthly Labor Review*, pp. 1–27. Retrieved from https://www.bls.gov/opub/mlr/2013/article/pdf/labor-force-projections-to-2022-the-labor-force-participation-rate-continues-to-fall.pdf.
76. Skirbekk, V., & Kc, S. (2012). Fertility-reducing dynamics of women's social status and educational attainment. *Asian Population Studies*, 8(3), 251–264. https://doi.org/10.1080/17441730.2012.714667.

77. The World Bank (2016). World development report 2016: Digital dividends. Washington, DC: The World Bank. https://www.worldbank.org/en/publication/wdr2016. Accessed 1 June 2021.
78. Bowles, J. 2021 (2014). The computerisation of European jobs. *Bruegel*. July 24. https://www.bruegel.org/2014/07/the-computerisation-of-european-jobs/. Accessed 1 June 2021.
79. Manyika, J., Lund, S., Chui, M., Bughin, J., Woetzel, J., Batra, P., et al. (2017). Jobs lost, jobs gained: Workforce transitions in a time of automation. McKinsey Global Institute. https://www.mckinsey.com/global-themes/future-of-organizations-and-work/what-the-future-of-work-will-mean-for-jobs-skills-and-wages. Accessed 1 June 2021.
80. Autor, D. H., Levy, F., & Murnane, R. J. (2003). The skill content of recent technological change: An empirical exploration. *The Quarterly Journal of Economics*, 118(4), 1279–1333. https://doi.org/10.1162/003355303322552801.
81. Brynjolfsson, E., & McAfee, A. (2015, July/August). Will humans go the way of horses? Labor in the second machine age. *Foreign Affairs*, p. 8. Retrieved from https://www.foreignaffairs.com/articles/2015-06-16/will-humans-go-way-horses.
82. Pew Research Center (2014). AI, robotics, and the future of jobs. Washington, DC: Pew Research Center. http://www.pewinternet.org/2014/08/06/future-of-jobs/. Accessed 1 June 2021.

9

An Era of Choice: Childbearing Has Become More Planned

- Contraception has improved and proliferated in the last decades. Thanks in part to family planning programs and the Internet, people have more knowledge about reproduction compared with previous generations. Women and men have also generally gained more autonomy with regard to their reproductive choices. As a result, whether and when one becomes a parent has become more a matter of choice than of chance. In this chapter, I discuss statistics on planned versus unplanned pregnancies, trends in contraceptive use and abortion, and why even in developed countries a significant number of pregnancies are still unintentional.

Contraception Key to Fertility Decline

Technological progress in contraception has been essential for fertility decline since the 1950s [1–3]. Several contraceptive technologies were first developed and implemented in Western countries and later spread to the rest of the world [4–6]. Latex was invented in 1920, making way for the invention of the first modern male condoms. In 1960, the first contraceptive pill was approved for use by the United States Food and

V. Skirbekk, *Decline and Prosper!*,
https://doi.org/10.1007/978-3-030-91611-4_9

Drug Administration, allowing women to reliably control their reproduction for the first time in history. In 1968, the first intrauterine devices (IUD) were approved for use; the first contraceptive implant (Norplant) was introduced in 1990; the first injectable method (Depo-Provera) was approved in 1992; and the "morning after pill" was approved for use in the United States in 1999. Contraception continues to become not only more effective, but also safer (e.g., the hormonal level of contraceptive pills has decreased over time [7]).

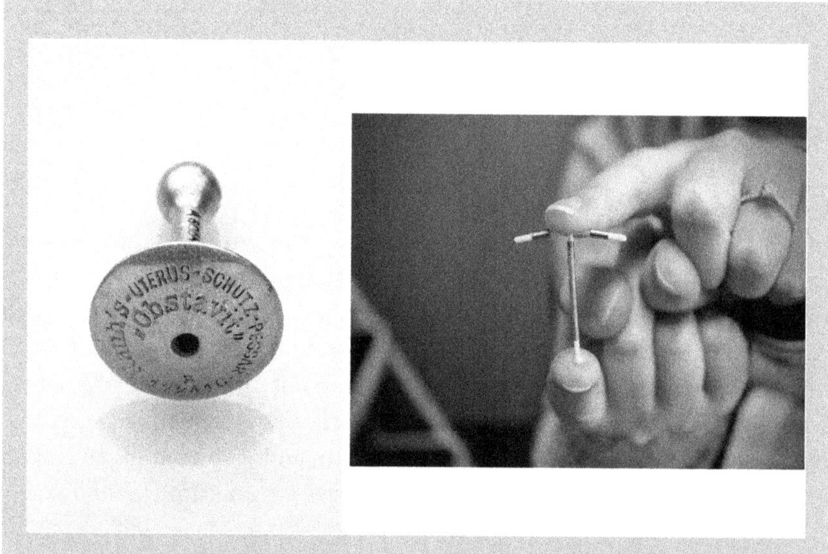

Intrauterine contraceptive device from the late 1920s (left) and today (right). Left image: Stem pessary, Germany, 1925–1935. Science Musuem, London. Attribution 4.0 International (CC BY 4.0), https://wellcomecollection.org/works/xkv7b3cb. Right image: Robin Marty, CC BY 2.0, https://creativecommons.org/licenses/by/2.0, via Wikimedia Commons.

Figure 9.1 displays the effectiveness of different contraceptive methods based on data from the Demographic and Health Surveys [8]. The figure shows the 36-month failure rate for each method—that is, the median number of women who become pregnant within three years. As can be seen in the figure, modern contraceptives are much more

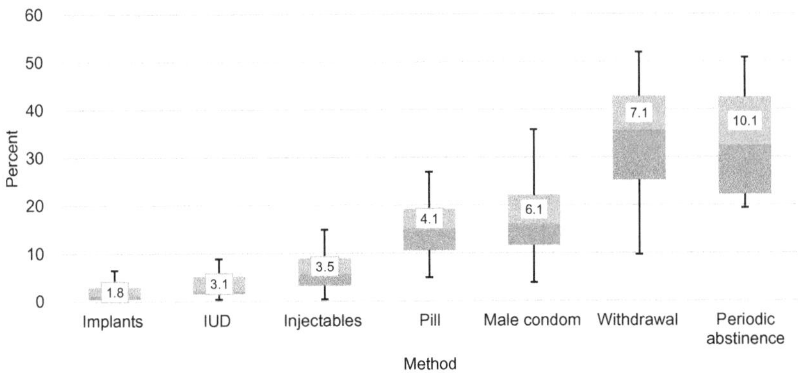

Fig. 9.1 Failure rates of different contraceptive methods. Displayed is the minimum, middle 50% (gray), median, and maximum estimates of the failure rate. Adapted from [9]

effective than traditional methods like periodic abstinence (i.e., calendar method; abstaining from sex on the days when a woman is most fertile) or withdrawal. More than 30 women practicing withdrawal or periodic abstinence can expect to become pregnant within three years. In comparison, the failure rate of the male condom and the contraceptive pill is less than half that of withdrawal or periodic abstinence, and the failure rate is even lower for implants, IUDs, and injectables. Figure 9.1 makes it easy to understand just how huge the impact of modern contraception has been on fertility—at least for people with access to it.

Two-Thirds of People Now Use Contraception Globally

Nationally representative surveys began measuring contraceptive use in the 1950s and, since the early 1980s, information about contraceptive practices has been available for well over half the world's population [10]. Data shows that the proportion of people using contraception globally almost doubled between 1970 and 2015, from 36% in 1970 to 64% in 2015, with most of the increase occurring before the mid-1990s. Nevertheless, sizeable increases were observed after 1990 as well. In 2010,

63% of the world population used contraception, up from 55% in 1990 [11]. There was a small global decrease in the proportion of people who wanted modern contraception but could not access it during the same period. Still, many people continue to rely on traditional and less effective methods (e.g., abstinence, withdrawal) [12, 13]. According to data from 2009, 7% of global couples were relying on traditional methods, and another 12% would like to use contraception but do not [14]. If the 215 million couples relying either on traditional methods or no contraception at all had been using modern contraception, global fertility would have been significantly lower.

The majority of couples—more than 80%—use some form of birth control that regulates female as opposed to male fertility [14]. The preponderance of female-based methods is both a cause and a consequence of the gender division in contraceptives, whereby women are disproportionately responsible for preventing pregnancy [15, 16]. As women tend to be more careful about their reproduction, female-administered as opposed to male-administered contraceptives are more likely to be effective in preventing unintended pregnancies. There has also been a shift away from sterilization and an increase in long-acting but reversible contraceptive methods like the IUD and implants in some countries. Among United States women aged 15–44, for instance, the proportion using long-acting reversible contraceptive methods increased from 6 to 14% between 2008 and 2014, while sterilization decreased from 37 to 28% [17].

The spread of effective and often subsidized (or free) contraceptives implies that most people on the planet now have the option to control their reproduction, at least theoretically. However, large regional and country variations in contraception use remain. The prevalence of contraception use is much lower in Africa (33%) than in other world regions (59% in Oceania, 68% in Asia, 69% in Europe, 73% in Latin America and the Caribbean, and 75% in North America) [10]. As with fertility, contraception use varies highly across the African countries: Contraceptive prevalence is over 50% in 17 countries (e.g., 75.7% in Mauritius, 68.2% in Morocco) but below 20% in an equal number of countries (e.g., 16% in Nigeria and less than 10% in Chad, Guinea, and South Sudan in 2015) [10]. Also in Europe, where contraception use is generally high, prevalence is below 50% in Montenegro, Bosnia and Herzegovina, and Macedonia [10].

"Women can now give up contraceptive methods. I have travelled to Europe and elsewhere and have seen the harmful effects of birth control."

—John Magufuli, President of Tanzania between 2015 and 2021, in 2018 [18]. The average woman in Tanzania has more than five children.

As shown in Fig. 9.2, there are also large regional differences regarding which contraceptive methods are used the most. Female sterilization is common in Asia and the Americas (between 30 and 40%), but infrequent in Africa and Europe (below 7%) [11]. The contraceptive pill, on the other hand, is used by just 10% of Asian couples, while it is the most popular contraceptive method in Africa and Europe where over 30% of couples use the pill. Using condoms is common in Europe (28%) but rare in Africa (8%). The use of contraceptives with relatively

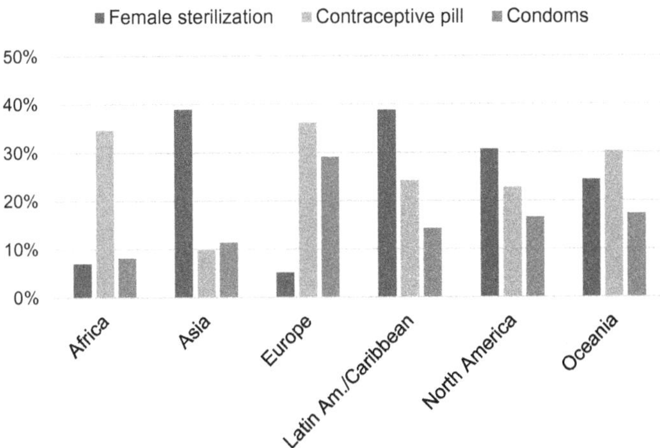

Fig. 9.2 Percent of couples using modern contraception who use female sterilization, the contraceptive pill, and condoms by world region. Based on [11]

high failure rates also remains common among some (sub)populations. Modern contraceptive methods constituted less than half of all contraceptive use in many of the countries in Middle Africa and Southern Europe [10]. Withdrawal is widely practiced in Southern Europe, while in Middle Africa the rhythm method is more common [19].

How individuals perceive the risks of unplanned pregnancy and sexually transmitted diseases [20] and sexual and reproductive education [21, 22] influence whether people use contraception. Education, affluence, urbanization, and regional development are other key factors that predict whether contraception is available and used [23–25]. Relationship quality can also influence contraceptive use. Women in abusive or violent relationships use contraceptives less frequently, according to evidence from the state of Michigan in the United States [26]. Norms and attitudes can be important, whereby more traditional communities tend to be more negative toward birth control [27, 28]. Qualitative interviews in Timor-Leste, for example, suggest that women are constrained by their families and traditions and therefore rarely access contraception freely [29]. Other reasons why people do not use contraception despite wanting to prevent pregnancy include infrequent sexual activity (e.g., due to labor migration) and fear of health side effects [19]. Many Italians use withdrawal as a contraceptive method because they fear the negative health effects of the contraceptive pill [3].

Abortion Decreases Unintended Fertility

All in all, abortion laws have generally been liberalized over the past decades [30]. Induced abortion is defined as either *therapeutic* (in order to prevent harm or save the woman's life) or *elective* (to avoid unwanted childbearing). Most countries in the world now allow abortion in order to save a woman's life (97%). About a third of countries allow abortion on the basis of a woman's request, including the United States, Canada, most European countries, and China [30]. About 25% of the world's population live in countries that never allow abortion or allow it only to save the mother's life, including most countries in Latin America, the greater Middle East, approximately half of the countries of Africa and seven countries in the Asia–Pacific region. In Europe, abortion is never allowed in Malta and the Vatican and only allowed to save a mother's life in the Northern Ireland [30].

Recent data put the worldwide abortion rate at 35 abortions per 1000 women aged 15–44 years for each year between 2010 and 2014, compared with 40 abortions per 1000 women aged 15–44 in 1990–1994 [31]. However, since 1990, abortion rates declined significantly only in developed but not in developing countries [31]. The majority of abortions worldwide now occur in developing countries, and nearly all (97%) unsafe abortions—that is, abortions performed by people without the necessary skills or in a setting that does not conform to minimum medical standards—are performed in low-income countries. The abortion rate in countries with restrictive abortion laws has been found to be about the same as in countries with more liberal laws [31]. However, abortions are much less safe in countries with restrictive laws. About 67,000 women died from complications from unsafe abortions annually, mostly in countries with highly restrictive abortion laws. Globally, it has been estimated that three out of the four abortions conducted between 2010 and 2014 in countries with highly restrictive abortion laws were unsafe, significantly higher than in countries with less restrictive laws [32]. The use of dangerous methods by untrained individuals is relatively common in several regions in Africa [32].

> "Nobody likes abortion, even when safe and legal. It's not what any woman would choose for a happy time on Saturday night. But nobody likes women bleeding to death on the bathroom floor from illegal abortions, either. What to do?"
>
> —Margaret Atwood, author of the best-selling novel *The Handmaid's Tale* [33]

Most abortions are the result of an unintended pregnancy. In the group of countries where abortion is prohibited altogether or allowed only to save a woman's life, one study estimated that 48% of unintended pregnancies ended in abortion in 2010–2014 compared with 69% in countries where abortion is allowed on request [34]. Some have argued that liberalization of abortion laws combined with the increased possibility to test for chromosome deviations in utero (e.g., Down's syndrome) may lead to more abortions [31]. However, worldwide only few women report that fetal defects motivated their decision to have an abortion—at least according to older data from 1998 [35]. In a study from 2005, just around 2% of a sample of abortion patients in the United States reported having the abortion due to fetal abnormalities [36]. The rate of worldwide abortions due to fetal abnormalities probably remains quite low for three reasons: due to the low incidence of birth abnormalities in the first place, the fact that most women obtain abortions before fetal abnormalities could be identified, and that fetal abnormalities are generally not detected in developing countries where the majority of abortions take place [35].

Research has found that the legalization of abortion is associated with declines in population growth [37], and abortions are also likely to impact the timing and overall level of contemporary fertility [31, 34]. One study assessed the effect of a government ban on abortion in Romania, which lasted from 1966 to 1989. Abortion and family planning were legalized after the fall of communism in 1989. Fertility decreased by 30% within six months [38]. Abortion has likely contributed to a decrease in unplanned births and births to mothers in difficult life circumstances [39, 40] and to a decrease in births to adolescent mothers in particular [41]. Abortion is relatively common among teens—even if most abortions occur later in the reproductive window. In the United States, by age 20, 4.6% of women will have had an abortion, and 19% will have done so by age 30 according to one study [41].

Family Planning Reduces Unplanned Pregnancies

Family planning refers to informing individuals about reproduction, sex, contraception, and options for dealing with an unintended pregnancy. Globally, in 2015, 166 out of 197 governments (84%) provided direct support for family planning (i.e., family planning services were provided through government-run facilities or outlets), up from 63% in 1976. The majority of governments (76%) now also provide sex and reproductive education in schools [42]. It is, however, difficult to evaluate the effects of reproductive education and family planning initiatives on fertility and unintended pregnancies. Often, it cannot be ruled out that any changes in fertility would have happened without intervention, or that the people who receive and/or seek out reproductive education are different from people who do not (e.g., with regard to socioeconomic status). One analysis of family planning programs implemented in Matlab, Bangladesh, in 1977 [43] found that villages that were part of the program experienced an additional 17% decline in fertility compared with other villages. A United States-based study examined the relationship between school-based sex education and teenage sexual behavior from 1991 to 2013. The study concluded that school-based sex education raised contraceptive use and also lowered the prevalence of chlamydia among teens [44]. Another study based on data from 17 Latin American countries observed between 1997 and 2012 found that countries with school-based sex education and legal access to abortion (under one or more restrictions) had lower adolescent fertility rates [45].

With the expansion of the Internet, people can more easily and anonymously acquire information on sex, reproduction, and contraception. The Internet may be a particularly important source of reproductive knowledge in contexts where information about sex is restricted, or for individuals who feel uncomfortable asking questions. Research has provided some indirect support for the hypothesis that Internet access improves fertility control (e.g., getting pregnant when one wants to, avoiding pregnancy when one doesn't). One study suggested that the spread of broadband Internet in the 1999–2007 period in the United States contributed to the decline in adolescent fertility—regions that first got broadband Internet experienced more rapid decline [46]. Another study in Germany in the late 2000s found that the expansion of broadband Internet led to a decline in pregnancies in early adulthood, but also to a rise in childbearing for women aged 25 and above—and a slight overall increase in fertility [47].

Three Out of Four Births Are Planned

The proliferation of effective contraception and pregnancy termination techniques as well as improved sex education and accessible information have together decreased the number and proportion of unintended pregnancies and births [48]—and reduced the number of teenage births in particular [49]. *Unintended pregnancies* are defined as pregnancies that, at the time of conception, are either mistimed (the mother wanted the pregnancy to occur at a later point in time) or unwanted (the mother did not want it to occur at that time or any other time in the future). Typically, in research, a pregnancy is classified as "unintended" based on how a woman answers a retrospective survey question about whether or not they wanted a pregnancy at the time of conception. It is important to differentiate between unintended pregnancies and unintended *births*, as many unintended pregnancies end in abortion and some end in miscarriage. The number/proportion of unintended births is thus often much lower than the number/proportion of unintended pregnancies. Differentiating between unintended births and unintended pregnancies is also important for drawing conclusions about the population's supply of and demand for contraception and/or abortion.

For every year in the 2010s, globally more than 200 million pregnancies took place each year, out of which around 140 million resulted in a live birth [50]. About six out of ten pregnancies were unintended [11, 34, 51], but only about one out of four births was unintended [34]. Of the 85 million unintended pregnancies in 2012, about half ended in abortion, 13% ended in miscarriage, and 38% (32 million) led to birth [52]. Together, these statistics indicate that while most contemporary *births* are planned, the proportion of unintended pregnancies remains substantial and often results in abortion. Globally, there has been a moderate decrease in unintended pregnancy over the last few decades. Based on data from 105 countries, one study estimated that the global unintended pregnancy rate fell from 74 per 1000 women aged 15–44 years in 1990–1994 to 62 in 2010–2014, a decrease of 17% [34]. It is difficult, however, to determine the extent to which the decrease in unintended pregnancies is because pregnancies have become more planned versus the overall decline in pregnancies per se.

Whether pregnancies are planned or unintended has important consequences. Women who become pregnant unintentionally may experience negative emotions and poor mental health, and they often have difficulty achieving their education and career goals. As a major contributor to socioeconomic inequality, unintended pregnancies also have important implications for the population as a whole [53, 54]. Particularly adolescent mothers faced with an unintended pregnancy are at risk for dropping out of school. Especially in developing countries, many unintended pregnancies result in unsafe abortions [55], with dire consequences for women's health. For couples, unplanned births are often a source of conflict and decreased satisfaction, and also increase the risk that the relationship will end. Unintended children also tend to have worse physical and mental health, difficult relationships with their parents, and poorer educational outcomes, effects that can be observed not only in infancy but also throughout childhood and young adulthood [56, 57].

Planned Childbearing: Still Room for Improvement

Contraceptive technology has improved tremendously since the 1950s. People are now able to control their own reproduction safely and reliably. And many people do: Today, more than three out of four births are planned. However, despite improvements in contraceptive technology, contraceptive access, the liberalization of abortion laws, and widespread government support for family planning initiatives, four out of ten global pregnancies are still unintended. Most unintended pregnancies occur in developing regions where many women are unable to exercise control over their own reproduction, and where abortion is legally restricted. As a result, unintended pregnancies often end in unsafe abortions. This is a major health risk for women, particularly in poorer countries.

According to a 2020 report from the United Nations, almost half of the women in 57 low- to middle-income countries have no decision-making power regarding their health, contraceptive use, or sex lives [58].

Better sexual and reproductive health services are needed to help women avoid unintended pregnancies and ensure healthy outcomes. Access to modern contraception has improved tremendously, but there is still work to be done, particularly regarding women's reproductive autonomy. The Internet and long-acting, reversible contraceptive methods offer new opportunities to improve autonomous, controlled, and informed childbearing choices.

References

1. Sanderson, W. C. (1987). Below-replacement fertility in nineteenth century America. *Population and Development Review*, 13(2), 305–313. https://doi.org/10.2307/1973195.
2. Lavely, W., & Freedman, R. (1990). The origins of the Chinese fertility decline. *Demography*, 27(3), 357–367. https://doi.org/10.2307/2061373.
3. Dereuddre, R., Van de Putte, B., & Bracke, P. (2016). Ready, willing, and able: Contraceptive use patterns across Europe. *European Journal of Population*, 32(4), 543–573. https://doi.org/10.1007/s10680-016-9378-0.
4. Silies, E.-M. (2015). Taking the Pill after the 'sexual revolution': Female contraceptive decisions in England and West Germany in the 1970s. *European Review of History: Revue européenne d'histoire*, 22(1), 41–59. https://doi.org/10.1080/13507486.2014.983431.
5. Flandrin, J.-L. (1975). Contraception, marriage, and sexual relations in the Christian west. In R. Forster, & O. Ranum (Eds.), *Biology of man in history* (pp. 23–47). Baltimore and London: Johns Hopkins University Press.
6. Tentler, L. W. (2004). *Catholics and contraception: An American history*. Ithaca and London: Cornell University Press.
7. Riddle, J. M. (1997). *Eve's herbs: A history of contraception and abortion in the West*. Cambridge, MA and London: Harvard University Press.

8. The Demographic and Health Surveys Program (2020). Demographic and Health Surveys. ICF International. https://www.dhsprogram.com/. Accessed 31 May 2021.
9. Polis, C. B., Sarah E. K., Bankole, A., Onda, T., Croftand, T. N., & Singh, S. (2016). Contraceptive failure rates in the developing world: An analysis of Demographic and Health Survey Data in 43 countries. New York: Guttmacher Institute. https://www.guttmacher.org/report/contraceptive-failure-rates-in-developing-world#appendixa. Accessed 31 May 2021.
10. United Nations Department of Economic and Social Affairs Population Division (2015). Trends in contraceptive use worldwide 2015. New York: United Nations. https://www.un.org/en/development/desa/population/publications/pdf/family/trendsContraceptiveUse2015Report.pdf. Accessed 31 May 2021.
11. Alkema, L., Kantorova, V., Menozzi, C., & Biddlecom, A. (2013). National, regional, and global rates and trends in contraceptive prevalence and unmet need for family planning between 1990 and 2015: A systematic and comprehensive analysis. *The Lancet*, 381(9878), 1642–1652. https://doi.org/10.1016/S0140-6736(12)62204-1.
12. Carmichael, G. A. (2016). Analysis of fertility. *Fundamentals of demographic analysis: Concepts, measures and methods* (pp. 247–298). Cham: Springer. https://doi.org/10.1007/978-3-319-23255-3_6.
13. Hertrich, V. (2017). Trends in age at marriage and the onset of fertility transition in sub-Saharan Africa. *Population and Development Review*, 43(S1), 112–137. https://doi.org/10.1111/padr.12043.
14. Reading, B. F. (2012, March 27). Growth in world contraceptive use stalling; 215 million women's needs still unmet. Retrieved from http://www.earth-policy.org/mobile/releases/highlights26. Accessed 31 May 2021.
15. Bertotti, A. M. (2013). Gendered divisions of fertility work: Socioeconomic predictors of female versus male sterilization. *Journal of Marriage and Family*, 75(1), 13–25. https://doi.org/10.1111/j.1741-3737.2012.01031.x.
16. Kimport, K. (2018). More than a physical burden: Women's mental and emotional work in preventing pregnancy. *Journal of Sex Research*, 55(9), 1096–1105. https://doi.org/10.1080/00224499.2017.1311834.
17. Kavanaugh, M. L., & Jerman, J. (2018). Contraceptive method use in the United States: Trends and characteristics between 2008, 2012 and 2014. *Contraception*, 97(1), 14–21. https://doi.org/10.1016/j.contraception.2017.10.003.

18. Tanzania's President Magufuli calls for end to birth control (2018, September 10). *BBC News*. Retrieved from https://www.bbc.com/news/world-africa-45474408.
19. Sedgh, G., & Hussain, R. (2014). Reasons for contraceptive nonuse among women having unmet need for contraception in developing countries. *Studies in Family Planning*, 45(2), 151–169. https://doi.org/10.1111/j.1728-4465.2014.00382.x.
20. Blessing Ngcobo, N., Maharaj, P., & Nzima, D. (2018). Men's motivation for contraceptive use in Inanda Township, KwaZulu-Natal, South Africa. *Culture, Health & Sexuality*, 1-11. https://doi.org/10.1080/13691058.2018.1521992.
21. Starrs, A. M., Ezeh, A. C., Barker, G., Basu, A., Bertrand, J. T., Blum, R., et al. (2018). Accelerate progress—Sexual and reproductive health and rights for all: Report of the Guttmacher–Lancet Commission. *The Lancet*, 391(10140), 2642–2692. https://doi.org/10.1016/S0140-6736(18)30293-9.
22. Amo-Adjei, J., Mutua, M., Athero, S., Izugbara, C., & Ezeh, A. (2017). Improving family planning services delivery and uptake: Experiences from the "Reversing the Stall in Fertility Decline in Western Kenya Project". *BMC Research Notes*, 10(1), 498. https://doi.org/10.1186/s13104-017-2821-4.
23. Allotey, P. A., Diniz, S., DeJong, J., Delvaux, T., Gruskin, S., & Fonn, S. (2011). Sexual and reproductive health and rights in public health education. *Reproductive Health Matters*, 19(38), 56–68. https://doi.org/10.1016/S0968-8080(11)38577-1.
24. Singh, S., Remez, L., Sedgh, G., Kwok, L., & Onda, T. (2018). Abortion worldwide 2017: Uneven progress and unequal access. https://www.guttmacher.org/report/abortion-worldwide-2017. Accessed 31 May 2021.
25. Mutumba, M., Wekesa, E., & Stephenson, R. (2018). Community influences on modern contraceptive use among young women in low and middle-income countries: A cross-sectional multi-country analysis. *BMC Public Health*, 18(1), 430. https://doi.org/10.1186/s12889-018-5331-y.
26. Kusunoki, Y., Barber, J. S., Gatny, H. H., & Melendez, R. (2018). Physical intimate partner violence and contraceptive behaviors among young women. *Journal of Women's Health*, 27(8), 1016–1025. https://doi.org/10.1089/jwh.2016.6246.
27. Wusu, O. (2015). Religious influence on non-use of modern contraceptives among women in Nigeria: Comparative analysis of 1990 and 2008 NDHS.

Journal of Biosocial Science, 47(05), 593–612. https://doi.org/10.1017/S0021932014000352.

28. Hill, N. J., Siwatu, M., & Robinson, A. K. (2014). "My religion picked my birth control": The influence of religion on contraceptive use. *Journal of Religion and Health*, 53(3), 825–833. https://doi.org/10.1007/s10943-013-9678-1.
29. Wallace, H. J., McDonald, S., Belton, S., Miranda, A. I., da Costa, E., da Conceicao Matos, L., et al. (2018). What influences a woman's decision to access contraception in Timor-Leste? Perceptions from Timorese women and men. *Culture, Health & Sexuality*, 1–16. https://doi.org/10.1080/13691058.2018.1433330.
30. United Nations Department of Economic and Social Affairs Population Division (2014). Abortion policies and reproductive health around the world. https://www.un.org/en/development/desa/population/publications/pdf/policy/AbortionPoliciesReproductiveHealth.pdf. Accessed 31 May 2021.
31. Sedgh, G., Bearak, J., Singh, S., Bankole, A., Popinchalk, A., Ganatra, B., et al. (2016). Abortion incidence between 1990 and 2014: Global, regional, and subregional levels and trends. *The Lancet*, 388(10041), 258–267. https://doi.org/10.1016/S0140-6736(16)30380-4.
32. Ganatra, B., Gerdts, C., Rossier, C., Johnson Jr, B. R., Tunçalp, Ö., Assifi, A., et al. (2017). Global, regional, and subregional classification of abortions by safety, 2010–14: Estimates from a Bayesian hierarchical model. *The Lancet*, 390(10110), 2372–2381. https://doi.org/10.1016/S0140-6736(17)31794-4.
33. Beaumont, P. H., Amanda (2018, August 3). How The Handmaid's Tale dressed protests across the world. *The Guardian*. Retrieved from https://www.theguardian.com/world/2018/aug/03/how-the-handmaids-tale-dressed-protests-across-the-world.
34. Bearak, J., Popinchalk, A., Alkema, L., & Sedgh, G. (2018). Global, regional, and subregional trends in unintended pregnancy and its outcomes from 1990 to 2014: Estimates from a Bayesian hierarchical model. *The Lancet Global Health*, 6(4), e380–e389. https://doi.org/10.1016/S2214-109X(18)30029-9.
35. Bankole, A., Singh, S., & Haas, T. (1998). Reasons why women have induced abortions: Evidence from 27 countries. *International Family Planning Perspectives*, 24(3), 117–152. https://doi.org/10.2307/3038208.
36. Finer, L. B., Frohwirth, L. F., Dauphinee, L. A., Singh, S., & Moore, A. M. (2005). Reasons US women have abortions: Quantitative and qualitative

perspectives. *Perspectives on Sexual and Reproductive Health*, 37(3), 110–118. https://doi.org/10.1363/psrh.37.110.05.
37. Tietze, C. (1975). The effect of legalization of abortion on population growth and public health. *Family Planning Perspectives*, 123–127.
38. Pop-Eleches, C. (2010). The supply of birth control methods, education, and fertility evidence from Romania. *Journal of Human Resources*, 45(4), 971–997. https://doi.org/10.3368/jhr.45.4.971.
39. Pilecco, F. B., Teixeira, L. B., Vigo, Á., Dewey, M. E., & Knauth; D. R. (2014). Lifetime induced abortion: A comparison between women living and not living with HIV. *PLoS One*, 9(4), e95570. https://doi.org/10.1371/journal.pone.0095570.
40. Santelli, J. S., Song, X., Garbers, S., Sharma, V., & Viner, R. M. (2017). Global trends in adolescent fertility, 1990–2012, in relation to national wealth, income inequalities, and educational expenditures. *Journal of Adolescent Health*, 60(2), 161–168. https://doi.org/10.1016/j.jadohealth.2016.08.026.
41. Jones, R. K., & Jerman, J. (2017). Population group abortion rates and lifetime incidence of abortion: United States, 2008–2014. *American Journal of Public Health*, 107(12), 1904–1909. https://doi.org/10.2105/AJPH.2017.304042.
42. United Nations Department of Economic and Social Affairs Population Division (2018). World population policies 2015: Highlights. New York: United Nations. https://www.un.org/en/development/desa/population/publications/pdf/policy/WPP2015/WPP2015_Highlights.pdf. Accessed 31 May 2021.
43. Joshi, S., & Schultz, T. P. (2013). Family planning and women's and children's health: Long-term consequences of an outreach program in Matlab, Bangladesh. *Demography*, 50(1), 149–180. https://doi.org/10.1007/s13524-012-0172-2.
44. Bass, B. (2016). The effect of state mandated sex education on teenage sexual behaviors and health. ESSPRI Working Paper Series, Paper 20161. University of California Irvine. https://www.esspri.uci.edu/files/docs/2016/ESSPRI%20Working%20Paper%2020161%20Brittany%20Bass.pdf. Accessed 31 May 2021.
45. Avellaneda, C. N., & Dávalos, E. J. A. J. o. S. E. (2017). Identifying the macro-level drivers of adolescent fertility rate in Latin America: The role of school-based sexuality education. 12(4), 358–382. https://doi.org/10.1080/15546128.2017.1372830.

46. Guldi, M., & Herbst, C. M. (2017). Offline effects of online connecting: The impact of broadband diffusion on teen fertility decisions. *Journal of Population Economics*, 30(1), 69–91. https://doi.org/10.1007/s00148-016-0605-0.
47. Billari, F. C., Giuntella, O., & Stella, L. (2019). Does broadband internet affect fertility? *Population Studies*, 73(3), 297–316. https://doi.org/10.1080/00324728.2019.1584327.
48. Kantorová, V., Biddlecom, A., & Newby, H. (2014). Keeping pace with population growth. *The Lancet*, 384(9940), 307–308. https://doi.org/10.1016/S0140-6736(14)61130-2.
49. Singh, S., Sedgh, G., & Hussain, R. (2010). Unintended pregnancy: Worldwide levels, trends, and outcomes. *Studies in family planning*, 41(4), 241–250. https://doi.org/10.1111/j.1728-4465.2010.00250.x.
50. United Nations (2017). World Population Prospects 2017. United Nations. https://population.un.org/wpp/Download/Archive/Standard/. Accessed 26 May 2021.
51. Guttmacher Institute (2014, September 17). New study finds that 40% of pregnancies worldwide are unintended. Retrieved from https://www.guttmacher.org/news-release/2014/new-study-finds-40-pregnancies-worldwide-are-unintended. Accessed 25 May 2021.
52. Sedgh, G., Singh, S., Shah, I. H., Åhman, E., Henshaw, S. K., & Bankole, A. (2012). Induced abortion: Incidence and trends worldwide from 1995 to 2008. *The Lancet*, 379(9816), 625–632. https://doi.org/10.1016/S0140-6736(11)61786-8.
53. Sonfield, A., Hasstedt, K., Kavanaugh, M. L., & Anderson, R. (2013). The social and economic benefits of women's ability to determine whether and when to have children. New York. www.guttmacher.org/pubs/social-economic-benefits.pdf. Accessed 31 May 2021.
54. Logan, C., Holcombe, E., Manlove, J., & Ryan, S. (2007). The consequences of unintended childbearing. Washington, DC: C. Trends. https://www.michigan.gov/documents/mdch/The_Consequences_of_Unintended_Childbearing_296516_7.pdf. Accessed 31 May 2021.
55. Tsui, A. O., McDonald-Mosley, R., & Burke, A. E. (2010). Family planning and the burden of unintended pregnancies. *Epidemiologic Reviews*, 32(1), 152–174. https://doi.org/10.1093/epirev/mxq012.
56. de La Rochebrochard, E., & Joshi, H. (2013). Children born after unplanned pregnancies and cognitive development at 3 years: Social differentials in the United Kingdom Millennium Cohort. *American Journal of Epidemiology*, 178(6), 910–920. https://doi.org/10.1093/aje/kwt063.

57. Nguyen, C. V. (2018). The long-term effects of mistimed pregnancy on children's education and employment. *Journal of Population Economics*, 31(3), 937–968. https://doi.org/10.1007/s00148-018-0697-9.
58. United Nations Population Fund (2020, April 9). Staggering numbers of women unable to exercise decision-making over their own bodies, new UNFPA report shows. *Africa Renewal*. Retrieved from https://www.un.org/africarenewal/news/staggering-numbers-women-unable-exercise-decision-making-over-their-own-bodies-new-unfpa-report.

10

Fertility Preferences: How Many Children Do People Want?

Because childbearing has become more controlled, how many children people actually have has become increasingly dependent on how many children they *want*. In this chapter, I therefore discuss fertility preferences, how they have changed over time, how they vary across world regions, and the gap between preferred and actual fertility.

Measuring Fertility Ideals and Intentions

People have ideas about how many children one "should" ideally have, how many children they would ideally like to have themselves, and how many children they actually plan or expect to have, given their circumstances. I refer to these three concepts respectively as *general fertility ideals*, *personal fertility ideals*, and *fertility intentions*. Fertility ideals—particularly personal ones—reflect optimal family size under "ideal conditions" (e.g., good health, stable relationship, no work-family conflict, economic stability) and hence reflect more general pro- or anti-natalist societal norms [1, 2]. In contrast, fertility intentions reflect how many children one actually plans to have considering one's own, perhaps

V. Skirbekk, *Decline and Prosper!*,
https://doi.org/10.1007/978-3-030-91611-4_10

less-than-ideal life circumstances. It should be noted that scholars sometimes use the terms fertility ideals and intentions somewhat differently, use other labels, or make further distinctions (e.g., fertility intentions versus expectations) that I won't discuss here.

Fertility ideals and intentions are each measured with survey questions. General fertility ideals can be measured with questions such as "Generally speaking, what do you think is the ideal number of children for a family?" as in the Eurobarometer Survey. In the Demographic and Health Surveys, personal fertility ideals are measured with separate items for women with and without living children. Women without living children are asked, "If you could choose exactly the number of children to have in your whole life, how many would that be?" Women who already have living children are asked, "If you could go back to the time when you did not have any children and could choose exactly the number of children to have in your life, how many would that be?" Empirically, general and personal fertility ideals tend to be very similar [3]. The National Longitudinal Survey of Youth assessed fertility intentions with the question "How many (more) children do you expect to have?"

There is some debate with regard to how well survey questions can really capture people's "true" fertility ideals and intentions. Individuals generally respond to survey items about their fertility ideals and intentions with a concrete number. However, in poorer countries and in more traditional settings, many people answer that reproduction is outside of their control (e.g., that it is up to destiny, God will decide) [4, 5]. Some people may inflate the number of children they originally wanted in order to avoid conceding that one or more existing children were unintended. In other words, they may adjust their ideals and intentions to match their actual family size. People may also sometimes feel pressured to report in a way that conforms to social norms about how many children one "should" have, as certain answers may be expected from family members, community leaders, or society at large. Moreover, unexpected changes in one's life circumstances—a loss of a job or the dissolution of a partnership—may change one's fertility ideals and intentions. Thus, survey responses are not necessarily stable over time. Nevertheless, survey data on fertility ideals and intentions are highly useful for tracking general trends in perceptions of ideal family size and also for identifying gaps between fertility ideals and actual fertility outcomes.

Ideal Family Size Has Shrunk

Fertility ideals have shrunk gradually over time, along with people's own fertility intentions [6–8]. In Europe, ideal family size fell from 2.5 children in 1979 to 2.2 children in 2012 [8]. Fertility ideals have decreased to a similar degree across educational groups [8–10]. Similar trends have been observed in other parts of the world as well, for example in the Philippines, where members of the 1950s cohort perceived four children as ideal, while the 1990s cohort perceived just two children as ideal [11].

Over time, fertility ideals appear to converge around two children. In many places, there is a stigma against childlessness as well as concerns about the consequences of having/being an only child [12, 13]. At the same time, having "too many" children is widely believed to threaten a family's material well-being, limit parents' ability to adequately nurture each child, and contribute to overpopulation and environmental degradation. There is also evidence that people around the world believe that having few children is key to advancing society ("developmental idealism"). In 1798, Thomas Malthus famously warned against the dangers of "excess" fertility among the poor [14]. The perceived need to reduce fertility among the poor was a key impetus for the fight to make contraception universally available [15, 16].

In sum, there appear to be simultaneous pressures to have more than one child, but also not to have "too many" children, resulting in a strong normative two-child ideal [17]. In the United States, the two-child ideal rapidly gained popularity in the late 1960s/early 1970s. Since then, around half of United States Americans say that two is the ideal number of children [7]. Like their American counterparts, Europeans mostly prefer to have two or sometimes three children, and few prefer to have zero, one, or more than three [8]. Six out of ten European women consider two children as ideal, and the proportion is very similar in different European regions. The two-child ideal appears to become common as countries develop. Data from 18 countries in Latin

America and the Caribbean, South Asia, South-east Asia, as well as Turkey, Morocco, and Namibia shows that the share of women desiring two children jumped from 36 to 46% between 1990 and 2008 [8]. In the United States and Europe, the literature suggests that norms against childlessness and only children are weakening while fewer want larger families with three or more children [8, 18].

There are also populations that have not experienced a decline in ideal family size, and where fertility ideals remain much higher than two children. In Pakistan, for instance, fertility ideals have hovered around 4 children for the past four decades [19]. In Africa there tends to be a preference for larger families than in most other world regions, although fertility ideals have declined in Africa as elsewhere. According to recent data, ideal family size is above five children in most African countries. In comparison, ideal family size exceeds five children in just a few countries in Asia and Latin America and is below four in half of the countries (combining both regions) [6]. The median ideal family size in Africa is currently 4.6 children, comparable with median ideal family size in Asia at the beginning of the demographic transition [6]. Still, there is quite a bit of variation across the African countries. In sub-Saharan Africa in the mid-2000s, men's fertility ideals ranged from four children among men in Malawi to 14 children among men in Chad, while women's fertility ideals ranged from four children in Zimbabwe to nine children in Niger [20].

Social Differences in Ideal and Intended Family Size

While family size ideals have generally shrunk over time, research has pointed to a number of persistent social differences with regard to perceptions of the ideal family. Gender differences in fertility preferences are commonplace [21, 22]. Women often prefer to have fewer children than their husbands in poorer countries [19, 23, 24]. In Senegal, for instance, married men prefer to have more than nine children, while women would prefer fewer than six children [25]. In Pakistan, spousal disagreement in ideal family size declined between 1990 and 2012—yet when disagreement occurred, it was usually that the husband wanted another child when the wife did not [26]. In some European countries, particularly countries in which the state offers financial support for having and raising children, the opposite is true: Women often tend to want more children than men [27].

Fertility ideals and intentions also tend to differ across socioeconomic groups. In poorer countries, people with higher income and more education tend to prefer relatively fewer children. In India, women with no schooling consider 2.6 children to be ideal, compared with 1.8 children for women with 12 or more years of schooling. Similarly, mean ideal family size is 2.5 children among Indian women in the lowest wealth quintile, compared with 2.0 children among women in the highest quintile. A similar pattern is observed among men [28]. Differences across socioeconomic groups tend to be less pronounced in richer countries, and often those with higher education prefer as many children as those with less education [29]. In Europe, countries with a higher proportion of highly educated women of reproductive age actually have higher average fertility intentions (e.g., women intend to have a mean of 2.4 children in Sweden versus 1.9 children in Portugal) [29]. Migrant populations often have higher fertility ideals than the "native" population, probably because migrants tend to move from high to low fertility countries. Over time, migrants tend to adjust their fertility ideals toward the ideals of the host population [30, 31].

Finally, fertility ideals and intentions often differ between younger and older adults. In India, women aged 40–49 indicate an ideal family size of 2.4 children compared with 1.9 children among women aged 15–19 [28]. In Japan, older people think that people should have bigger families than younger people [32]. Differences between older and younger adults may reflect differences between members of different generations, but may also reflect how ideals and intentions may change over the life course as people get older. People might decide they want another child if his or her children do not have the desired gender or gender composition (e.g., someone with only daughters might decide that they want to try for a son, or vice versa), or they might adjust their personal ideals and intentions downward after a difficult pregnancy, birth, or parental experience. A person's personal fertility ideals and intentions may also change with his or her partnership status. The few studies which have followed how individuals' personal fertility ideals and intentions change as they get older indicate, however, that fertility ideals and intentions do not appear to change very much with age per se [17, 33, 34]. One study assessed individuals' fertility intentions a total of 16 times over a 27-year period, beginning in 1978 when the respondents were aged 14–21 years old and ending when respondents were aged 41–50 years. The study found that people's fertility intentions decreased only slightly as they aged. Interestingly, the greatest decline was before age 30 and not at older ages as respondents approached the end of their reproductive life spans [17]. Differences between younger and older respondents may therefore reflect primarily changes in preferred family size *across generations* as opposed to changes in preferred family size as people get older. The age difference in Japan, for instance, appears to be at least partly due to the increasing cost of childbearing which has made having more children more difficult for younger generations [32].

Low Fertility Role Models

Why have fertility ideals and intentions decreased over time? The same factors that have contributed to lower fertility including education, the cost of childbearing, and lack of a partner have likely made smaller families more attractive. Another reason for shrinking fertility ideals may be due to "low fertility role models"—that is, people who have been unusually successful and also remained childless or had relatively few children. Western history is rife with low fertility role models: Composers Frederic Chopin, Johannes Strauss and Ludwig van Beethoven, scientists Nicolaus Copernicus, Isaac Newton, and Leonardo da Vinci, United States presidents James Buchanan and James Polk, writer and activist Gloria Steinham, and actress Katharine Hepburn were all childless. In the late 2010s, the heads of the three largest European economies, Angela Merkel, Emmanuel Macron, and Theresa May [35] as well as the Indian Prime Minister Narendra Modi were all childless. Contemporary Indian low fertility role models include journalist Barkha Dutt and actress Shabana Azmi, who are both childless. Artists, writers, and other creative professionals also often have very low fertility [36]. Some people may perceive that the success and creativity of these individuals followed from the fact that they did not have children.

> *"I could not... have had this life and lived it with the level of intensity that is required to do [my] show the way it's done."*
> *—Oprah Winfrey, hugely successful American talk show host and media mogul on why she did not have children [37]*

Television can also influence fertility ideals and intentions through role modeling [38]. Relatively low family size is common among the relatively wealthy, educated characters often portrayed in television series and films [39, 40]. *Shuga*, a television program which aired in 40 African countries between 2009 and 2019, reached up to 550 million viewers and addressed themes such as safe sex, unwanted pregnancies, and sexually transmitted diseases [41]. Several popular Latin American soap operas had storylines linking family size to economic outcomes. In the late 1970s, a storyline of the Mexican telenovela *Acompáñame* [Accompany Me] contrasted the fates of two sisters. Pampered, rich, and selfish Raquel had just one child out of fear that more children would destroy her body; her son was unloved and neglected. Her sister, Esperanza, married a promising young man. She did not believe in contraceptives and her family grew "too large." Several of her children were psychotic and criminals, the family bickered constantly, and they were forced to move into a rundown shack [42]. Television may also have contributed to a general shift in the relative value of childbearing vis-à-vis material well-being and self-actualization. Fictional television characters and "real" media personalities often display high levels of consumption (e.g., by flaunting their wealth and success) [43]. Television shows often tend to focus on young adults without children and emphasize their leisure, relationships, and self-actualization which may not be compatible with having many children [44].

While television and other media are often cited as important sources of cultural change, in practice it is very difficult to determine how media affects people's attitudes and behavior. There is at least some weak evidence that television has affected fertility ideals and intentions, not only as a source of information but also as a "competing activity" (i.e., an activity that reduces the opportunity for childbearing). In Brazil, women living in areas with television access have significantly lower fertility compared to others, especially women of lower socioeconomic status and in the middle to end of their reproductive window [45]. In Bangladesh, a study based on data from 2010 to 2011 found that television watchers desire fewer children, are more likely to use contraceptives, and are less likely to have had a birth in the two years before the survey [46]. In Cote D'Ivoire, a study concluded that access to mass media portraying examples of female autonomy led to significantly lower fertility [47]. An Indonesian study suggested that the introduction of electricity accounted for about 18% to 24% of the overall decline in fertility, primarily through increased exposure to television [48]. In the mid-1990s, mainland stations of Radio Tanzania broadcast a radio soap on family planning. Data about the effects of the radio soap opera was gathered in five annual surveys. The soap opera was found to have strong effects on listeners' family planning efficacy and behaviors (e.g., talking with their spouses and peers about contraception) [49]. Another study using birth records found that a month-long television blackout in Zanzibar in 2008 caused a significant increase in the number of births [50]. Some have argued that soap operas were the largest driving force behind Mexican fertility decline [51]. In the United States, the reality show *16 and Pregnant* portrayed the challenges of becoming and being a teenage mother and may have contributed to a decline in the teen birth rate in 2009–2010 [52, 53]. Since the early 2000s, maternity and child-focused online blogs and Instagram accounts have proliferated, often romanticizing the joys of childbearing [54, 55]. It is, however, currently unknown whether the popularity of such "mom blogs" will contribute to an upswing in fertility ideals.

Gaps Between Fertility Ideals and Actual Fertility

People who state that they intend to have more children early in life generally have more children [56]. However, the relationship between how many children wants and how many one actually ends up having is far from perfect. Fertility intentions in low fertility regions such as Europe or East Asia tend to lie close to replacement fertility (i.e., around two children), while actual fertility tends to be much lower [9]. As a result, in low fertility contexts, people often have fewer children than they would prefer to have according to differences between the TFR and average ideal family size. The TFR is around 0.2–0.3 fewer children lower than average ideal family size in the United States, the United Kingdom, or Norway [17, 57, 58]. In Singapore, the gap between the TFR of around 1.2 and the ideal fertility (which is typically two children) is greater still [59]. In South Korea, fertility ideals have been slightly above replacement since the mid-1980s, but actual fertility has been below 1.3 since 2001 [60]. The ideal versus actual "fertility gap" has been used to argue that many low fertility societies constrain young women and men from realizing their fertility ideals [61, 62].

"Is there any certainty to anyone's life? If my son or daughter would die, then we would only have one child. For that I decided that we will have another child. My mother, my sister also told me, "If you have two sons, then you have two sticks to walk with in your old age".
—Nazmin, a Bangladeshi woman, on why she wanted a third child [63]

In contrast to low fertility countries, in high fertility contexts, people often have more children than they say they would ideally like to have. With the exception of several African countries, estimates for countries in early stages of the demographic transition suggest that ideal family size is seldom above three children [64]. In contrast, fertility at this stage for most non-Western countries has often been around 6–7 children, suggesting that people often considerably overshoot their own ideals [65]. Part of the discrepancy between ideal and actual family size during early stages of the demographic transition appears to be explained by the fact that few people immediately adapt their fertility behavior to the decline in infant and child mortality. Instead, people purposefully have "extra" births because they (in most cases wrongly) expect that some of their children will die [66].

Most People Want Smaller (but Not Too Small) Families

As childbearing becomes more controlled, fertility depends more and more on how many children people want to have. Globally, having two children has become the dominant ideal. Along with sociodemographic development, low fertility role models have likely played a role in shrinking ideal family size.

If people were able to have the number of children they personally want to have, people in more developed countries would generally be having more children, while people in less developed countries would generally be having fewer children. There are of course exceptions—particularly in parts of Africa, where fertility ideals remain very high, often higher than actual fertility. Implementing integrated policies which seek to increase understanding about the consequences of different fertility choices, as well as empower people to achieve their own informed, personal fertility ideals would be an admirable goal.

In both high and low fertility countries, men and women often disagree about ideal family size. In poorer countries, men tend to want more children than women, and men also typically do less of the work related to childrearing. In richer countries, men are often expected to participate more in childrearing, and the gender difference is reversed; women often want slightly more children than men. The gap between ideal and actual fertility in both poorer and richer settings thus tends to be higher for women than for men in both poorer and richer settings, and may hence reflect how a particular gender role distribution manifests itself in different socioeconomic settings.

References

1. Trent, R. B. (1980). Evidence bearing on the construct validity of "ideal family size". *Population and Environment*, 3(3), 309–327. https://doi.org/10.1007/BF01255345.
2. Philipov, D., & Bernardi, L. (2012). Concepts and operationalisation of reproductive decisions implementation in Austria, Germany and Switzerland. *Comparative Population Studies*, 36(2–3). https://doi.org/10.12765/CPoS-2011-14.
3. Testa, M. R., & Grilli, L. (2006). The influence of childbearing regional contexts on ideal family size in Europe. *Population*, 61(1–2), 99–127. https://doi.org/10.3917/pope.601.0099.
4. Frye, M., & Bachan, L. (2017). The demography of words: The global decline in non-numeric fertility preferences, 1993–2011. *Population Studies*, 71(2), 187–209. https://doi.org/10.1080/00324728.2017.1304565.
5. Wawire, S. N., Jensen, A.-M., & Mumah, J. N. (2013, April 11–13). Differences in fertility desires between men and women: The role of gender context (Paper presented at the Population Association of America, New Orleans, Louisiana). https://paa2013.princeton.edu/papers/132636.
6. Bongaarts, J., & Casterline, J. (2013). Fertility transition: Is sub-Saharan Africa different? *Population and Development Review*, 38, 153–168. https://doi.org/10.1111/j.1728-4457.2013.00557.x.
7. Gallup (2013). Desire to have children (full survey results). https://news.gallup.com/poll/164618/desire-children-norm.aspx. Accessed 29 May 2021.
8. Sobotka, T., & Beaujouan, É. (2014). Two is best? The persistence of a two-child family ideal in Europe. *Population and Development Review*, 40(3), 391–419. https://doi.org/10.1111/j.1728-4457.2014.00691.x.
9. Testa, M. R., & Rampazzo, F. (2017). Intentions and childbearing. Vienna Institute of Demography Working Papers No. 07/2017. Vienna. http://hdl.handle.net/10419/175539.
10. Van Keep, P. (1977). Ideal family size in 5 European countries. *Family Planning Resume*, 1(1), 89–90.
11. Schoumaker, B. (2016). Fixed or moving targets? Consistency of desired number of children within cohorts across surveys in DHS and predicting

fertility changes (Paper presented at the European Association for Population Studies Conference, Mainz, Germany). https://epc2016.princeton.edu/papers/161222.
12. Veenhoven, R., & Verkuyten, M. (1989). The well-being of only children. *Adolescence*, 24(93), 155–166.
13. Dufner, M., Back, M. D., Oehme, F. F., & Schmukle, S. C. (2020). The end of a stereotype: Only children are not more narcissistic than people with siblings. *Social Psychological and Personality Science*, 11(3), 416–424. https://doi.org/10.1177/1948550619870785.
14. Levin, S. M. (1966). Malthus and the idea of progress. *Journal of the History of Ideas*, 92–108. https://doi.org/10.2307/2708310.
15. Wardell, D. (1980). Margaret Sanger: Birth control's successful revolutionary. *American Journal of Public Health*, 70(7), 736–742. https://doi.org/10.2105/ajph.70.7.736.
16. Connell, E. B. (1999). Contraception in the prepill era. *Contraception*, 59(1), 7S–10S. https://doi.org/10.1016/s0010-7824(98)00130-9.
17. Morgan, S. P., & Rackin, H. (2010). The correspondence between fertility intentions and behavior in the United States. *Population and Development Review*, 36(1), 91–118. https://doi.org/10.1111/j.1728-4457.2010.00319.x.
18. Hagewen, K. J., & Morgan, S. P. (2005). Intended and ideal family size in the United States, 1970–2002. *Population and Development Review*, 31(3), 507–527. https://doi.org/10.1111/j.1728-4457.2005.00081.x.
19. Wazir, M. A. (2018). Fertility preferences in Pakistan. In S. Gietel-Basten, J. Casterline, & M. K. Choe (Eds.), *Family demography in Asia* (pp. 247–259). Cheltenham and Northampton: Edward Elgar Publishing. https://doi.org/10.4337/9781785363559.00021.
20. Madsen, E. L. 2021 (2015) What's behind West and Central Africa's youthful demographics? High desired family size. *New Security Beat*. Environmental Change and Security Program May 11. https://www.newsecuritybeat.org/2015/05/whats-west-central-africas-youthful-demographics-high-desired-family-size/. Accessed 30 May 2021.
21. Golmakani, N., Fazeli, E., Taghipour, A., & Shakeri, M. T. (2015). Relationship between gender role attitude and fertility rate in women referring to health centers in Mashhad in 2013. *Iranian Journal of Nursing and Midwifery Research*, 20(2), 269–274. http://ijnmr.mui.ac.ir/index.php/ijnmr/article/view/1180.
22. Brinton, M. C., Bueno, X., Oláh, L., & Hellum, M. (2018). Postindustrial fertility ideals, intentions, and gender inequality: A comparative qualitative

analysis. *Population and Development Review*, 44(2), 281–309. https://doi.org/10.1111/padr.12128.
23. Jensen, A.-M., Khasakhala, A. A., Odwe, G., & Wawire, S. (2015). Fertility and poverty in western and coast villages of Kenya. http://erepository.uonbi.ac.ke/bitstream/handle/11295/88679/Khasakhala_Fertility%20and%20Poverty.%20Project%20Report%202015.pdf?sequence=1&isAllowed=y. Accessed 31 May 2021.
24. Farré, L. (2013). The role of men in the economic and social development of women: Implications for gender equality. *The World Bank Research Observer*, 28(1), 22–51. https://doi.org/10.1093/wbro/lks010.
25. Doepke, M., & Tertilt, M. (2018). Women's empowerment, the gender gap in desired fertility, and fertility outcomes in developing countries. IZA Discussion Paper No. 11262. https://ssrn.com/abstract=3111136
26. Bashir, S., & Guzzo, K. (2019). Changing gender roles and spousal agreement on fertility intentions. PIDE Working Papers No. 165. https://mail.pide.org.pk/pdf/Working%20Paper/WorkingPaper-165.pdf. Accessed 31 May 2021.
27. Billingsley, S., Neyer, G., & Wesolowski, K. (2018). The influence of family policies on women's childbearing: A longitudinal micro-data analysis of 21 countries. Stockholm Research Reports in Demography. https://www.su.se/polopoly_fs/1.393546.1530869888!/menu/standard/file/WP_2018_04.pdf. Accessed 31 May 2021.
28. International Institute for Population Sciences (2017). National Family Health Survey-4. http://rchiips.org/nfhs/nfhs4.shtml. Accessed 31 May 2021.
29. Testa, M. R. (2014). On the positive correlation between education and fertility intentions in Europe: Individual-and country-level evidence. *Advances in Life Course Research*, 21, 28–42. https://doi.org/10.1016/j.alcr.2014.01.005.
30. Carlsson, E. (2017) Fertility intentions of the children of immigrants in Sweden. MA thesis, Stockholm University. https://su.diva-portal.org/smash/get/diva2:1150927/FULLTEXT01.pdf.
31. Kraus, E. K., & Castro-Martín, T. (2018). Does migrant background matter for adolescents' fertility preferences? The Latin American 1.5 generation in Spain. *European Journal of Population*, 34(3), 277–312. https://doi.org/10.1007/s10680-017-9427-3.
32. Skirbekk, V., Matsukura, R., & Ogawa, N. (2015). What are the prospects for continued low fertility in Japan? In N. Ogawa, & I. H. Shah (Eds.),

Low fertility and reproductive health in East Asia (pp. 75–100). Dordrecht: Springer.

33. Kuhnt, A.-K., Kreyenfeld, M., & Trappe, H. (2017). Fertility ideals of women and men across the life course. In M. Kreyenfeld, & D. Konietzka (Eds.), *Childlessness in Europe: Contexts, causes, and consequences* (pp. 235–251). Cham: Springer. https://doi.org/10.1007/978-3-319-44667-7_11.
34. Hayford, S. R. (2009). The evolution of fertility expectations over the life course. *Demography*, 46(4), 765–783. https://doi.org/10.1353/dem.0.0073.
35. Raber, J. O. (2014). *Famous—But no children.* New York: Algora Publishing.
36. Hoem, J. M., Neyer, G., & Anderson, G. (2006). Education and childlessness. The relationship between educational field, educational level, and childlessness among Swedish women born in 1955–59. *Demographic Research*, 14(15), 330–331. https://doi.org/10.4054/DemRes.2006.14.15.
37. ABC News (2010, December 9) The Barbara Walters special. *A Barbara Walters special: Oprah, the next chapter*.
38. La Ferrara, E. (2016). Mass media and social change: Can we use television to fight poverty? *Journal of the European Economic Association*, 14(4), 791–827. https://doi.org/10.1111/jeea.12181.
39. Wang, H., & Singhal, A. (2016). East Los High: Transmedia edutainment to promote the sexual and reproductive health of young Latina/o Americans. *American Journal of Public Health*, 106(6), 1002–1010.
40. Billari, F. C., Giuntella, O., & Stella, L. (2019). Does broadband internet affect fertility? *Population Studies*, 73(3), 297–316. https://doi.org/10.1080/00324728.2019.1584327.
41. Booker, N. A., Miller, A. N., & Ngure, P. (2016). Heavy sexual content versus safer sex content: A content analysis of the entertainment education drama Shuga. *Health Communication*, 31(12), 1437–1446. https://doi.org/10.1080/10410236.2015.1077691.
42. Basten, S. (2010). Television and fertility. *Finnish Yearbook of Population Research*, 45, 67–82. https://journal.fi/fypr/article/download/45054/11332/0.
43. Feasey, R. (2017). The hierarchy of celebrity childbirth stories. *Celebrity Studies*, 8(2), 278–293. https://doi.org/10.1080/19392397.2016.1266955.
44. Ryan, K. M., Springer, N. J., Macey, D. A., & Erickson, M. (Eds.) (2016). Friends, lovers, co-workers, and community: Everything I know about relationships I learned from television. Lanham, MD: Lexington Books.

45. La Ferrara, E., Chong, A., & Duryea, S. (2012). Soap operas and fertility: Evidence from Brazil. *American Economic Journal: Applied Economics*, 4(4), 1–31. https://doi.org/10.1257/app.4.4.1.
46. Rahman, M., Curtis, S. L., Chakraborty, N., & Jamil, K. (2017). Women's television watching and reproductive health behavior in Bangladesh. *SSM-Population Health*, 3, 525–533. https://doi.org/10.1016/j.ssmph.2017.06.001.
47. Peters, J., & Vance, C. (2011). Rural electrification and fertility—Evidence from Côte d'Ivoire. *The Journal of Development Studies*, 47(5), 753–766. https://doi.org/10.1080/00220388.2010.527954.
48. Grimm, M., Sparrow, R., & Tasciotti, L. (2015). Does electrification spur the fertility transition? Evidence from Indonesia. *Demography*, 52(5), 1773–1796. https://doi.org/10.1007/s13524-015-0420-3.
49. Rogers, E. M., Vaughan, P. W., Swalehe, R. M., Rao, N., Svenkerud, P., & Sood, S. (1999). Effects of an entertainment-education radio soap opera on family planning behavior in Tanzania. *Studies in Family Planning*, 30(3), 193–211. https://doi.org/10.1111/j.1728-4465.1999.00193.x.
50. Burlando, A. (2014). Power outages, power externalities, and baby booms. *Demography*, 51(4), 1477–1500. https://doi.org/10.1007/s13524-014-0316-7.
51. Ehrlich, P. R., & Ornstein, R. E. (2010). *Humanity on a tightrope: Thoughts on empathy, family, and big changes for a viable future*. Lanham, MD: Rowman & Littlefield.
52. Kearney, M. S., & Levine, P. B. (2015). Media influences on social outcomes: The impact of MTV's 16 and pregnant on teen childbearing. *American Economic Review*, 105(12), 3597–3632. https://doi.org/10.1257/aer.20140012.
53. Jaeger, D. A., Joyce, T. J., & Kaestner, R. (2018). A cautionary tale of evaluating identifying assumptions: Did reality TV really cause a decline in teenage childbearing? *Journal of Business & Economic Statistics*, 1–10. https://doi.org/10.1080/07350015.2018.1497510.
54. Strif, E. (2005). "Infertile me:" The public performance of fertility treatments in internet weblogs. *Women & Performance: A Journal of Feminist Theory*, 15(2), 189–206. https://doi.org/10.1080/07407700508571511.
55. Sterling, E. W. (2013) From no hope to fertile dreams: Procreative technologies, popular media, and the culture of infertility. PhD thesis, Georgia State University. https://scholarworks.gsu.edu/cgi/viewcontent.cgi?article=1069&context=sociology_diss.

56. Beaujouan, E., & Berghammer, C. (2019). The gap between lifetime fertility intentions and completed fertility in Europe and the United States: A cohort approach. *Population Research and Policy Review*, 38, 1–29. https://doi.org/10.1007/s11113-019-09516-3.
57. Berrington, A., & Pattaro, S. (2014). Educational differences in fertility desires, intentions and behaviour: A life course perspective. *Advances in Life Course Research*, 21, 10–27. https://doi.org/10.1016/j.alcr.2013.12.003.
58. Noack, T., & Østby, L. (2002). Free to choose—But unable to stick to it? Norwegian fertility expectations and subsequent behaviour in the following 20 years. In M. Macura, & G. Beets (Eds.), *Dynamics of fertility and partnership in Europe–Insights and lessons from comparative research, Vol. II* (pp. 103–116). New York and Geneva: United Nations. https://unece.org/DAM/pau/_docs/ffs/FFS_V2_DynamicsFertilityPartenrshipEurope.pdf.
59. Yap, M. T., & Gee, C. (2018). Fertility preferences in Singapore. In S. Gietel-Basten, J. Casterline, & M. K. Choe (Eds.), *Family demography in Asia* (pp. 291–304). Cheltenham and Northampton: Edward Elgar Publishing. https://doi.org/10.4337/9781785363559.
60. Choe, M. K., & Park, K. T. (2018). How is the decline of fertility related to fertility preference in South Korea? In S. Gietel-Basten, J. Casterline, & M. K. Choe (Eds.), *Family demography in Asia* (pp. 305–322). Cheltenham and Northampton: Edward Elgar Publishing. https://doi.org/10.4337/9781785363559.00025.
61. Greulich, A., Thévenon, O., & Guergoat-Larivière, M. (2016). Securing women's employment: A fertility booster in European countries? CES Working Papers 2016.24. https://halshs.archives-ouvertes.fr/halshs-01306103/document. Accessed 31 May 2021.
62. Thévenon, O. (2011). Family policies in OECD countries: A comparative analysis. *Population and Development Review*, 37(1), 57–87. https://doi.org/10.1111/j.1728-4457.2011.00390.x.
63. Gipson, J. D., & Hindin, M. J. (2007). 'Marriage means having children and forming your family, so what is the need of discussion?' Communication and negotiation of childbearing preferences among Bangladeshi couples. *Culture, Health & Sexuality*, 9(2), 185–198. https://doi.org/10.1080/13691050601065933.
64. Mauldin, W. P. (1965). Fertility studies: Knowledge, attitude, and practice. *Studies in Family Planning*, 1(7), 1–10. https://doi.org/10.2307/1964765.
65. Keilman, N., Tymicki, K., & Skirbekk, V. (2014). Measures for human reproduction should be linked to both men and women. *International*

Journal of Population Research, 2014(908385). https://doi.org/10.1155/2014/908385.
66. Bhatia, J. C. (1978). Ideal number and sex preference of children in India. *Journal of Family Welfare*, 24(4), 3–16.

11

Delaying Parenthood, for Better and for Worse

One of the most remarkable trends in contemporary fertility is the postponement of parenthood. Whereas childbearing in the late teens and early twenties was the norm in the mid-twentieth century, today more and more women are in their late twenties or thirties when they have their first child. The delay in parenthood is reflected in both a decrease in the number and proportion of children born to adolescent mothers and a shift in "peak fertility" toward the early 30s in many countries. Delayed parenthood has come along with a number of benefits in terms of being able to realize other life aims and activities that are difficult to combine with childbearing. At the same time, however, many people in Western countries may be "waiting too long" and as a result may fail to realize their own fertility ideals. In this chapter, I discuss the delay in parenthood and some of its positive and negative consequences.

V. Skirbekk, *Decline and Prosper!*,
https://doi.org/10.1007/978-3-030-91611-4_11

People Are Postponing Parenthood All Over the World

Many of the world's richest countries have seen the primary period of childbearing shift from the early twenties to the early thirties. Since 1970, fertility in the OECD countries has generally declined among women aged 20–29 (primarily between 1970 and 1995), while in several countries it has also slightly increased among women aged 30–34 and 35–39. Many men and women in richer countries are delaying marriage and childbearing until the late twenties, early thirties, or even later—and some forego childbearing altogether [1, 2]. In all OECD countries with available data, the mean age at first birth increased between 1995 and 2017 by at least two years [3]. In many developed economies like the United States, there are more births to women above than those below age 30 [4]. The postponement of childbearing in most developing countries has also been substantial. The proportion of women having their first birth before age 20 has declined in 17 of 30 sub-Saharan countries [5], while the age at first birth rose between the early 1990s and 2010 by at least a year in Asia, North Africa, Central Africa, and Western Africa [6]. For the majority of the countries with data on male fertility between 2004 and 2008, the average age at childbearing ranged from age 30 to 35 and few men became fathers after 50 [7].

The postponement of fertility is partly captured by the dramatic global decline in births to adolescent mothers—that is, mothers under 20 years old. Fertility among people in their teens and early 20s has fallen for decades, a development which is projected to continue in the years to come [8, 9]. Globally, the fertility rate of women aged 15–19 has decreased from 66 per 1000 women in 1960 to 42.5 in 2017 [10]. Although adolescent fertility has declined in all world regions and in almost all countries, it remains high in some areas. Furthermore, it is important to note that while the global *rate* of adolescent fertility may have declined, the actual number of births to adolescents has not, due to the large—and in some cases, growing—population of adolescents (around 16% of the world population).

Today, almost all adolescent births occur in developing countries. By the time they are 19 years old, half of adolescent girls in developing countries are sexually active, about 40% are married, and close to 20% have children [11]. In terms of absolute numbers, the most adolescent births happen in India, Bangladesh, Nigeria, Brazil, and Indonesia due to their large adolescent populations [12]. Sub-Saharan Africa stands out as a global outlier in terms of teenage fertility, with a regional adolescent fertility rate of 103 births per 1000 women [10]. According to the most recent data available, adolescent fertility is over 150 births per 1000 women in Angola, Chad, Equatorial Guinea, Mali, and Niger compared with under 10 births per 1000 women in most Western European and East Asian countries [10]. The highest rates of fertility to women under age 15 are likewise found in sub-Saharan Africa, where one out of ten girls in Chad, Guinea, Mali, Mozambique, Niger, and Sierra Leone has children before reaching age 16 [13]. Poor socioeconomic development, a high burden of disease, limited investments in contraceptive use and family planning, and an erosion of the fertility-inhibiting effects of postpartum practices such as breastfeeding or sexual abstinence have all contributed to relatively high levels of adolescent fertility in sub-Saharan Africa [14].

Higher proportions of women also marry during adolescence in Africa, especially in sub-Saharan Africa [11]. While marriage before age 18 has declined over time in Africa, the proportion of girls who marry before their 15th birthday has remained unchanged for twenty years for 31 African countries and has even increased in a few countries [15]. Within countries, adolescent pregnancies are concentrated among disadvantaged groups with high levels of poverty and poor educational and economic opportunities. Overall, the adolescent birth rate is much higher among adolescents in rural areas, with less education or in poor households, and is lower among adolescents in urban areas, with higher levels of education or in wealthier households [12].

In many countries, early childbearing is not seen as a problem. The vast majority of adolescent births in developing countries occur within the context of marriage and are hence probably intended [11]. Even in developed countries like the United States, adolescent births were not considered a social problem until the 1960s [16]. Adolescent pregnancies can at least sometimes be viewed as part of a larger adolescent identity project in which teens seek ways to achieve status and meaning [17].

In some settings, becoming a parent is one way that young women can access the legal protections and social opportunities reserved for adults. Becoming a parent may in fact be the only way for some young women—especially those with few educational and occupational opportunities—to achieve any status at all. Young married women (and men) may feel social pressure to have a birth soon after getting married as a way to prove their fecundity, secure their marriage, and gain respect.

That said, about half of adolescent pregnancies in the developing world [11] and an even higher proportion in richer countries (e.g., 72% in Canada [18]) are *unintended*. Adolescents who want to avoid pregnancy may not be able to do so because they lack adequate knowledge or access to modern contraception, or because they lack the self-confidence or autonomy to use it [11]. Many adolescent pregnancies are the result of coercion and sexual violence. Relative to older women, adolescents are more likely to be subject to physical and/or sexual violence from an intimate partner [19]. The World Health Organization estimates that, globally, 29% of ever-partnered women aged 15–19 have experienced physical or sexual intimate partner violence, and the overall prevalence of intimate partner is even higher in Africa, the Eastern Mediterranean Region, and South East Asia [20]. One study of 12- to 19-year-old women in four countries found that, in Malawi, 38% were "not willing at all" at their first sexual experience; the same was reported by lower, but still substantial, proportions of 12- to 19-year-olds in Ghana (30%), Uganda (23%), and Burkina Faso (15%) [21].

Education Decisive for Fertility Postponement

Family planning programs between the 1990s to the mid-2010s have been related to substantial reductions in adolescent fertility [22]. Nevertheless, many popular interventions aimed at improving adolescents' reproductive health (and reduce unintended adolescent births) have proven ineffective [23]. In contrast, there is little controversy that young women's educational attainment—especially their secondary school attendance—is closely related to adolescent fertility. In both developing and developed countries, more education (as reflected in more years of schooling and/or higher enrolment rates) is associated with lower teenage fertility, also in quasi-experimental studies on the effects of universal extensions to compulsory education [24–29]. The study on an education reform in Norway cited earlier found that one additional year of schooling reduced the chance of teenage pregnancy by eight percentage points [28]. Increasing the length of compulsory education in Turkey [29] and Argentina [30] had similar effects on teenage fertility. Other studies based on data from over 50 low- and middle-income countries found that the proportion of women aged 15–24 studying was inversely related to the proportion who were married or mothers [31, 32], while another found that decreases in adolescent fertility between 1990 and 2012 were greater in countries where national income grew more, educational expenditure increased, and there were better job opportunities and less income inequality [33].

While most scholars agree that young women's educational attainment is associated with particularly adolescent fertility, whether education *causes* teenage fertility (and if so, how) is still a matter of debate. One Argentinian study found evidence that education has both a "human capital effect" (whereby one additional year of schooling causes a decline of 30 births per 1000 girls) and also a weaker incarceration effect (whereby an increase of one percentage point in the enrollment rate reduces 3 births per 1000 girls) [30]. Another primary mechanism by which education appears to affect adolescent fertility is by delaying marriage [32, 34]. A Senegalese study, for instance, found that women tend to delay marriage until they have completed school; hence, longer schooling is associated with a delay in the timing of marriage and thereby also childbearing [34].

No matter how much pressure [my family] may create, I do not want to have any children for 2-3 years.... This is because I am still a student. I am not even earning any money, and my wife is a student.... Therefore, I think that if my wife becomes a mother, her entire time will be spent in nourishing her child. She won't have any time for her education.... I tell my wife not to be under any pressure and to study as long as she wants to.... My parents are uneducated, and the trend in this village is to give birth immediately after getting married. My parents want me to follow the trend. If my wife doesn't get pregnant, people will start talking against her and may question her fertility."

—A newly married man in Nepal, aged 21, on why he wants to delay having his first child [35]

Educational expansion is thought to be a main driver not only of the reduction in adolescent fertility, but also of the delay in childbearing to the late 20s and 30s in many richer countries. The same basic mechanisms appear to apply: Prior to having children, people often seek to ensure a certain standard of living, which necessitates completing education, finding suitable employment with long-term prospects, and securing an adequate income. In developed countries, more and more people pursue tertiary degrees (e.g., between 24 and 68% of 25- to 34-year-olds in the OECD countries in 2014 [36]). Achieving a secure position on the labor market may take several more years after that. A key reason why people are having children later is that they are entering their first consensual union and marrying later in countries all over the world [37]: Just as the European pattern of late marriage was associated with lower fertility in the 1800s, being older at the time of marriage continues to be an important driver of global fertility. The postponement of marriage is at least partly due to the fact that people all over the world are spending more years in education [38–40].

Delay Due to the Labor Market

Over the past couple of decades, a significant proportion of young people have become "stuck in adolescence" or *NEETS* (Not in Education, Employment, or Training). In the United States, they are called *twixters*, in Spain *mileuristas*, in Japan *freeters* or *parasite singles*. Germany calls them *Generation Praktikum* and France has its *Génération précaire*. The OECD has been tracking NEETS since the late 1990s. Although NEETS are often viewed as selfish, lazy, and unwilling to take on adult roles, their prevalence suggests that structural factors outside individual control at least partially explain why so many young people are not engaged in either education or employment [41]. According to the available data, NEETS have consistently represented between 13 and 16% of the population of 15- to 29-year-olds in the OECD countries between 1998 and 2018. The proportion of NEETS varies widely across countries, ranging from under 10% in countries like Iceland, The Netherlands, and Switzerland to over 20% in Turkey, Brazil, and Italy [42]. Because they are unable to establish themselves on the job market, NEETS are unable to gain their financial independence and may hence delay marriage and fertility.

Even young people who do manage to establish themselves on the job market may find it difficult to gain financial independence because they often work at insecure and low-paying jobs. Relative to older workers, younger workers are more likely to lose their job in periods of economic downturn, and they are much more likely than older workers to be employed temporarily or informally [43]. Across the OECD countries, the relative earnings of young people also declined between the 1980s and the 2000s [44]. Low earnings at younger ages often lead to "scarring" for life, implying that people who begin working at a relatively low wage are likely to have a relatively low wage also in midlife and beyond [45].

Slow and difficult transitions to the workforce as well as the low-quality of jobs for many youths are important reasons why many young people fail to establish their own homes in early adulthood. It should be noted, however, that poor labor market outcomes can also sometimes *speed up* childbearing, as the opportunity costs of childbearing may be lower for people who are poorly integrated in the labor market. Poor integration in the labor market has been found to delay the transition to first births in Germany, but not necessarily in the UK [46]. The relationship between labor market integration and the transition to parenthood appears to depend on the institutional context, gender, and level of education.

At the same time that poor labor market opportunities have made it more difficult for younger people to establish a family, the labor market may also incentivize women to have children later in life. Earning typically increases rapidly in the first two decades of working life, and women who have children "early" tend to have worse career outcomes [47]. In developed countries like the United States, some companies (e.g., Yahoo) encourage young professional women to freeze their eggs so that they can first make a career before having children [48, 49]. Some men and women who delay childbearing to the late 30s may unwillingly end up childless due to their advanced age [50], insufficient knowledge of or access to fertility treatment [51–53], and/or the limited efficacy of assisted reproductive technologies (ART).

Why Age Matters—For Men and for Women

Adolescent childbearing is associated with a number of serious health consequences for adolescent parents and their babies. A review of 18 studies from sub-Saharan Africa found that adolescents had an increased risk of low birth weight, pre-eclampsia/eclampsia, preterm birth, and maternal and perinatal mortality [54]. Pregnancy and delivery can cause health problems for young adolescents whose bodies are still maturing [55]. Globally, pregnancy and childbirth complications are an important cause of death among girls aged 15–19 years [56]. All-cause mortality for adolescent parents tends to be higher also in richer countries. In Japan, women who had a child before age 19 were 1.17 times more likely to die within a 14-year period than those who delayed childbearing to age 20–24 [57].

Adolescent fertility is also associated with negative social and economic outcomes, including low income and poor housing [58], partnership instability and a greater likelihood of being a single parent, and also less education among the parents [59, 60]. However, more recent studies indicate that adolescent fertility is more a *consequence* than a *cause* of socioeconomic disadvantage; the same factors that "cause" teenage fertility also cause poor socioeconomic outcomes [54, 61]. Most studies and public health campaigns have focused on the negative effects of adolescent women's fertility, but some research suggests that adolescent men's fertility also has negative effects. Teenage fathers feel less competent, exhibit worse childrearing behaviors, and have worse father-child relationships, even as some men exhibit more adult behavior as they enter parenthood [62, 63].

At the other end of the age spectrum, delaying childbearing for "too long" is also associated with a number of negative consequences. Women and men who initiate childbearing late have a lower ability to conceive, and there are greater health risks for the offspring [64, 65]. While a woman aged 20–24 has a 86% likelihood of conceiving within one year, the chance of conceiving within one year drops to 52% among women aged 35–39 [66]. The risk of infertility increases with advanced age in a non-linear manner, becoming much stronger at the late 30s and early 40s. Even as some of the risks of being an older mother are exaggerated, older maternal and paternal age are both related to several fertility-related problems, including decreased fecundity, an increased risk of spontaneous abortion, genetic diseases including Down's syndrome, and pregnancy complications including preeclampsia [67–69].

Women and men may delay having children in part because they overestimate their chances of having children later in life. Media often report on women who conceive relatively late, even if many may have conceived through in vitro fertilization and/or have not used their own oocytes [70–72]. More than half of the famous women whose pregnancies or births were mentioned in magazines Cosmopolitan, People, and US We*ekly* were over the age of 35 [73]. Media reports rarely mention the difficulty of conceiving at older ages, the use of ART, semen or egg donations, surrogate mothers and their costs or negative side effects—creating the false impression that childbearing is always easy at later ages [74, 75]. Men might wrongly assume that their longer biological reproductive window means that they can put off having children, when in fact very few men have children after age 50. Population level surveys suggest that the vast majority of women have unrealistic or misinformed expectations about the effectiveness of ART [76]. For instance, a study of Chinese university students found that 92% underestimated age-related fertility decline and 66% overestimated the success rate of fertility treatment [77]. Similarly, a Swedish survey found that science postgraduates (without children) generally wanted two or three children, but also that approximately half of the respondents had overly optimistic perceptions of their chances to conceive by means of in vitro fertilization

[78]. Furthermore, the costs of childbearing with ART can be very high. In some countries, reproductive technologies are free with some restrictions (e.g., Colombia and Israel [79, 80]), but in most countries they are very expensive, even when they are partially subsidized through national health insurance schemes. In some countries, the costs of assisted reproduction are so high that they are out of reach for large proportions of the population [81, 82].

Most People Prefer to Delay Childbearing…Somewhat

Preferences for the timing of childbearing may be also changing, though many still see relatively early childbearing as "ideal." A Gallup survey from 2013 found that, on average, Americans saw age 25 as the ideal age for women and age 27 as the ideal age for men to have their first child, while only 3% thought that it was ideal for women to wait until she was 30 or older; highly educated respondents perceived the ideal ages as somewhat older [83]. Another United States survey found that about 60% of women who had their first child between 35 and 39 said they wish they had been younger [84]. In Europe, survey findings from 2006 put the perceived ideal age for having a first child around 25 for both men and women [85]. The ideal age range for having children appears to be rather consistent across countries, at least in Europe: generally somewhere between ages 19 and 40 for women, and somewhere between ages 20 and 45 or 50 for men [86, 87]. Thus, what people consider as the "appropriate" reproductive life span is considerably shorter than the actual biological reproductive life span; people also tend to have their child later than they themselves perceive as "ideal." While perceptions of the appropriate reproductive life span are very similar across countries, attitudes toward late childbearing (i.e., women who have children after age 40) appear to vary quite a bit [87]. In countries where people have more negative attitudes toward late childbearing, ART are less accessible and fewer women aged 40 and older actually have children [87].

Why wait? In an article written for *Cosmopolitan Magazine*, author Devon Corneal—a lawyer who had her first child at age 35—advises:

> *"Wait until you've lived, achieved, traveled, met the right person or decided you never will and are ready to go it alone, but do not be bullied into having babies. It's OK if you don't have kids yet because you want to be young and unconstrained or if things just haven't worked out for you yet. (It's also OK if you decide not to have kids at all.) Stop freaking out. Don't feel the need to explain. If there are things you want to do, do them. Work crazy hours, get the dream job, quit the job and travel, go back to school, party like the world is ending, fall in love more than once, break up, get married or don't, sleep late and live. Don't have kids because your parents suggest it, your doctor scares you or the Internet decides that 30 is the new 50. Don't rush into a lifelong commitment because you are worried or afraid or want to fit in. Ignore the voices in your head that say you will be alone or lonely or incomplete. Ignore the voices in the media that tell you to hurry up. Doing anything out of fear is a bad idea; having children before you're ready because you're afraid that it's now or never is a recipe for disaster of Titanic proportions [88]."*

In the absence of historical data, it is difficult to say for sure whether the perceived ideal ages for starting a family, or social perceptions of "reproductive deadlines," have been delayed over time. Developmental research on "emerging adulthood" [89] has shown that, in Western countries, the ages between 18 and 25 or even through the early 30s now often entail a period of freedom and exploration, including travel, education, experiments in work and love, and delayed entry into what have historically been the markers of adulthood: marriage, a steady job, and children [89]. It therefore seems likely that, regardless of what people think the ideal age for *other* people to have children might be, the average age people see as ideal for starting a family *themselves* is likely to be delayed even more. Indeed, men and women commonly wait until they have finished with education to have children, and the age of school completion is increasing rapidly for women in countries all over the world [24, 90, 91].

The Risks and Rewards of Postponed Fertility

Delaying parenthood from the teens to the twenties has allowed more individuals—particularly women—to realize their potential in other areas of life. Surveys also suggest that delaying pregnancy to at least the mid-twenties tends to be in line with people's preferences. The reduction in adolescent pregnancies is related to improved health, opportunities, and welfare of both children and adults. Delaying parenthood generally allows prospective parents to make more informed and rational fertility decisions, but there is also a risk of waiting too long, and hence having problems conceiving, having fewer children than one would ideally like to have, or negative health outcomes. ART are only moderately effective at best, as well as stressful and expensive. Making sure that people are informed about their chances of conceiving later in life, together with reducing some of the barriers for childbearing in the twenties and thirties, might be effective for reducing unwanted childlessness.

References

1. Thornton, A., & Young-DeMarco, L. (2001). Four decades of trends in attitudes toward family issues in the United States: The 1960s through the 1990s. *Journal of Marriage and Family*, 63(4), 1009–1037. https://doi.org/10.1111/j.1741-3737.2001.01009.x.
2. Blair-Loy, M. (2009). *Competing devotions: Career and family among women executives*. Cambridge, MA: Harvard University Press.
3. OECD Family Database (2019). SF2.3: Age of mothers at childbirth and age-specific fertility. Paris. https://www.oecd.org/els/soc/SF_2_3_Age_mothers_childbirth.pdf. Accessed 28 May 2021.
4. Women in 30s now having more babies than younger moms in U.S. (2017, May 18). *Bloomberg*. Retrieved from https://www.bloomberg.com/news/articles/2017-05-17/women-in-30s-now-having-more-babies-than-younger-moms-in-us.
5. Westoff, C. F. (2003). Trends in marriage and early childbearing in developing countries. DHS Comparative Reports No. 5. Calverton, MD: ORC

Macro. https://www.dhsprogram.com/publications/publication-CR5-Comparative-Reports.cfm. Accessed 28 May 2021.

6. Bongaarts, J., Mensch, B. S., & Blanc, A. K. (2017). Trends in the age at reproductive transitions in the developing world: The role of education. *Population Studies*, 71(2), 139–154. https://doi.org/10.1080/00324728.2017.1291986.
7. Keilman, N., Tymicki, K., & Skirbekk, V. (2014). Measures for human reproduction should be linked to both men and women. *International Journal of Population Research*, 2014(908385). https://doi.org/10.1155/2014/908385.
8. United Nations (1973). The determinants and consequences of population trends: New summary of findings on interaction of demographic, economic and social factors. Population studies no. 50. New York: United Nations.
9. United Nations (2017). World Population Prospects 2017. United Nations. https://population.un.org/wpp/Download/Archive/Standard/. Accessed 26 May 2021.
10. The World Bank Adolescent fertility rate (births per 1,000 women ages 15–19). https://data.worldbank.org/indicator/SP.ADO.TFRT?view=chart. Accessed 28 May 2021.
11. Darroch, J. E., Woog, V., Bankole, A., & Ashford, L. S. (2016). Adding it up: Costs and benefits of meeting the contraceptive needs of adolescents. New York: G. Institute. https://www.guttmacher.org/report/adding-it-meeting-contraceptive-needs-of-adolescents. Accessed 28 May 2021.
12. Loaiza, E., & Liang, M. (2013). Adolescent pregnancy: A review of the evidence. New York: United Nations Population Fund. https://www.unfpa.org/sites/default/files/pub-pdf/ADOLESCENT%20PREGNANCY_UNFPA.pdf. Accessed 28 May 2021.
13. Neal, S., Matthews, Z., Frost, M., Fogstad, H., Camacho, A. V., & Laski, L. (2012). Childbearing in adolescents aged 12–15 years in low resource countries: A neglected issue. New estimates from demographic and household surveys in 42 countries. *Acta Obstetricia et Gynecologica Scandinavica*, 91(9), 1114–1118. https://doi.org/10.1111/j.1600-0412.2012.01467.x.
14. Schoumaker, B. (2017). African fertility changes. In H. Groth, & J. F. May (Eds.), *Africa's population: In search of a demographic dividend* (pp. 197–211). Springer International.
15. Koski, A., Clark, S., & Nandi, A. J. P. (2017). Has child marriage declined in sub-Saharan Africa? An analysis of trends in 31 countries. *Population and Development Review*, 43(1), 7–29. https://doi.org/10.1111/padr.12035.

16. Furstenberg, F. F. J. (2003). Teenage childbearing as a public issue and private concern. *Annual Review of Sociology*, 29(1), 23–39. https://doi.org/10.1146/annurev.soc.29.010202.100205.
17. Cashdollar, S. E. (2018). Neither accidental nor intended: Pregnancy as an adolescent identity project among Hispanic teenage mothers in Doña Ana County, New Mexico. *Journal of Adolescent Research*, 33(5), 598–622. https://doi.org/10.1177/0743558417712014.
18. Sekharan, V. S., Kim, T. H. M., Oulman, E., & Tamim, H. (2015). Prevalence and characteristics of intended adolescent pregnancy: An analysis of the Canadian maternity experiences survey. *Reproductive Health*, 12(1), 101. https://doi.org/10.1186/s12978-015-0093-9.
19. Stöckl, H., March, L., Pallitto, C., Garcia-Moreno, C., & WHO Multi-country Study Team (2014). Intimate partner violence among adolescents and young women: Prevalence and associated factors in nine countries: A cross-sectional study. *BMC Public Health*, 14, 751–751. https://doi.org/10.1186/1471-2458-14-751.
20. World Health Organization (2013). Global and regional estimates of violence against women: Prevalence and health effects of intimate partner violence and non-partner sexual violence. Geneva: World Health Organization. https://www.who.int/reproductivehealth/publications/violence/978 9241564625/en/. Accessed 28 May 2021.
21. Moore, A. M., Awusabo-Asare, K., Madise, N., John-Langba, J., & Kumi-Kyereme, A. (2007). Coerced first sex among adolescent girls in sub-Saharan Africa: Prevalence and context. *African Journal of Reproductive Health*, 11(3), 62–82. https://doi.org/10.2307/25549732.
22. Kuang, B., & Brodsky, I. (2016). Global trends in family planning programs, 1999–2014. *International Perspectives on Sexual and Reproductive Health*, 42(1), 33–44. https://doi.org/10.1363/42e0316.
23. Chandra-Mouli, V., Lane, C., & Wong, S. (2015). What does not work in adolescent sexual and reproductive health: A review of evidence on interventions commonly accepted as best practices. *Global Health, Science and Practice*, 3(3), 333–340. https://doi.org/10.9745/GHSP-D-15-00126.
24. Tan, P. L. (2017). The impact of school entry laws on female education and teenage fertility. *Journal of Population Economics*, 30(2), 503–536. https://doi.org/10.1007/s00148-016-0609-9.
25. Duflo, E., Dupas, P., & Kremer, M. (2015). Education, HIV, and early fertility: Experimental evidence from Kenya. *The American Economic Review*, 105(9), 2757–2797. https://doi.org/10.1257/aer.20121607.

26. Güneş, P. M. (2016). The impact of female education on teenage fertility: Evidence from Turkey. *The B.E. Journal of Economic Analysis & Policy*, 16(1), 259–288. https://doi.org/10.1515/bejeap-2015-0059.
27. Silles, M. A. (2009). The causal effect of education on health: Evidence from the United Kingdom. *Economics of Education Review*, 28(1), 122–128. https://doi.org/10.1016/j.econedurev.2008.02.003.
28. Monstad, K., Propper, C., & Salvanes, K. G. (2008). Education and fertility: Evidence from a natural experiment. *Scandinavian Journal of Economics*, 110(4), 827–852. https://doi.org/10.1111/j.1467-9442.2008.00563.x.
29. Kirdar, M. G., Tayfur, M. D., & Koç, Ī. (2018). The effect of compulsory schooling laws on teenage marriage and births in Turkey. *Journal of Human Capital*, 12(4). https://doi.org/10.1086/700076.
30. Alzúa, M. L., & Velázquez, C. (2017). The effect of education on teenage fertility: Causal evidence for Argentina. *IZA Journal of Development and Migration*, 7(1), 7. https://doi.org/10.1186/s40176-017-0100-8.
31. Esteve, A., Spijker, J., Riffe, T., & García, J. (2012). Spousal and parental roles among female student populations in 55 low-and middle-income countries. *Vienna Yearbook of Population Research*, 10, 77–94. https://doi.org/10.1553/populationyearbook2012s07.
32. McQueston, K., Silverman, R., & Glassman, A. (2013). The efficacy of interventions to reduce adolescent childbearing in low-and middle-income countries: A systematic review. *Studies in Family Planning*, 44(4), 369–388. https://doi.org/10.1111/j.1728-4465.2013.00365.x.
33. Santelli, J. S., Song, X., Garbers, S., Sharma, V., & Viner, R. M. (2017). Global trends in adolescent fertility, 1990–2012, in relation to national wealth, income inequalities, and educational expenditures. *Journal of Adolescent Health*, 60(2), 161–168. https://doi.org/10.1016/j.jadohealth.2016.08.026.
34. Marchetta, F., & Sahn, D. E. (2016). The role of education and family background in marriage, childbearing, and labor market participation in Senegal. *Economic Development and Cultural Change*, 64(2), 369–403. https://doi.org/10.1086/683982.
35. Diamond-Smith, N., Plaza, N., Puri, M., Dahal, M., Weiser, S. D., & Harper, C. C. (2020). Perceived conflicting desires to delay the first birth: A household-level exploration in Nepal. *International Perspectives on Sexual and Reproductive Health*, 46, 125–133. https://doi.org/10.1363/46e9420.

36. OECD (2020). Educational attainment of 25–64 year-olds (2019). https://www.oecd-ilibrary.org/education/educational-attainment-of-25-64-year-olds-2019_75230926-en. Accessed 28 May 2021.
37. Jones, G. W., & Gubhaju, B. (2009). Factors influencing changes in mean age at first marriage and proportions never marrying in the low-fertility countries of East and Southeast Asia. *Asian Population Studies*, 5(3), 237–265. https://doi.org/10.1080/17441730903351487.
38. Schneider, D., Harknett, K., & Stimpson, M. (2018). What explains the decline in first marriage in the United States? Evidence from the panel study of income dynamics, 1969 to 2013. *Journal of Marriage and Family*, 80(4), 791–811. https://doi.org/10.1111/jomf.12481.
39. Hertrich, V. (2017). Trends in age at marriage and the onset of fertility transition in sub-Saharan Africa. *Population and Development Review*, 43(S1), 112–137. https://doi.org/10.1111/padr.12043.
40. Kalmijn, M. (2013). The educational gradient in marriage: A comparison of 25 European countries. *Demography*, 50(4), 1499–1520. https://doi.org/10.1007/s13524-013-0229-x.
41. Lőrinc, M., Ryan, L., D'Angelo, A., & Kaye, N. (2020). De-individualising the 'NEET problem': An ecological systems analysis. *European Educational Research Journal*, 19(5), 412–427. https://doi.org/10.1177/1474904119880402.
42. OECD (2021). Youth not in employment, education or training (NEET) (indicator). https://data.oecd.org/youthinac/youth-not-in-employment-education-or-training-neet.htm. Accessed 28 May 2021.
43. OECD (2010). *Off to a good start? Jobs for youth*. Paris: OECD.
44. Sanderson, W. C., Skirbekk, V., & Stonawski, M. (2014). Young adults failure to thrive syndrome. *Finnish Yearbook of Population Research*, 48, 169–187. https://doi.org/10.23979/fypr.40934.
45. Gregg, P., & Tominey, E. (2005). The wage scar from male youth unemployment. *Labour Economics*, 12(4), 487–509. https://doi.org/10.1016/j.labeco.2005.05.004.
46. Schmitt, C. (2012). Labour market integration, occupational uncertainty, and fertility choices in Germany and the UK. *Demographic Research*, 26, 253–292. https://doi.org/10.4054/DemRes.2012.26.12.
47. England, P., Bearak, J., Budig, M. J., & Hodges, M. J. (2016). Do highly paid, highly skilled women experience the largest motherhood penalty? *American Sociological Review*, 81(6), 1161–1189. https://doi.org/10.1177/0003122416673598.

48. Rottenberg, C. (2017). Neoliberal feminism and the future of human capital. *Signs: Journal of Women in Culture and Society*, 42(2), 329–348. https://doi.org/10.1086/688182.
49. Datta, M. (2017). Egg freezing on company dollars: Making biological clock irrelevant. *DePaul Journal of Women, Gender and the Law*, 6, 119.
50. Te Velde, E., Habbema, D., Leridon, H., & Eijkemans, M. (2012). The effect of postponement of first motherhood on permanent involuntary childlessness and total fertility rate in six European countries since the 1970s. *Human Reproduction*, 27(4), 1179–1183. https://doi.org/10.1093/humrep/der455
51. ESHRE Capri Workshop Group (2001). Social determinants of human reproduction. *Human Reproduction*, 16(7), 1518–1526. https://doi.org/10.1093/humrep/16.7.1518.
52. Bunting, L., Tsibulsky, I., & Boivin, J. (2012). Fertility knowledge and beliefs about fertility treatment: Findings from the International Fertility Decision-making Study. *Human Reproduction*, 28(2), 385–397. https://doi.org/10.1093/humrep/des402.
53. Gormack, A. A., Peek, J. C., Derraik, J. G., Gluckman, P. D., Young, N. L., & Cutfield, W. S. (2015). Many women undergoing fertility treatment make poor lifestyle choices that may affect treatment outcome. *Human Reproduction*, 30(7), 1617–1624. https://doi.org/10.1093/humrep/dev094.
54. Grønvik, T., & Sandøy, I. F. (2018). Complications associated with adolescent childbearing in Sub-Saharan Africa: A systematic literature review and meta-analysis. *PLoS One* 13(9), e0204327. https://doi.org/10.1371/journal.pone.0204327.
55. Bearinger, L. H., Sieving, R. E., Ferguson, J., & Sharma, V. (2007). Global perspectives on the sexual and reproductive health of adolescents: Patterns, prevention, and potential. *The Lancet*, 369(9568), 1220–1231. https://doi.org/10.1016/S0140-6736(07)60367-5.
56. World Health Organization (2016). Causes of death among adolescents. https://www.who.int/maternal_child_adolescent/data/causes-death-adolescents/en/. Accessed 29 May 2021.
57. Sakai, T., Sugawara, Y., Watanabe, I., Watanabe, T., Tomata, Y., Nakaya, N., et al. (2017). Age at first birth and long-term mortality for mothers: The Ohsaki cohort study. *Environmental Health and Preventive Medicine*, 22(1), 24. https://doi.org/10.1186/s12199-017-0631-x.
58. Hoffman, S. D., & Maynard, R. A. (Eds.) (2008). *Kids having kids: Economic costs & social consequences of teen pregnancy* (2nd Ed.). Washington, DC: The Urban Institute.

59. Furstenberg, F. F., Brooks-Gunn, J., & Morgan, S. P. (1988). *Adolescent mothers in later life*. Cambridge: Cambridge University Press.
60. McLanahan, S., Tach, L., & Schneider, D. (2013). The causal effects of father absence. *Annual Review of Sociology*, 39, 399–427. https://doi.org/10.1146/annurev-soc-071312-145704
61. Skirbekk, V., Kohler, H.-P., & Prskawetz, A. (2004). Birth month, school graduation, and the timing of births and marriages. *Demography*, 41(3), 547–568. https://doi.org/10.1353/dem.2004.0028.
62. Sriyasak, A. (2016). Becoming a Thai teenage parent. PhD thesis, Mälardalen University.
63. Dariotis, J. K., Pleck, J. H., Astone, N. M., & Sonenstein, F. L. (2011). Pathways of early fatherhood, marriage, and employment: A latent class growth analysis. *Demography*, 48(2), 593. https://doi.org/10.1007/s13524-011-0022-7.
64. Nilsen, A. B. V., Waldenström, U., Rasmussen, S., Hjelmstedt, A., & Schytt, E. (2013). Characteristics of first-time fathers of advanced age: A Norwegian population-based study. *BMC Pregnancy and Childbirth*, 13(29). https://doi.org/10.1186/1471-2393-13-29.
65. Stene, L. C., Magnus, P., Lie, R. T., Søvik, O., & Joner, G. (2001). Maternal and paternal age at delivery, birth order, and risk of childhood onset type 1 diabetes: Population based cohort study. *BMJ*, 323(7309), 369. https://doi.org/10.1136/bmj.323.7309.369.
66. Hendershot, G. E., Mosher, W. D., & Pratt, W. F. (1982). Infertility and age: An unresolved issue. *Family Planning Perspectives*, 14(5), 287. https://doi.org/10.2307/2134890.
67. Kneale, D., & Joshi, H. (2008). Postponement and childlessness: Evidence from two British cohorts. *Demographic Research*, 19, 1935–1968. https://doi.org/10.4054/DemRes.2008.19.58.
68. Schmidt, L., Sobotka, T., Bentzen, J. G., & Andersen, A. N. (2011). Demographic and medical consequences of the postponement of parenthood. *Human Reproduction Update*, 18(1), 29–43. https://doi.org/10.1093/humupd/dmr040.
69. Falster, K., Hanly, M., Banks, E., Lynch, J., Chambers, G., Brownell, M., et al. (2018). Maternal age and offspring developmental vulnerability at age five: A population-based cohort study of Australian children. *PLoS One*, 15(4), e1002558. https://doi.org/10.1371/journal.pmed.1002558.
70. Blázquez, A., García, D., Rodríguez, A., Vassena, R., & Vernaeve, V. (2016). Use of donor sperm in addition to oocyte donation after repeated implantation failure in normozoospermic patients does not improve live

birth rates. *Human Reproduction*, 31(11), 2549–2553. https://doi.org/10.1093/humrep/dew226.

71. Moustafa, S., Skrip, L., Mutlu, L., & Pal, L. (2015). Geographical variability in outcome of donor egg IVF suggests ecological implications for ART success. A retrospective cohort analysis of 71, 182 donor egg IVF cycles. *Fertility and Sterility*, 104(3), e138. https://doi.org/10.1016/j.fertnstert.2015.07.427.
72. Almeling, R. (2007). Selling genes, selling gender: Egg agencies, sperm banks, and the medical market in genetic material. *American Sociological Review*, 72(3), 319–340. https://doi.org/10.1177/000312240707200301.
73. Cohen, C. (2017, October 30). The crazy, conflicting fertility advice about when women should have children. *The Telegraph*. Retrieved from http://www.telegraph.co.uk/women/life/the-crazy-conflicting-advice-about-when-women-should-have-childr/.
74. Wood, M. (2008). Celebrity older mothers: Does the media give women a false impression? *British Journal of Midwifery*, 16(5), 326–326. https://doi.org/10.12968/bjom.2008.16.5.29197.
75. Hine, G. (2013). The changing shape of pregnancy in New Zealand women's magazines: 1970–2008. *Feminist Media Studies*, 13(4), 575–592. https://doi.org/10.1080/14680777.2012.655757.
76. Goold, I. (2017). Trust women to choose: A response to John a Robertson's 'Egg freezing and Egg banking: Empowerment and alienation in assisted reproduction'. *Journal of Law and the Biosciences*, 4(3), 507–541. https://doi.org/10.1093/jlb/lsx020.
77. Chan, C., Chan, T., Peterson, B., Lampic, C., & Tam, M. (2014). Intentions and attitudes towards parenthood and fertility awareness among Chinese university students in Hong Kong: A comparison with Western samples. *Human Reproduction*, 30(2), 364–372. https://doi.org/10.1093/humrep/deu324.
78. Skoog Svanberg, A., Lampic, C., Karlström, P.-O., & Tydén, T. (2006). Attitudes toward parenthood and awareness of fertility among postgraduate students in Sweden. *Gender Medicine*, 3(3), 187–195. https://doi.org/10.1016/S1550-8579(06)80207-X.
79. Audibert, C., & Glass, D. (2015). A global perspective on assisted reproductive technology fertility treatment: An 8-country fertility specialist survey. *Reproductive Biology and Endocrinology*, 13(1), 133. https://doi.org/10.1186/s12958-015-0131-z.
80. Lande, Y., Seidman, D. S., Maman, E., Baum, M., & Hourvitz, A. (2015). Why do couples discontinue unlimited free IVF treatments? *Gynecological*

Endocrinology, 31(3), 233–236. https://doi.org/10.3109/09513590.2014.982082.
81. Widge, A. (2005). Seeking conception: Experiences of urban Indian women with in vitro fertilisation. *Patient Education and Counseling*, 59(3), 226–233. https://doi.org/10.1016/j.pec.2005.07.014.
82. Christiansen, T., Erb, K., Rizvanovic, A., Ziebe, S., Englund, A. L. M., Hald, F., et al. (2014). Costs of medically assisted reproduction treatment at specialized fertility clinics in the Danish public health care system: Results from a 5-year follow-up cohort study. *Acta Obstetricia et Gynecologica Scandinavica*, 93(1), 64–72. https://doi.org/10.1111/aogs.12293.
83. Saad, L. (2013, November 8). Americans see 25 as ideal age for women to have first child. *Gallup*. Retrieved from http://news.gallup.com/poll/165770/americans-ideal-age-women-first-child.aspx.
84. Late 20s, early 30s the best age to have a baby, according to survey of women (2010). *New York Daily News*. Retrieved from http://www.nydailynews.com/life-style/late-20s-early-30s-best-age-baby-survey-women-article-1.170801.
85. Testa, M. R. (2007). Childbearing preferences and family issues in Europe: Evidence from the Eurobarometer 2006 survey. *Vienna Yearbook of Population Research*, 5, 357–379. https://doi.org/10.1553/populationyearbook2007s357.
86. Liefbroer, A. C., Merz, E.-M., & Testa, M. R. (2015). Fertility-related norms across Europe: A multi-level analysis. In D. Philipov, A. Liefbroer, & J. Klobas (Eds.), *Reproductive decision-making in a macro-micro perspective* (pp. 141–163). Dordrecht: Springer. https://doi.org/10.1007/978-94-017-9401-5_6.
87. Billari, F. C., Goisis, A., Liefbroer, A. C., Settersten, R. A., Aassve, A., Hagestad, G., et al. (2011). Social age deadlines for the childbearing of women and men. *Human Reproduction*, 26(3), 616–622. https://doi.org/10.1093/humrep/deq360.
88. Corneal, D. (2013, December 23). Why you should wait to have children. *Cosmopolitan*. Retrieved from https://www.cosmopolitan.com/lifestyle/advice/a5237/why-you-should-wait-to-have-children/.
89. Arnett, J. J. (2015). *Emerging adulthood: The winding road from the late teens through the twenties* (2nd Ed.). New York: Oxford University Press.

90. Neels, K., Murphy, M., Bhrolcháin, M. N., & Beaujouan, É. (2017). Rising educational participation and the trend to later childbearing. *Population and Development Review*, 43(4), 667–693. https://doi.org/10.1111/padr.12112.
91. Barro, R. J., & Lee, J.-W. (2015). *Education matters: Global schooling gains from the 19th to the 21st century*. New York: Oxford University Press.

12

Finding a Mate: Contemporary Partnership and Conception

In many countries, marriage is no longer considered a prerequisite for childbearing, and the number of cohabitating couples and children born outside of marriage are both on the rise. Advances in assisted reproductive technologies (ART) have also made it increasingly feasible to have a child in the absence of a partner or within the context of a same-sex union. In this chapter, I discuss trends in partnerships and conception and why they matter for fertility.

Let's Talk About Sex……and Assisted Reproductive Technology

Most conceptions are the result of sexual intercourse. Recently, there have been concerns that people in many of the world's richer countries—particularly in Japan—are having less sex. Data suggests that almost half of married couples in Japan are "sexless" (i.e., having sex less than once a month). Even among Japanese couples who are trying to conceive, about one out of three is sexless [1]. Representative surveys suggest that sexual

V. Skirbekk, *Decline and Prosper!*,
https://doi.org/10.1007/978-3-030-91611-4_12

frequency has also decreased over the past decade(s) in the United States [2, 3], Australia [4], and the United Kingdom [5], but not in France [6]. The observed decrease in sexual frequency in some countries appears to be driven primarily by the decrease in marriage, as married people tend to have more sex than unmarried people. Additional reasons for the decrease in sexual frequency may include increases in singlehood, stress, financial difficulties, alternative time use, and consumption of pornography [7, 8].

While by far most babies are still conceived through heterosexual intercourse, people are increasingly turning to ART. *ART* refers to all procedures that increase the likelihood of establishing a pregnancy, including in vitro fertilization (where sperm is combined with an egg outside of the body), intracytoplasmic sperm injection (where sperm is injected into the cytoplasm of an egg), fertility-enhancing treatments (e.g., hormones that stimulate the release of an egg), and surrogacy (when a woman carries out a pregnancy for another party, typically using her own egg and the initiating man's sperm) [9, 10].

The first "test tube" baby was born in England in 1978. Since then, it is estimated that over 9 million babies conceived through IVF have been born worldwide. [11]

The first baby conceived through in vitro fertilization was born in 1978. Since then, the share of people using ART has increased considerably, partly due to increased access and more effective methods but also due to the postponement of childbearing and problems conceiving in later life. Globally, more than a million babies born between 2008 and 2010 were conceived using ART [12], representing roughly 2 to 3% of all infants born. The highest proportions of newborns conceived through ART have been observed in Denmark (e.g., in the mid-2010s, around 8% of all newborns [13]). The use of ART (number of initiated cycles) and the number of babies born via ART increased by almost 9.5 and 9.1% per annum, respectively, during the 3-year period [12]. ART is also increasingly used preventively. Patients are routinely offered the opportunity to freeze semen or oocytes when a medical condition or intervention might reduce their fertility [14]. Freezing semen or oocytes also allows individuals the opportunity to have children later in life [15–17]. Surrogacy is typically used by heterosexual couples when the woman (and in some cases also the man) cannot conceive—and in a minority of cases for a single male or for a same-sex male couple [18, 19]. Surrogacy users tend to be from richer, Western countries, while surrogate mothers are often from poorer nations such as in India [20–22].

The success rates of ART remain, on the whole, rather low. It is estimated that only about one out of four cycles of non-donor in vitro fertilization results in a pregnancy, and just under one out of five cycles results in a live birth [12]. Success rates are particularly low for women in their late 30s and still lower for women in their 40s [23–25]. The Human Fertilization and Embryology Authority, the independent regulator of fertility treatment in the United Kingdom, estimates that in vitro fertilization with one's own fresh eggs has a success rate around 30% for women aged under 35, but under 10% for women aged 40 and older [25]. Another recent study of women aged 45 years and older using in vitro fertilization with their own eggs found that over 97% failed to conceive [26].

Marriage Still Predicts Fertility

Traditionally, marriage has been the primary mechanism by which societies regulated sex and childbearing. Marriage and childbearing continue to be closely intertwined in contemporary society, even in more socially-liberal countries where sex outside of marriage, cohabitation, and alternative family constellations are widely accepted. Some men and women marry because they are expecting a child, others because they already have a child together, or most commonly, because they seek to have children [27, 28]. Although some people do marry with the explicit intention *not* to have children [29], the majority of people in most populations perceive childbearing as an important, or even essential, part of a marriage, even in low fertility contexts such as China [30]. Most of men and women who are married have children; for example, almost 90% of married men and women in Germany have children versus 25 to 30% of never married men and women [31]. Moreover, infertility raises the risk of marital break-up, especially in high fertility societies [32], while out-of-wedlock fertility raises the likelihood of marriage both in richer [33, 34] and in poorer settings [35, 36].

Today, most babies are still born within the context of a heterosexual marriage (e.g., in 2016, 85% of all babies born globally were born to a married mother [37]). Nevertheless, there has been a gradual decoupling of marriage from childbearing in many of the world's richer countries, where the proportion of children born to unwed mothers has increased dramatically. In 1970, less than 10% of children born in most OECD countries were born to an unwed mother. The OECD average had increased to 23.1% by 1995 and to 39.7% by 2016 [38]. The Netherlands, Norway, and Slovenia have seen the largest increases, where the proportion of children born outside of marriage has increased by roughly 50 percentage points since 1970. Today, more than 40% of births in the OECD countries occur outside of marriage [38]. In 11 OECD countries (Chile, Denmark, Estonia, France, Iceland, Mexico, The Netherlands, Norway, Portugal, Slovenia, and Sweden), more than half of children are born outside of marriage, with rates particularly high in Mexico (67%), Iceland (70%), and Chile (73%) [38]. Rates remain below 10% in Greece and Israel, and below 5% in Japan, Korea, and Turkey [38]. In some countries, it is disproportionally women with lower socioeconomic status who have children outside of marriage, including in the United States [39, 40].

Most people consider it best to have children within the context of a stable partnership, and few people intentionally decide to become parents on their own. ART has theoretically expanded opportunities for singles to have their own biological children with donated sperm or eggs and surrogacy. However, the overwhelming majority of women (and men) who use ART are people within stable partnerships [25, 41, 42]. ART may be, however, an increasingly popular option for single women approaching the end of their reproductive life span in richer countries where legislation allows. In the United Kingdom, the proportion of in vitro fertilization clients without a partner increased by 4% between 2007 and 2017, and these clients were also more likely to be above age 40 (50%) [25].

The Decrease and Delay in Marriage

Given that globally most babies are born to married couples, it is highly relevant that fewer people are getting married and staying married, and that those who do marry are getting married later. In Central and Southern Asia, Eastern and South-Eastern Asia and Northern Africa and Western Asia, long-lasting heterosexual marriages continue to be nearly universal. In most developed countries and in Latin America and the Caribbean, however, marriage rates are decreasing, cohabitation is increasing, and there are higher rates of divorce [43, 44]. Globally, the average age at which women got married for the first time was delayed from age 21.9 around 1990 to 23.3 years around 2010 [44]. Women typically marry in their early 20s in Central and Southern Asia, sub-Saharan Africa and Latin America and the Caribbean. In Eastern and South-Eastern Asia, Oceania (excluding Australia and New Zealand) and Northern Africa and Western Asia, women marry later, around age 25. Women marry latest in Europe and Northern America and Australia and New Zealand (late 20s to early 30s) [44]. The delay in marriage is important because people who marry younger tend to have more children, and this seems to hold true in different contexts as supported by findings from sub-Saharan Africa, Latin America, and East Asia [45–47].

Part of the global postponement of marriage is reflected in a marked decrease in child marriage (e.g., marriage before age 18). Child marriage continues to be far more common among young girls than among young boys—and mainly occurs in poorer countries [48]. The marriage of girls below 18 is legally permitted in 23 of 191 countries (12%) where data on minimum age laws is available and unambiguous; 99 countries (52%) permit girls under the age of 18 to be married with parental consent [48]. Over the past 25 years, the proportion of girls married before the age of 18 declined worldwide from 25.0 to 20.8%, and the proportion of girls married before the age of 15 decreased from 7.1 to 5.0% [44]. Both in terms of proportions and number, most child marriages take place in rural sub-Saharan Africa and South Asia.

Globally, the share of never married men and women has also increased, indicating that people are not only delaying marriage but also foregoing it altogether. Globally, the proportion of women aged 45–49 who never married increased from 3.1% around 1990 to 4.3% around 2010, and hence remain just a small minority [44]. The share of never married women aged 45–49 is, however, over 10% in Australia and New Zealand, Latin America and the Caribbean, and Europe and Northern America. Some high-income East Asian countries have witnessed steep increases in non-marriage among women (e.g., 16.1% in Japan and 12.8% in Singapore around 2010). Some countries in sub-Saharan Africa also have high shares of never married women in their late 40s, including Botswana (32.3%), Namibia (31.1%), and South Africa (26.4%)—even while marriage remains more or less universal in much of the region as a whole [44].

Choosing the Single Life in Japan

A very high proportion of young adults in Japan are single. According to a 2015 survey people aged 18–34, 69.8% of unmarried men and 59.1% of unmarried women were not involved in a steady relationship. Approximately half of the singles interviewed had no intention of looking for a girlfriend or boyfriend [49].

36-year-old Riku Inamoto explains why he intends to remain single: "I have two things in my life that take up all my time: my work and my hobbies," he says. "I can't stop work, so if I get married, I will lose my hobbies, which means I will have no fun. That would be a terrible life." [50]

The Spread of Cohabitation

A large part of the decrease in marriage and the increase in births to unwed mothers in developed countries can be explained by the increase in *cohabitation*, that is, the state of living together and having a sexual relationship without being married. Cohabitation has by now become the dominant living form in early adult life in Western countries and in most of Latin America [51]. While in Brazil 13% of women aged 25–29 cohabited 1980, 39.3% did so by 2000 [52, 53]. Also in Asia, cohabitation has become increasingly common. In the Philippines, the proportion of people cohabiting increased from 2% in 2000 to more than 8% in the 2010s [54]. Cohabitation has also become more commonplace in China [55–57], where just over 10% of men and women who married for the first time in the 1990s had lived together with their partner prior to marrying, compared with over 40% of men and women who married for the first time in the 2010s [56]. Nevertheless, in most countries, cohabiting couples continue to lack many of the legal rights associated with marriage (e.g., inheritance rights, pension entitlements) [58].

The increase in cohabitation reflects changes in the strength of traditional family norms and attitudes toward marriage, and the lower need to marry for economic reasons [46, 59, 60]. In several parts of the world, weddings are the most costly single event in a person's lifetime [61, 62], and some people cohabit but do not marry because they cannot afford a "proper" wedding. In the United States, for instance, many see a lack of financial resources as a reason for not marrying [63]. In Latin America, scholars have distinguished between cohabiting for "traditional reasons" (due to economic limitations) and "modern reasons" (due to personal preferences) [52].

For many, cohabitation precedes marriage, while for others, cohabitation offers a preferable alternative to marriage [27, 28, 64]. In Japan, most cohabiting unions result in marriage or dissolve—suggesting that cohabitation has become a prelude rather than an alternative to marriage [65]. In Europe, most cohabitating couples who have children marry: A study of family formation sequences since the 1970s found that, in each of the 11 European countries studied, more than 60% of women who had a child within a cohabiting union married within three years of the first birth, suggesting that marriage remains the predominant institution for raising children even in contexts where cohabitation is socially accepted [66]. It has been argued that marriage can seal a cohabitating couple's commitment to the cooperative joint project of raising economically successful children [67].

In terms of its implications for fertility, people who cohabit tend to have more children than single people, but fewer children than married people [68]. Many of the births born to unwed mothers are in fact born to cohabiting as opposed to unpartnered mothers. In the United States, for instance, the share of women who have ever cohabited has nearly doubled over the past 25 years, and most non-marital births now occur to cohabiting rather than to unpartnered mothers at all levels of education [67].

What Makes a Good Mate?

In many parts of the world, families and communities heavily influence—if not completely decide—who marries whom, and when. A study from the early 1980s found that among 142 cultures studied globally, 130 cultures (92%) had some form of arranged marriage system [69]. Though it is somewhat difficult to assess the extent to which contemporary marriages are arranged versus fully self-chosen (e.g., some argue that online dating represents a modern form of arranged marriage, where algorithms rather than parents influence and choose potential marital partners [70]), data suggests that arranged marriages (where parents or elders decide who the children should marry) continue to represent a large proportion, possibly a majority of global marriages. One assessment from 2012 found that 53% of global marriages were arranged [71], although the proportion is declining over time [72]. Arranged marriages are dominant in several of the most populous parts of the world, including large parts of Africa and the Indian subcontinent. Marriages are sometimes arranged when the children are infants or before they are even born. In contexts where families and communities do the deciding, marriages often have a social and political dimension, representing the formal bonding of two families, communities, or even countries [73–75]. Marriage can also offer a means of consolidating resources and power and increasing cooperation. For individuals who seek to migrate to higher income countries, "sham" or "pro-forma" marriage can also be a means of ensuring visas, citizenship, or access to economic benefits [76–78]. In many contexts, what makes a marriage mate therefore depends more on political and social factors and much less on individuals' personal characteristics or preferences.

According to data from 2011–2012, two-thirds of Indian women did not meet their husband until their wedding day [79].

In some cultures, a "good mate" may well be a member of the family. Although having children with a closely-related relative is associated with a number of negative health outcomes, *consanguineous* or *kin marriage* (i.e., marriage between genetic relatives) remains common in many cultures. Kin marriage may be used as a way to maintain religious and cultural traditions, strengthen alliances, and maintain wealth within the family [80, 81]. Marital traditions are often transmitted across generations and influence decisions also in younger generations [82, 83]. Cousin marriage is particularly common in Northern Africa, the Middle East, as well as Nigeria, Pakistan, Iraq, Iran, and Afghanistan [84]. Historically, kin marriage was also common in Western cultures, not least among European nobility, but is now uncommon and often illegal [85, 86]. However, kin marriage continues to be relatively frequent in some migrant communities [85, 87, 88]. In Norway, for instance, about half of migrants from Pakistan are registered as married to their cousins, and their children are twice as likely to have a genetic disorder and die within the first year than the children of couples who are not genetically related [88]. Improved knowledge on the adverse negative health effects of consanguineous reproduction has stimulated an increase in social norms and legal regulations restricting marriage between close kin in several countries [89–92].

Particularly in the West, establishing a romantically fulfilling relationship is often seen as the basis for family formation [75, 93]. There is a lower ideal and emphasis of romantic relationships as a basis for a family in, for example, India than in Western countries such as the United States [94]. In contexts where women and men seek out their own partner, women and men tend to seek out mates with particular traits. Some have argued that, in contexts where individuals choose their own mate, women seek men that can provide adequate resources (signaled by a man's wealth, income, and education), while men look for women with high reproductive capability (signaled by, for instance, their age and attractiveness) [95]. Others have argued that individual mate choices reflect a "likes-attract" pattern, whereby both men and women seek out partners with similar characteristics to themselves (i.e., assortative mating) [96].

There is ample evidence to support both hypotheses. One experimental study found that online dating profiles which described the woman as attractive and the man as financially successful elicited the most interest [97], while another study found that women, but not men, "liked" opposite-sex Tinder candidates based on their educational level [98]. Men with more limited financial resources are less likely to marry [99], even though women are increasingly rich themselves. The majority of women in the richest nations on the planet (including the United States and Norway) still prefer partners with higher income, while men give less importance to female earnings when they look for a partner and potential mother of their children [95, 100]. Not only do many women seek to marry men with high socioeconomic status [101], women also appear to prefer physically stronger men when choosing a husband [102] or a sexual partner [103]. Physical strength may act as a cue of a man's ability to provide for and protect the family, emotional strength, and competence [104]. Men with higher physical strength are generally believed to have higher positions and status within organizations, independent of their actual status [105]. Women also appear to prefer men who have higher levels of the personality traits of agreeableness, conscientiousness, and emotional stability according to Czech and Brazilian data [106]. As evidence of assortative mating, several studies have found that women and men tend to form unions with those who are similar to themselves. Couples' education levels tend to be highly similar [107, 108]. Individuals also tend to marry individuals who are more similar in terms of income [109], religion [110], and personality [111].

Problems Establishing a Partnership

The dream of finding the perfect partner might be a key reason why (Western) childbearing takes place so late and occurs at such low levels relative to many other cultures. Becoming an ideal partner (e.g., with high levels of education and wealth) as well as finding an ideal partner can both be lengthy procedures. Long and multiple dating periods often precede settling on a single partner—and hence fertility tends to be lower [112, 113]. In many countries, women are expected to take a subordinate role to their husbands or devote more of their time to housework and childrearing once they get married. In such contexts, some women delay marriage or prefer not to marry at all [114]. Many men and women prefer the man to be the main "breadwinner," even in socially progressive countries like Norway [100]. In many of the world's richer countries, women are, however, outperforming men in education [115], at the same time that men's wages have stagnated, creating a shortage of "attractive" marriage partners for both men and women. The gendered division of labor and the social expectation for women to "marry up" are particularly strong in East Asian contexts. At the same time, cohabitation and childbearing outside of marriage remain relatively rare in East Asia. Together, these social norms contribute to extremely low birth rates in the East Asian countries [44].

1 in 562

The odds a single person finding a partner with the desired characteristics on any given day in the United Kingdom [116].

It has long been accepted as a truism that women are more selective when choosing their sexual and romantic partners, particularly when looking for potential co-parents [95, 117]. Though some have challenged whether this is truly the case [118], many women in the world's richer countries appear to seek *Mr. Perfect*, while their male counterparts are more willing to accept *Ms. Goodenough*. A study based on the online dating platform Tinder found, for instance, that in a random female/male Tinder interaction, the man is 6.2 times more likely to "like" the woman than vice versa [119]. Analysis of data from the OKCupid online dating platform found that men ranked most women on the website as being close to average with regard to their physical attractiveness. Women, on the other hand, rated 80% of men as worse-looking than average [120].

There is also evidence that women are becoming more selective over time. In one of my own studies, we used Norwegian data to analyze how men's fertility was related to their personality traits. Norway is one of the few countries with good data on men's fertility, and we were able to link the fertility data with survey data on personality traits. We reasoned that women would prefer to have children with men with low levels of neuroticism. Neuroticism, particularly among males, is associated with lower education, poorer salaries, higher alcohol intake, greater risks of substance abuse, and criminal offenses [121–124]. Neuroticism has also been linked to delayed parenthood in previous research [125]. Our analysis showed that men with higher neuroticism had lower fertility, but only for men born after 1956. There was no relationship between men's neuroticism and their fertility for men born earlier. Our results therefore suggest that women in Norway are getting more selective, and that personality traits have become more important determinants of men's fertility [126].

One commonly voiced concern is that screen time may be negatively impacting contemporary union and family formation. In richer countries, people spend an average of 11 hours a day—two-thirds of all waking hours—in front of screens (including television, smartphones, and computers) [127]. There has been concern that screen time might be displacing time spent engaging in the behaviors that ultimately result in union formation and childbearing. Increased screen time may have come at the cost of less physical proximity to others, social interaction, dating, sex, physical activity, and quality sleep, all of which may depress fertility [128–130]. Evidence from Swedish Time Use Surveys from 1990 to 2011 indicate that while online time increased, time spent on social activities, activities with other people, and offline hobbies consistently declined [128]. In another study, time spent gaming predicted less time with others, less relationship satisfaction, and more relationship uncertainty [131]. Excessive screen time may also cause physiological problems decreasing fertility (e.g., laptops may create heat that worsens semen production; radiation from mobile phones might be linked to lower fecundity [132, 133]). The Internet, gaming, and the increase in physically-isolating communication are thought to be major contributors to the phenomenon of modern recluses [134–136]. The Japanese

Health, Labor and Welfare Ministry uses the term *hikikomori* to define the condition as well as people who haven't left their homes or interacted with others for at least six months. *Hikikomori* is a particularly Japanese phenomenon, but similar phenomena have been observed in other countries as well [135].

On the face of things, high levels of gaming seem to be associated with lower national fertility rates, where countries such as Japan, Western nations, and China tend to have among the highest shares playing computer games [130, 137, 138]. Empirically, however, it is currently difficult to conclude whether screen time is truly getting in the way of union formation and childbearing. So far, most existing research on computer use and fertility is either based on small surveys, or fails to control for other potentially confounding factors (e.g., the availability of contraception increased at the same that computers became more commonplace). Identifying a causal link between screen time and union formation and/or fertility is difficult, as not having a partner or children might also lead to more screen time.

Same-Sex Couples

In many developed countries, the social acceptance of same-sex couples has increased considerably over the last decades. By the 2010s, marriage between two same-sex partners was legally recognized in 28 countries, primarily North America and Europe but also including several Latin American countries (Argentina, Brazil, Costa Rica Colombia, Ecuador, Mexico, and Uruguay), Israel, South Africa, and Taiwan [139]. Changing social attitudes and legal regulations have gone along with increases in the proportion of people openly living in same-sex partnerships. In some countries, non-heterosexual individuals and couples represent small but significant shares of the population. In 2011–2013 in the United States, 1.3% of women and 1.9% of men identified themselves as "homosexual, gay, or lesbian" and another 5.5% of women and 2.0% of men identified as bisexual (0.9% of women and 1.0% of men said "don't know" or "refused") [140]. In Canada, in 2011, 0.8% of all couples were same-sex couples [141]. In a Dutch 2001 survey, 1.5% of men self-identified as gay, 0.6% as bisexual, and 97.9% as heterosexual, while among women, 1.5% self-identified as gay, 1.2% as bisexual, and 97.3% as heterosexual [142].

Despite the increase of people openly living with a same-sex partner, homosexual men and women remain a minority. The fertility of same-sex couples hence has rather limited effects on the fertility of a population as a whole. Increasing acceptance of non-heterosexual orientations has thus probably not contributed to changes in overall fertility rates [143], nor has the extension of marriage laws to include homosexual couples influenced marriage rates much according to a Dutch study [144]. Moreover, fertility among non-heterosexual people remains low. Some homosexual individuals may have their own biological children through heterosexual conceptions. Homosexuals from older cohorts may have previously been part of a heterosexual partnership, as indicated by Danish data [145]. Theoretically at least, homosexual women can have biological children using ART and donated semen, while homosexual men can have biological children with donated eggs and female surrogacy [18, 146]. However, many countries only legally allow or subsidize ART for married, heterosexual couples. Even in contexts where homosexuals can access ART, the proportion of homosexual men and women who have children through ART is low. According to a recent report on in vitro fertilization in the United Kingdom, for instance, just 5.9% of cycles were undertaken by women with a female partner [25].

Same Now as It Was Then: Late and Low Marriage Lowers Fertility

Despite loosening norms about sex, marriage, and homosexuality and the increased availability of ART, the vast majority of the world's children are still the product of sexual intercourse between a husband and a wife. The global decline and delay in marriage has therefore been a major driver of delayed and lower fertility. Most people appear to prefer to first establish themselves financially, establish a long-term relationship with a partner, then have children, in that order. The situation today is thus quite reminiscent of how the European pattern of late marriage often led to later and lower fertility already in the 1700 and 1800s.

The lack of a stable partnership appears to be one of the main reasons why many people in the low fertility countries tend to have fewer children than they would ideally like to have. Helping people to find a partner earlier in their reproductive window may therefore be crucial for reducing unwanted childlessness. In many contexts, men and particularly women postpone marriage in the hope of finding a "perfect" partner. Women's educational gains have had an empowering effect and raised their expectations for their marriage and their partners. Encouraging equity in the household and reducing the dominance of the male breadwinner norm may be particularly important for encouraging stable partnerships in the low fertility countries. It is important that legal and economic systems allow women and men to support a family without being dependent on transfers from others.

References

1. Moriki, Y., Hayashi, K., & Matsukura, R. (2015). Sexless marriages in Japan: Prevalence and reasons. In N. Ogawa, & I. Shah (Eds.), *Low fertility and reproductive health in East Asia* (pp. 161–185). Dordrecht: Springer. https://doi.org/10.1007/978-94-017-9226-4_9.
2. Twenge, J. M., Sherman, R. A., & Wells, B. E. (2017). Declines in sexual frequency among American adults, 1989–2014. *Archives of Sexual Behavior*, 46(8), 1–13. https://doi.org/10.1007/s10508-017-0953-1.
3. Stone, L. 2021 (2018). Sexlessness is rising but not for the reasons Incels claim. Institute for Family Studies, May 14. https://ifstudies.org/blog/male-sexlessness-is-rising-but-not-for-the-reasons-incels-claim. Accessed 29 May 2021.
4. de Visser, R. O., Richters, J., Rissel, C., Badcock, P. B., Simpson, J. M., Smith, A. M. A., et al. (2014). Change and stasis in sexual health and relationships: Comparisons between the first and second Australian studies of health and relationships. *Sexual Health*, 11(5), 505-509. https://doi.org/10.1071/SH14112.

5. Wellings, K., Palmer, M. J., Machiyama, K., & Slaymaker, E. (2019). Changes in, and factors associated with, frequency of sex in Britain: Evidence from three National Surveys of Sexual Attitudes and Lifestyles (NATSAL). *BMJ*, 365, l1525. https://doi.org/10.1136/bmj.l1525.
6. Bajos, N., Bozon, M., Beltzer, N., Laborde, C., Andro, A., Ferrand, M., et al. (2010). Changes in sexual behaviours: From secular trends to public health policies. *AIDS*, 24(8), 1185–1191. https://doi.org/10.1097/QAD.0b013e328336ad52.
7. Kim, J. H., Tam, W. S., & Muennig, P. (2017). Sociodemographic correlates of sexlessness among American adults and associations with self-reported happiness levels: Evidence from the US General Social Survey. *Archives of Sexual Behavior*, 46(8), 2403–2415. https://doi.org/10.1007/s10508-017-0968-7.
8. Hirayama, M. (2019). Developments in information technology and the sexual depression of Japanese youth since 2000. *International Journal of the Sociology of Leisure*, 2(1–2), 95–119. https://doi.org/10.1007/s41978-019-00034-2.
9. Keep, L. 2021 (2019, October 22). Surrogacy facts and myths: How much do you know? *Independent Lens*. http://www.pbs.org/independentlens/blog/surrogacy-facts-and-myths-how-much-do-you-know/. Accessed 29 May 2021.
10. Jadva, V., Gamble, N., Prosser, H., & Imrie, S. (2019). Parents' relationship with their surrogate in cross-border and domestic surrogacy arrangements: Comparisons by sexual orientation and location. *Fertility and Sterility*, 111(3), 562–570. https://doi.org/10.1016/j.fertnstert.2018.11.029.
11. European Society of Human Reproduction and Embryology. (2021). ART fact sheet. https://www.eshre.eu/Press-Room/Resources. Accessed 19 May 2021.
12. Dyer, S., Chambers, G. M., de Mouzon, J., Nygren, K. G., Zegers-Hochschild, F., Mansour, R., et al. (2016). International committee for monitoring assisted reproductive technologies world report: Assisted reproductive technology 2008, 2009 and 2010. *Human Reproduction*, 31(7), 1588–1609. https://doi.org/10.1093/humrep/dew082.
13. Lassen, T. H., Iwamoto, T., Jensen, T. K., & Skakkebæk, N. E. (2015). Trends in male reproductive health and decreasing fertility: Possible influence of endocrine disrupters. In N. Ogawa, & I. Shah (Eds.), *Low fertility and reproductive health in East Asia* (pp. 117–135). Dordrecht: Springer. https://doi.org/10.1007/978-94-017-9226-4_7.

14. Wood, G., Hayden, R., & Tanrikut, C. (2017). Successful sperm extraction and live birth after radiation, androgen deprivation and surgical castration for treatment of metastatic prostate cancer. *Andrologia*, 49(1), e12578.
15. Baldwin, K. (2019). The experience of freezing eggs for social reasons. *Egg freezing, fertility and reproductive choice* (pp. 87–118). Bingley: Emerald Publishing Limited.
16. Kılıç, A., & Göçmen, İ. (2018). Fate, morals and rational calculations: Freezing eggs for non-medical reasons in Turkey. *Social Science & Medicine*, 203, 19–27. https://doi.org/10.1016/j.socscimed.2018.03.014.
17. Kroløkke, C., Petersen, T. S., Herrmann, J. R., Bach, A. S., Adrian, S. W., Klingenberg, R., et al. (2019). Delay: On the use of freezing for non-medical reasons. *The cryopolitics of reproduction on ice: A new Scandinavian ice age* (pp. 73–94). Bingley: Emerald Publishing Limited. https://doi.org/10.1108/978-1-83867-042-920191005.
18. Carone, N., Baiocco, R., & Lingiardi, V. (2017). Single fathers by choice using surrogacy: Why men decide to have a child as a single parent. *Human Reproduction*, 32(9), 1871–1879. https://doi.org/10.1093/humrep/dex245.
19. Söderström-Anttila, V., Wennerholm, U.-B., Loft, A., Pinborg, A., Aittomäki, K., Romundstad, L. B., et al. (2016). Surrogacy: Outcomes for surrogate mothers, children and the resulting families—A systematic review. *Human Reproduction Update*, 22(2), 260–276. https://doi.org/10.1093/humupd/dmv046.
20. Eriksen, L. M. (2018). It starts with wanting children: Norwegian parents' experiences with commercial surrogacy in the USA. MA thesis, University of Oslo. https://www.duo.uio.no/bitstream/handle/10852/64041/eriksen_master.pdf?sequence=1&isAllowed=y.
21. Scherman, R., Misca, G., Rotabi, K., & Selman, P. (2016). Global commercial surrogacy and international adoption: Parallels and differences. *Adoption & Fostering*, 40(1), 20–35. https://doi.org/10.1177/0308575915626376.
22. Twine, F. W. (2015). *Outsourcing the womb: Race, class and gestational surrogacy in a global market*. New York: Routledge.
23. Wyndham, N., Figueira, P. G. M., & Patrizio, P. (2012). A persistent misperception: Assisted reproductive technology can reverse the "aged biological clock". *Fertility and Sterility*, 97(5), 1044–1047. https://doi.org/10.1016/j.fertnstert.2012.02.015.

24. Ylänne, V. (2017). Representations of ageing and infertility in the twenty-first-century British press. In G. Davis, & T. Loughran (Eds.), *The Palgrave handbook of infertility in history* (pp. 509–535). London: Palgrave Macmillan. https://doi.org/10.1057/978-1-137-52080-7_26.
25. Human Fertilisation and Embryology Authority. (2019). Fertility trends 2017: Trends and figures. https://www.hfea.gov.uk/media/3189/fertility-treatment-2017-trends-and-figures.pdf. Accessed 29 May 2021.
26. Gunnala, V., Irani, M., Melnick, A., Rosenwaks, Z., & Spandorfer, S. (2018). One thousand seventy-eight autologous IVF cycles in women 45 years and older: The largest single-center cohort to date. *Journal of Assisted Reproduction and Genetics*, 35, 435–440. https://doi.org/10.1007/s10815-017-1088-y.
27. Klärner, A., & Knabe, A. (2017). On the normative foundations of marriage and cohabitation: Results from group discussions in eastern and western Germany. *Demographic Research*, 36, 1637–1666. https://doi.org/10.4054/DemRes.2017.36.53.
28. Jones, G. (2018). What is driving marriage and cohabitation in low fertility countries? In D. J. Poston (Ed.), *Low fertility regimes and demographic and societal change* (pp. 149–166). Cham: Springer.
29. Carroll, L. (2018). The intentionally childless marriage. In N. Sappleton (Ed.), *Voluntary and involuntary childlessness: The joys of otherhood?* (pp. 217–235). Bingley: Emerald Publishing Limited. https://doi.org/10.1108/978-1-78754-361-420181010.
30. Chow, N., & Lum, T. (2008). Trends in family attitudes and values in Hong Kong. F. r. s. t. t. C. P. U. H. K. S. Government. https://hub.hku.hk/bitstream/10722/159856/1/Content.pdf?accept=1. Accessed 29 May 2021.
31. Kreyenfeld, M., & Konietzka, D. (2017). Childlessness in East and West Germany: Long-term trends and social disparities. In M. Kreyenfeld, & D. Konietzka (Eds.), *Childlessness in Europe: Contexts, causes, and consequences* (pp. 97–114). Cham: Springer. https://doi.org/10.1007/978-3-319-44667-7_5.
32. Fledderjohann, J. (2017). Difficulties conceiving and relationship stability in Sub-Saharan Africa: The case of Ghana. *European Journal of Population*, 33(1), 129–152. https://doi.org/10.1007/s10680-016-9401-5.
33. Steele, F., Kallis, C., Goldstein, H., & Joshi, H. (2005). The relationship between childbearing and transitions from marriage and cohabitation in Britain. *Demography*, 42(4), 647–673. https://doi.org/10.1353/dem.2005.0038.

34. Lichter, D. T., Michelmore, K., Turner, R. N., & Sassler, S. (2016). Pathways to a stable union? Pregnancy and childbearing among cohabiting and married couples. *Population Research and Policy Review*, 35(3), 377–399. https://doi.org/10.1007/s11113-016-9392-2.
35. Meekers, D., & Gage, A. J. (2017). Marriage patterns and the demographic dividend. In H. Groth, & J. May (Eds.), *Africa's population: In search of a demographic dividend* (pp. 251–265). Cham: Springer. https://doi.org/10.1007/978-3-319-46889-1_16.
36. Widyastari, D. A., Isarabhakdi, P., Vapattanawong, P., & Völker, M. (2019). Rethinking early childbearing in Indonesia: Is it preceded by a premarital first birth? *International Journal of Adolescent Medicine and Health*. https://doi.org/10.1515/ijamh-2019-0055.
37. Chamie, J. 2021 (2017, March 16). Out-of-wedlock births rise worldwide. *YaleGlobal Online*. The Macmillan Center, Yale University. https://archive-yaleglobal.yale.edu/content/out-wedlock-births-rise-worldwide.
38. OECD. (2020). SF2.4: Share of births outside of marriage. https://www.oecd.org/social/family/SF_2_4_Share_births_outside_marriage.pdf. Accessed 29 May 2021.
39. Perelli-Harris, B., Sigle-Rushton, W., Kreyenfeld, M., Lappegård, T., Keizer, R., & Berghammer, C. (2010). The educational gradient of childbearing within cohabitation in Europe. *Population and Development Review*, 36(4), 775–801. https://doi.org/10.1111/j.1728-4457.2010.00357.x.
40. Duncan, S., & Edwards, R. (Eds.) (2013). *Single mothers in international context: Mothers or workers?* London and New York: Routledge.
41. De Jonge, C., & Barratt, R. (2002). *Assisted reproductive technology: Accomplishments and new horizons*. London: Cambridge University Press.
42. Präg, P., Sobotka, T., Lappalainen, E., Miettinen, A., Rotkirch, A., Takács, J., et al. (2017). Childlessness and assisted reproduction in Europe. Families and Societies Working Paper Series, 69. http://www.familiesandsocieties.eu/wp-content/uploads/2017/02/WP69Pragetal2017.pdf. Accessed 29 May 2021.
43. Lesthaeghe, R. (2014). The second demographic transition: A concise overview of its development. *Proceedings of the National Academy of Sciences*, 111(51), 18112–18115. https://doi.org/10.1073/pnas.1420441111.

44. United Nations Women (2019). *Progress of the world's women 2019–2020: Families in a changing world*. New York: U. N. Women. https://www.unwomen.org/en/digital-library/progress-of-the-worlds-women. Accessed 29 May 2021.
45. Hertrich, V. (2017). Trends in age at marriage and the onset of fertility transition in Sub-Saharan Africa. *Population and Development Review*, 43(S1), 112–137. https://doi.org/10.1111/padr.12043.
46. Laplante, B., Martín, T. C., Cortina, C., & Fostik, A. L. (2016). The contributions of childbearing within marriage and within consensual union to fertility in Latin America, 1980–2010. *Demographic Research*, 34, 827–844. https://doi.org/10.4054/DemRes.2016.34.29.
47. Straughan, P. (2015). Marriage and parenthood in Singapore. In D. Chan (Ed.), *50 years of social issues in Singapore* (pp. 61–73). Singapore: World Scientific. https://doi.org/10.1142/9789814632621_0004.
48. Arthur, M., Earle, A., Raub, A., Vincent, I., Atabay, E., Latz, I., et al. (2018). Child marriage laws around the world: Minimum marriage age, legal exceptions, and gender disparities. *Journal of Women, Politics & Policy*, 39(1), 51–74. https://doi.org/10.1080/1554477X.2017.1375786.
49. Yukiko, A. (2018). Japan's unmarried masses face mounting obstacles to matrimony. https://www.nippon.com/en/features/c05601/. Accessed 29 May 2021.
50. Dickens, A. Why Japanese men are choosing the single life. *Flash Pack*. Retrieved from https://www.flashpack.com/travel/why-japanese-men-choosing-single-life-japan/
51. Esteve, A., Lesthaeghe, R. J., López-Colás, J., López-Gay, A., & Covre-Sussai, M. (2016). Cohabitation in Brazil: Historical legacy and recent evolution. In A. Esteve, & R. J. Lesthaeghe (Eds.), *Cohabitation and marriage in the Americas: Geo-historical legacies and new trends* (pp. 217–245). Cham: Springer. https://doi.org/10.1007/978-3-319-31442-6_8.
52. Covre-Sussai, M., Meuleman, B., Botterman, S., & Matthijs, K. (2015). Traditional and modern cohabitation in Latin America: A comparative typology. *Demographic Research*, 32(32), 873–914. https://doi.org/10.4054/DemRes.2015.32.32.
53. Esteve, A., Lesthaeghe, R., & López-Gay, A. (2012). The Latin American cohabitation boom, 1970–2007. *Population and Development Review*, 38(1), 55–81. https://doi.org/10.1111/j.1728-4457.2012.00472.x.
54. Kobayashi, K., & Kampen, R. (2015). Cohabitation in Asia. In S. R. Quah (Ed.), *Routledge handbook of families in Asia* (pp. 377–397). Abingdon, Oxon, and New York: Routledge.

55. Zhang, Y. (2017). Premarital cohabitation and marital dissolution in postreform China. *Journal of Marriage and Family*, 79(5), 1435–1449. https://doi.org/10.1111/jomf.12419.
56. Yu, J., & Xie, Y. (2015). Cohabitation in China: Trends and determinants. *Population and Development Review*, 41(4), 607–628. https://doi.org/10.1111/j.1728-4457.2015.00087.x.
57. Nauck, B., Gröpler, N., & Yi, C.-C. (2017). How kinship systems and welfare regimes shape leaving home: A comparative study of the United States, Germany, Taiwan, and China. *Demographic Research*, 36, 1109–1148. https://doi.org/10.4054/DemRes.2017.36.38.
58. Pleasence, P., & Balmer, N. J. (2012). Ignorance in bliss: Modeling knowledge of rights in marriage and cohabitation. *Law & Society Review*, 46(2), 297–333. https://doi.org/10.1111/j.1540-5893.2012.00490.x.
59. Covre-Sussai, M., Meuleman, B., Van Bavel, J., & Matthijs, K. (2014). Measuring gender equality in family decision making in Latin America: A key towards understanding changing family configurations. *Genus*, 69(3), 47–73. https://www.jstor.org/stable/genus.69.3.47
60. Ellison, C. G., Wolfinger, N. H., & Ramos-Wada, A. I. (2012). Attitudes toward marriage, divorce, cohabitation, and casual sex among working-age Latinos: Does religion matter? *Journal of Family Issues*, 34(3), 295–322. https://doi.org/10.1177/0192513X12445458.
61. Cleuziou, J., & Ohayon, I. (2017, September). My big fat very expensive wedding. Ceremonial inflation in Central Asia. *Le Monde Diplomatique*. Retrieved from https://mondediplo.com/2017/09/11tajikistan.
62. Das, U. R. (2016, February 16). The big fat wedding industry in India: Recap of 2015 and outlook for 2016. *Business Insider (India)*. Retrieved from https://www.businessinsider.in/The-Big-Fat-Wedding-Industry-in-India-Recap-of-2015-and-outlook-for-2016/articleshow/51008952.cms.
63. Edin, K. (2000). What do low-income single mothers say about marriage? *Social Problems*, 47(1), 112–133. https://doi.org/10.1525/sp.2000.47.1.03x0282v.
64. Lesthaeghe, R. (2010). The unfolding story of the second demographic transition. *Population and Development Review*, 36(2), 211–251. https://doi.org/10.1111/j.1728-4457.2010.00328.x.
65. Raymo, J. M., Iwasawa, M., & Bumpass, L. (2009). Cohabitation and family formation in Japan. *Demography*, 46(4), 785–803. https://doi.org/10.1353/dem.0.0075.
66. Perelli-Harris, B., Kreyenfeld, M., Sigle-Rushton, W., Keizer, R., Lappegard, T., Jasilioniene, A., et al. (2012). Changes in union status during

the transition to parenthood in eleven European countries, 1970s to early 2000s. *Population Studies*, 66(2), 167–182. https://doi.org/10.1080/00324728.2012.673004.

67. Lundberg, S., Pollak, R. A., & Stearns, J. (2016). Family inequality: Diverging patterns in marriage, cohabitation, and childbearing. *Journal of Economic Perspectives*, 30(2), 79–102. https://doi.org/10.1257/jep.30.2.79
68. Laplante, B., & Fostik, A. L. (2015). Two period measures for comparing the fertility of marriage and cohabitation. *Demographic Research*, 32, 421–442. https://doi.org/10.4054/DemRes.2015.32.14.
69. Broude, G. J., & Greene, S. J. (1983). Cross-cultural codes on husband-wife relationships. *Ethnology*, 22(3), 263–280. https://doi.org/10.2307/3773467.
70. Batabyal, A. A. (2018, April 5). How online dating is like having an arranged marriage. *Quartz India*. Retrieved from https://qz.com/india/1245343/how-online-dating-is-like-having-an-indian-arranged-marriage/
71. Statistic Brain. (2018). Arranged/forced marriage statistics. https://www.statisticbrain.com/arranged-marriage-statistics/. Accessed 29 May 2021.
72. Patton, G. C., Olsson, C. A., Skirbekk, V., Saffery, R., Wlodek, M. E., Azzopardi, P. S., et al. (2018). Adolescence and the next generation. *Nature*, 554(7693), 458–466. https://doi.org/10.1038/nature25759.
73. Millett, K. (2016). *Sexual politics*. New York: Columbia University Press.
74. Curran, K. (2016). *Marriage, performance, and politics at the Jacobean court*. London: Routledge.
75. Coontz, S. (2005). *Marriage, a history: How love conquered marriage*. New York: Viking Penguin.
76. Wolf, K. (2016). Marriage migration versus family reunification: How does the marriage and migration history affect the timing of first and second childbirth among Turkish immigrants in Germany? *European Journal of Population*, 32(5), 731–759. https://doi.org/10.1007/s10680-016-9402-4.
77. Wagner, R. (2015). Family life across borders: Strategies and obstacles to integration. *Journal of Family Issues*, 36(11), 1509–1528. https://doi.org/10.1177/0192513X14558299.
78. Wray, H., Agoston, A., & Hutton, J. (2014). A family resemblance? The regulation of marriage migration in Europe. *European Journal of Migration and Law*, 16(2), 209–247. https://doi.org/10.1163/15718166-12342054.

79. Soy, N. F., & Sahoo, H. (2016). Marriage arrangements and customs in India. *Social Science Spectrum*, 2(4), 248–262.
80. Bittles, A. H. (2015). The prevalence and outcomes of consanguineous marriage in contemporary societies. In A. Shaw, & A. Raz (Eds.), *Cousin marriages: Between tradition, genetic risk and cultural change* (p. 33). New York and Oxford: Berghahn.
81. Small, N., Bittles, A. H., Petherick, E. S., & Wright, J. (2017). Endogamy, consanguinity and the health implications of changing marital choices in the UK Pakistani community. *Journal of Biosocial Science*, 49(4), 435–446. https://doi.org/10.1017/S0021932016000419.
82. Harkness, G., & Khaled, R. (2014). Modern traditionalism: Consanguineous marriage in Qatar. *Journal of Marriage and Family*, 76(3), 587–603. https://doi.org/10.1111/jomf.12106.
83. Allendorf, K., & Pandian, R. K. (2016). The decline of arranged marriage? Marital change and continuity in India. *Population and Development Review*, 42(3), 435–464. https://doi.org/10.1111/j.1728-4457.2016.00149.x.
84. Rijpma, A., & Carmichael, S. G. (2016). Testing Todd and Matching Murdock: Global data on historical family characteristics. *Economic History of Developing Regions*, 31(1), 10–46. https://doi.org/10.1080/20780389.2015.1114415.
85. Baykara-Krumme, H. (2016). Consanguineous marriage in Turkish families in Turkey and in Western Europe. *International Migration Review*, 50(3), 568–598.
86. Bittles, A. H. (1990). Consanguineous marriage: Current global incidence and its relevance to demographic research.
87. Shaw, A. (2015). British Pakistani cousin marriages and the negotiation of reproductive risk. In A. Shaw, & A. Raz (Eds.), *Cousin marriages: Between tradition, genetic risk and cultural change* (pp. 113–129). Oxford and New York: Berghahn.
88. Surén, P., Grjibovski, A., & Stoltenberg, C. (2007). *Inngifte i Norge: omfang og medisinske konsekvenser* [Consanguineous marriage in Norway: Prevalence and medical consequences]. Oslo: Norwegian Institute of Public Health. https://fhi.brage.unit.no/fhi-xmlui/handle/11250/2711781. Accessed 29 May 2021.
89. Bener, A., & Mohammad, R. R. (2017). Global distribution of consanguinity and their impact on complex diseases: Genetic disorders from an endogamous population. *Egyptian Journal of Medical Human Genetics*, 18(4), 315–320. https://doi.org/10.1016/j.ejmhg.2017.01.002.

90. Chisholm, J. S., & Bittles, A. H. (2015). Consanguinity and the developmental origins of health and disease. *Journal of Evolutionary Medicine*, 3(4). https://doi.org/10.4303/jem/235909.
91. Anwar, W. A., Khyatti, M., & Hemminki, K. (2014). Consanguinity and genetic diseases in North Africa and immigrants to Europe. *The European Journal of Public Health*, 24(suppl 1), 57–63. https://doi.org/10.1093/eurpub/cku104.
92. Tadmouri, G. O., Nair, P., Obeid, T., Al Ali, M. T., Al Khaja, N., & Hamamy, H. A. (2009). Consanguinity and reproductive health among Arabs. *Reproductive Health*, 6(1), 17. https://doi.org/10.1186/1742-4755-6-17.
93. Muraco, J. A., & Curran, M. A. (2012). Associations between marital meaning and reasons to delay marriage for young adults in romantic relationships. *Marriage & Family Review*, 48(3), 227–247. https://doi.org/10.1080/01494929.2012.665013.
94. Medora, N. P., Larson, J. H., Hortacsu, N., Hortagsu, N., & Dave, P. (2002). Perceived attitudes towards romanticism; a cross-cultural study of American, Asian-Indian, and Turkish young adults. *Journal of Comparative Family Studies*, 33(2), 155–178. https://doi.org/10.3138/jcfs.33.2.155.
95. Buss, D. M. (1989). Sex differences in human mate preferences: Evolutionary hypotheses tested in 37 cultures. *Behavioral and Brain Sciences*, 12(1), 1–14. https://doi.org/10.1017/S0140525X00023992.
96. Buston, P. M., & Emlen, S. T. (2003). Cognitive processes underlying human mate choice: The relationship between self-perception and mate preference in Western society. *Proceedings of the National Academy of Sciences*, 100(15), 8805–8810. https://doi.org/10.1073/pnas.1533220100.
97. Strassberg, D. S., & English, B. L. (2015). An experimental study of men's and women's personal ads. *Archives of Sexual Behavior*, 44(8), 2249–2255. https://doi.org/10.1007/s10508-014-0428-6.
98. Neyt, B., Vandenbulcke, S., & Baert, S. (2018). Education level and mating success: Undercover on Tinder. IZA Discussion Paper No. 11933. https://ssrn.com/abstract=3294148. Accessed 29 May 2021.
99. Jokela, M., Rotkirch, A., Rickard, I. J., Pettay, J., & Lummaa, V. (2010). Serial monogamy increases reproductive success in men but not in women. *Behavioral Ecology*, 21(5), 906–912. https://doi.org/10.1093/beheco/arq078.

100. Line Tomter (2008, February 21). *Kvinner vil at mannen skal tjene mest* [Women want the man to earn most]. *NRK*. Retrieved from http://www.nrk.no/okonomi/vil-at-mannen-skal-tjene-mest-1.4879831.html
101. Greenwood, J., Guner, N., Kocharkov, G., & Santos, C. (2014). Marry your like: Assortative mating and income inequality. *The American Economic Review*, 104(5), 348–353. https://doi.org/10.1257/aer.104.5.348.
102. Skirbekk, V., Hardy, M., & Strand, B. H. (2018). Women's spousal choices and a man's handshake: Evidence from a Norwegian study of cohort differences. *SSM - Population Health*, 5, 1–7. https://doi.org/10.1016/j.ssmph.2018.04.004.
103. Gallup, A. C., White, D. D., & Gallup, G. G. (2007). Handgrip strength predicts sexual behavior, body morphology, and aggression in male college students. *Evolution and Human Behavior*, 28(6), 423–429. https://doi.org/10.1016/j.evolhumbehav.2007.07.001.
104. Powers, R. S., & Reiser, C. (2005). Gender and self-perceptions of social power. *Social Behavior and Personality: An International Journal*, 33(6), 553–568. https://doi.org/10.2224/sbp.2005.33.6.553.
105. Lukaszewski, A. W., Simmons, Z. L., Anderson, C., & Roney, J. R. (2016). The role of physical formidability in human social status allocation. *Journal of Personality and Social Psychology*, 110(3), 385–406. https://doi.org/10.1037/pspi0000042.
106. Valentova, J. V., Štěrbová, Z., Bártová, K., & Varella, M. A. C. (2016). Personality of ideal and actual romantic partners among heterosexual and non-heterosexual men and women: A cross-cultural study. *Personality and Individual Differences*, 101, 160–166. https://doi.org/10.1016/j.paid.2016.05.048.
107. Trimarchi, A., Schnor, C., & Van Bavel, J. (forthcoming). Educational assortative mating and nonmarital childbearing within cohabitation-Evidence from four European contexts. In S. Walper, E.-V. Wendt, & F. Schmahl (Eds.), *Partnership relations from adolescence to adulthood: Psychological and sociological perspectives*. Springer.
108. Verbakel, E., & Kalmijn, M. (2014). Assortative mating among Dutch married and cohabiting same-sex and different-sex couples. *Journal of Marriage and Family*, 76(1), 1–12. https://doi.org/10.1111/jomf.12084.
109. Olivo-Villabrille, M. (2017). Assortative marriages and household income inequality. https://molivo.net/wp-content/uploads/AssortativeMarriages.pdf. Accessed 29 May 2021.

110. McClendon, D. (2016). Religion, marriage markets, and assortative mating in the United States. *Journal of Marriage and Family*, 78(5), 1399–1421. https://doi.org/10.1111/jomf.12353.
111. Štěrbová, Z., Bártová, K., Nováková, L. M., Varella, M. A. C., Havlíček, J., & Valentova, J. V. (2017). Assortative mating in personality among heterosexual and male homosexual couples from Brazil and the Czech Republic. *Personality and Individual Differences*, 112, 90–96. https://doi.org/10.1016/j.paid.2017.02.036.
112. Andersson, G., & Kolk, M. (2016). Trends in childbearing, marriage and divorce in Sweden: An update with data up to 2012. *Finnish Yearbook of Population Research*, 50, 21–30. https://doi.org/10.23979/fypr.52483.
113. Jones, G. W., & Gubhaju, B. (2009). Factors influencing changes in mean age at first marriage and proportions never marrying in the low-fertility countries of East and Southeast Asia. *Asian Population Studies*, 5(3), 237–265. https://doi.org/10.1080/17441730903351487.
114. McDonald, P. (2000). Gender equity in theories of fertility transition. *Population and Development Review*, 26(3), 427–439. https://doi.org/10.1111/j.1728-4457.2000.00427.x.
115. Barro, R. J., & Lee, J. W. (2013). A new data set of educational attainment in the world, 1950–2010. *Journal of Development Economics*, 104, 184–198. https://doi.org/10.1016/j.jdeveco.2012.10.001.
116. Third City. (2021). We discovered the odds of finding love—And how to improve them. https://thirdcity.co.uk/one-in-562-the-odds-of-finding-love/. Accessed 29 May 2021.
117. Fletcher, G. J., Kerr, P. S., Li, N. P., & Valentine, K. A. (2014). Predicting romantic interest and decisions in the very early stages of mate selection: Standards, accuracy, and sex differences. *Personality and Social Psychology Bulletin*, 40(4), 540–550. https://doi.org/10.1177/0146167213519481.
118. Finkel, E. J., & Eastwick, P. W. (2009). Arbitrary social norms influence sex differences in romantic selectivity. *Psychological Science*, 20(10), 1290–1295. https://doi.org/10.1111/j.1467-9280.2009.02439.x
119. "Worst online dater". 2021 (2015, March 25). Tinder Experiments II: Guys, unless you are really hot you are probably better off not wasting your time on Tinder—A quantitative socio-economic study. https://medium.com/@worstonlinedater/tinder-experiments-ii-guys-unless-you-are-really-hot-you-are-probably-better-off-not-wasting-your-2ddf370a6e9a. Accessed 29 May 2021.

120. OKCupid. 2021 (2009, November 17). Your looks and your inbox. https://theblog.okcupid.com/your-looks-and-your-inbox-8715c0f1561e. Accessed 29 May 2021.
121. Koorevaar, A. M. L., Comijs, H. C., Dhondt, A. D. F., van Marwijk, H. W. J., van der Mast, R. C., Naarding, P., et al. (2013). Big Five personality and depression diagnosis, severity and age of onset in older adults. *Journal of Affective Disorders*, 151(1), 178–185. https://doi.org/10.1016/j.jad.2013.05.075.
122. Sutin, A. R., Costa, P. T., Miech, R., & Eaton, W. W. (2009). Personality and career success: Concurrent and longitudinal relations. *European Journal of Personality*, 23(2), 71–84. https://doi.org/10.1002/per.704.
123. Gelissen, J., & de Graaf, P. M. (2006). Personality, social background, and occupational career success. *Social Science Research Network*, 35, 702–706. https://doi.org/10.1016/j.ssresearch.2005.06.005.
124. Judge, T. A., Higgins, C. A., Thoresen, C. J., & Barrick, M. R. (1999). The Big Five personality traits, general mental ability, and career success across the life span. *Personnel Psychology*, 52(3), 621–652. https://doi.org/10.1111/j.1744-6570.1999.tb00174.x.
125. Reis, O., Dörnte, M., & von der Lippe, H. (2011). Neuroticism, social support, and the timing of first parenthood: A prospective study. *Personality and Individual Differences*, 50(3), 381–386. https://doi.org/10.1016/j.paid.2010.10.028.
126. Skirbekk, V., & Blekesaune, M. (2013). Personality traits increasingly important for male fertility: Evidence from Norway. *European Journal of Personality*, 28(6), 521–552. https://doi.org/10.1002/per.1936.
127. Hessel, R. (2017). 11 hours a day in front of a screen. This is what it's doing to your eyes. World Economic Forum. https://www.weforum.org/agenda/2016/09/staring-down-the-dangers-of-the-digital-workplace/. Accessed 29 May 2021.
128. Vilhelmson, B., Elldér, E., & Thulin, E. (2018). What did we do when the Internet wasn't around? Variation in free-time activities among three young-adult cohorts from 1990/1991, 2000/2001, and 2010/2011. *New Media & Society*, 20(8), 2898–2916. https://doi.org/10.1177/1461444817737296.
129. Sayer, L. C. (2016). Trends in women's and men's time use, 1965–2012: Back to the future? In S. McHale, V. King, J. Van Hook, & A. Booth (Eds.), *Gender and couple relationships* (pp. 43–77). Cham: Springer. https://doi.org/10.1007/978-3-319-21635-5_2.

130. Zhang, M., Tillman, D. A., & An, S. A. (2017). Global prevalence of sleep deprivation in students and heavy media use. *Education and Information Technologies*, 22(1), 239–254. https://doi.org/10.1007/s10639-015-9440-2.
131. Limke-McLean, A. (2018). The cost of war: Attachment and MMO gamers' online and offline relationships. *Journal of Relationships Research*, 9. https://doi.org/10.1017/jrr.2018.14.
132. Jung, A., & Schuppe, H. C. (2007). Influence of genital heat stress on semen quality in humans. *Andrologia*, 39(6), 203–215. https://doi.org/10.1111/j.1439-0272.2007.00794.x.
133. Adams, J. A., Galloway, T. S., Mondal, D., Esteves, S. C., & Mathews, F. (2014). Effect of mobile telephones on sperm quality: A systematic review and meta-analysis. *Environment International*, 70, 106–112. https://doi.org/10.1016/j.envint.2014.04.015.
134. Kato, T. A., Kanba, S., & Teo, A. R. (2018). Hikikomori: Experience in Japan and international relevance. *World Psychiatry: Official Journal of the World Psychiatric Association*, 17(1), 105–106. https://doi.org/10.1002/wps.20497.
135. Kato, T. A., Shinfuku, N., Sartorius, N., & Kanba, S. (2011). Are Japan's hikikomori and depression in young people spreading abroad? *The Lancet*, 378(9796), 1070. https://doi.org/10.1016/S0140-6736(11)61475-X.
136. Harding, C. (2018). Hikikomori. *The Lancet Psychiatry*, 5(1), 28–29. https://doi.org/10.1016/S2215-0366(17)30491-1.
137. Bucksch, J., Sigmundova, D., Hamrik, Z., Troped, P. J., Melkevik, O., Ahluwalia, N., et al. (2016). International trends in adolescent screen-time behaviors from 2002 to 2010. *Journal of Adolescent Health*, 58(4), 417–425. https://doi.org/10.1016/j.jadohealth.2015.11.014.
138. Algan, Y., & Fortin, N. M. (2018). Computer gaming and the gender math gap: Cross-country evidence among teenagers. In S. W. Polachek, & K. Tatsiramos (Eds.), *Transitions through the labor market: Work, occupation, earnings and retirement* (pp. 183–228). Bingley: Emerald Publishing Limited. https://doi.org/10.1108/S0147-912120180000046006.
139. Hamilton, F., & La Diega, G. N. (Eds.). (2020). *Same-sex relationships, law and social change*. London: Routledge.
140. Copen, C. E., Chandra, A., & Febo-Vazquez, I. (2016). Sexual behavior, sexual attraction, and sexual orientation among adults aged 18–44 in the United States: Data from the 2011–2003 National Survey of Family

Growth. *National Health Statistics Reports*, 88. https://stacks.cdc.gov/view/cdc/37398.
141. Statistics Canada. (2015). Same-sex couples and sexual orientation... by the numbers. https://www.statcan.gc.ca/eng/dai/smr08/2015/smr08_203_2015. Accessed 29 May 2021.
142. Sandfort, T. G., Bakker, F., Schellevis, F. G., & Vanwesenbeeck, I. (2006). Sexual orientation and mental and physical health status: Findings from a Dutch population survey. *American Journal of Public Health*, 96(6), 1119–1125. https://doi.org/10.2105/AJPH.2004.058891.
143. Eydal, G. B., & Gíslason, I. V. (2014). Family policies: The case of Iceland. In M. Robila (Ed.), *Handbook of family policies across the globe* (pp. 109–124). New York: Springer.
144. Trandafir, M. (2014). The effect of same-sex marriage laws on different-sex marriage: Evidence from The Netherlands. *Demography*, 51(1), 317–340. https://doi.org/10.1007/s13524-013-0248-7.
145. Priskorn, L., Holmboe, S., Jacobsen, R., Jensen, T., Lassen, T., & Skakkebaek, N. (2012). Increasing trends in childlessness in recent birth cohorts–a registry-based study of the total Danish male population born from 1945 to 1980. *International Journal of Andrology*, 35(3), 449–455. https://doi.org/10.1111/j.1365-2605.2012.01265.x.
146. Gerkowicz, S., Crawford, S., Hipp, H., Boulet, S., Kissin, D., & Kawwass, J. (2017). Assisted reproductive technology with donor sperm: National trends and perinatal outcomes. *Fertility and Sterility*, 108(3), e72.

13

Money Matters: The Economics of Fertility

When people consider whether they should have a(nother) child, they often consider whether they can afford it. High childrearing costs and economic insecurity tend to delay and/or depress fertility, but not always. In this chapter, I review economic theories of fertility, some of the costs associated with having children, and how one's own economic situation and the economy at large are related to fertility.

Economic Approaches to Fertility

Economic approaches construe fertility behavior as the outcome of a rational decision-making process that aims to maximize a person, couple's and family's well-being, taking into account both the costs and benefits of having a child at a particular moment in time. Parents are thought to derive well-being or "utility" from both the quantity and "quality" of their offspring (e.g., their children's educational attainment and potential for labor market success) [1, 2]. Economic theories of childbearing often focus exclusively on the *financial* costs and benefits of childrearing (and not, e.g., the psychological costs and benefits)

V. Skirbekk, *Decline and Prosper!*,
https://doi.org/10.1007/978-3-030-91611-4_13

and are sometimes based on the unrealistic assumption that fertility is perfectly controllable (recall that four out of ten global pregnancies are unplanned). While economic approaches to fertility clearly have their weaknesses, they are nevertheless helpful for describing and predicting fertility outcomes given that potential parents do tend to make fertility decisions that seem economically feasible and also bring about the most favorable balance of costs and benefits.

From an economic perspective, children can be seen (a) as by-products of other desirable activities (marriage, sex); (b) as consumption "goods" which directly increase parents' well-being (e.g., through children's provision of paid and domestic work, families representing a basic form of social security at older ages, better quality of life); and/or (c) as investments which indirectly increase parents' well-being (e.g., the possibility of having grandchildren, social interaction, practical help, and possibly financial support to parents in old age) [2]. Potential parents must then weigh these benefits against the direct costs (e.g., the costs of additional housing and food, day care, and education) and indirect costs (e.g., lower maternal labor force participation, career interruption, stress, and time use), which may mean reducing consumption of other goods.

Whereas children once contributed to the family economy at a relatively young age, in modern economies children represent a financial burden for a very long period, often for more than twenty years [3, 4]. Furthermore, as incomes and particularly women's participation in the labor market increase, so have the *opportunity costs* of having children (i.e., the benefits foregone when one chooses to have children). Hence, the loss in consumption associated with childrearing tends to increase during the demographic transition [5, 6]. In other words, having children requires a greater economic sacrifice. Fertility decline may therefore act as a response to peoples' decreasing demand for children compared to other goods [7, 8], or indicate a shift in preferences from many children toward fewer, but higher "quality".

How Much Do Children Cost?

Having children comes along with many obvious financial costs, including everything from the costs of pre-natal care, childbirth, food, diapers, clothing, health care, housing, day care, and education. The opportunity costs of children include not only the loss of income incurred when a parent stops working or reduces working hours to care for children, but also the loss of potential income incurred when a parent takes a lower-paying job in order to avoid work-family conflict, when career prospects decline as a result of having children, and/or reductions in future pension payments.

The Australian Tooth Fairy paid twice as much per tooth in 2015 ($6) as in 2005 ($3). That's about $120 in tooth fairy money per child [9].

It is difficult to estimate and compare how much children cost in different countries for several reasons. First, the costs of children vary according to parental preferences and standards, which may also change as a result of having children. For instance, families with more income also tend to spend more on children, particularly for child care, education, and miscellaneous expenses [10]. Cultural norms also influence what is considered "essential" for a child, how much and on what parents spend, and whether the public or the private sector pays for child care. It is also difficult to determine which proportion of goods shared by the entire family (e.g., housing, a bigger car) should be attributed to a child. Bigger families generate economies of scale, so that the cost of having each additional child may be progressively less. Economies of scale occur especially after the birth of a third child and are mainly due to reduced marginal increases in housing expenditure from having an additional child [11].

Several approaches have been used to estimate the financial costs of having children. One approach is to calculate the cost of a standard "basket" of goods and services that a child of a given age is deemed to need.

Another approach is to compare the household expenditures of individuals/couples with and without children who have the same standard of living. Finally, opinion surveys can be used to measure the *subjective* costs of children, that is, how much people believe children cost. One major finding is that a child under 14 consumes the equivalent of 20 to 30% of the household budget of a childless couple [11]. Importantly, the estimate includes neither the opportunity costs of having children, nor the expenses associated with supporting an adolescent and/or young adult child (e.g., tertiary education). People in low fertility countries often perceive having (more) children as too expensive. Many people in Japan [12] and China [13] cite the high cost of children as a key reason for why they do not plan to have (more) children.

Given the lack of a universally accepted method for calculating the costs of childrearing, it is not necessarily valid nor helpful to compare estimates of the total cost of childrearing across countries. It is much more feasible to estimate and compare the costs of particular expenses, such as food or day care. Food is the second largest childrearing expense in the United States [10]. In most high-income countries, feeding children is relatively cheap: In 2018 in the United States, for instance, households in the middle income quintile spent just about 15% of their income on food [14]. In contrast, in many developing countries such as the countries in sub-Saharan Africa, the majority of households spend about half of the household budget on food [15]. In richer countries where women and especially mothers typically participate in the labor market, day care is a major childrearing expense. In the OECD countries in 2018, the cost of day care as a percentage of household income for a couple with average wages ranged from under 5% (Czech Republic, Korea, Austria, Cyprus, Italy, Estonia, Hungary, Sweden, Germany, Iceland, Greece, and Spain) to over 30% (Australia, United States, United Kingdom, and New Zealand) [16].

Over the past fifty years, the average cost of attending a four-year university in the United States has almost tripled from 10,561 USD per year in 1963–1964 to 28,123 USD per year in 2018–2019 (inflation adjusted; in 2018–2019 dollars) [17].

The age at which children become financially independent also varies across countries. Using data from 42 countries, one study examined the age at which the average person began producing more than he or she consumed (the age at which the so-called *life cycle surplus* began) [18]. This study considered people's income from paid work as well as the estimated monetary value of any unpaid labor in the home. The age at which the life cycle surplus began ranged from 22 years in Cambodia and Colombia to 35 years in Ghana (see Fig. 13.1). For the majority of the analyzed countries, production did not exceed consumption until the second half of the 20s. One reason why people now tend to consume more than they earn until their mid-20s is because people are spending more time in school.

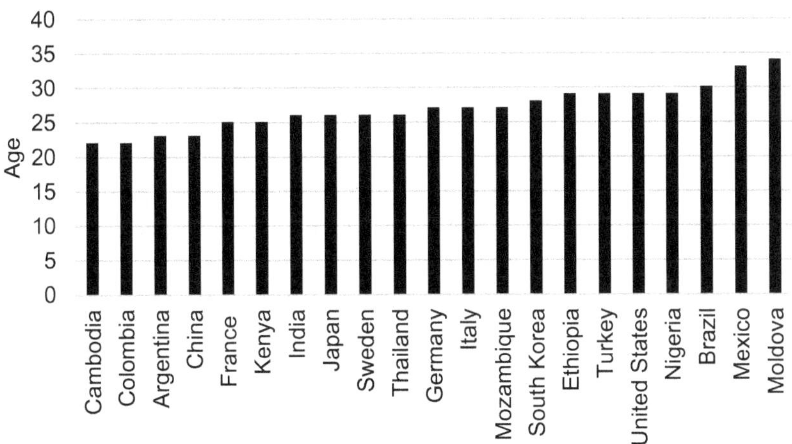

Fig. 13.1 Age at which the life cycle surplus begins in different countries. Own analyses based on data from the National Transfer Accounts Project [www.ntaccounts.org]. Cross-country comparability may be limited due to methodological differences and when data was collected, which ranged from 1997 to 2016

High Costs of Children Can Drive Down Fertility

> *"It would have been nice to have children and start a family, but after a lot of soul-searching, I decided against it. It would mean too much sacrifice and suffering on my part. It's a shame, because I love kids, but they're luxuries I can't afford. I'll just have to make do with my nieces and nephews."*
>
> *—Yoo Nara, age 37, resident of Seoul, South Korea in 2021 [19]*

High and increasing costs of having children are thought to be a major reason why fertility declines and stays low. Already in eighteenth- and nineteenth-century Sweden, young adults—particularly those from landless and semi-landless families—responded to moderate and large increases in food prices by reducing their fertility [20]. Another study from Bangladesh concluded that the growing direct and opportunity costs of raising children did more to reduce fertility than either mortality decline or cultural change [21]. A study of 11 European countries found that fertility tends to be higher in more rural and more affordable regions [22]. The high cost of children's education has been identified as an important driver of low fertility in East Asia [23], where the cost of raising and educating children has become so high that many East Asian couples decide to have no or just one child [24].

One of the biggest costs of childrearing is housing, which accounts for the largest share of total childrearing expenses in the United States [10]. Especially in societies where establishing a household separate from one's parents is seen as a pre-requisite for marriage and starting a family, high housing costs may be one reason that people have delayed and decreased fertility. Housing prices in many urban regions around the world including in the countries of South America, India, and France have increased rapidly since the 1980s [25–27]. The rise in housing prices has disproportionately affected younger people, as they are the least likely to own a house, have a high and secure income, or be in a stable relationship where housing costs can be shared; they are also often unable to obtain a mortgage [28, 29]. The high cost of housing may explain why fertility tends to be low in urban centers. Housing costs and young adults' incomes influence when young people move out of the parental home and the number of children they have [30, 31]. Increasing housing prices have been related to fertility decline in Malaysia [32]. Low housing security has been shown to lead to a delay in having a first child in Italy [33]. In the Nordic countries, people who have more housing space available are more likely to have (additional) children [34–36], while high housing prices in Britain have been shown to be detrimental to the fertility of people who rent [37].

There is also some evidence that fertility is higher among groups for whom the (relative) costs of childrearing are lower. The opportunity costs of having children are particularly high for highly educated women who have high earning potential but are, as women, often expected to assume primary responsibility for child care. One study concluded that the opportunity costs of having children are more than three times as important as low wealth levels for explaining low fertility among highly educated American women [38]. Access to high-quality and low-cost day care is thought to be a central driver of fertility in low fertility countries, especially for highly educated women who might otherwise have to make major career sacrifices in order to have children. The high availability of low-cost day care is thought to explain why there is little difference between the fertility of people with less and more education in the Nordic countries, while the high cost of day care may explain why fertility is highly and inversely related to education in North America and East Asia [39–42]. An increase in child care availability in Japan from 2000 to 2010 led to a small but significant increase in the fertility rate of women aged 25–39 living in regions where the propensity for women to work was high [43]. Another analysis based on German data from 1998 to 2010 similarly concluded that a 10 percentage point increase in public child care coverage was related to a 3.2% increase in the birth rate [44], though some studies have not found evidence that fertility change in low fertility settings is related to child care access [45]. Whether or not the availability of affordable daycare affects fertility depends upon parents' willingness to entrust an institution to take care of their children. Trust in child care institutions may be low in some contexts, including in many Italian regions [46].

Do Richer People Have More Children?

In contexts where the costs of childrearing constrain fertility, it would seem reasonable to assume that people with more financial resources would want and have more children (or, as economists would put it, greater financial resources should go along with a greater demand for children). The relationship between financial resources and fertility is, however, far from straightforward. For one thing, an individual's financial resources are often highly correlated with his or her education, but financial resources and education can have opposite relationships with fertility. In one of my own studies, I combined data from several hundred studies from around the world to analyze the relationship between wealth/income and education on the one hand, and fertility on the other hand. I found that individuals and groups with higher levels of education often had fewer children than their less-educated peers, although there was less of a difference in more developed countries. In contrast, individuals and groups with higher wealth and income tended to have about the same fertility as individuals and groups who were less well-off [47]. Studies that assess the relationship between financial resource and fertility without controlling for education may therefore come to erroneous conclusions. The relationship between financial resources and fertility also appears to depend on whether one considers wealth (e.g., accumulated assets and inherited wealth) or income. Both greater wealth and higher income make it easier to afford (additional) children, but only higher income is associated with higher opportunity costs [48].

Of course, people base their fertility decisions not only on their current, but also on their expected future economic situation. Young people tend to have uncertain employment, also in regions with strong welfare states such as Europe [49–51]. The precarious employment of many young people at least partially explains why current cohorts of young people in wealthier countries tend to delay fertility to their late 20s and 30s [52, 53]. According to classic economic models of work division, women contribute more to "household production" (e.g., taking care of the home and children) while men provide more economic resources, especially after having children [54, 55]. Economic uncertainty may thus depress men's fertility more than women's fertility [56]. In some settings, however, economic insecurity actually may encourage people to have *more* children [57, 58]. In contexts where there are few opportunities for high-income jobs and no welfare provisions, children can represent a basic form of social security.

It's Still the Economy, Stupid

Fertility is not only affected by an individual's own economic situation, but also by the regional and national economy as a whole. In general, fertility tends to be pro-cyclical; that is, people tend to want and also have fewer children during economic recessions. Unexpected economic "booms" can increase fertility; as an example, improved economic conditions from the fracking boom in the United States appear to have led to increases in both non-marital and marital fertility [59].

Many people do not marry before they can afford to do so, and marriage among those with lower education and lower income in the United States tends to decline when their economic situation has deteriorated [60]. The Great Recession starting in 2008 had particularly large and negative effect on the fertility of young people, who often chose to postpone or depress childbearing [61, 62]. Rapid decreases in housing wealth have also been found to significantly reduce the likelihood of having another child [63]. One study found that a sudden decrease in fertility may in fact *predict* economic downturn, potentially because individuals perceive negative changes in the economy and accordingly reduce their fertility before the downturn can be picked up by standard economic indicators [64]. The effects of economic downturn on fertility are typically limited to the short term, however. Once the economy has recovered, people begin having children again, assuming that they are still within their reproductive windows.

In some settings, people and particularly women with less education [61, 65, 66] tend to have *more* children during recessions. A recession may reduce the opportunity costs of having a child for women who are already unemployed and/or see little potential for career advancement. This is consistent with economic fertility theory asserting that lower male income tends to decrease fertility, while lower female income tends to increase fertility [1, 67]. The stress and despair experienced during a recession may also sometimes lead to an increase in unprotected sex [59]. In Nigeria, economic recessions have been found to reduce contraception use and potentially increased fertility in Lagos, the capital [68].

Making Childbearing More Affordable

In contexts where fertility represents a highly controlled and purposeful decision, economic models do a good job explaining when people have children, and how many children they have. Whereas once children provided a net economic benefit to the family already at a young age and acted as a key source of economic security, today having children typically necessitates major financial investment and foregoing consumption for more than two decades. Housing, education, food, and day care represent just a few of the costs of childrearing. While it is difficult to quantify how much children cost, there is enough evidence to conclude that many of the costs of childrearing have increased over time (e.g., housing) and also that the costs of childrearing vary substantially across countries. The possibility of financially supporting a large family—or even a small family—may soon be out of reach for much of the population.

In most countries today, people generally have more children when the costs of childbearing are lower, when they are economically secure, and when the economy is going well. Exploding housing prices and recessions often affect young people the most, due to their insecure positions on the labor market and low incomes. Traditionally, men's economic resources and economic security have mattered more for fertility than women's, but that is probably changing as more women participate in the work force, take on highly paid jobs, and make essential financial contributions to the family.

In the low fertility countries, policies that reduce the explicit and opportunity costs of childbearing and make housing more affordable might help more people realize their own fertility ideals. In the high fertility countries, stronger welfare systems might reduce fertility by displacing the role of children as an informal source of economic security. Clearly, though, costs are just one determining factor; measures that make childbearing more affordable and/or less necessary as sources of financial security may not affect some of the other major determinants of fertility such as having a stable partnership or the cultural/individual valuation of children.

References

1. Becker, G. S. (1991). *A treatise on the family*. Cambridge, MA: Harvard University Press.
2. Werding, M. (2014). Children are costly, but raising them may pay: The economic approach to fertility. *Demographic Research*, S16(8), 253–276. https://doi.org/10.4054/DemRes.2014.30.
3. Buchmann, M. C., & Kriesi, I. (2011). Transition to adulthood in Europe. *Annual Review of Sociology*, 37, 481–503. https://doi.org/10.1146/annurev-soc-081309-150212.
4. Patton, G. C., Olsson, C. A., Skirbekk, V., Saffery, R., Wlodek, M. E., Azzopardi, P. S., et al. (2018). Adolescence and the next generation. *Nature*, 554(7693), 458–466. https://doi.org/10.1038/nature25759.
5. Lee, R. (2003). The demographic transition: Three centuries of fundamental change. *The Journal of Economic Perspectives*, 17(4), 167–190. https://doi.org/10.1257/089533003772034943.
6. Gustafsson, S. (2001). Optimal age at motherhood: Theoretical and empirical considerations on postponement of maternity in Europe. *Journal of Population Economics*, 14(2), 225–247. https://doi.org/10.1007/s001480000051.
7. Schultz, T. P. (1974). *Fertility determinants: A theory, evidence, and application to policy evaluation*. Santa Monica, CA: RAND.
8. Becker, G. S. (1964). *Human capital*. Chicago: University of Chicago Press.
9. Core Data Research, & Real Insurance. (2015). The Australian Family Survey Data Report. https://assets-au-01.kc-usercontent.com/1f0619a0-4164-0241-3335-de16f4a2d9f3/f796583a-559b-4cf0-ac18-e43ebc455b8e/media-release-real-aussie-families-full-report.pdf. Accessed 28 May 2021.

10. Lino, M., Kuczynski, K., Rodriguez, N., & Schap, T. (2017). Expenditures on children by families, 2015. Miscellaneous Report No. 1528-2015.Washington, DC: United States Department of Agriculture, & Center for Nutrition Policy and Promotion. https://fns-prod.azureedge.net/sites/default/files/crc2015_March2017.pdf. Accessed 28 May 2021.
11. Letablier, M.-T., Luci, A., Math, A., & Thévenon, O. (2009). The costs of raising children and the effectiveness of policies to support parenthood in European countries: A literature review. E. Communities. https://ec.europa.eu/social/BlobServlet?docId=2268&langId=en. Accessed 28 May 2021.
12. Skirbekk, V., Matsukura, R., & Ogawa, N. (2015). What are the prospects for continued low fertility in Japan? In N. Ogawa, & I. H. Shah (Eds.), *Low fertility and reproductive health in East Asia* (pp. 75–100). Dordrecht: Springer.
13. Hancock, T. (2018, January 18). China births fall despite relaxation of one-child policy. *Financial Times*. Retrieved from https://www.ft.com/content/835c057e-fc5c-11e7-9b32-d7d59aace167
14. United States Department of Agriculture / Economic Research Service. (2018). Food spending and share of disposable income spent on food across U.S. households, 2018. https://www.ers.usda.gov/data-products/chart-gallery/gallery/chart-detail/?chartId=58372. Accessed 28 May 2021.
15. Lozano-Gracia, N., & Young, C. (2014). Housing consumption and urbanization. Washington, DC: W. B. Group. http://documents.shihang.org/curated/zh/998081468003944551/pdf/WPS7112.pdf. Accessed 28 May 2021.
16. OECD. (2019). Net childcare costs. https://www.oecd-ilibrary.org/content/data/e328a9ee-en. Accessed 28 May 2021.
17. National Center for Education Statistics. (2019). Table 330.10. Average undergraduate tuition and fees and room and board rates charged for full-time students in degree-granting postsecondary institutions, by level and control of institution: Selected years, 1963–64 through 2018–19. United States Department of Education. https://nces.ed.gov/programs/digest/d19/tables/dt19_330.10.asp. Accessed 28 May 2021.
18. Lee, R., & Mason, A. (2011). *Population aging and the generational economy: A global perspective*. Cheltenham, UK: Edward Elgar.
19. McCurry, J. (2021, January 15). 'Luxuries I can't afford': Why fewer women in South Korea are having children. *The Guardian*. Retrieved from https://www.theguardian.com/world/2021/jan/15/luxuries-i-cant-afford-why-fewer-women-in-south-korea-are-having-children

20. Bengtsson, T., & Dribe, M. (2006). Deliberate control in a natural fertility population: Southern Sweden, 1766–1864. *Demography*, 43(4), 727–746. https://doi.org/10.1353/dem.2006.0030.
21. Shenk, M. K., Towner, M. C., Kress, H. C., & Alam, N. (2013). A model comparison approach shows stronger support for economic models of fertility decline. *Proceedings of the National Academy of Sciences*, 110(20), 8045–8050. https://doi.org/10.1073/pnas.1217029110.
22. Riederer, B., & Buber-Ennser, I. (2019). Regional context and realization of fertility intentions: The role of the urban context. *Regional studies*, 53(12), 1669–1679.
23. Anderson, T., & Kohler, H.-P. (2013). Education fever and the East Asian fertility puzzle: A case study of low fertility in South Korea. *Asian Population Studies*, 9(2), 196–215. https://doi.org/10.1080/17441730.2013.797293.
24. Tan, P. L., Morgan, S. P., & Zagheni, E. (2016). A case for "reverse one-child" policies in Japan and South Korea? Examining the link between education costs and lowest-low fertility. *Population Research and Policy Review*, 35(3), 327–350. https://doi.org/10.1007/s11113-016-9390-4.
25. Lennartz, C., Arundel, R., & Ronald, R. (2016). Younger adults and homeownership in Europe through the global financial crisis. *Population, Space and Place*, 22(8), 823–835. https://doi.org/10.1002/psp.1961.
26. Knoll, K., Schularick, M., & Steger, T. (2017). No price like home: Global house prices, 1870–2012. *American Economic Review*, 107(2), 331–353. https://doi.org/10.1257/aer.20150501.
27. Slater, T. (2017). Planetary rent gaps. *Antipode*, 49(S1), 114–137. https://doi.org/10.1111/anti.12185.
28. Whitehead, C., & Williams, P. (2017). Changes in the regulation and control of mortgage markets and access to owner-occupation among younger households. OECD Social, Employment, and Migration Working Papers No. 196. Paris: OECD. https://read.oecd-ilibrary.org/social-issues-migration-health/changes-in-the-regulation-and-control-of-mortgage-markets-and-access-to-owner-occupation-among-younger-households_e16ab00e-en#page2. Accessed 28 May 2021.
29. OECD. (2008). *Growing unequal? Income distribution and poverty in OECD countries*. Paris: OECD. http://www.oecd.org/els/socialpoliciesanddata/growingunequalincomedistributionandpovertyinoecdcountries.htm. Accessed 28 May 2021.
30. Fukuda, S. (2009). Leaving the parental home in post-war Japan: Demographic changes, stem-family norms and the transition to adulthood.

Demographic Research, 20, 731–816. https://doi.org/10.4054/DemRes.2009.20.30.

31. Cobb-Clark, D. A. (2008). Leaving home: What economics has to say about the living arrangements of young Australians. *Australian Economic Review*, 41(2), 160–176. https://doi.org/10.1111/j.1467-8462.2008.00488.x.
32. Li, W. W. (2017). House price determinants and their impact on consumption and fertility. PhD thesis, Universiti Putra Malaysia. https://core.ac.uk/reader/227536383.
33. Vignoli, D., Rinesi, F., & Mussino, E. (2013). A home to plan the first child? Fertility intentions and housing conditions in Italy. *Population, Space and Place*, 19(1), 60–71. https://doi.org/10.1002/psp.1716.
34. Kulu, H., Vikat, A., & Andersson, G. (2007). Settlement size and fertility in the Nordic countries. *Population Studies*, 61(3), 265–285. https://doi.org/10.1080/00324720701571749.
35. Kulu, H. (2013). Why do fertility levels vary between urban and rural areas? *Regional Studies*, 47(6), 895–912. https://doi.org/10.1080/00343404.2011.581276.
36. Ström, S. (2010). Housing and first births in Sweden, 1972–2005. *Housing Studies*, 25(4), 509–526. https://doi.org/10.1080/02673031003711519.
37. Aksoy, C. (2015). Short-term effects of house prices on birth rates. EBRD Working Paper No. 192. https://papers.ssrn.com/sol3/papers.cfm?abstract_id=2846173. Accessed 28 May 2021.
38. Baudin, T., De La Croix, D., & Gobbi, P. E. (2015). Fertility and childlessness in the United States. *The American Economic Review*, 105(6), 1852–1882. https://doi.org/10.1257/aer.20120926.
39. Kravdal, Ø. (2016). Not so low fertility in Norway—A result of affluence, liberal values, gender-equality Ideals, and the welfare state. In R. Rindfuss, & M. Choe (Eds.), *Low fertility, institutions, and their policies* (pp. 13–47). Cham: Springer. https://doi.org/10.1007/978-3-319-32997-0_2.
40. Thévenon, O. (2011). Family policies in OECD countries: A comparative analysis. *Population and Development Review*, 37(1), 57–87. https://doi.org/10.1111/j.1728-4457.2011.00390.x.
41. Brauner-Otto, S. R. (2016). Canadian fertility trends and policies: A story of regional variation. In R. Rindfuss, & M. Choe (Eds.), *Low fertility, institutions, and their policies* (pp. 99–130). Cham: Springer.

42. Lam, G., Yan, Y., & Tu, E. J.-C. (2017). Significance of family-friendly measures on fertility in Hong Kong. *Asian Education and Development Studies*, 6(2), 125–137. https://doi.org/10.1108/AEDS-02-2016-0017.
43. Fukai, T. (2017). Childcare availability and fertility: Evidence from municipalities in Japan. *Journal of the Japanese and International Economies*, 43, 1–18. https://doi.org/10.1016/j.jjie.2016.11.003.
44. Bauernschuster, S., Hener, T., & Rainer, H. (2013). Does the expansion of public child care increase birth rates? Evidence from a low-fertility country. Ifo Working Paper No. 158. Munich: Leibniz Institute for Economic Research at the University of Munich. https://www.ifo.de/DocDL/IfoWorkingPaper-158.pdf. Accessed 28 May 2021.
45. Lee, G. H., & Lee, S. P. (2014). Childcare availability, fertility and female labor force participation in Japan. *Journal of the Japanese and International Economies*, 32, 71–85. https://doi.org/10.1016/j.jjie.2014.01.002.
46. Aassve, A., Billari, F. C., & Pessin, L. (2016). Trust and fertility dynamics. *Social Forces*, 1–30. https://doi.org/10.1093/sf/sow080.
47. Skirbekk, V. (2008). Fertility trends by social status. *Demographic Research*, 18(5), 145–180. https://doi.org/10.4054/DemRes.2008.18.5.
48. Ager, P., Herz, B., & Brueckner, M. (2019). Structural change and the fertility transition. *Review of Economics and Statistics*, 1–45. https://doi.org/10.1162/rest_a_00851.
49. Willcocks, L. P., & Lacity, M. C. (2015, September 15). Businesses will increasingly use robots to deal with the explosion of data. *LSE Business Review*. Retrieved from https://blogs.lse.ac.uk/businessreview/2015/09/15/businesses-will-increasingly-use-robots-to-deal-with-the-explosion-of-data/.
50. Autor, D. H. (2015). Why are there still so many jobs? The history and future of workplace automation. *The Journal of Economic Perspectives*, 29(3), 3–30. https://doi.org/10.1257/jep.29.3.3.
51. Brynjolfsson, E., & McAfee, A. (2015, July/August). Will humans go the way of horses? Labor in the second machine age. *Foreign Affairs*, p. 8. Retrieved from https://www.foreignaffairs.com/articles/2015-06-16/will-humans-go-way-horses.
52. Nathan, M., & Pardo, I. (2017). Fertility postponement and regional patterns of dispersion in age at first birth. *Comparative Population Studies*, 44, 1–17. https://doi.org/10.12765/CPoS-2019-07.
53. Tanturri, M. L. (2013). Why fewer babies? Understanding and responding to low fertility in Europe. In A. Abela, & J. Walker (Eds.), *Contemporary*

issues in family studies (pp. 136–150). John Wiley & Sons. https://doi.org/10.1002/9781118320990.ch10.
54. England, P., & Farkas, G. (2017). *Households, employment, and gender: A social, economic, and demographic view*. New York: Routledge.
55. Lundberg, S. (2008). Gender and household desicion-making. In F. Bettio, & A. Verashchagina (Eds.), *Frontiers in the economics of gender* (pp. 116–134). New York: Routledge.
56. Tölke, A., & Diewald, M. (2003). Insecurities in employment and occupational careers and their impact on the transition to fatherhood in Western Germany. *Demographic Research*, 9, 41–68. https://doi.org/10.4054/DemRes.2003.9.3.
57. Schoumaker, B. (2017). African fertility changes. In H. Groth, & J. F. May (Eds.), *Africa's population: In search of a demographic dividend* (pp. 197–211). Springer International.
58. Garenne, M. (2017). Record high fertility in sub-Saharan Africa in a comparative perspective. *African Population Studies*, 31(2). https://doi.org/10.11564/31-2-1043.
59. Kearney, M. S., & Wilson, R. (2018). Male earnings, marriageable men, and nonmarital fertility: Evidence from the fracking boom. *Review of Economics and Statistics*, 100(4), 678–690. https://EconPapers.repec.org/RePEc:tpr:restat:v:100:y:2018:i:4:p:678-690.
60. Cherlin, A. J. (2014). *Labor's love lost: The rise and fall of the working-class family in America*. New York: Russell Sage Foundation.
61. Sobotka, T., Skirbekk, V., & Philipov, D. (2011). Economic recession and fertility in the developed world. *Population and Development Review*, 37(2), 267–306. https://doi.org/10.1111/j.1728-4457.2011.00411.x.
62. Cherlin, A., Cumberworth, E., Morgan, S. P., & Wimer, C. (2013). The effects of the Great Recession on family structure and fertility. *The Annals of the American Academy of Political and Social Science*, 650(1), 214–231. https://doi.org/10.1177/0002716213500643.
63. Lovenheim, M. F., & Mumford, K. J. (2012). Do family wealth shocks affect fertility choices? Evidence from the housing market. *Review of Economics and Statistics*, 95(2), 464–475. https://doi.org/10.1162/REST_a_00266.
64. Buckles, K., Hungerman, D., & Lugauer, S. (2021). Is fertility a leading economic indicator? *The Economic Journal*, 131(634), 541–565. https://doi.org/10.1093/ej/ueaa068.

65. Liepmann, H. (2018). The impact of a negative labor demand shock on fertility. *Labour Economics*, 54, 210–224. https://doi.org/10.1016/j.labeco.2018.07.003.
66. Wood, J., Vergauwen, J., & Neels, K. (2015). Economic conditions and variation in first birth hazards in 22 European countries between 1970 and 2005. In M. Koenraad, K. Neels, C. Timmerman, & J. Haers (Eds.), *Population change in Europe, the Middle-East and North Africa: Beyond the demographic divide*. London and New York: Routledge.
67. Day, C. (2018). Inverse J effect of economic growth on fertility: A model of gender wages and maternal time substitution. *Journal of Family and Economic Issues*, 39, 1–11. https://doi.org/10.1007/s10834-018-9578-3.
68. Wright, K., Wright, E., Ottun, T., Oyebode, M., Sarma, V., & Chung, S. (2018). Economic recession and family planning uptake: Review of a Nigerian health institution. *Tropical Journal of Obstetrics and Gynaecology*, 35(2), 147–152. https://doi.org/10.4103/TJOG.TJOG_82_17.

14

Fertility in the Aftermath of Disaster

Natural disasters and ethno-political conflicts not only put people's immediate physical and mental health at risk, but also their desire and opportunity to reproduce. Sometimes natural disasters and conflicts lead to earlier and higher fertility, and sometimes they delay and depress fertility. In this chapter, I review the research on how and why catastrophes such as natural disasters and ethno-political conflicts affect fertility. I also discuss why climate change and high levels of population displacement are making the effects of catastrophes on fertility ever more relevant.

Catastrophic Events and Fertility

Catastrophic events—natural or man-made—can affect fertility in both the short and long terms. When assessing the effects of different catastrophes on fertility, it is helpful to distinguish between natural disasters and ethno-political conflicts. A *natural disaster* is a biologic, climate-related, or geophysical event that "overwhelms local capacity, necessitating a request at the national or international level for external assistance; an

V. Skirbekk, *Decline and Prosper!*,
https://doi.org/10.1007/978-3-030-91611-4_14

unforeseen and often sudden event that causes great damage, destruction and human suffering" [1]. Examples include floods, droughts, hurricanes, earthquakes, landslides, famines, tsunamis, and volcanic eruptions. *Ethno-political conflicts* refer to ongoing states of hostility and opposition between two or more groups of people [2, 3]. Ethno-political conflicts might be over governmental power, or natural resources such as land, water, or oil. Many ethno-political conflicts concern group identity and intangible resources like respect, rights, and recognition. Some examples of ethno-political conflicts include the conflicts between Israeli Jews and Palestinian Arabs, Northern Ireland Catholics and Protestants, Houthis and government forces in Yemen, Rohingya Muslim and Rakhine Buddhist communities in Myanmar, Christian-Muslim conflicts in Egypt, and the Boko Haram insurgence in Nigeria.

Large shares of the world population live in world regions that are susceptible to conflicts and natural disasters, including many populous regions in South Asia and sub-Saharan Africa [4, 5]. Natural disasters have also become more common over the course of the last half-century: Between 2008 and 2017, there were an average of 348 natural disasters each year [1]. There were three times as many natural disasters from 2000 through 2009 as there were from 1980 through 1989 [6]. The number of natural disasters—particularly major ones—further increased during the 2010s [7]. Projections foresee that natural disasters will happen more frequently in the decades ahead [8].

It is more difficult to quantify the frequency of ethno-political conflicts, given that they can range from intergroup rivalry to full-on wars. Globally, the number and severity of armed conflicts have both generally declined since the Cold War [3], though religious-based conflicts have become more common in recent years [9, 10]. Data suggests that political turbulence, conflicts, and the loss of livelihoods in many regions of the world have dramatically increased the number of displaced people since the 1960s and since the early 1980s in particular [6, 11]. The United Nations estimates that by the end of 2018, 70.8 million individuals were forcibly displaced worldwide as a result of persecution, conflict, violence, or human rights violations [11]. The increases in natural disasters and forcibly displaced persons suggest that catastrophic events have become more relevant for understanding contemporary fertility patterns and will likely become even more relevant in the future.

Catastrophes often increase fertility. For example, childbearing increased following the earthquakes in Izmit, Turkey, in 1999; Gujarat, India, in 2001; and in North-West Frontier, Pakistan, in 2005 [12]. Fertility also rose after the Red River Flooding in North Dakota in the United States in 1997 [13], and a 27% increase in births was observed nine to 15 months after a major earthquake in the Italian village of L'Aquila [14]. However, catastrophes can also sometimes depress fertility. Famine and economic and political upheaval decreased fertility in Ethiopia in both the short and long terms [15], and hurricane warnings in the United States were related to more than a 2% decrease in births 9 and 10 months later [16].

When do catastrophes increase fertility, and when do they depress it? The socioeconomic context in which a catastrophe takes place is a decisive factor. All else held equal, a catastrophe is likely to have a larger and more long-term positive effect on fertility in poorer countries where children provide a basic form of social security. In countries with higher levels of education, income, and contraceptive use, people may prefer to delay and depress fertility until conditions are better or—if conditions do not improve—to forego childbearing altogether. The impact of the violent ethno-political conflicts in Rwanda and Bosnia-Herzegovina in the 1990s illustrates how the consequences of catastrophes depend on the socioeconomic context in which they take place. The ethno-political conflict caused fertility to increase in Rwanda, while fertility levels fell in Bosnia where the population had a much higher level of education and higher use of modern contraceptives [17]. A global analysis found that armed conflict tended to increase fertility in poorer countries but not in richer countries, suggesting that conflict may act as a deterrent to the demographic transition in poor countries [18].

The net effect of catastrophes on fertility also depends on characteristics of the disaster itself [19], including whether the disaster is apt to reoccur, and whether it is short or long-lasting. Recurring and/or longer-lasting disasters are apt to decrease fertility (e.g., as observed in Ethiopia during the long periods of war and famine from the 1970s to the 1990s [15]), whereas short-term, one-off disasters are apt to result in fertility increases, as observed after the 1995 Oklahoma City Bombings in the United States [20].

Disaster-Related Pro-Natalism

Catastrophic events can affect fertility through many different and sometimes opposing mechanisms. One way in which catastrophic events can affect fertility is by increasing pro-natalistic norms and preferences. According to terror management theory [21], being reminded of one's own mortality often leads people to try to psychologically distance themselves from the threat of death. Childbearing is one way that people deny death by achieving a sort of symbolic immortality: Children not only provide a literal continuation of one's genes, but also carry valued aspects of the self (e.g., one's cultural heritage, worldview, religion, and possessions) into the future. A number of psychological studies have shown that reminding people of their mortality often increases people's family values and their desire for offspring [22]. Indeed, studies have often documented temporary jumps in fertility and family values following disasters. After the 2001 September 11 attacks in the United States, there was a spike in patriotism and national unity, and divorce rates fell [23]. The increase in fertility in Oklahoma Country following the 1995 Oklahoma City Bombings has been partly attributed to a shift toward more traditional family values, as many people prioritized family goals ahead of careers and other life aims in the wake of the disaster [20].

"Competitive demography".

The population of India's northwestern region of Ladakh consists of Muslims and Buddhists. In recent years, the topic of family planning in Ladakh has become highly politicized and linked to conflict between the two communities. Many Buddhists worry that their population is declining and are convinced that Muslims are "outbreeding" them. As a result, there is growing pro-natalist sentiment among Buddhists.

One lama from Zangskar explained:

> *"We need more births...we need to be more influential...I told the villagers that we should have more children: 6 per family at least. No problem, we have a school, we have a gonpa [Buddhist college], we have a nunnery. We can take more people, there's no problem, I told them. More people is more power. 500 people, 500 power. 1,000 people, 1,000 power. Then only we will be heard." [24]*

Sometimes post-disaster pro-natalism may be more of a practical than an emotional coping response. In the wake of disaster, people may purposefully hasten or increase fertility in order to offset population losses and "rebuild" their own families and community. People in regions with more extreme weather events often want and have more children [25]. This finding supports the idea that individuals increase fertility in order to "replace" children who have already died, but also to ensure adequate family size in the case that some children will die in the future [12].

Several studies have supported the idea that "mortality shocks" (i.e., when a lot of people die at one time) can increase fertility. In post-Khmer Rouge Cambodia, marital fertility increased substantially after the fall of the regime under which 25% of the population had died [26]. In Indonesia, women without children initiated childbearing earlier in communities with higher tsunami-related mortality [27]. The drive to replenish or increase the population may be especially important within the context of intergroup conflict as people seek to increase the power of their own group. In conflict-ridden areas, women may sometimes face pressure from the community to fulfill their "duty" to have babies and hence boost the size of their own group, as in post-war Yugoslavia [28]. The Palestinian-Israeli conflict has been found to be an important cause of sustained high fertility among both Israelis and Palestinians, and to be a central reason why Palestinian fertility rose in Gaza during the 1990s Intifada [29].

Disasters Can Affect "Opportunities" for Conception—Wanted or Not

A second way that catastrophic events can affect fertility is by affecting the opportunities for conception. Disasters may lower fecundity, as suggested by declines in sperm quality following the 1995 Kobe earthquake in Japan [30] or the 2008 Wenchuan earthquake in China [31]. There is also some evidence that disasters can affect the frequency of intercourse. Sex can provide comfort [32] and may increase when people are "bunkered down" together during a disaster [33], but may also decrease as a result of apathy and depression.

Disasters sometimes lower access to contraceptives and abortion if supply chains are disrupted or health clinics cannot fully function. There was an increase in unprotected sex following Hurricane Ike in 2008 in Texas, especially among Black women due to the lack of access to contraceptives [34]. The 2010 Haiti earthquake reduced use of injectable contraceptives—the most widely used form of modern contraption in Haiti—and increased unintended pregnancies and fertility [35]. Access to reproductive health services also decreased in conflict-ridden regions between 1970 and 2015, according to an international assessment [18]. There are, however, exceptions; one study of severe natural disasters in Indonesia between 1994 and 2012 found no evidence that natural disasters were related to contraceptive access or fertility [36].

Armed conflicts can depress fertility by decreasing the availability of men, at least temporarily, if many young men are mobilized for warfare, as observed in Eritrea during the 1998–2000 border conflict with Ethiopia [37]. In the longer term, high war-related male mortality can cause distorted sex ratios and decrease fertility [38]. A lack of men was related to lower fertility in Russia following World War II [39] and in the European countries during both world wars [40, 41], and more recently following the 1994 genocide in Rwanda where local decreases in the proportion of men were associated with lower fertility [42].

In the aftermath of a disaster, many women resort to transactional sex—that is, the exchange of sex for gifts or benefits—to survive.

Describing life post-earthquake, one Haitian woman reported, "Many women exchange sexual favors for distribution cards, kits. Me, I do it, too - if not, how would I feed my children?" [43]

Finally, natural disasters and especially armed conflict are often associated with the sexual exploitation of women and rape [44–46], as well as a worsening of women's reproductive autonomy [18]. Young women are particularly vulnerable. Pre-marital first sexual intercourse increased during the violent conflicts in Rwanda [47]. Due to a lack of alternatives, young women may be married earlier, such as in Iraq, where adolescent fertility rose by 30% during the 2003–2011 war [48]. The United Nations has reported an alarming rate of child marriage among contemporary Syrian refugees in Lebanon, much higher than the rate of child marriage among Syrians before the crisis [49].

Disasters Can Cause Economic Malaise and Uncertainty About the Future

Over the longer term, catastrophes affect fertility by disrupting the economy and creating uncertainty about the future. Uncertainty about the future makes it difficult for people to predict the costs and benefits of childbearing [50], and may adversely affect their confidence that they will be able to ensure the welfare of any future children. In richer contexts, the post-disaster economic situation may thus be associated with delay and decreased fertility, similar to the slump in fertility often observed during economic recessions [51]. The economic malaise and uncertainty that follow a disaster tend to have the opposite effect in poorer settings. Not only are poorer people more likely to experience catastrophic events, they also lose a greater share of their wealth as a result of a disaster and receive less support from their governments in the wake of such events [52]. Disasters may thus be a major cause of poverty and worsened long-term prospects.

In developing countries, parents often reduce their investments in education in the aftermath of a disaster in order to maintain more immediately essential consumption (e.g., food) [53]. In Afghanistan, nearly half of school age children did not attend education because of war, widespread poverty, and cultural factors [54]. Schools may also be more directly affected by catastrophic events: In 2012, nearly 600 schools in the North Kivu Province in the Democratic Republic of Congo were looted or damaged during conflicts [55]. In Syria, the ongoing conflict intertwined with the more recent COVID-19 pandemic has led to the widespread closure of schools and other educational facilities [56]. In the long term, disasters can thus affect fertility by decreasing educational attainment.

Fertility of Displaced Persons

Catastrophes often lead to forced displacement, and the fertility of forced migrants often differs from that of the host population. High fertility has been observed among Palestinian refugees in the 1980s and 1990s (in some periods more than seven children per woman [57]) and displaced persons in Ethiopian camps originating mainly from South Sudan, Somalia, Eritrea, and Sudan (around 4.6 children per woman) [58]. In Turkey, the fertility of Syrian migrants in 2018 was 5.3 births per women, much higher than the TFR of native Turkish women (2.3 children per woman) [59] and almost twice the TFR of Syrian women in Syria (2.8 children per woman) [60]. Many recent Asian and African migrants in Europe, where significant shares have refugee status, have considerably higher fertility compared to the native populations [61, 62].

Forced migrant's fertility may differ from that of non-migrants for several reasons [63, 64]. For refugees living indefinitely in camps or entrenched areas with limited outside contact, having children may be one of the few opportunities for self-realization. According to qualitative interviews, the high fertility among displaced Syrians in Lebanon is due at least in part to the unaffordability of contraceptives. Lebanon has a privatized health system, while contraceptives are free in Syria [65]. Some forced migrants may become more religious and traditional [66], which may raise fertility [67, 68]. Much of the difference between the fertility of forced migrants and "natives" in the host country probably has little to do with the experience of forced migration per se, however. Rather, the higher fertility of forced migrants probably has more to do with the fertility patterns in their country of origin [69–71] and their socioeconomic characteristics. The people who were forced to migrate from Finnish Karelia in the 1940s following Soviet annexation provide a unique opportunity to study the causal effects of forced displacement on fertility, as everyone had to leave the area, no one had the opportunity to eventually return, and data is available for the entire population. There is no evidence that forced migration in Finland affected fertility patterns for either women or men [72].

In the longer term, the fertility of migrants (forced or voluntary) often gradually converges to that of the host population [69, 73–75], as observed among migrants in Sweden [73] and Germany [69], Afghan refugees in Iran [74], and refugees from Mozambique in South Africa [75]. Assimilation is not, however, automatic. The extent to which migrants adopt the fertility patterns of the host country depends upon their level of integration in the new society. Some characteristics relevant for fertility like religious affiliation may be rather resistant to change. Despite co-residing for many generations, there are substantial fertility differences between religious groups in Bulgaria [76, 77].

Looming Threats: Pandemics and Global Warming

Pandemics and global warming are likely to affect the global fertility patterns of the future. Compared to epidemics (such as the annual flu), pandemics (such as the 1918–1920 Spanish flu or the COVID-19 virus beginning in 2019) affect a far greater share of the world population and often result in higher mortality [78, 79]. People in poor health (with lower ability to conceive, lower capacity to take care of children, and fewer expected years of remaining life) might decide to have fewer children [80–82]. A pandemic may cause people to at least temporarily abstain from childbearing. The Zika outbreak in 2015/2016 caused many Brazilian women to postpone pregnancies due to the risk of their children facing developmental challenges [83]. The COVID-19 pandemic beginning in 2019 is projected to depress fertility in richer countries but raise it in less developed countries [84].

> Pandemics can also potentially affect fertility by decreasing the opportunities for dating and sex (e.g., due to quarantines). According to a YouGov poll of adults in the United Kingdom, 18% of actively dating singles stopped dating completely due to the COVID-19 outbreak, while 20% of adults had less sex as a result of the government-imposed lockdown. Just a minority (8%) reported having more sex [85].

Another looming threat is global warming. Global warming is increasing the frequency of natural disasters including floods, drought, hurricanes, earthquakes, landslides, and famines [86, 87]. More frequent natural disasters will likely negatively impact the global economy and public health, increase displacement, and cause anxiety about the future—which may in turn affect fertility. Global warming is likely to affect fertility particularly in more traditional, higher fertility regions of the world because they are more vulnerable to the effects of climate change [88]. A recent survey found that 88% of people from 26 countries around the world, including Russia, Indonesia, Philippines, Kenya, Brazil, and the United States, see climate change as a threat—commonly as the *greatest* threat—to their nation, and these percentages have been rapidly rising in recent years [89]. The prospect of climate change already appears to be influencing people's fertility intentions and behavior. In richer countries, a small but vocal group of young people are vowing not to have children because of climate change, either as a form of protest or to avoid exacerbating the problem [90–92].

Disasters Are Becoming More Relevant for Understanding Fertility

Catastrophes can increase, but also sometimes decrease, fertility via several different mechanisms. People in richer contexts tend to decrease fertility in the wake of a disaster, while people in poorer contexts tend to increase fertility. If the global increase in educational attainment [93] and access to contraception [94], and the global decrease in absolute poverty [95] continue, future disasters will be more apt to depress fertility. But this won't happen automatically.

There is some indication that the frequency and severity of ethno-political conflicts are, for the world as a whole, generally decreasing. But this may not be true for particular regions, and there is no guarantee that the global decrease will continue. Global warming is likely to increase the frequency of natural disasters, particularly in world regions which already have high fertility. For many reasons, fertility being just one of them, it is critical that governments and the world community work to prevent ethno-political conflicts and prepare for natural disasters. World leaders need to actively work against competitive demography in areas of ethno-political conflict. Policies that slow population growth (e.g., investments in education and family planning resources) and hence reduce the strain on the environment [96] as well as improve access to contraception, education, and social safety nets would reduce countries' vulnerability to future disasters.

References

1. Centre for Research on the Epidemiology of Disaster. (2019). *Natural disasters 2018: A chance to prepare*. Brussels: CRED. https://www.cred.be/publications. Accessed 27 May 2021.
2. Ellis, D. (2015). Ethno-political conflict. In R. K. Pachauri (Ed.), *The international encyclopedia of interpersonal communication* (pp. 1–10). https://doi.org/10.1002/9781118540190.wbeic024.

3. Dupuy, K., Gates, S., Nygård, H. M., Strand, H., & Urdal, H. (2016). Trends in armed conflict, 1946–2014. Conflict Trends 2-2017.Oslo: P. R. I. Oslo. https://www.prio.org/Publications/Publication/?x=8937. Accessed 26 May 2021.
4. Bremner, J. (2017). Population, food security, and climate change: Africa's challenges. In H. Groth, & J. May (Eds.), *Africa's population: In search of a demographic dividend* (pp. 403–414). Cham: Springer.
5. Mondal, M. S. H. (2019). The implications of population growth and climate change on sustainable development in Bangladesh. *Jamba: Journal of Disaster Risk Studies*, 11(1), 1–10. https://doi.org/10.4102/jamba.v11i1.535.
6. Leaning, J., & Guha-Sapir, D. (2013). Natural disasters, armed conflict, and public health. *New England Journal of Medicine*, 369(19), 1836–1842. https://doi.org/10.1056/NEJMra1109877.
7. Coronese, M., Lamperti, F., Keller, K., Chiaromonte, F., & Roventini, A. (2019). Evidence for sharp increase in the economic damages of extreme natural disasters. *Proceedings of the National Academy of Sciences*, 116(43), 21450–21455. https://doi.org/10.1073/pnas.1907826116.
8. Pachauri, R. K., Allen, M. R., Barros, V. R., Broome, J., Cramer, W., Christ, R., et al. (2014). *Climate change 2014: Synthesis report. Contribution of Working Groups I, II and III to the fifth assessment report of the Intergovernmental Panel on Climate Change*. Geneva: IPCC.
9. Isaacs, M. (2016). Sacred violence or strategic faith? Disentangling the relationship between religion and violence in armed conflict. *Journal of Peace Research*, 53(2), 211–225. https://doi.org/10.1177/0022343315626771.
10. Karakaya, S. (2015). Religion and conflict: Explaining the puzzling case of "Islamic Violence". *International Interactions*, 41(3), 509–538. https://doi.org/10.1080/03050629.2015.1016158.
11. United Nations High Commissioner for Refugees. (2019). Global trends: Forced displacement in 2018. https://www.unhcr.org/5d08d7ee7.pdf. Accessed 27 May 2021.
12. Finlay, J. E. (2009). Fertility response to natural disasters: The case of three high mortality earthquakes. Policy Research Working Paper. Washington, DC: W. Bank. http://documents.worldbank.org/curated/en/118031468284119109/Fertility-response-to-natural-disasters-the-case-of-three-high-mortality-earthquakes.
13. Tong, V. T., Zotti, M. E., & Hsia, J. (2011). Impact of the Red River catastrophic flood on women giving birth in North Dakota, 1994–2000.

Maternal and Child Health Journal, 15(3), 281–288. https://doi.org/10.1007/s10995-010-0576-9.
14. Carta, G., D'Alfonso, A., Colagrande, I., Catana, P., Casacchia, M., & Patacchiola, F. (2012). Post-earthquake birth-rate evaluation using the brief cope. *The Journal of Maternal-Fetal & Neonatal Medicine*, 25(11), 2411–2414. https://doi.org/10.3109/14767058.2012.697945.
15. Lindstrom, D. P., & Berhanu, B. (1999). The impact of war, famine, and economic decline on marital fertility in Ethiopia. *Demography*, 36(2), 247–261. https://doi.org/10.2307/2648112.
16. Evans, R., Hu, Y., & Zhao, Z. (2007). The fertility effect of catastrophe: U.S. hurricane births. *Journal of Population Economics*, 23(1), 1–36. https://doi.org/10.1007/s00148-008-0219-2.
17. Staveteig, S. E. (2011). Genocide, nuptiality, and fertility in Rwanda and Bosnia-Herzegovina. PhD thesis, University of California, Berkeley. http://escholarship.org/uc/item/0t58z112#page-3.
18. Urdal, H., & Che, C. P. (2013). War and gender inequalities in health: The impact of armed conflict on fertility and maternal mortality. *International Interactions*, 39(4), 489–510. https://doi.org/10.1080/03050629.2013.805133.
19. Omori, T., & Fujimori, T. (2010). Recurring natural disasters and their psychological influence on the survivors. *Yokohama Journal of Social Sciences*, 15(4), 491–502. https://ynu.repo.nii.ac.jp/index.php?action=pages_view_main&active_action=repository_action_common_download&item_id=3058&item_no=1&attribute_id=20&file_no=1&page_id=59&block_id=74.
20. Rodgers, J. L., John, C. A. S., & Coleman, R. (2005). Did fertility go up after the Oklahoma City bombing? An analysis of births in metropolitan counties in Oklahoma, 1990–1999. *Demography*, 42(4), 675–692. https://doi.org/10.1353/dem.2005.0034.
21. Greenberg, J., Solomon, S., & Pyszczynski, T. (1997). Terror management theory of self-esteem and cultural worldviews: Empirical assessments and conceptual refinements. In M. P. Zanna (Ed.), *Advances in experimental social psychology, vol. 29* (pp. 61–139). Academic Press. https://doi.org/10.1016/S0065-2601(08)60016-7.
22. Greenberg, J., Vail, K., & Pyszczynski, T. (2014). Terror management theory and research: How the desire for death transcendence drives our strivings for meaning and significance. *Advances in motivation science, Vol. 1* (pp. 85–134). San Diego: Elsevier Academic Press.

23. Cohan, C. L., Cole, S. W., & Schoen, R. (2009). Divorce following the September 11 terrorist attacks. *Journal of Social and Personal Relationships*, 26(4), 512–530. https://doi.org/10.1177/0265407509351043.
24. Aengst, J. (2013). The politics of fertility: Population and pronatalism in Ladakh. *Himalaya*, 32, 23–34.
25. Brown, D. L., & Schafft, K. A. (2011). *Rural people and communities in the 21st century: Resilience and transformation.* Cambridge and Malden: Polity.
26. Heuveline, P., & Poch, B. (2007). The phoenix population: Demographic crisis and rebound in Cambodia. *Demography*, 44(2), 405–426. https://doi.org/10.1353/dem.2007.0012.
27. Nobles, J., Frankenberg, E., & Thomas, D. (2015). The effects of mortality on fertility: Population dynamics after a natural disaster. *Demography*, 52(1), 15–38. https://doi.org/10.1007/s13524-014-0362-1.
28. Eifler, C., & Seifert, R. (Eds.) (2009). *Gender dynamics and post-conflict reconstruction.* Frankfurt, Berlin, Bern, Brussels, New York, Oxford, and Vienna: Peter Lang.
29. Khawaja, M., & Randall, S. (2006). Intifada, Palestinian fertility and women's education. *Genus*, 62(1), 21–51. http://www.jstor.org/stable/29789295.
30. Fukuda, M., Fukuda, K., Shimizu, T., Yomura, W., & Shimizu, S. (1996). Kobe earthquake and reduced sperm motility. *Human Reproduction*, 11(6), 1244–1246. https://doi.org/10.1093/oxfordjournals.humrep.a019365.
31. Chen, X. M., Chen, S. M., Yue, H. X., Lin, L., Wu, Y. B., Liu, B., et al. (2016). Semen quality in adult male survivors 5 years after the 2008 Wenchuan earthquake. *Andrologia*, 48(10), 1274–1280. https://doi.org/10.1111/and.12573.
32. Greenberg, J. M., Smith, K. P., Kim, T. Y., Naghdechi, L., & IsHak, W. W. (2017). Sex and quality of life. In W. W. IsHak (Ed.), *The textbook of clinical sexual medicine* (pp. 539–572). Cham: Springer.
33. Birnbaum, G., Hirschberger, G., & Goldenberg, J. (2011). Desire in the face of death: Terror management, attachment, and sexual motivation. *Personal Relationships*, 18(1), 1–19. https://doi.org/10.1111/j.1475-6811.2010.01298.x.
34. Leyser-Whalen, O., Rahman, M., & Berenson, A. B. (2011). Natural and social disasters: Racial inequality in access to contraceptives after Hurricane Ike. *Journal of Women's Health*, 20(12), 1861–1866. https://doi.org/10.1089/jwh.2010.2613.

35. Behrman, J. A., & Weitzman, A. (2016). Effects of the 2010 Haiti earthquake on women's reproductive health. *Studies in Family Planning*, 47(1), 3–17. https://doi.org/10.1111/j.1728-4465.2016.00045.x.
36. Riese, H., & Vitri, R. (2018). Born in the wake of disaster: A quantitative study of the effect on total fertility rates of severe natural disasters between 1994 and 2012 in Indonesian provinces. BA thesis, Uppsala University. http://urn.kb.se/resolve?urn=urn:nbn:se:uu:diva-355250.
37. Blanc, A. K. (2004). The role of conflict in the rapid fertility decline in Eritrea and prospects for the future. *Studies in Family Planning*, 35(4), 236–245. https://doi.org/10.1111/j.0039-3665.2004.00028.x.
38. Keilman, N., Tymicki, K., & Skirbekk, V. (2014). Measures for human reproduction should be linked to both men and women. *International Journal of Population Research*, 2014(908385). https://doi.org/10.1155/2014/908385.
39. Brainerd, E. (2017). The lasting effect of sex ratio imbalance on marriage and family: Evidence from World War II in Russia. *Review of Economics and Statistics*, 99(2), 229–242. https://doi.org/10.1162/REST_a_00649.
40. Winter, J. M. (1992). War, family, and fertility in twentieth-century Europe. In J. R. Gillis, L. A. Tilly, & D. Levine (Eds.), *The European experience of declining fertility, 1850–1970 : The quiet revolution* (pp. 291–309). Oxford: Blackwell.
41. Hajnal, J. (1947). The analysis of birth statistics in the light of the recent international recovery of the birth-rate. *Population Studies*, 1(2), 137–164. https://doi.org/10.1080/00324728.1947.10415527.
42. Kraehnert, K., Brück, T., Di Maio, M., & Nisticò, R. (2018). The effects of conflict on fertility: Evidence From the genocide in Rwanda. *Demography*, 56(3), 935–968. https://doi.org/10.1007/s13524-019-00780-8.
43. United Nations High Commissioner for Refugees. (2011). Driven by desperation: Transactional sex as a survival strategy in Port-au-Prince IDP camps. https://www.humanitarianresponse.info/sites/www.humanitarianresponse.info/files/documents/files/Haiti%20UNHCR%20Study%20on%20Transactional%20Sex.pdf. Accessed 27 May 2021.
44. Danjibo, N., & Akinkuotu, A. (2019). Rape as a weapon of war against women and girls. *Gender and Behaviour*, 17(2), 13161–13173.
45. Corbin, J. N. (2019). Effect of armed conflict and displacement on women's social, cultural and economic roles and responsibilities in Northern Uganda. *Journal of Refugee Studies*, fez015. https://doi.org/10.1093/jrs/fez015.

46. Undelikwo, V., Michael, & Ihwo, I. (2019). The impact of disaster on the reproductive health of women and girls in Nigeria. *Canadian Social Sciences*, 15(3), 42–48. https://doi.org/10.3968/10890.
47. Lindskog, E. E. (2016). Violent conflict and sexual behavior in Rwanda. *Population, Space and Place*, 22(3), 241–254. https://doi.org/10.1002/psp.1881.
48. Cetorelli, V. (2014). The effect on fertility of the 2003–2011 war in Iraq. *Population and Development Review*, 40(4), 581–604. https://doi.org/10.1111/j.1728-4457.2014.00001.x.
49. United Nations Population Fund. (2017, January 31). New study finds child marriage rising among most vulnerable Syrian refugees. Retrieved from https://www.unfpa.org/news/new-study-finds-child-marriage-rising-among-most-vulnerable-syrian-refugees. Accessed 28 May.
50. Williams, N. E., Ghimire, D. J., Axinn, W. G., Jennings, E. A., & Pradhan, M. S. (2012). A micro-level event-centered approach to investigating armed conflict and population responses. *Demography*, 49(4), 1521–1546. https://doi.org/10.1007/s13524-012-0134-8.
51. Sobotka, T., Skirbekk, V., & Philipov, D. (2011). Economic recession and fertility in the developed world. *Population and Development Review*, 37(2), 267–306. https://doi.org/10.1111/j.1728-4457.2011.00411.x.
52. Hallegatte, S., Vogt-Schilb, A., Bangalore, M., & Rozenberg, J. (2017). *Unbreakable; building the resilience of the poor in the face of natural disasters*. Washington, DC: World Bank.
53. Karim, A., & Noy, I. (2016). Poverty and natural disasters: A regression meta-analysis. *Review of Economics and Institutions*, 7(2), 1–26. https://doi.org/10.5202/rei.v7i2.222.
54. UNICEF. (2018, June 8). Ongoing conflict leaves nearly half of children in Afghanistan out of school. Retrieved from https://www.unicef.org/rosa/press-releases/ongoing-conflict-leaves-nearly-half-children-afghanistan-out-school. Accessed 28 May 2021.
55. UNICEF. (2012, December 10). DR Congo: Over 600 schools looted or damaged by conflict this year. Retrieved from https://www.unicef.org/media/media_66599.html. Accessed 28 May 2021.
56. UNICEF. (2020). Whole of Syria humanitarian situation report mid-year 2020. https://www.unicef.org/media/77481/file/Whole-of-Syria-SitRep-Mid-Year-2020.pdf. Accessed 28 May 2021.
57. Khawaja, M. (2003). The fertility of Palestinian women in Gaza, the West Bank, Jordan and Lebanon. *Population*, 58(3), 273–302. https://doi.org/10.2307/3246675.

58. Haile, G., & Mekonnen, W. (2018). 2.4-O8 Correlates of fertility among refugee women in Ethiopia. *European Journal of Public Health*, 28(suppl_1), cky047. 069. https://doi.org/10.1093/eurpub/cky047.069.
59. Hacettepe University Institute of Population Studies. (2019). 2018 Turkey Demographic and Health Survey. Ankara: Hacettepe University Institute of Population Studies, & T.R. Presidency of Turkey Directorate of Strategy and Budgetand TÜBİTAK. http://www.hips.hacettepe.edu.tr/eng/tdhs2018/TDHS_2018_main_report.pdf. Accessed 28 May 2021.
60. United Nations. (2019). World Population Prospects 2019. https://population.un.org/wpp/. Accessed 25 May 2021.
61. Coleman, D. A., & Dubuc, S. (2010). The fertility of ethnic minorities in the UK, 1960s–2006. *Population Studies*, 64(1), 19–41. https://doi.org/10.1080/00324720903391201.
62. Sobotka, T. (2008). The rising importance of migrants for childbearing in Europe. *Demographic Research, Special Collection 7: Childbearing trends and policies in Europe*, 19, 225–248. https://doi.org/10.4054/DEMRES.2008.19.9.
63. Hervitz, H. M. (1985). Selectivity, adaptation, or disruption? A comparison of alternative hypotheses on the effects of migration on fertility: The case of Brazil. *International Migration Review*, 19(2), 293–317. https://doi.org/10.2307/2545774.
64. Singley, S. G., & Landale, N. S. (1998). Incorporating origin and process in migration-fertility frameworks: The case of Puerto Rican women. *Social Forces*, 76(4), 1437–1464. https://doi.org/10.2307/3005841.
65. Kabakian-Khasholian, T., Mourtada, R., Bashour, H., Kak, F. E., & Zurayk, H. (2017). Perspectives of displaced Syrian women and service providers on fertility behaviour and available services in West Bekaa, Lebanon. *Reproductive health matters*, 25(sup1), 75–86. https://doi.org/10.1080/09688080.2017.1378532.
66. Connor, P. (2014). *Immigrant faith: Patterns of immigrant religion in the United States, Canada, and Western Europe*. New York and London: NYU Press.
67. McQuillan, K. (2004). When does religion influence fertility? *Population and Development Review*, 30(1), 25–56. https://doi.org/10.1111/j.1728-4457.2004.00002.x.
68. Hackett, C., Stonawski, M., Potančoková, M., Grim, B. J., & Skirbekk, V. (2015). The future size of religiously affiliated and unaffiliated populations. *Demographic Research*, 32, 829–842. https://doi.org/10.4054/DemRes.2015.32.27.

69. Milewski, N. (2010). *Fertility of immigrants: A two-generational approach in Germany*. Berlin and Heidelberg: Springer.
70. Pew Research Center. (2015). The future of world religions: Population growth projections, 2010–2050. Washington, DC: P. R. Center. https://www.pewforum.org/2015/04/02/religious-projections-2010-2050/. Accessed 26 May 2021.
71. Mussino, E., & Ortensi, L. E. (2018). The same fertility ideals as in the country of origin? A study of the personal ideal family size among immigrant women in Italy. *Comparative Population Studies-Zeitschrift für Bevölkerungswissenschaft*, 43, 243–274. https://doi.org/10.12765/CPoS-2019-03en.
72. Saarela, J., & Skirbekk, V. (2019). Forced migration in childhood and subsequent fertility: The Karelian displaced population in Finland. *Population, Space and Place*, 25(6), e2223. https://doi.org/10.1002/psp.2223.
73. Andersson, G. (2004). Childbearing after migration: Fertility patterns of foreign-born women in Sweden. *International Migration Review*, 38(2), 747–774. https://doi.org/10.1111/j.1747-7379.2004.tb00216.x.
74. Abbasi-Shavazi, M. J., Hugo, G., Sadeghi, R., & Mahmoudian, H. (2015). Immigrant–native fertility differentials: The Afghans in Iran. *Asian and Pacific Migration Journal*, 24(3), 273–297. https://doi.org/10.1177/0117196815594718.
75. Ibisomi, L., Williams, J., Collinson, M. A., & Tollman, S. (2014). The stall in fertility decline in rural, northeast, South Africa: The contribution of a self-settled, Mozambican, refugee sub-population. *African Population Studies*, 28, 590–600. https://doi.org/10.11564/28-0-517.
76. Stonawski, M., Potančoková, M., & Skirbekk, V. (2015). Fertility patterns of native and migrant Muslims in Europe. *Population, Space and Place*, 22(6), 552–567. https://doi.org/10.1002/psp.1941.
77. Westoff, C. F., & Frejka, T. (2007). Religiousness and fertility among European Muslims. *Population and Development Review*, 33(4), 785–809. https://doi.org/10.2307/25487622.
78. Panovska-Griffiths, J., Grieco, L., van Leeuwen, E., Baguelin, M., Pebody, R., & Utley, M. (2019). Are we prepared for the next influenza pandemic? Lessons from modelling different preparedness policies against four pandemic scenarios. *Journal of Theoretical Biology*, 481, 223–232. https://doi.org/10.1016/j.jtbi.2019.05.003.
79. Porter, R. M., Goldin, S., Lafond, K. E., Hedman, L., Ungkuldee, M., Kurzum, J., et al. (2020). Does having a seasonal influenza program facilitate pandemic preparedness? An analysis of vaccine deployment during the

2009 pandemic. *Vaccine*, 38(5), 1152–1159. https://doi.org/10.1016/j.vaccine.2019.11.025.
80. Weller, N. M., & Kronenfeld, J. J. (2017). Infertility utilization and women's self-rated health. *Journal of the Indiana Academy of the Social Sciences*, 19(1), article 13. https://digitalcommons.butler.edu/jiass/vol19/iss1/13/.
81. Ventimiglia, E., Capogrosso, P., Boeri, L., Serino, A., Colicchia, M., Ippolito, S., et al. (2015). Infertility as a proxy of general male health: Results of a cross-sectional survey. *Fertility and Sterility*, 104(1), 48–55. https://doi.org/10.1016/j.fertnstert.2015.04.020.
82. Dey, I., & Wasoff, F. (2010). Another child? Fertility ideals, resources and opportunities. *Population Research and Policy Review*, 29(6), 921–940. https://doi.org/10.1007/s11113-009-9174-1.
83. Diniz, D., Medeiros, M., & Madeiro, A. (2017). Brazilian women avoiding pregnancy during Zika epidemic. *Journal of Family Planning and Reproductive Health Care*, 43(1), 80–80. https://doi.org/10.1136/jfprhc-2016-101678.
84. Aassve, A., Cavalli, N., Mencarini, L., Plach, S., & Bacci, M. L. (2020). The COVID-19 pandemic and human fertility. *Science*, 369(6502), 370–371. https://doi.org/10.1126/science.abc9520.
85. YouGov.. (2020). YouGov survey results: Sex and dating under COVID-19. https://docs.cdn.yougov.com/l2llsos027/YouGov%20-%20dating.pdf. Accessed 27 May 2021.
86. Bouwer, L. M. (2013). Projections of future extreme weather losses under changes in climate and exposure. *Risk Analysis*, 33(5), 915–930. https://doi.org/10.1111/j.1539-6924.2012.01880.x.
87. Huang, C., Barnett, A. G., Wang, X., Vaneckova, P., FitzGerald, G., & Tong, S. (2011). Projecting future heat-related mortality under climate change scenarios: A systematic review. *Environmental Health Perspectives*, 119(12), 1681–1690. https://doi.org/10.1289/ehp.1103456.
88. Skirbekk, V., de Sherbinin, A., Adamo, S., Navarro, J., & Chai-Onn, T. (2020). Religious affiliation and environmental challenges in the 21st century. *Journal of Religion and Demography*, 7(2), 238–271. https://doi.org/10.1163/2589742X-12347110.
89. Fagan, M., & Huang, C. (2019, April 18). A look at how people around the world view climate change. Retrieved from https://www.pewresearch.org/fact-tank/2019/04/18/a-look-at-how-people-around-the-world-view-climate-change/. Accessed 28 May 2021.

90. Koropeckyj-Cox, T., Çopur, Z., Romano, V., & Cody-Rydzewski, S. (2018). University students' perceptions of parents and childless or child-free couples. *Journal of Family Issues*, 39(1), 155–179. https://doi.org/10.1177/0192513X15618993.
91. Rieder, T. N. (2016). *Toward a small family ethic: How overpopulation and climate change are affecting the morality of procreation.* Springer International.
92. Hunt, E. (2019, March 12). BirthStrikers: Meet the women who refuse to have children until climate change ends. *The Guardian.* Retrieved from https://www.theguardian.com/lifeandstyle/2019/mar/12/birthstrikers-meet-the-women-who-refuse-to-have-children-until-climate-change-ends
93. Barro, R. J., & Lee, J. W. (2013). A new data set of educational attainment in the world, 1950–2010. *Journal of Development Economics*, 104, 184–198. https://doi.org/10.1016/j.jdeveco.2012.10.001.
94. Alkema, L., Kantorova, V., Menozzi, C., & Biddlecom, A. J. S. (2013). National, regional, and global rates and trends in contraceptive prevalence and unmet need for family planning between 1990 and 2015: A systematic and comprehensive analysis. *The Lancet*, 381(9878), 1642–1652. https://doi.org/10.1016/S0140-6736(12)62204-1.
95. Asadullah, M. N., & Savoia, A. (2018). Poverty reduction during 1990–2013: Did millennium development goals adoption and state capacity matter? *World Development*, 105, 70–82. https://doi.org/10.1016/j.worlddev.2017.12.010.
96. Ezeh, A. C., Bongaarts, J., & Mberu, B. (2012). Global population trends and policy options. *The Lancet*, 380(9837), 142–148. https://doi.org/10.1016/S0140-6736(12)60696-5.

15

New Times, Old Beliefs: Religion and Contemporary Fertility

Religious institutions played a huge role in lowering Western fertility in the eighteenth century by delaying marriage, limiting pre- and extramarital fertility, and spreading education. But does religion still matter today? Although many scholars have long predicted that religion would soon cease to meaningfully influence life outcomes, there is substantial evidence that religion remains very relevant for understanding contemporary fertility—even in the secularized West. In this chapter, I describe how and why religion matters for fertility, and why the importance of religion is probably *increasing* over time.

The Relationship Between Religion and Fertility—Then and Now

Scholars in the latter part of the twentieth century have tended to ignore the role of religion for fertility, particularly in Western countries which are typically highly secularized and where religion is considered a private

V. Skirbekk, *Decline and Prosper!*,
https://doi.org/10.1007/978-3-030-91611-4_15

matter [3, 4]. However, as more recent studies have found, contemporary fertility continues to be strongly related to both *religious affiliation* (whether a person self-identifies as, e.g., Muslim, Christian, Hindu, Jewish, or Buddhist) and *religiosity* (the extent to which individuals are devoted to a religious faith as indicated by, e.g., being religiously unaffiliated or affiliated, how often a person attends religious services, or how important a person perceives religion to be for his/her daily life) [5, 6, 7, 8, 9, 10]. Independent of a person's *own* faith, the dominant religion and religiosity of a country can also be a powerful cultural force that shapes individuals' fertility-related attitudes and behaviors.

People who are more religious tend to want and have more children, also after accounting for sociodemographic and geographic differences [7, 11, 12, 13, 14, 15]. Ideal fertility and actual fertility are strongly related to religiosity even among women with doctoral degrees [7]. So far, most of the evidence on the positive relationship between religiosity and fertility is from Western countries and hence based primarily on samples of Christians, but higher fertility has also been found among more devout Jews [16] and Muslims [17] in Israel, as well as more devout Muslims in Europe [18].

The most basic way to demonstrate the relationship between religion and fertility is to compare the TFR of religiously affiliated versus religiously unaffiliated women. My colleagues and I integrated more than 2500 surveys, registers, and censuses to produce the first global dataset on religious affiliation by age and sex, covering 199 nations and more than 99% of the global population [19]. This unique global dataset contained information on how people defined their own religious beliefs. Using this dataset, we estimated that, globally between 2010 and 2015, the TFR of unaffiliated women was 1.7 children per woman, whereas the TFR of women affiliated with any religion was 2.6 children [19]. The largest affiliated/unaffiliated fertility difference was observed in Asia, a region that encompasses both highly religious individuals who tend to have many children and secular individuals with low fertility. Interestingly, we found no evidence of a difference between the religiously affiliated and unaffiliated in Latin America.

Fertility also differs across religious denominations, as shown using data from Europe [15, 20], Asia, Africa, and Latin America

[8]. Fertility is generally higher among Muslims and Christians than followers of other religions. Based on the global data set described above, we found that global average fertility was 1.6 children per woman among Buddhists, 2.4 children per woman among Hindus and Jews, 2.7 among Christians, and 3.1 among Muslims [19]. In many countries, Muslims marry and initiate childbearing at younger ages [18, 22, 23] and ultimately have more children as shown in an analysis of data from 30 developing countries in Asia, Africa, and Latin America [8]. Other studies confirm that Muslims tend to prefer larger families and have more children than members of other religious groups for example in India, Malaysia, Thailand, and the Philippines [23]. Much of the relationship between Muslim affiliation and fertility appears to be explained by education, which tends to be considerably lower among Muslims relative to other religious groups—particularly in poorer countries [24].

Across the European countries, the TFR of Muslims is 47% higher than the national average [25]. Much of the fertility difference has little to do with religious doctrine, but more to do with the fact that many Muslims in Europe or their parents come from countries with higher fertility. Although migrants tend to adapt to the fertility patterns of their host country over time [26, 27, 28, 29, 30], fertility differences between "native" Europeans (primarily Christians or non-religious) and certain migrant groups (often Muslims from high fertility countries) can persist also in the longer term [31, 32].

Why Does Religion Affect Fertility?

Religion continues to affect fertility via many of the same pathways as in the eighteenth century. Perhaps most importantly for contemporary fertility, religious affiliation and religiosity are associated with particularly women's education and work experiences. In the eighteenth century, religious authorities stimulated women's education in Europe. Today, women who are more religious tend to have somewhat lower education and employment levels, which in turn influence their fertility [33, 34, 35]. Traditional interpretations of Islam and Christianity emphasize the importance of women's familial roles, which may encourage affiliated families to invest less in daughters' education and affiliated women to pursue less education, be housewives, and have more children [36, 37].

Religion can also affect sexual behavior, contraception, and abortion [38, 39, 40]. Most major religions discourage sex outside of marriage, but people's attitudes and behaviors toward pre- and extramarital sex are nevertheless associated with their religious affiliation. One study based on data from 31 developing countries found that ever-married Muslims and Hindus were less likely than ever-married Christians and Jews to report premarital sex [41]. Married Muslims were also less likely to report having had extramarital sex than adherents of all other major religions except Buddhists. International surveys suggest that Muslim respondents also tend to be more opposed to abortion than people affiliated with other religions [42]. Religious affiliation also continues to predict the prevalence and duration of breastfeeding, which suppresses conception [43, 44].

So far, there have been two instances in which the Catholic Church has officially condoned the use of contraception. In the early 1960s, Pope Paul VI allowed nuns in the then-Belgian Congo to take the contraceptive pill when rape was being used as a weapon of war. More recently in 2016, Pope Francis suggested that women who live in countries threatened by the Zika virus could use contraception, saying that "avoiding pregnancy is not an absolute evil" [1].

Of all the world's major religious groups, only Roman Catholicism officially prohibits the use of contraception. Officially, only the rhythm method for birth spacing is allowed. Protestant Christians tend to have lower fertility than Catholics in some countries such as Northern Ireland [45]. In the United States, the higher fertility of the Catholics in recent years has been mainly driven by Hispanic immigration (even if there was a period in the 1970s when Catholic and Protestant fertility rates converged) [3, 46]. The persistent difference between Catholics and Protestant in some countries is thought to be at least partly due to differences in how the respective institutions approach contraception: a greater degree of prohibition by the Catholic church versus a more "pragmatic" approach by the Protestant church [47]. Orthodox Judaism is also rather restrictive with regard to contraception; contraception is generally considered acceptable only when a pregnancy would threaten a woman's mental or physical health; and methods that least interfere with the sex act are the most preferred [48].

Contrary to what many people assume, Islam does not officially prohibit the use of contraception. Historically, coitus interruptus has been permitted in the Qur'an; today, the official stance is that married couples can use modern contraceptive methods as long as they are reversible and do not induce abortion [48]. Many Islamic scholars and Muslim followers argue that the absence of an explicit prohibition of contraception in the Qur'an allows them to use several forms of family planning [49, 50, 51]. Sometimes contraception has been tangled up with inter-group conflict; it has sometimes been argued that birth control is part of a Western conspiracy to reduce the number of Muslims in countries such as Iran [52] or Pakistan [53].

> *(The mother) should not get pregnant (if she is breastfeeding). It is according to Islam. The child has the right to be breastfed. Once child is weaned, then she can get pregnant.*
> *—Married man in Kabul, Afghanistan, in 2007 [2]*

The world's religions also take different official stances with regard to abortion. Most mainstream schools of Protestant Christianity, Judaism, and Islam allow abortion under some circumstances (e.g., typically to save the mother's life, rape, incest, and sometimes for economic reasons). Both Hinduism and Buddhism officially condemn abortion, but also emphasize that it is the mother who must decide what is moral or not. Hinduism is generally opposed to ending life—the sacred texts and traditions within Hinduism teach that one should minimize harm to others and oneself. Abortion is permitted on certain grounds in India and Nepal, the two Hindu majority countries. Only Catholicism and the most conservative schools of Christianity, Judaism, and Islam prohibit abortion under all or nearly all circumstances. Catholicism does allow for medical procedures that will save a mother's life even when it is foreseeable that a pregnancy will be terminated as an indirect and unintended result [48].

Naturally, people do not always follow the official stance of their religion. According to 2014 data, the abortion rate among Catholic women in the United States was about the same as the overall national rate [39], and a survey from the same year showed that about half of United States' Catholics and Muslims indicated that they believed that abortion should be legal in all or most cases [54]. On the societal level, a diversity of abortion laws can also be observed in Catholic- and Muslim-dominant countries. In the Catholic-dominated Latin American countries, as of 2021 abortion was completely banned in 9 out of 48 countries and dependencies, but available on request in 9 out of 48 countries/dependencies; laws in the rest of the countries/dependencies landed somewhere in between the two extremes [55]. All Muslim-majority countries currently allow abortions to save a woman's life; 18 out of 47 allow abortions *only* to save a woman's life; 19 allow abortion under a number of other conditions; and 10 allow abortion on request [56]. Tunisia, for example, liberalized its abortion laws in 1973, before France, Germany, or the United States. In Tunisia, abortion is permitted upon request within 12 weeks of conception and is provided without charge within the scope of the public healthcare system [56].

Buddhism—The Low Fertility Religion

Being more religious generally goes along with higher fertility. This rule does not appear to apply to Buddhists, however. Buddhism is a widespread religion in many Asian countries, including many low fertility countries such as Japan, China, Taiwan, and South Korea. Unlike the Abrahamic religions, Buddhism does not stress the importance of either marriage or procreation. Marriage is viewed positively, but it is not seen as a religious duty [48]. Large families are not encouraged and childlessness or small families are not frowned upon [57, 58, 59]. There is also no formal Buddhist doctrine prohibiting contraception or abortion [48, 60], and there is little religious opposition to sexual and contraceptive freedom [61]. The Buddhist religious leader Dalai Lama encourages family planning, stating that "...precious human life is now overcrowding the world. As a result, not only is it a question of survival of a single human being but that of the entire humanity. Therefore, the conclusion is that family planning is necessary provided that it is based on non-violent principles" [62]. Within Buddhism, sexual impulses are thought to hinder enlightenment. Siddhartha, the founder of Buddhism, provides a "low fertility role model": He chose to cease childbearing and become celibate (he had one child prior to doing so) in order to attain spiritual enlightenment.

In one study, we examined fertility differences between self-identified Buddhists and unaffiliated people in six countries with large Buddhist populations [6]. We examined differences in period fertility in India, Cambodia, and Nepal and differences in cohort fertility in Mongolia, Thailand, and Japan. We found that, after controlling for education, region of residence, age, and marital status, Buddhist affiliation was either negatively or not associated with fertility. That is, Buddhists had lower or the same fertility as their unaffiliated peers. Other recent studies have likewise found that fertility was unrelated to being Buddhist in Japan, Korea, and Singapore [63] or in Japan, Korea, and Taiwan [64]. In our study, there was no evidence that more devout Buddhists in Japan had higher fertility than less devout Buddhists [6].

The Future of (No) Religion

Secularization at the societal level is defined as the gradual distancing of a society from religious values and institutions; at the individual level, secularism refers to people's indifference for religious doctrine or beliefs [65, 66, 67]. Globally in 2015, there were slightly fewer than 1.2 billion atheists, agnostics, and people who did not identify with any particular religion, representing about 16% of the global population [19]. The religiously unaffiliated are expected to continue to increase as a share of the population in much of Europe and North America, following rapid shifts from Christianity to no religion in these regions [19]. Secularization could be an important reason for the overall decline in fertility in the United States [21], as well as the convergence between Catholics' and Protestants' fertility in the United States [3] and Northern Ireland [45]. Using cross-sectional data from 1985 to 1999 in Spain, one study found that fertility differences between practicing and non-practicing Catholic women increased over time, because fertility decline occurred only among the latter group [10].

While Western countries are likely to become more secularized, religion does not show signs of disappearing globally. In fact, the world population as a whole is becoming *more* religious, and the trend toward greater religiosity is stronger among young adults [21]. My colleagues and I have estimated that 83% of the world population was affiliated with a religion in 2010, and we expect that the proportion will increase to 87% by 2050 [68]. The increase in the proportion of religiously affiliated people is primarily due to the projected growth of the African population, where many people have a high religious affiliation and high fertility. Thus, the world may become more religiously polarized in the years to come, with some parts of the world remaining highly traditional and religious and other regions turning increasingly secular [68, 69, 70, 71]. This is not only likely to cause political tension, but could also bring about demographic tension as some countries may be younger and subject to resource scarcity, while other more secular countries will experience aging and population decline.

Most people inherit their religious affiliation from their parents. Low fertility among secular and certain religious communities may therefore imply that their populations will decline or eventually disappear. One example is the Zoroastrian or Parsi religion, a millennium-old religion originating in what is now Iran. Many Zoroastrians have high status positions in business and leadership, particularly in India. Strict regulations against marrying outside of the religion and high childlessness have led to decreases in the Zoroastrian population since it was first counted in 1941, decreasing from 71,630 in 1981 to just 57,264 in 2011 [72, 73, 74]. Given current trends, the Zoroastrians may even be at risk of disappearing altogether. Due to their low fertility, secular individuals in the world's richer countries might become a minority due to the cumulative effect of immigration from religious countries and the higher fertility of religious people [4]. Across all religions, the fertility of more conservative groups (e.g., Orthodox Jews, Dutch orthodox Calvinists, Finnish Laestadians, and Salafist Sunni Muslims) tends to be much higher than that of more moderate groups [75]. The TFR of secular Jewish Americans has been far below replacement levels for many decades, while Jewish conservative groups have very high fertility [76]. It has been projected that 49% of the population of 0- to 14-year-olds in Israel will be comprised of Ultra-orthodox Jews by 2065 [77] due to the much higher fertility of the Ultra-orthodox relative to less conservative Jews. All of these projections, however, entail a considerable degree of uncertainty.

Religion and the Future of Fertility

Religion continues to influence fertility, also when socioeconomic factors such as economic development is accounted for. Religion continues to affect fertility via many of the same mechanisms as in the past: namely, by affecting people's educational attainment, their family values, and their sexual practices. Muslims tend to have the highest fertility followed by Christians and Hindus, and people who are more religious and conservative tend to have more children—except for Buddhists, who have as low or lower fertility than people unaffiliated with any religion.

Secularization may be one reason why fertility has declined in the West. Globally, however, the proportion of people with a religious affiliation is growing. It seems highly likely that religion and religiosity will continue to be important determinants of fertility for the time ahead. The relative effect of religion on fertility may even increase over time as educational differences shrink, absolute poverty declines, and the potential to control fertility increases, meaning that people have more freedom to behave in line with their religious beliefs.

References

1. Wooden, C. (2016, February 19). In Zika outbreak, contraceptives may be 'lesser evil,' pope says. *The Catholic Telegraph*. Retrieved from https://

www.thecatholictelegraph.com/in-zika-outbreak-contraceptives-may-be-lesser-evil-pope-says/32076.

2. Haider, S., Todd, C., Rahimi, S., Azfar, P., Morris, J., & Miller, S. (2009). Childbearing and contraceptive decision making amongst Afghan men and women: A qualitative analysis. *Health Care for Women International*, 30(10), 935–953. https://doi.org/10.1080/07399330903052129.
3. Westoff, C. F., & Jones, E. F. (1979). The end of "Catholic" fertility. *Demography*, 16(2), 209–217. https://doi.org/10.2307/2061139.
4. Kaufmann, E. (2010). Shall the religious inherit the Earth: Demography and politics in the twenty-first century. London: Profile Books.
5. McClendon, D. (2016). Religion, marriage markets, and assortative mating in the United States. *Journal of Marriage and Family*, 78(5), 1399–1421. https://doi.org/10.1111/jomf.12353.
6. Skirbekk, V., Stonawski, M., Fukuda, S., Spoorenberg, T., Hackett, C., & Muttarak, R. (2015). Is Buddhism the low fertility religion of Asia? *Demographic Research*, 32(1), 1–28. https://doi.org/10.4054/DemRes.2015.32.1.
7. Buber-Ennser, I., & Skirbekk, V. (2016). Researchers, religion and childlessness. *Journal of Biosocial Science*, 1–15. https://doi.org/10.1017/S0021932015000188.
8. Heaton, T. B. (2011). Does religion influence fertility in developing countries. *Population Research and Policy Review*, 30(3), 449–465. https://doi.org/10.1007/s11113-010-9196-8.
9. Goujon, A., Malenfant, É. C., & Skirbekk, V. (2013). Towards a Catholic North America? In S. D. Brunn (Ed.), *The changing world religion map* (pp. 1689–1709). Dordrecht: Springer. https://doi.org/10.1007/978-94-017-9376-6_89.
10. Adsera, A. (2006). Marital fertility and religion in Spain, 1985 and 1999. *Population Studies*, 60(2), 205–221. https://doi.org/10.1080/00324720600684817.
11. Dilmaghani, M. (2019). Religiosity, secularity and fertility in Canada. *European Journal of Population*, 35(2), 403–428. https://doi.org/10.1007/s10680-018-9487-z.
12. Morency, J. -D., Caron Malenfant, É., & MacIsaac, S. (2017). Immigration and diversity: Population projections for Canada and its regions, 2011 to 2036. Ottawa: M. o. I. S. Canada). https://www150.statcan.gc.ca/n1/pub/91-551-x/91-551-x2017001-eng.htm. Accessed 27 May 2021.

13. Berghammer, C. (2012). Church attendance and childbearing: Evidence from a Dutch panel study, 1987–2005. *Population Studies*, 66(2), 197–212. https://doi.org/10.1080/00324728.2012.655304.
14. Philipov, D., & Berghammer, C. (2007). Religion and fertility ideals, intentions and behaviour: A comparative study of European countries. *Vienna Yearbook of Population Research*, 5, 271–305. https://doi.org/10.1553/populationyearbook2007s271.
15. Peri-Rotem, N. (2016). Religion and fertility in Western Europe: Trends across cohorts in Britain, France and The Netherlands. *European Journal of Population*, 32(2), 231–265. https://doi.org/10.1007/s10680-015-9371-z.
16. Okun, B. S. (2017). Religiosity and fertility: Jews in Israel. *European Journal of Population*, 33(4), 475–507. https://doi.org/10.1007/s10680-016-9409-x.
17. Schellekens, J., & Atrash, A. a. (2018). Religiosity and marital fertility among Muslims in Israel. *Demographic Research*, 39(34), 911–926. https://doi.org/10.4054/DemRes.2018.39.34.
18. Westoff, C. F., & Frejka, T. (2007). Religiousness and fertility among European Muslims. *Population and Development Review*, 33(4), 785–809. https://doi.org/10.2307/25487622.
19. Pew Research Center. (2017). The changing global religious landscape. Washington, D.C.: P. R. Center. https://www.pewforum.org/2017/04/05/the-changing-global-religious-landscape/. Accessed 27 May 2021.
20. Goujon, A., Jurasszovich, S., & Potancokova, M. (2017). Religious denominations in Vienna & Austria: Baseline study for 2016—scenarios until 2046. Vienna Institute of Demography working papers, 9/2017.Vienna: A. A. o. Sciences. https://www.oeaw.ac.at/fileadmin/subsites/Institute/VID/IMG/Publications/Working_Papers/WP2017_09.pdf. Accessed 27 May 2021.
21. Stonawski, M., Skirbekk, V., Hackett, C., Potančoková, M., Connor, P., & Grim, B. (2015). Global population projections by religion: 2010–2050. In B. J. Grim, T. M. Johnson, V. Skirbekk, & G. A. Zurlo (Eds.), *Yearbook of International Religious Demography 2015* (pp. 99–116). Leiden: Brill. https://doi.org/10.1163/9789004297395_004.
22. Stonawski, M., Potančoková, M., & Skirbekk, V. (2015). Fertility patterns of native and migrant Muslims in Europe. *Population, Space and Place*, 22(6), 552–567. https://doi.org/10.1002/psp.1941.
23. Morgan, S. P., Stash, S., Smith, H. L., & Mason, K. O. (2002). Muslim and Non-Muslim differences in female autonomy and fertility: Evidence

from four Asian countries. *Population and Development Review*, 28(3), 515–537. https://doi.org/10.1111/j.1728-4457.2002.00515.x.
24. McClendon, D., Hackett, C., Potančoková, M., Stonawski, M., & Skirbekk, V. (2018). Women's education in the Muslim world. *Population and Development Review*, 44(2), 311–342. https://doi.org/10.1111/padr.12142.
25. Pew Research Center (2011). The future of the global Muslim population. Projections for 2010–2030. Washington, D.C.: P. R. Center. http://www.pewforum.org/The-Future-of-the-Global-Muslim-Population.aspx. Accessed 27 May 2021.
26. Milewski, N. (2010). *Fertility of immigrants: A two-generational approach in Germany*. Berlin, Heidelberg: Springer.
27. Guarin, A., & Bernardi, L. (2015). First child among immigrants and their descendants in Switzerland. In H. Kuluand, & T. Hannemann (Eds.), *Country-specific case studies on fertility among the descendants of immigrants* (pp. 150–171). http://www.familiesandsocieties.eu/wp-content/uploads/2015/08/WP39KuluEtAl2015.pdf.
28. Andersson, G. (2004). Childbearing after migration: Fertility patterns of foreign-born women in Sweden. *International Migration Review*, 38(2), 747–774. https://doi.org/10.1111/j.1747-7379.2004.tb00216.x.
29. Abbasi-Shavazi, M. J., Hugo, G., Sadeghi, R., & Mahmoudian, H. (2015). Immigrant–native fertility differentials: The Afghans in Iran. *Asian and Pacific Migration Journal*, 24(3), 273–297. https://doi.org/10.1177/0117196815594718.
30. Ibisomi, L., Williams, J., Collinson, M. A., & Tollman, S. (2014). The stall in fertility decline in rural, northeast, South Africa: The contribution of a self-settled, Mozambican, refugee sub-population. *African Population Studies*, 28, 590–600. https://doi.org/10.11564/28-0-517.
31. Coleman, D. A., & Dubuc, S. (2010). The fertility of ethnic minorities in the UK, 1960s–2006. *Population Studies*, 64(1), 19–41. https://doi.org/10.1080/00324720903391201.
32. Dubuc, S. (2014). Fertility of immigrants. In B. F., & B. S. (Eds.), *Encyclopedia of migration* (pp. 1–8). Dordrecht: Springer. https://doi.org/10.1007/978-94-007-6179-7_69-1.
33. Hajj, M., & Panizza, U. (2009). Religion and education gender gap: Are Muslims different? *Economics of Education Review*, 28(3), 337–344. https://doi.org/10.1016/j.econedurev.2008.01.007.
34. García-Muñoz, T., & Neuman, S. (2012). Is religiosity of immigrants a bridge or a buffer in the process of integration? A comparative study of

Europe and the United States. IZA Discussion Paper No. 6384. Rochester, NY: S. S. R. Network. https://papers.ssrn.com/sol3/papers.cfm?abstract_id=2019436. Accessed 27 May 2021.
35. Lehrer, E. L. (2004). Religion as a determinant of economic and demographic behavior in the United States. *Population and Development Review*, 30(4), 707–726. https://doi.org/10.2307/3657335.
36. Sherkat, D. E. (2000). "That they be keepers of the home": The effect of conservative religion on early and late transitions into housewifery. *Review of Religious Research*, 41(3), 344–358. https://doi.org/10.2307/3512034.
37. Heaton, T. B. (2013). Religion and socioeconomic status in developing nations: A comparative approach. *Social Compass*, 60(1), 97–114. https://doi.org/10.1177/0037768612471772.
38. Wusu, O. (2015). Religious influence on non-use of modern contraceptives among women in Nigeria: Comparative analysis of 1990 and 2008 NDHS. *Journal of Biosocial Science*, 47(05), 593–612. https://doi.org/10.1017/S0021932014000352.
39. Jerman, J., Jones, R. K., & Onda, T. (2016). Characteristics of U.S. abortion patients in 2014 and changes since 2008. New York: G. Institute. https://www.guttmacher.org/report/characteristics-us-abortion-patients-2014. Accessed 27 May 2021.
40. Agadjanian, V., Yabiku, S. T., & Fawcett, L. (2009). History, community milieu, and Christian-Muslim differentials in contraceptive use in sub-Saharan Africa. *Journal for the Scientific Study of Religion*, 48(3), 462–479. https://doi.org/10.1111/j.1468-5906.2009.01460.x.
41. Adamczyk, A., & Hayes, B. E. (2012). Religion and sexual behaviors: Understanding the influence of Islamic cultures and religious affiliation for explaining sex outside of marriage. *American Sociological Review*, 77(5), 723–746. https://doi.org/10.1177/0003122412458672.
42. Jelen, T. G. (2014). The subjective bases of abortion attitudes: A cross national comparison of religious traditions. *Politics and Religion*, 7(3), 550–567. https://doi.org/10.1017/S1755048314000467.
43. Bernard, J. Y., Cohen, E., & Kramer, M. S. (2016). Breast feeding initiation rate across Western countries: Does religion matter? An ecological study. *BMJ Global Health*, 1(4), e000151. https://doi.org/10.1136/bmjgh-2016-000151.
44. Burdette, A. M., & Pilkauskas, N. V. (2012). Maternal religious involvement and breastfeeding initiation and duration. *American Journal of Public Health*, 102(10), 1865–1868. https://doi.org/10.2105/AJPH.2012.300737.

45. McGregor, P., & McKee, P. (2016). Religion and fertility in contemporary Northern Ireland. *European Journal of Population*, 32(4), 599–622. https://doi.org/10.1007/s10680-016-9399-8.
46. Skirbekk, V., Kaufmann, E. P., & Goujon, A. (2010). Secularism, fundamentalism, or Catholicism? The religious composition of the United States to 2043. *Journal for the Scientific Study of Religion*, 49(2), 293–310. https://doi.org/10.1111/j.1468-5906.2010.01510.x.
47. McQuillan, K. (2004). When does religion influence fertility? *Population and Development Review*, 30(1), 25–56. https://doi.org/10.1111/j.1728-4457.2004.00002.x.
48. Srikanthan, A., & Reid, R. (2008). Religious and cultural influences on contraception. *Journal of Obstetrics and Gynaecology Canada*, 30, 129–137. https://doi.org/10.1016/S1701-2163(16)32736-0.
49. Shabaik, S. A., Awaida, J. Y., Xandre, P., & Nelson, A. L. (2019). Contraceptive beliefs and practices of American Muslim women. *Journal of Women's Health*, 28(7), 976–983. https://doi.org/10.1089/jwh.2018.7500.
50. Nadeem, M., & Sher, M. K. (2017). Modern reproductive technologies, aesthetic surgery and cotnraceptionin Islamic law: A case study of Khyber Pakhtunkhwa. *Journal of Law and Society*, 48(70). http://journals.uop.edu.pk/papers/Jan%202017%20---%208.pdf.
51. Shaikh, S. d. (2003). Family planning, contraception and abortion in Islam. In D. C. Maguire (Ed.), *Sacred choices: The case for contraception and abortion in world religions* (pp. 105–128). New York, Oxford: Oxford University Press. https://doi.org/10.1093/acprof:oso/9780195160017.003.0005.
52. Yaghmai, M. (2015) The reversal of Iran's family planning program (from 2005 to present) as a new nationalist project. Masters thesis, Leiden University. https://hdl.handle.net/1887/35995.
53. Ataullahjan, A., Mumtaz, Z., & Vallianatos, H. (2019). Family planning in Pakistan: A site of resistance. *Social Science & Medicine*, 230, 158–165. https://doi.org/10.1016/j.socscimed.2019.04.021.
54. Pew Research Center. (2014). Views about abortion by religious group. Washington, D.C.: P. R. Center. https://www.pewforum.org/religious-landscape-study/views-about-abortion/. Accessed 27 May 2021.
55. Center for Reproductive Rights. (2021). The world's abortion laws. https://maps.reproductiverights.org/worldabortionlaws. Accessed 27 May 2021.
56. Shapiro, G. (2013). Abortion law in Muslim-majority countries: An overview of the Islamic discourse with policy implications. *Health Policy and Planning*, 29(4), 483–494. https://doi.org/10.1093/heapol/czt040.

57. Falk, N. A. (1980). The case of the vanishing nuns: The fruits of ambivalence in ancient Indian Buddhism. In N. A. Falk, & R. M. Gross (Eds.), *Unspoken worlds: Women's religious lives* (pp. 207–224). San Francisco: Harper & Row.
58. Faure, B. (2009). *The power of denial: Buddhism, purity, and gender*. Princeton: Princeton University Press.
59. Knodel, J., Gray, R. S., Sriwatcharin, P., & Peracca, S. (1999). Religion and reproduction: Muslims in Buddhist Thailand. *Population Studies*, 53(2), 149–164. https://doi.org/10.1080/00324720308083.
60. Knodel, J. E., Chamratrithirong, A., & Debavalya, N. (1987). *Thailand's reproductive revolution: Rapid fertility decline in a third-world setting*. Madison: University of Wisconsin Press.
61. Keown, D. (Ed.) (1999). Buddhism and abortion. Honolulu: University of Hawaii Press.
62. Tibetan Women's Association. (1995). An interview with His Holiness the Dalai Lama: July 20, 1995, private office Dharamsala. *Dolma: The Voice of Tibetan Women,* pp. 34–38.
63. Kojima, H. (2014). The effects of religion on fertility-related attitudes and behavior in Japan, South Korea and Singapore. *Waseda Studies in Social Sciences*, 15(1), 1–26. https://core.ac.uk/reader/144446252.
64. Bessey, D. (2018). Religion and Fertility in East Asia: Evidence from the East Asian Social Survey. *Pacific Economic Review*, 23(3), 517–532. https://doi.org/10.1111/1468-0106.12209.
65. Martin, D. (1978). *A general theory of secularization.* New York: Harper & Row.
66. Tschannen, O. (1991). The secularization paradigm: A systematization. *Journal for the Scientific Study of Religion*, 30(4), 395–415. https://doi.org/10.2307/1387276.
67. Bruce, S. (2011). *Secularization: In defence of an unfashionable theory*. Oxford: Oxford University Press.
68. Hackett, C., Stonawski, M., Potančoková, M., Grim, B. J., & Skirbekk, V. (2015). The future size of religiously affiliated and unaffiliated populations. *Demographic Research*, 32, 829–842. https://doi.org/10.4054/DemRes.2015.32.27.
69. Stonawski, M., Skirbekk, V., Kc, S., & Goujon, A. (2010). Projections of religiosity for Spain. Eurostat/UNECE Work Session on Demographic Projections, 28–30 April, Lisbon. https://doi.org/10.2785/50697.
70. McGrath, P. (2003). Religiosity and the challenge of terminal illness. *Death Studies*, 27(10), 881–899. https://doi.org/10.1080/716100343.

71. Pew Research Center (2015). The future of world religions: Population growth projections, 2010–2050. Washington, D.C.: P. R. Center. https://www.pewforum.org/2015/04/02/religious-projections-2010-2050/. Accessed 26 May 2021.
72. Pandey, R., & Yadav, N. (2015). Fertility decline: A statistical demographic review of Parsi community. *Bulletin of Mathematical and Statistical Research*, 3(4), 104–122.
73. Shroff, Z., & Castro, M. C. (2011). The potential impact of intermarriage on the population decline of the Parsis of Mumbai, India. *Demographic Research*, 25, 545–564. https://doi.org/10.4054/DemRes.2011.25.17.
74. Unisa, S., Bhagat, R. B., Roy, T. K., & Upadhyay, R. B. (2008). Demographic transition or demographic trepidation? The case of Parsis in India. *Economic and Political Weekly*, 43(1), 61–65. www.jstor.org/stable/40276446.
75. Kaufmann, E. (2015). Sacralization by stealth? In E. P. Kaufmann, & W. B. Wilcox (Eds.), *Whither the child?: Causes and consequences of low fertility* (pp. 135–156). New York: Routledge.
76. Schmelz, U. O., & Della Pergola, S. (1988). *Basic trends in American Jewish demography*. New York: American Jewish Committee.
77. Grave-Lazi, L. (2017, May 21). Israel's population to reach 20 million by 2065. *The Jerusalem Post*. Retrieved from http://www.jpost.com/Israel-News/Report-Israels-population-to-reach-20-million-by-2065-492429.

16

Contemporary Fertility from an Evolutionary Perspective: Are the Fittest Still Surviving?

Evolutionary approaches assert that human behavior is driven by the motivation to survive, to reproduce, and to ensure the survival of one's offspring. From an evolutionary perspective, the low fertility in many countries today thus seems rather perplexing. At least two phenomena need to be explained. First, why has human fertility in many countries declined to below replacement levels, if people are genetically programmed to have as many children as they can? Second, why do people continue to strive for higher social status, even though status is no longer or even negatively related to fertility? In this chapter, I review evolutionary approaches to fertility and consider how adaptive low fertility and status-seeking are from an evolutionary perspective.

Evolutionary Approaches to Childbearing

In his seminal 1859 book *On the Origin of Species*, Charles Darwin described how differences in survival and reproductive success drive natural evolution in all species [1]. Darwin essentially argued that evolution is driven by differential net reproduction, whereby plants or animals

V. Skirbekk, *Decline and Prosper!*,
https://doi.org/10.1007/978-3-030-91611-4_16

with advantageous traits have more surviving offspring than their peers who lack the advantageous traits. Over time, the subpopulation which lacks the advantageous traits declines and eventually dies out. In lay terms, the theory of evolution by natural selection is often described as "survival of the fittest," with "fitness" being captured by an individual's propensity to survive and transmit his or her genes to subsequent generations.

Evolutionary theories have been refined and adapted since Darwin. One important development is evolutionary life-history theory, which describes the life trajectory an organism as the result of a process of selective resource allocation. Resources are finite, and resources used for one purpose cannot be used for another purpose. Organisms thus have to navigate a series of trade-offs at the molecular, physiological, and behavioral levels, including whether to invest in one's own survival versus reproduction, in current versus future reproduction, and in the quantity versus quality of offspring. Evolutionary life-history theory predicts that natural selection optimizes such trade-offs to maximize *inclusive fitness*, that is, the production of long-term genetic descendants [4].

The trade-off between reproduction and own survival is highly relevant whenever resources are very constrained, but less relevant when survival is relatively certain. With regard to the trade-off between current and future fertility, it may be adaptive to delay reproduction whenever it increases one's future reproductive potential. For example, delaying fertility (and thereby truncating the time available for reproduction) may be adaptive if it means that resources can be allocated toward securing a superior mate, which would ultimately increase the quantity and quality of one's future offspring. The third major trade-off is between offspring quantity and quality. Individuals can invest their resources in either producing many offspring who each have a relatively low chance of surviving and reproducing themselves, or they can produce fewer offspring which have a higher probability of surviving and reproducing. In historic settings characterized by high infant and child mortality, and large and sudden mortality shocks (e.g., due to an epidemic), from an evolutionary perspective it would generally make more sense to maximize offspring quantity. The alternative strategy of fewer offspring but investing more resources in each child makes more sense only when mortality is relatively low (and hence the potential return of investments in child quality is higher) [8, 9].

Another important development in evolutionary theory is the idea that culture, like genes, is likewise subject to an evolutionary process. According to the dual inheritance approach [11], each new human inherits not only genetic material but also a set of socially learned information ("culture"). Cultural traits that are (1) linked to survival, (2) related to having a greater a number of surviving offspring, and (3) transmitted to children (from parents, kin, and the community) are—from an evolutionary perspective—advantageous and should become more prevalent in the population over time.

Current evolutionary approaches acknowledge that the extent to which a genetic or a cultural trait is adaptive depends on the context. In safe and resource-rich settings where survival can more or less be taken for granted, for instance, the trade-off between one's own survival and reproduction becomes less relevant. Evolution should thus favor traits that increase reproduction. This is precisely the pattern observed in the average age at menarche, which ranges from around 12 years of age in healthy populations but up to 18 years in poorly nourished, less healthy populations; globally, the age of menarche is also decreasing over time as health and nutrition improve [13–15]. The optimal number of children depends on factors such as the extent to which group members share in the burden of childcare, or the costs of ensuring that a child obtains the group's particular standard for "quality". Sharing the burden means that fewer resources must be deterred from other activities (e.g., own survival) in order to have children.

How Do Evolutionary Perspectives Explain Low Fertility?

For evolution scholars, contemporary low fertility is a bit of a puzzle. Why do people in the world's richest countries have the fewest babies, when the trade-off between own survival and reproduction is more or less irrelevant, and nearly all children survive to reproductive age? Several hypotheses attempt to explain how natural selection could have led to the demographic transition and below replacement fertility in particular [18]. According to one hypothesis, low fertility is evolutionarily adaptive because changes in the environment have made high levels of parental investment critical to offspring success. Parents thus optimize fitness by producing fewer children with higher levels of investment. If this hypothesis is correct, one would expect to find evidence that people who had very few but also very many children would have the fewest surviving long-term descendants. However, studies based on past generations have generally found that people who had more children also had more (great-)grandchildren [19, 20, 21]. There is thus little evidence that the demographic transition happened as a result of people behaving in a way that optimized the long-term survival of their genetic material. It is nevertheless possible that the number of children that maximizes long-term genetic survival has changed between past generations (for which we have data) and contemporary generations (which we cannot yet observe).

A second, contrasting hypothesis is that below replacement fertility is a maladaptive by-product of rapid environmental change. Selection processes adapt human traits to past but not present environments. Some human traits—status-seeking or sex drive, for instance—may have been evolutionarily adaptive in the past, but maladaptive or ineffective in the current era. Contemporary low fertility might thus be the result of an "adaptive lag." If this hypothesis is correct, cultural and genetic evolution will eventually result in higher fertility as human traits "catch up" with the new environment. Because modern contraception has broken the link between sex drive and procreation, my colleagues and I have argued that the continued desire for children may reflect a cultural lag—that is, people continue to have children because that's what people have always done in the past; their preferences have not yet caught up with their environment [22]. According to our argument, there is no reason why fertility should stop falling further if preferences and norms change to match the current environment.

A third hypothesis is that fertility has declined because of cultural evolutionary processes. People tend to imitate the traits (such as low fertility) of culturally successful individuals, and the traits that lead to cultural success may not necessarily correspond with success from an evolutionary perspective. Today, more education increases the likelihood of cultural success, but also depresses fertility. It has recently been argued that spread of cultural traits that increase survival but represses fertility—such as valuing education—could explain the onset of the demographic transition [23]. In a high mortality context, natural selection will favor traits associated with higher reproduction. If there is transmission of a cultural trait that reduces mortality, the death rate will decrease. In turn, the population density will increase, which also increases the rate of further cultural transmission. Eventually, cultural transmission of the low reproduction trait will outpace the transmission of traits through reproduction.

A final, contentious hypothesis concerns whether selection may, under certain circumstances, favor low fertility because it is advantageous for *group* (as opposed to individual) survival [24]. There may in fact be circumstances in which having fewer or no children would enable the survival for at least some members of the species, whereas having many children would result in extinction [25]. For example, it is presumed that high fertility contributed to rapid decline of the Rapa Nui people of Easter Island because the quickly growing population could not be supported by the fragile ecosystem [26, 27]. Today, this same reasoning is sometimes used to justify the decision not to have children in order to avoid exacerbating the threat of human-driven climate change [28].

Fertility is Genetically Heritable

In order to examine how processes of biological natural selection are acting on fertility over time, one first needs to determine whether fertility is genetically heritable. The heritability of a fertility trait, such as the number of children or age at first birth, can be examined in family and twin studies. In family studies, researchers assess the correlation of a trait between multiple generations of a family (e.g., parents and their children and/or grandchildren). In twin studies, researchers examine the extent to which monozygotic (i.e., identical) and dizygotic (i.e., fraternal) twins differ with regard to a particular trait or phenotype in order to determine the extent to which a particular trait is shaped by genes, shared environment, and unique environment (and sometimes their interaction). Recent advances in DNA analysis now allow researchers to analyze large *biobanks* (i.e., biological samples, typically blood or saliva) in order to find out whether particular genetic variants are more common in people with a particular trait (e.g., age at menopause, diseases related to reproduction).

By now, there is ample evidence from multiple family, twin, and biobank studies that there are genetically heritable components not only of many common diseases affecting fertility (e.g., endometriosis), but also the age at menarche and menopause, age at first birth, and total lifetime fertility [29, 30, 31, 32, 33]. There also appear to be specific genetic components associated with educational attainment [34] and religiosity [35], two major determinants of fertility. However, inherited factors typically only explain small shares of the variation in fertility behavior, and the pathways by which genes affect childbearing are often poorly understood [32, 36].

So far, there is evidence that natural selection is acting in some human populations to reduce age at first birth, to increase age at last birth, and also to increase age at menopause [37]. It thus seems that natural selection is favoring high fertility genetic traits. For most of our history, humans have lived under conditions of high mortality. Given that biological natural selection favors traits adaptive for past environments, it is not entirely surprising that biological natural selection would favor high fertility. Because reproductive success is composed of survival and reproduction, in low mortality contexts (where there is little variation in survival), one would expect that processes of natural selection would be stronger for reproductive parameters [37].

Inspired by his cousin Charles Darwin's book On the Origin of the Species, *British scientist Francis Galton inspired the eugenics movement. Galton believed that "desirable" human qualities were mostly if not entirely hereditary, and hence that one could improve the genetic stock of the human race by limiting the fertility of people with "inferior" traits [2]. Eugenic ideas were part of mainstream thinking in many countries up until the middle of the twentieth century [3], and motivated measures that coercively limited the fertility of people with physical and mental health conditions, poor people, criminals, different racial groups, and people considered to be "deviants" all around the world.*

Today, many people continue to espouse the idea that that people with serious health conditions should not have children. Data indicate, for instance, that the majority of people in Libya [5], Yemen, and Tanzania [6] believe that people with epilepsy should not have children. Nearly one-third (31%) of Indians [7] and about nine out of ten Zimbabwean women (89%) [10] believe that people who are HIV positive should not have children. More than one-third of Irish respondents believed that people with mental health difficulties should not be allowed to have children [12], while in Italy around half of the relatives of individuals with schizophrenia think they should not have children [16].

Given the continued prevalence of eugenic ideas, it is no wonder that people generally seek partners in good health. In Nigeria, genotypes for sickle cell disease have become an important criterion for partner selection [17]. In 2019, one recently married Nigerian women reported, "Before I met my current partner, I was always on the lookout for someone whose genotype was compatible with mine. All my dates had the 'what is your genotype?' question." DNA tests in Nigeria are now common in dating to avoid the risk of having children with sickle cell disease.

Climbing the Social Ladder, Then and Now

Another puzzle for evolutionary theorists is why the relationship between status and fertility has reversed in contemporary populations. Status-striving is assumed to be a biological instinct and a major driver of human behavior [38]. Evolutionary theories of status-striving are based on the notion that men with higher social status in hierarchical groups tend to have more sexual access to women—and thereby have more offspring. For women, in the past it made sense to have children with high-status men, as high-status men could provide more resources and protection and thereby better ensure one's own survival and the survival of one's children.

The process of status-striving has, however, changed over time. Historically, social status tended to be determined early in life through the inheritance of a name, caste, or wealth, and social mobility was limited. The caste system dominated social organization in many South Asian societies, where the caste one was born into determined occupational type, social position, who one could marry and also ones social and legal rights, and changing caste was generally impossible [39].

When status is determined early in life, there is no trade-off between investing in status and investing in reproduction. Over time, however, social systems have become more meritocratic; there are now more opportunities for social advancement during one's own life time through education, career, or the accumulation of wealth. Acquiring status in a meritocratic system often involves huge investments of time and energy during adulthood, and may hence be at odds with establishing a family. Moreover, as the average levels of education and wealth increase across generations, members of younger generations must invest more and more in order to keep up with their peers. As a result, childbearing is postponed to increasingly older ages. People may wind up having fewer children in part because there are fewer years of reproductive life left after one has attained the preferred status.

From the mid-twentieth century onward, higher social status (e.g., higher education, higher career status) has generally been associated with *lower* fertility [40]. From an evolutionary perspective, there is less incentive for women to seek out high-status males, as almost all children survive to reproductive age in any case. When considering the evolutionary aim to pass on one's genetic material, striving for success in contemporary society may thus be misguided. One could therefore conclude that people in contemporary societies may be working too hard to achieve something that makes little sense in evolutionary terms.

Ironically, the same individuals and populations who will eventually win the genetic evolutionary game may be the same individuals and populations who lose, or at least not win, the contemporary race for status and material well-being. The most reproductively "successful" people are religious and conservative, from poorer countries; rural, poor, less educated, living in unsafe and poor health environments characterized by poverty, with low levels of happiness and greater exposure to environmental risks [41, 42]. People who are well-educated, more liberal, wealthy, and living in urban and/or relatively wealthy regions have fewer children. Their cultural legacy—including the preference for particular lifestyles, achievement, and standard of living—may be greater than their genetic legacy.

Trade-off Between Social and Evolutionary "Success"

Evolutionary theory predicts that we all seek to survive and reproduce—so why are people having fewer children? Natural selection favors genetic and cultural traits that are adaptive for environments of the past. Humans have evolved in settings with high mortality; hence, it makes sense that biological selection seems to favor genetic traits associated with high fertility. There is, for instance, evidence that the length of the female reproductive window is lengthening. Cultural traits may spread faster than genetic traits due to modern technology and the increased diffusion of ideas.

Some human traits may have become maladaptive over time. Historically, humans may have been motivated sought to climb the social ladder in order to have more surviving children. In the contemporary world, social status is either unrelated or negatively related to fertility. Most species (99%) that have ever lived on the planet are now extinct [43], and there is no guarantee that our species will survive in the long term. As humans' material well-being increases and fertility drops, we may get rich *and* die trying. Adjusting our fertility to best fit with the conditions of our current and future environment is important for ensuring our longer-term survival. Very low fertility implies a greater risk of extinction, but high population growth will also put us at risk. Potentially, under the current conditions low, but not too low, fertility may be best for ensuring that not only our genetic, but also our cultural traits survive long into the future.

References

1. Darwin, C. (1859). *On the origin of the species*. London: John Murray.
2. Gillham, N. W. (2001). Sir Francis Galton and the birth of eugenics. *Annual Review of Genetics*, 35, 83–101. https://doi.org/10.1146/annurev.genet.35.102401.090055.
3. Marks, J. (1993). Historiography of eugenics. *American Journal of Human Genetics*, 52(3), 650–652.
4. Hill, K. (2005). Life history theory and evolutionary anthropology. *Evolutionary Anthropology: Issues, News, and Reviews*, 2, 78–88. https://doi.org/10.1002/evan.1360020303.
5. Taher, Y. A., Al-Gamati, M. A., Samud, A. M., & El-Taher, F. E. (2018). Knowledge and attitudes toward epilepsy among Libyan parents resident in Tripoli. *Libyan Journal of Medical Sciences*, 2(3), 102. https://doi.org/10.4103/LJMS.LJMS_37_18.
6. Winkler, A. S., Mayer, M., Schnaitmann, S., Ombay, M., Mathias, B., Schmutzhard, E., et al. (2010). Belief systems of epilepsy and attitudes toward people living with epilepsy in a rural community of northern Tanzania. *Epilepsy & Behavior*, 19(4), 596–601. https://doi.org/10.1016/j.yebeh.2010.09.023.
7. Jain, M., Sinha, R., Kar, S. K., & Yadav, M. (2017). A questionnaire survey of stigma related to human immunodeficiency virus infection/acquired immunodeficiency syndrome among healthy population. *Community Acquired Infection*, 4(1), 6–11. https://doi.org/10.4103/2225-6482.203265.
8. Vining, D. R. (1986). Social versus reproductive success: the central theoretical problem of human sociobiology. *Behavioral and Brain Sciences*, 9(01), 167–187. https://doi.org/10.1017/S0140525X00021968.
9. Liu, J., & Lummaa, V. (2014). An evolutionary approach to change of status–fertility relationship in human fertility transition. *Behavioral Ecology*, 25(1), 102–109. https://doi.org/10.1093/beheco/art091.
10. Feldman, R., & Maposhere, C. (2003). Safer sex and reproductive choice: Findings from "positive women: Voices and choices" in Zimbabwe. *Reproductive Health Matters*, 11(22), 162–173. https://doi.org/10.1016/s0968-8080(03)02284-5.
11. Boyd, R., & Richerson, P. (1985). *Culture and the evolutionary process*. Chicago: University of Chicago Press.

12. Mentally ill 'ought not have children' - survey (2007, September 28). *Irish Times*. Retrieved from https://www.irishtimes.com/news/mentally-ill-ought-not-have-children-survey-1.967070.
13. Kirk, K. M., Blomberg, S. P., Duffy, D. L., Heath, A. C., Owens, I. P., & Martin, N. G. (2001). Natural selection and quantitative genetics of life-history traits in Western women: A twin study. *Evolution*, 55(2), 423–435. https://doi.org/10.1111/j.0014-3820.2001.tb01304.x.
14. Song, Y., Ma, J., Agardh, A., Lau, P. W., Hu, P., & Zhang, B. (2015). Secular trends in age at menarche among Chinese girls from 24 ethnic minorities, 1985 to 2010. *Global Health Action*, 8(1), 26929. https://doi.org/10.3402/gha.v8.26929.
15. Wyshak, G., & Frisch, R. E. (1982). Evidence for a secular trend in age of menarche. *New England Journal of Medicine*, 306(17), 1033–1035. https://doi.org/10.1056/NEJM198204293061707.
16. Fiorillo, A., De Rosa, C., Malangone, C., Luciano, M., Giacco, D., Del Vecchio, V., et al. (2011). Views of general public, mental health professionals and patients' relatives about schizophrenia: An Italian multi-centric survey. *European Psychiatry*, 26(S2), 532–532. https://doi.org/10.1016/S0924-9338(11)72239-8.
17. Salaudeen, A. (2019, July 11). In Nigeria, your genetic makeup can decide if you get a second date *CNN*. Retrieved from https://edition.cnn.com/2019/07/10/health/genotype-dating-nigeria-intl/index.html.
18. Mulder, M. B. (1998). The demographic transition: Are we any closer to an evolutionary explanation? *Trends in Ecology & Evolution*, 13(7), 266–270.https://doi.org/10.1016/S0169-5347(98)01357-3.
19. Fox, G. A. (2005). Extinction risk of heterogeneous populations. *Ecology*, 86(5), 1191–1198. https://doi.org/10.1890/04-0594.
20. Hamza, K., Jagers, P., & Klebaner, F. C. (2014). On the establishment, persistence, and inevitable extinction of populations. *Journal of Mathematical Biology*, 72(4), 797–820. https://doi.org/10.1007/s00285-015-0903-2.
21. Kolk, M., & Skirbekk, V. (2019). Fading family lines—Women and men without children, grandchildren and great-grandchildren in 19th , 20th , and 21st century Northern Sweden. Stockholm Research Reports in Demography.Stockholm: S. University. https://su.figshare.com/articles/preprint/Fading_family_lines_-_Women_and_men_without_children_grandchildren_and_great-grandchildren_in_19th_20th_and_21st_century_Northern_Sweden/9778685/1.

22. Lutz, W., Skirbekk, V., & Testa, M. R. (2006). The low-fertility trap hypothesis: Forces that may lead to further postponement and fewer births in Europe. *Vienna Yearbook of Population Research*, 167–192. http://www.iiasa.ac.at/Admin/PUB/Documents/RP-07-001.pdf.
23. Wodarz, D., Stipp, S., Hirshleifer, D., & Komarova, N. L. (2020). Evolutionary dynamics of culturally transmitted, fertility-reducing traits. *Proceedings of the Royal Society B: Biological Sciences*, 287(1925), 20192468. https://doi.org/10.1098/rspb.2019.2468.
24. Nowak, M. A., Tarnita, C. E., & Wilson, E. O. (2010). The evolution of eusociality. *Nature*, 466(7310), 1057–1062. https://doi.org/10.1038/nature09205.
25. Orlov, S., Rovenskaya, E., Cantele, M., Stonawski, M., & Skirbekk, V. (2021). Modelling social status and fertility decisions under differential mortality. In J. L. Haunschmied, R. M. Kovacevic, W. Semmler, & V. M. Veliov (Eds.), *Dynamic Economlc Problems with Regime Switches* (pp. 111–135). Cham: Springer. https://doi.org/10.1007/978-3-030-54576-5_5.
26. De la Croix, D., & Dottori, D. (2008). Easter Island's collapse: a tale of a population race. *Journal of Economic Growth*, 13(1), 27–55. https://doi.org/10.1007/s10887-007-9025-z.
27. Hunt, T. L., & Lipo, C. P. (2006). Late colonization of Easter Island. *Science*, 311(5767), 1603–1606. https://doi.org/10.1126/science.1121879.
28. Hunt, E. (2019, March 12). BirthStrikers: Meet the women who refuse to have children until climate change ends. *The Guardian*. Retrieved from https://www.theguardian.com/lifeandstyle/2019/mar/12/birthstrikers-meet-the-women-who-refuse-to-have-children-until-climate-change-ends.
29. Barban, N., Jansen, R., de Vlaming, R., Vaez, A., Mandemakers, J. J., Tropf, F. C., et al. (2016). Genome-wide analysis identifies 12 loci influencing human reproductive behavior. *Nature Genetics*, 48(12), 1462–1472. https://doi.org/10.1038/ng.3698.
30. Briley, D. A., Tropf, F. C., & Mills, M. C. (2017). What explains the heritability of completed fertility? Evidence from two large twin studies. *Behavior Genetics*, 47(1), 36–51. https://doi.org/10.1007/s10519-016-9805-3.
31. Tropf, F. C., Barban, N., Mills, M. C., Snieder, H., & Mandemakers, J. J. (2015). Genetic influence on age at first birth of female twins born in the UK, 1919–68. *Population Studies*, 69(2), 129–145. https://doi.org/10.1080/00324728.2015.1056823.

32. Mills, M. C., & Tropf, F. C. (2015). The biodemography of fertility: A review and future research frontiers. *Kolner Zeitschrift fur Soziologie und Sozialpsychologie*, 67(Suppl 1), 397–424. https://doi.org/10.1007/s11577-015-0319-4.
33. Blossfeld, H.-P., Klijzing, E., Mills, M., & Kurz, K. (Eds.) (2006). Globalization, uncertainty and youth in society: The losers in a globalizing world. London: Routledge.
34. Kong, A., Frigge, M. L., Thorleifsson, G., Stefansson, H., Young, A. I., Zink, F., et al. (2017). Selection against variants in the genome associated with educational attainment. *Proceedings of the National Academy of Sciences*, 114(5), E727–E732. https://doi.org/10.1073/pnas.1612113114.
35. Eaves, L. J., Hatemi, P. K., Prom-Womley, E. C., & Murrelle, L. (2008). Social and genetic influences on adolescent religious attitudes and practices. *Social Forces*, 86(4), 1621–1646. https://doi.org/10.1353/sof.0.0050.
36. Kim, Y., & Lee, J. J. (2019). The genetics of human fertility. *Current Opinion in Psychology*, 27, 41–45. https://doi.org/10.1016/j.copsyc.2018.07.011.
37. Stearns, S. C., Byars, S. G., Govindaraju, D. R., & Ewbank, D. (2010). Measuring selection in contemporary human populations. *Nature Reviews Genetics*, 11(9), 611–622. https://doi.org/10.1038/nrg2831.
38. Von Rueden, C., Gurven, M., & Kaplan, H. (2010). Why do men seek status? Fitness payoffs to dominance and prestige. *Proceedings of the Royal Society B: Biological Sciences*, 278(1715), 2223–2232. https://doi.org/10.1098/rspb.2010.2145.
39. Clark, G., & Landes, Z. (2013) Caste versus class: Social mobility in India, 1860–2012. http://www.econ.ucdavis.edu/faculty/gclark/research.html. Accessed 27 May 2021.
40. Skirbekk, V., & Kc, S. (2012). Fertility-reducing dynamics of women's social status and educational attainment. *Asian Population Studies*, 8(3), 251–264. https://doi.org/10.1080/17441730.2012.714667.
41. Welle, T., & Birkmann, J. (2015). The World Risk Index–An approach to assess risk and vulnerability on a global scale. *Journal of Extreme Events*, 2(01), 1550003. https://doi.org/10.1142/S2345737615500037.
42. Zwolinski, J. (2019). Happiness around the world. In K. D. Keith (Ed.), *Cross-Cultural Psychology: Contemporary Themes and Perspectives* (pp. 531–545). Hoboken, NJ: John Wiley & Sons. https://doi.org/10.1002/9781119519348.ch26.
43. Clayton, T., & Radcliffe, N. (2015). *Sustainability: A systems approach.* London: Routledge.

17

How Low Will It Go? Projecting Future Fertility

Demographers, national planners, and others with an interest in future trends want to know what fertility is going to look like in the future. Will fertility in all countries around the world eventually converge around replacement level? Will it continue to decline in the countries with high fertility? Will it rebound in the countries with the lowest fertility? In this chapter, I discuss projections of future fertility, how projections are made, and why some projections are probably wide off the mark.

How Do Demographers Make Projections?

A number of organizations make projections about how global, regional, and national population size, fertility, mortality, and migration will develop in the future. The United Nations' projections are the most widely used. Other national and international agencies including the World Bank, Eurostat, the United States Census Bureau, the Institute for Health Metrics Evaluation (IHME), and the International Institute for Applied Systems Analysis in Austria prepare their own projections. Most national governments also make projections for their own country.

V. Skirbekk, *Decline and Prosper!*,
https://doi.org/10.1007/978-3-030-91611-4_17

National level projections typically consider relevant factors such as existing regional differences, policy changes, local recessions, cultural factors (e.g., auspicious or unlucky birth years), or average educational length. For instance, projections of national fertility in Ethiopia need to account for the very high fertility in rural regions and the very low fertility observed in the capital Addis Abbeba, and shifts in the share of people that live in urban and rural regions over time [2, 3].

The United Nations increasingly uses probabilistic approaches [4, 5] that predict a likely range (e.g., there is an 80% chance that fertility will be between __ and __children per woman) as opposed to a specific point estimate. Assumptions about how fertility will develop in future are primarily based on past trends. The United Nations assumes that populations generally experience three phases of fertility: (i) a high fertility phase (prior to the demographic transition), where fertility remains high also after mortality declines, (ii) a transition to low fertility, and (iii) a low fertility phase with fertility close to the replacement level. The United Nations thus assumes that fertility patterns in populations further along in the demographic transition are more or less informative for how fertility in populations at earlier phases will develop in future [6]. Demographers have often been criticized for following a predominantly data-driven as opposed to theoretical approach when making assumptions about how fertility (and other demographic parameters) will develop in the future. The lack of theory is particularly relevant for projecting whether fertility will rebound or not in post-transition countries.

Policymakers and other planners use demographic projections to prepare adequate housing, health care, education, infrastructure, food, water, and energy as well as predict future economic development and military capacity. It would therefore seem to be in everyone's best interest to have accurate and reasonable projections. However, it is important to understand that projecting fertility (and other demographic parameters such as mortality or population size) is a highly sensitive task. Projecting high fertility may be problematic given the potential negative impacts of high population growth on development, public health, the environment, greenhouse gas emissions, and climate change. Projecting very low fertility may be just as problematic, given the difficulty of accepting that one's population group may eventually die out and/or that members of the society do not want to have more children under the current circumstances. Many people also (wrongly) assume that population aging—one of the consequences of low fertility—will have disastrous consequences on society. The people making projections may thus sometimes face pressure from politicians, funding bodies, and others to make certain kinds of assumptions (e.g., to assume that fertility will decrease in high fertility contexts, or rebound in low fertility contexts).

How Certain Are Fertility Projections?

A number of studies have assessed the accuracy of past fertility projections [7, 8, 9]. These studies have confirmed that past fertility projections have been far from certain. That said, demographic projections are generally more certain than, for instance, economic forecasts or projections of climate change [4, 10, 11, 12. One analysis of the United Nations' projections between 1950 and 1985 found that the projections overestimated global fertility (the crude birth rate) in the 1950s and 1960s, but underestimated fertility in the 1970s and 1980s [7]. The projections were particularly inaccurate for Asia, Northern and Latin America, and Oceania relative to other world regions. Interestingly, the analysis also suggested that it has been as difficult to accurately project fertility as it has been to accurately project mortality. Demographers' underestimation of the historical increase in life expectancy [8, 13, 14] has, however, received far more attention in the literature than their failure to accurately predict fertility.

Demographers often try to optimize fertility projections by consulting experts and by analyzing errors in previous projections. Still, fertility projections can only be as certain as the data and the assumptions on which they are based. Fertility projections tend to be less certain for developing countries than for more developed countries, partly due to differences in the availability of reliable data [7, 15]. Data inaccuracies are a particular problem in developing countries with weak registration systems [7, 15]. Projections about fertility in high fertility countries, particularly in sub-Saharan Africa, are less certain than projections about fertility in lower fertility countries [16], as fertility fluctuates within a narrower range. Longer-term projections also tend to be less accurate than shorter-term projections [7, 15]. Optimistically, the accuracy of the United Nations' projections improved between the 1950s and 1990s, in part due to the improvement in baseline data for developing countries [7].

The accuracy of longer-term projections greatly depends on the assumptions about how future fertility will change [15]. Most projections assume that fertility will have a smooth, gradual, and unidirectional trajectory. Demographers may therefore fail to predict "surprises," such as the unexpected sharp decline in birth rates in Iran between 1986 and 1996 [17, 18], the rapid fertility decrease in North America and Europe to below replacement levels from the 1960s [7], or the fertility increase in Egypt between 2005 and 2015 which occurred after six decades of decline due to stalled increases in education following the attempted revolution [19, 20, 21]. Many important factors such as economic development, family policies, trade regulations, and capital flows are very difficult to predict [22]. Furthermore, the assumption that high fertility countries will follow a similar trajectory as countries with different cultural contexts and who also experienced the demographic transition in a vastly different global context may not be tenable. Fertility decline in some sub-Saharan African countries stagnated in the late 1990s and early 2000s, and even increased again in some countries [23].

Some projections are based on unreasonable assumptions. In its most recent round of projections in 2019, Eurostat assumed that European (i.e., post-transition) fertility will converge around 1.83 children per woman [24]. This seems, however, unlikely given the fact that many Europeans do not start having children until their mid-30s, and that many of the drivers of low fertility are particularly strong in Europe (e.g., high male and female educational attainment, high contraceptive use, high housing prices, difficult labor markets for young people, and secularization). Moreover, period fertility in Europe has been far lower than 1.83 children for the preceding three decades. European fertility is thus likely to be far lower than the Eurostat projections would suggest. The IHME recently projected that world TFR will fall to 1.66 children per woman by 2100, and global population will reach a peak and eventually decline to a level of 8.8 billion. Fertility in Nigeria is projected to fall to 1.69, the Central African Republic to 1.34, Pakistan to 1.31, India to 1.29 and Afghanistan to 1.65 children per woman by the end of the century [25]. The IHME projection model, however, considers only contraception and education; other known determinants/concomitants of fertility including religion are ignored. The IHME projections therefore probably underestimate differences in how fertility will develop in secular versus religious countries and probably underestimate fertility and population growth.

Is Two the Magic Number?

The United Nations and most other projection-makers have historically assumed that fertility in all countries, regions, and the globe will eventually stabilize around the replacement level of (just over) two children per woman [26, 27]. There is, however, no particular reason to believe that there is something special about replacement level fertility [28, 29, 30, 31]. In 2017, fertility tended to be either considerably higher or lower than replacement level: 60 countries had a TFR of 1.79 or fewer children per woman, 138 countries had a TFR if 2.21 or more children per woman, and only there were only 44 countries in between [32]. Thus, so far there is no empirical basis for the assumption that countries will eventually meet in the middle around the replacement level—though the future could look different from the past.

Still, there is little theoretical reason to believe that fertility will converge around the replacement level. On the one hand, if low fertility represents an adaptive lag, fertility in post-demographic transition countries should increase as opposed to stabilize around the replacement level. Children from larger families will also gradually represent a larger share of the population, and they will inherit their parents' tendency to have bigger families [33], suggesting that fertility will increase. On the other hand, there is no reason to expect that the increases in education, contraception, and women's labor market participation will slow down or be reversed. Hence, there is no particular reason to believe that cohort fertility will rebound where it is already low [34]. Other theoretical approaches posit that women will not have (more) children so long as men remain unwilling to do an equal share of housework and childcare [35, 36]. This hypothesis is supported by evidence from highly developed countries, where, at least for some periods, countries with more egalitarian gender roles generally have higher fertility [35].

Some years ago, my colleagues and I put forth the low fertility trap hypothesis. We argued that once fertility stays low for a prolonged period, a series of mutually-reinforcing mechanisms make it ever less likely that birth rates will increase again in future [34, 37]. First, people's fertility preferences are influenced by what they have experienced in their own lives. People who come from smaller families, and who experienced fewer children in their social context will tend to see fewer children as the norm. The internalized low fertility norm is then reflected in their own reproductive behavior. Second, it is taking longer for young adults to become financially independent from their parents, and their economic outlook is less certain than in previous generations (e.g., due to high rates of unemployment among young adults in many of the world's richer countries). At the same time, young adults' material aspirations are probably higher than before (e.g., due to advertising, but also because of relatively high levels of parental wealth). We therefore expect each subsequent generation will have children later and smaller families. Finally, we have noted—un-controversially—that the age distribution of a population exerts an independent influence on the crude birth rate. Low fertility shifts the age structure of a population, so that fewer and fewer women enter reproductive age. As such, the total number of births in the population will decline, even with identical fertility rates as the previous generations of women. All three factors contribute to a "downward spiral" in births. Aspects of the low fertility trap hypothesis are—so far—consistent with the data.

At the same time that it is unlikely that fertility will rebound where it is already low, the end of reproduction—as portrayed in popular novels such as *Children of Men* and *A Handmaid's Tale* and their respective screen adaptions—is very unlikely. Historically, there is no precedent of fertility below 0.5 children per woman. One of the lowest period fertility levels ever recorded was in Vienna in 1934, when the TFR was just

0.61 children per woman, but it was preceded and succeeded by higher fertility [38]. More recently, fertility fell below one child per woman in many Spanish and Italian provinces in the 1990s [39], and the fertility of religiously unaffiliated women in Austria fell to 0.86 in 2001 (the last year religion was included in the census) [40]. In Asia, fertility in 2010 was just 1.04 children per woman in Hong Kong SAR and 0.89 in Taiwan. However, fertility ideals tend to be far higher than actual fertility even in populations with the lowest fertility. This implies that period fertility may increase as people who have delayed their fertility at least partially try to realize their fertility ideals toward the end of their reproductive windows. In some post-transition countries like France or Russia, period fertility has rebounded—partly following strong pro-natal policies [41, 42]. Furthermore, low fertility in certain subpopulations can be compensated by higher fertility in other subpopulations.

> *It's true that society would be greatly diminished without children, but it isn't right to create them just because we like having them around. People worry that we won't have enough workers to support pensioners, but economic systems are artificial and can be adjusted. We don't need to breed more wage slaves to prop up an obsolete system. If we go extinct, other species will have a chance to recover. I'll never see the day when there are no humans on the planet, but I can imagine what a magnificent world it would be—provided we go soon enough.*
>
> *—Les Knight, founder of the Voluntary Human Extinction Movement (VHMENT, pronounced "vehement"), in 2020 [1]*

What Will the Future of Fertility Look like?

In their most recent projections from 2019, the United Nations assumed that fertility in post-transition, low fertility countries will have a *maximum* of replacement level fertility, but not necessarily that fertility will stabilize around the replacement level [6]. The 2019 projections were informed by each country's own historical experience and also by the experiences of other low fertility countries. Countries that have experienced extended periods of low fertility are projected to maintain low fertility levels in the near future. According to the medium-variant projections, the United Nations expects that global fertility will fall from an average of 2.5 live births per woman in 2019 to 2.2 live births per woman in 2050, and to 1.9 live births per woman in 2100. In Europe and Northern America, total fertility is projected to increase slightly by the end of the century, from 1.7 live births per woman in 2019 to 1.8 in 2100. The World Bank similarly projects that global fertility will fall from 2.4 children per woman in 2020 to 2.2 children per woman in 2050 [43]. Based on continuing increases in women's education and contraceptive use in the coming years, the IHME projects that global fertility will drop below replacement level already by 2034 [25, 44]. All three projections find that the largest fertility declines will occur in sub-Saharan Africa [25, 43, 45]. The United Nations predicts that fertility in sub-Saharan Africa will reach the replacement level of 2.1 children per woman by 2100 [45] and IHME predicts it will decline below replacement already by 2063 [25, 44]. (The World Bank projects only until 2050, when sub-Saharan fertility is projected to be 3.1 children per woman [43].)

Projections typically focus on predicting how fertility will develop in a particular geographic region, or focus on what fertility would look like depending on changes in educational attainment [46]. My colleagues and I recently projected how fertility will develop for members of the world's eight major religions (see Fig. 17.1) [47]. Fertility currently differs across the world's major religions. The fluctuations in projected TFR by religion follow changes in the population sizes of different world regions. According to our projections, fertility differences across religious groups will gradually decrease. Nevertheless, in 2050, fertility will still be about 50% higher among Muslims and Christians compared to Buddhists and those without a religious affiliation in 2050. These fertility differentials will shift the world's religious landscape and also have implications for future fertility. In particular, greater shares of religious people in the population will push fertility upwards.

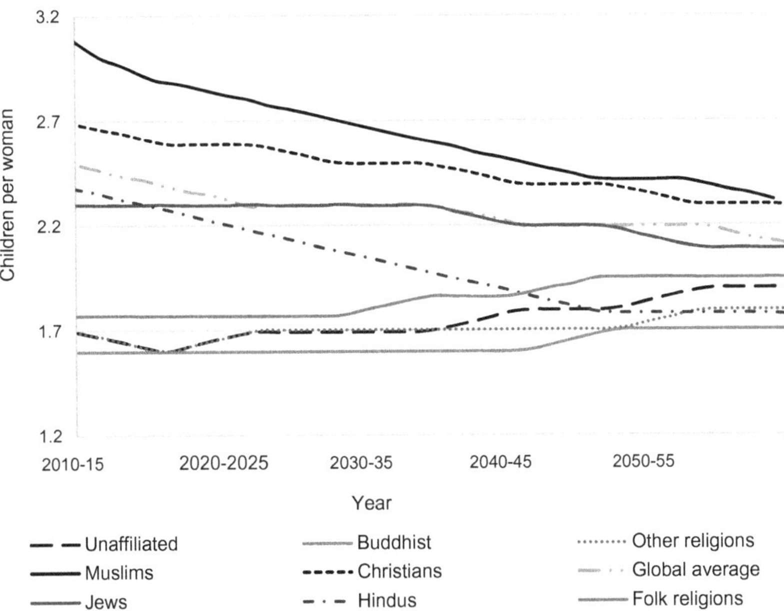

Fig. 17.1 Projected total fertility rate by religious affiliation. Based on [47]

The End of Reproduction is Unlikely, but so is a Return to Replacement Fertility in Richer Countries

Fertility projections are hugely important for adequately preparing society for the future. Improvements in data quality have made it easier to reliably predict fertility in the shorter term. Longer-term forecasts are more sensitive to the quality of the assumptions on which they are based. Most projections are based on the premise that all countries will follow more or less the same trajectory and that fertility will converge around the replacement level. These assumptions may, however, not hold.

While past experience has demonstrated that fertility can be surprising, it is still possible to make a number of general predictions about what the future of fertility will look like. It is highly unlikely that fertility will approach zero, and it is also unlikely that it will rebound to the levels observed prior to the demographic transition. But there is currently no particular reason to assume that fertility will rebound to replacement level in the world's richer countries, nor to assume that all countries will eventually converge around replacement level—or any other number. The future of fertility will depend to a considerable extent on how factors like female educational attainment, contraceptive use, changes in religious affiliation and adherence, and the cost of child-bearing develop, as well as unexpected economic and political events and natural disasters.

References

1. Knight, L. (2020, January 10). Experience: I campaign for the extinction of the human race. *The Guardian*. Retrieved from https://www.theguardian.com/lifeandstyle/2020/jan/10/i-campaign-for-the-extinction-of-the-human-race-les-knight.
2. Hailemariam, A. (2017). The second biggest African country undergoing rapid change: Ethiopia. In H. Groth, & J. F. May (Eds.), *Africa's population: In search of a demographic dividend* (pp. 53–69). Cham: Springer International.
3. Schmidt, E., Dorosh, P. A., Kedir Jemal, M., & Smart, J. (2018). Ethiopia's spatial and structural transformation: Public policy and drivers of change. ESSP working paper.International Food Policy Research International. https://www.ifpri.org/publication/ethiopias-spatial-and-structural-transformation-public-policy-and-drivers-change. Accessed 26 May 2021.
4. Raftery, A. E., Alkema, L., & Gerland, P. (2014). Bayesian population projections for the United Nations. *Statistical science: A review journal of the Institute of Mathematical Statistics*, 29(1), 58–68. https://doi.org/10.1214/13-STS419.
5. Skirbekk, V., Prommer, I., KC, S., Terama, E., Wilson, C. (2007). Report on methods for demographic projections at multiple levels of aggregation. PLUREL D1.2.1. https://core.ac.uk/download/pdf/52950131.pdf. Accessed 26 May 2021.
6. United Nations. (2019). World Population Prospects 2019: Methodology of the United Nations population estimates and projections. New

York: United Nations. https://population.un.org/wpp/Publications/Files/WPP2019_Methodology.pdf. Accessed 26 May 2021.
7. Keilman, N. (1998). How accurate are the United Nations world population projections? *Population and Development Review*, 24, 15–41. http://www.jstor.org/stable/2808049.
8. Keilman, N. (2019). Erroneous population forecasts. In T. Bengtsson, & N. Keilman (Eds.), *Old and New Perspectives on Mortality Forecasting* (pp. 95–111). Cham: Springer. https://doi.org/10.1007/978-3-030-05075-7_9.
9. Park, Y., & LaFrombois, M. E. H. (2019). Planning for growth in depopulating cities: An analysis of population projections and population change in depopulating and populating US cities. *Cities*, 90, 237–248. https://doi.org/10.1016/j.cities.2019.02.016.
10. Lee, J.-W., & Hong, K. (2012). Economic growth in Asia: Determinants and prospects. *Japan and the World Economy*, 24(2), 101–113. https://doi.org/10.1016/j.japwor.2012.01.005.
11. Pachauri, R. K., Allen, M. R., Barros, V. R., Broome, J., Cramer, W., Christ, R., et al. (2014). *Climate change 2014: synthesis report. Contribution of Working Groups I, II and III to the fifth assessment report of the Intergovernmental Panel on Climate Change*. Geneva: IPCC.
12. Carone, G., Costello, D., Guardia, D., Nuria, Mourre, G., Przywara, B., et al. (2005). The economic impact of ageing populations in the EU25 member states. Directorate General for Economic and Financial Affairs European Economy Economic Working Paper No. 236. Rochester, NY. Accessed 26 May 2021.
13. Wilson, T. (2012). Forecast accuracy and uncertainty of Australian Bureau of Statistics state and territory population projections. *International Journal of Population Research*, 1–16. https://doi.org/10.1155/2012/419824.
14. Armstrong, J. S., Green, K. C., & Graefe, A. (2015). Golden rule of forecasting: Be conservative. *Journal of Business Research*, 68(8), 1717–1731. https://doi.org/10.1016/j.jbusres.2015.03.031.
15. Population Reference Bureau (2001). Understanding and using population projections. Policy brief.Washington, D.C.: Population Reference Bureau. https://www.prb.org/understandingandusingpopulationprojections/. Accessed 26 May 2021.
16. United Nations (2019). World Population Prospects 2019. https://population.un.org/wpp/. Accessed 25 May 2021.

17. Erfani, A., & McQuillan, K. (2008). Rapid fertility decline in Iran: Analysis of intermediate variables. *Journal of Biosocial Science*, 40(3), 459–478. https://doi.org/10.1017/S002193200700243X.
18. Vahidnia, F. (2007). Case study: Fertility decline in Iran. *Population and Environment*, 28(4–5), 259–266. https://doi.org/10.1007/s11111-007-0050-9.
19. Ambrosetti, E., Angeli, A., & Novelli, M. (2019). Ideal family size and fertility in Egypt: An overview of recent trends. *Statistica*, 79(2), 223–244. https://doi.org/10.6092/issn.1973-2201/8811.
20. Goujon, A., & Al Zalak, Z. (2018). Why has fertility been increasing in Egypt? *Population & Societies*, 551, 1–4.
21. Radovich, E., el-Shitany, A., Sholkamy, H., & Benova, L. (2018). Rising up: Fertility trends in Egypt before and after the revolution. *PloS One*, 13(1), e0190148. https://doi.org/10.1371/journal.pone.0190148.
22. Götmark, F., & Andersson, M. (2020). Human fertility in relation to education, economy, religion, contraception, and family planning programs. *BMC Public Health*, 20(1), 1–17. https://doi.org/10.1186/s12889-020-8331-7.
23. Kebede, E., Goujon, A., & Lutz, W. (2019). Stalls in Africa's fertility decline partly result from disruptions in female education. *Proceedings of the National Academy of Sciences*, 116(8), 2891–2896. https://doi.org/10.1073/pnas.1717288116.
24. Eurostat (2019). Summary methodology of the 2018-based population projections (EUROPOP2018). Luxembourg: E. Commission. https://ec.europa.eu/eurostat/cache/metadata/Annexes/proj_esms_an26.pdf. Accessed 26 May 2021.
25. Vollset, S. E., Goren, E., Yuan, C.-W., Cao, J., Smith, A. E., Hsiao, T., et al. (2020). Fertility, mortality, migration, and population scenarios for 195 countries and territories from 2017 to 2100: A forecasting analysis for the Global Burden of Disease Study. *The Lancet*, 396(10258), 1285–1306. https://doi.org/10.1016/S0140-6736(20)30677-2.
26. United Nations. (2017). World Population Prospects 2017. United Nations. https://population.un.org/wpp/Download/Archive/Standard/. Accessed 26 May 2021.
27. United Nations. (2013). World fertility report 2012. New York: United Nations. https://www.un.org/development/desa/pd/content/world-fertility-report-2012. Accessed 26 May 2021.
28. Demeny, P. G. (1997). Replacement level fertility: The implausible endpoint of the demographic transition. In G. W. Jones, R. M. Douglas,

J. C. Caldwell, & R. M. D'Souza (Eds.), *The continuing demographic transition* (pp. 94–110). Oxford: Oxford University Press.
29. Skirbekk, V., & Kc, S. (2012). Fertility-reducing dynamics of women's social status and educational attainment. *Asian Population Studies*, 8(3), 251–264. https://doi.org/10.1080/17441730.2012.714667.
30. Frejka, T. (2017, December 4). Half the world's population reaching below replacement fertility. *N-IUSSP*. Retrieved from https://www.niussp.org/article/half-the-worlds-population-reaching-below-replacement-fertility/.
31. Zhao, Z., Xu, Q., & Yuan, X. (2017). Far below replacement fertility in urban China. *Journal of Biosocial Science*, 49(S1), S4–S19. https://doi.org/10.1017/S0021932017000347.
32. Central Intelligence Agency. (2017). *CIA World Factbook 2017*. Washington, D.C.: CIA.
33. Collins, J., & Page, L. (2019). The heritability of fertility makes world population stabilization unlikely in the foreseeable future. *Evolution and Human Behavior*, 40(1), 105–111. https://doi.org/10.1016/j.evolhumbehav.2018.09.001.
34. Lutz, W., Skirbekk, V., & Testa, M. R. (2006). The low-fertility trap hypothesis: Forces that may lead to further postponement and fewer births in Europe. *Vienna Yearbook of Population Research*, 167–192. http://www.iiasa.ac.at/Admin/PUB/Documents/RP-07-001.pdf.
35. McDonald, P. (2000). Gender equity in theories of fertility transition. *Population and Development Review*, 26(3), 427–439. https://doi.org/10.1111/j.1728-4457.2000.00427.x.
36. Yoon, S. -Y. (2016). Is gender inequality a barrier to realizing fertility intentions? Fertility aspirations and realizations in South Korea. *Asian Population Studies*, 12(2), 203–219. https://doi.org/10.1080/17441730.2016.1163873.
37. Lutz, W., & Skirbekk, V. (2005). Policies addressing the tempo effect in low-fertility countries. *Population and Development Review*, 31(4), 699–720. https://doi.org/10.1111/j.1728-4457.2005.00094.x.
38. Gisser, R., Grafinger, J., Haller, M., Kaufmann, A., Krämer, H., Ladstätter, J., et al. (1975). Bericht über die Situation der Frau in Österreich, Heft 4: Die persönliche Situation der Frau, Die·Freizeit der Frau [Report on the situation of women in Austria, vol 4: Womens' personal situation and leisure time]. Vienna: Bundeskanzleramt. https://www.parlament.gv.at/PAKT/VHG/XIII/III/III_00189/imfname_577633.pdf.
39. Sobotka, T. (2017). Post-transitional fertility: The role of childbearing postponement in fuelling the shift to low and unstable fertility levels.

Journal of Biosocial Science, 49(S1), S20–S45. https://doi.org/10.1017/S0021932017000323.

40. Goujon, A., Skirbekk, V., & Fliegenschnee, K. (2007). New times, old beliefs: Investigating the future of religions in Austria and Switzerland.
41. Pison, G. (2020). France has the highest fertility in Europe. *Population & Societies*, (3), 1–4. https://doi.org/10.3917/popsoc.575.0001.
42. Archangelskiy, V., Korotayev, A., & Shulgin, S. (2017). Modern fertility trends in Russia and the impact of the pro-natalist policies. *Sociological Studies*, 3(3), 43–50.
43. The World Bank. (2020). Population estimates and projections. https://databank.worldbank.org/reports.aspx?source=Health%20Nutrition%20and%20Population%20Statistics:%20Population%20estimates%20and%20projections. Accessed 26 May 2021.
44. Institute for Health Metrics and Evaluation. (2021). Total fertility rate, global, female, 1950–2100. University of Washington. https://vizhub.healthdata.org/population-forecast/. Accessed 14 June 2021.
45. United Nations. (2019). *World Population Prospects 2019: Highlights*. New York: U. Nations. https://www.un-ilibrary.org/content/publication/13bf5476-en. Accessed 26 May 2021.
46. Kc, S., Barakat, B., Goujon, A., Skirbekk, V., Sanderson, W. C., & Lutz, W. (2010). Projection of populations by level of educational attainment, age and sex for 120 countries for 2005–2050. *Demographic Research*, 22, 383–472. https://doi.org/10.4054/DemRes.2010.22.15.
47. Stonawski, M., Skirbekk, V., Hackett, C., Potančoková, M., Connor, P., & Grim, B. (2015). Global population projections by religion: 2010–2050. In B. J. Grim, T. M. Johnson, V. Skirbekk, & G. A. Zurlo (Eds.), *Yearbook of International Religious Demography 2015* (pp. 99–116). Leiden: Brill. https://doi.org/10.1163/9789004297395_004.

18

Fertility, Population Growth, and Population Composition

Fertility is becoming a more important driver of population growth. This is particularly true at advanced stages of the demographic transition, where mortality declines are slower and concentrated in post-reproductive ages. Population growth, in turn, impacts the environment and human welfare. Differences in fertility also eventually shift the characteristics of the global population. In this chapter, I discuss population growth and population shifts as two consequences of high and low fertility and differences in fertility across (sub)populations.

Population Growth Across Human Existence

For most of our existence, humans have been rather scarce. The eruption of the Toba volcano in what is now Sumatra in Indonesia about 70,000 years ago resulted in a genetic bottleneck [2, 3, 4] (i.e., when the population is greatly reduced in size, so that only a few individuals are able to pass on their genes to the next generation). The Toba eruption is thought to have reduced the human population to somewhere between 1,000 and 10,000 individuals [3, 7]. By the end of the last ice

V. Skirbekk, *Decline and Prosper!*,
https://doi.org/10.1007/978-3-030-91611-4_18

age about 11,700 years ago, the human population probably consisted of between 1 and 10 million people [8, 9], and somewhere between 150 and 300 million people by year 0 of the Christian calendar [11, 12, 13]. The size of the human population probably fluctuated frequently, just as it still does for most other species. Although most of the world had high fertility, high mortality constrained population growth to a modest level. A rise in population size in one period would often be offset by a rapid reduction in a subsequent period, resulting in slow, unstable, and uneven population growth and decline [11, 14, 15, 16, 17]. Recurrent plagues, famines, conflicts [18] and natural disasters limited population growth.

Between year 0 to around 1800, the size of the human population increased, but there were still several fluctuations and temporary decreases. Infectious disease slowed population growth; various outbreaks caused rapid reductions in population size. Several tens of millions of people died during the plague of Justinian (541–542). Up to 100 million people are thought to have died during the Black Death or bubonic plague (1347–1352), while the Spanish flu (1918–1920) took between 17 and 100 million lives. The deaths associated with these three plagues were numerous enough to cause temporary declines in the global population [19, 20, 21]. Following increased food production, more efficient societal organization, and improved living conditions, the global population probably reached close to half a billion individuals around the year 1500, and about one billion individuals by the first decade of the nineteenth century [12, 14, 15, 22].

Most of the increase in the global human population has occurred in just the past two centuries. Beginning around 1800, better hygiene, sanitation, and housing; the spread of new technologies (e.g., electricity, communication); increases in education and income; and improvements in the prevention and treatment of disease substantially prolonged human life [23, 24, 25, 26, 27]. Mortality continued to decline for infants, children, and young adults and, to a lesser extent, also for middle-aged and older people [28, 29]. Maternal mortality during childbirth fell at the same time that the health of women of reproductive age increased, raising their fecundity and extending their reproductive windows [30]. The widespread declines in mortality caused the global human population to increase from about 1 billion in 1800, to about 1.6 billion in 1900, and to around 3.5 billion in 1970 (see Fig. 18.1).

Population growth was very high in the last decades of the twentieth century. There were almost 6.1 billion humans on the planet in 2000. In 2020, the global human population was about 7.7 billion. By 2060, the world is likely to see its 10th billion human [29, 31]—a more than *two thousand-fold* increase in the population since the end of the last ice age, and more than a *one million-fold* increase since the last genetic bottleneck some 70,000 years ago. The exponential pace of human population growth observed in the last two centuries is unique to humans; similar rates of growth have never been observed in any other large mammal or primate. Humans have now become far more populous than any other larger mammal and dominate all but the most inhospitable regions of Earth.

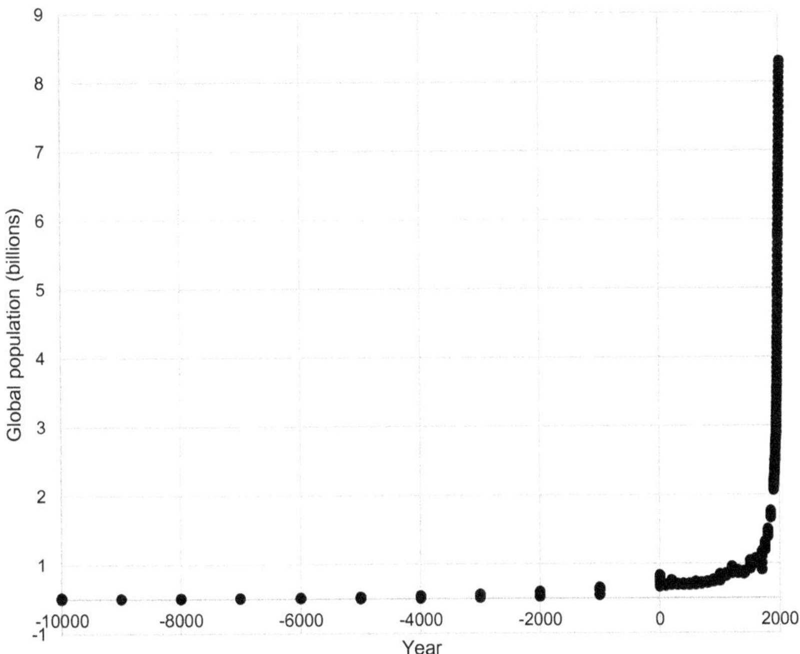

Fig. 18.1 Estimates of the global human population, 10,000 BCE through 2020. Based on [12]

After reaching a peak in the 1960s, annual population growth has since been slowing and may eventually stagnate in the course of the twenty-first century [31, 32]. Declining fertility and below replacement fertility in many countries have slowed down the rate of global population growth. High fertility in a number of very populous nations [31, 33] and an strong increases in life expectancy [34] act as upward pressures on the growth rate.

Fertility Now Matters More for Population Growth

As mortality and child mortality in particular have declined, fertility has become a much more important as a determinant of population growth. Fertility changes now impact population growth much more than they did before because the population is larger and average fertility is lower. In 1950, when global fertility was four children per woman and the number of newborns was around 40 million, a difference of 0.2 children per woman more or less would have implied about two million more or fewer births. In 2020, a difference of 0.2 children per woman would imply *13 million* more or fewer births. If the global TFR were to stabilize at 2.5 children per woman rather than at 1.5 children by end of the twenty-first century, it would more than quadruple the number of births. The human population would increase exponentially, as more children would produce more offspring in the next generation.

Differences in fertility have caused very different patterns of regional and national population growth. Rates of national population growth in Asia and Africa have tended to vastly exceed the rates of national population growth observed in most Western countries [31]. One example is Egypt, whose population increased from 4 million in 1805 to 93 million in 2017, more than a 20-fold increase [29, 35, 36]. Generally speaking, when the TFR is higher than the replacement level, population size will increase, and when it is less than the replacement level, population size will decrease. However, the relationship between fertility and population size also depends on mortality and the age structure of the population. A population with relatively high fertility and relatively high mortality can have a similar rate of population growth as a population with low fertility and low mortality. Compared to populations with an older age structure, populations with a younger age structure are likely to grow even if they have below replacement fertility, because relatively more people are having babies and relatively few people are dying.

Population growth in a specific region or country also depends on migration. High outmigration has strongly reduced population growth in countries such as Syria or Nepal, despite above replacement fertility. In contrast, high net immigration has meant that Germany has experienced population growth in spite of having below replacement fertility since around 1970 [31, 37]. *Natural population growth* occurs when births outnumber deaths [38]. Africa is experiencing strong natural population growth, while Europe is experiencing strong negative natural population growth. Due to low birth rates and/or outmigration, a number of countries (e.g., Lebanon, Cook Islands, Bulgaria) and particularly rural regions all over the world face declining populations and are being challenged to find ways to maintain the infrastructure and provide the population with adequate goods, services, and support.

Population Growth and Human Welfare: The Pessimists and Optimists

In 1798, as the human population was approaching a mere one billion, English demographer and pastor Thomas Malthus wrote that "the superior power of population cannot be checked without producing misery or vice" ([39], p. 11). *Malthusianism*—the view that, if left unchecked, population growth will ultimately result in human misery, mortality, and catastrophe [40, 41]—continues to influence perceptions of population growth. According to a pair of surveys conducted in the United States in 2014 [42], 59% of the general public and 82% of American scientists agreed that population growth will put a strain on natural resources.

Concerns about population growth are not unfounded. According to the 2018 edition of the United Nations World Water Development Report, by 2050 nearly six billion peoples will lack adequate access to clean water [43]. Feeding a growing population will increase the agricultural use of antibiotics, water, pesticides, and fertilizer as well as increase contact between humans and animals—all of which contribute to the emergence and spread of infectious disease [44]. One recent synthesis of the literature concluded that, since 1940, more than a quarter of all infectious human diseases were related to agricultural production [44]. The proportion of infectious diseases linked to agriculture will likely increase as agriculture expands and intensifies. Rapid population growth can also contribute to the "poverty trap" whereby poorer countries and poor families stay poor. With each additional child born, it gets more difficult for both parents to work, which limits the family budget, and the meager available resources also have to be shared between more people, leading to a continuation of poverty in subsequent generations [45, 46]. People in small and densely settled regions worry about overcrowding. Population growth is a major concern in Israel, one of the few wealthier countries with fertility far above the replacement level [47].

Malthusians have been criticized for underestimating the human ability to adapt [41, 48, 49, 50]. So far, technological and societal advances have been able to adequately increase agricultural yield and improve the production, storage, and preservation of food in order to support a human population far larger than Malthus probably ever imagined possible; living standards and life expectancy have both improved dramatically over the last two centuries [31, 51, 52]. Some see population growth as *good* for human welfare, arguing that population growth fuels economic development [53] and technological progress [54]. Greater population size is also often equated with greater social and political power, economic and military strength, and has been seen as a marker of a society's success and achievement [55]. High(er) fertility and population growth are thus sometimes spurred on by nationalism [56, 57], and population decline often creates a sense of alarm [58, 59].

Fertility, the Natural Environment, and Climate Change

Few would deny that humans have contributed to an immense loss of biodiversity and destruction of the natural environment [60, 61, 62]. Some scientists argue that the Earth has entered the "Anthropocene" Epoch, a geological era during which the Earth and its processes are substantially affected by human behavior [63, 64, 65]. The world's 7.7 billion people (as of 2019) represent just 0.01% of all that is alive, yet humans are thought to have caused the loss of half of all plants and 83% of all wild mammals at the same time that livestock's share of the world's biomass has increased [66]. The loss of biodiversity is attributable to several causes but the increases in the human population and human consumption levels are by far the biggest culprits [61, 66, 67].

About 60% of Earth's primate species, including apes, monkeys, gorillas, gibbons and lemurs, are threatened with extinction. About 75% have experienced recent population decline [1].

Population growth can exacerbate the destruction of ecosystems, pollution, and the exploitation of natural resources and it has clear implications for the pace of climate change [68, 69]. Carbon dioxide (CO_2) is the primary greenhouse gas contributing to global warming and climate change. Globally, CO_2 emissions in 2018 were 4.9 metric tons per capita, but ranged from very low emissions per capita in low income countries (e.g., Mali emitted 0.1 metric tons per capita) to several hundred times more in some in high income countries (44 metric tons per capita in Qatar) [70]. If regional per capita emissions were the same as today, but global fertility had followed the European pattern (i.e., fertility only moderately above the replacement level during the demographic transition), in 2010 the world's population would have been 4.8 billion instead of 6.9 billion, and total annual emissions would have been around 19% lower than what they were. China has drawn out its "One Child Policy Card" in climate negotiations [71], arguing that by reducing fertility it has also reduced its emissions based on counterfactual estimates of what emissions would have been had the One Child Policy not been in place [71, 72].

Experts often point out that the impact of population growth on the environment depends on a population's level of consumption and their per capita greenhouse gas emissions, as opposed to their population size per se [73, 74, 75, 76, 77]. By far most greenhouse gas emissions are produced in high income countries where fertility is already low. According to recent data, greenhouse gas emissions were 16.1 metric tons per capita in the United States, 9.4 in Japan, 8 in China, versus 1.9 in India, 1.6 in Albania, 1 in Angola, and 0.8 in Zimbabwe [78]. Indeed, most countries have either high fertility and low emissions, or low fertility and high emissions. Just a few countries have either both high fertility and high emissions (e.g., Israel and Saudi Arabia) or low fertility and low emissions (e.g., Armenia and Albania) [31, 78]. Thus, many of the countries experiencing rapid population growth are not experiencing large increases in emissions [79]. However, national emission levels are converging across the world as emissions decrease in richer countries and increase in emerging economies. China, where emissions more than tripled from about two tons per person in 2000 to almost seven tons in 2015 [80], is now the world's greatest CO_2 emitter, with around three times as much production-based greenhouse gas emissions as the European Union and almost twice that of the United States [81]. As countries become more similar with regard to their emissions, differences in their fertility become more important determinants of their population's impact on the planet.

In 2019, a YouGov survey asked adults in the United Kingdom: Do you think limiting the number of children you have for the sake of the planet is or is not necessary? More than half (53%) of respondents said "yes" [6].

Many people are optimistic that technological progress—together with effective policies—will eventually "fix" most contemporary environmental challenges [82, 83, 84]. Examples of past successes include the implementation of mandatory standards for automobiles in the

1950s which reduced smog, and the ban of chlorofluorocarbon gases in the 1990s which reduced greenhouse gas emissions [85]. New carbon capture technologies, better recycling technologies, an electrification of transport, and a shift toward greener energy production are just a few examples of changes that could significantly reduce the negative environmental impact of a larger population. Later born generations may also be more willing to adjust their lifestyles for the sake of sustainability [86, 87, 88]. Many of the world's developed nations have set an explicit goal to lower their emissions by signing the Kyoto Protocol or recommending regional or national emission targets. All else equal, reducing population growth would lower a country's emissions, help them meet their targets, and increase flexibility in addressing environmental sustainability [89, 90]. However, fertility is rarely discussed as a potential target for intervention, even though having one fewer child would be a much more effective way for individuals to reduce emissions than being vegetarian, not using a car, avoiding long distance flights, buying green energy, recycling or using low-energy lightbulbs [91].

If humans were to suddenly vanish, how soon would nature take over? Award-winning science writer Alan Weisman describes what would happen in New York City *[5]:*

Within 10 years: *Sidewalks crack and weeds invade. Hawks and falcons flourish, as do feral cats and dogs. The rat population, deprived of human garbage, crashes. Cockroaches, which thrive in warm buildings, disappear. Cultivated carrots, cabbages, broccoli and brussels sprouts revert to their wild ancestors.*

20 years: *Water-soaked steel columns supporting subway tunnels corrode and buckle. Bears and wolves invade Central Park.*

50 years: *Concrete chunks tumble from buildings, whose steel foundations begin to crumble. Indian Point nuclear reactors leak radioactivity into the Hudson River.*

100 years: *Oaks and maples re-cover the land.*

300 years: *Most bridges collapse.*

1000 years: *Hell Gate Bridge, built to bring the railroad across the East River, finally falls.*

10,000 years: *The Indian Point nuclear reactors continue to leak radioactivity into the Hudson River.*

> ***20,000 years:*** *Glaciers move relentlessly across the island of Manhattan and its environs, scraping the landscape clean.*

Shifting Characteristics of the Global Population

By the middle of the century, current high and low fertility rates will have dramatically shifted the characteristics of the global population, including its distribution across world regions. In 1820, almost 69% of world's population lived in Asia, 22.5% in Europe and North America, and just 7% in Africa and 1.5% in Latin America. By 2010, the distribution had changed to 60% in Asia, 16% in Europe and North America, 15% in Africa and 8.6% in Latin America. By the end of the century, the United Nations projects that nearly four in ten humans will be African, while the share of the world population in Asia, Europe and North America, and Latin Africa will be diminished to 43.5%, 10.6%, and 6.8%, respectively [31]. Sub-Saharan Africa is projected to become the most populous region around 2062, while India is projected to surpass China as the world's most populous country in the 2020s [92].

Earlier in this book I discussed how fertility differs across the world's major religious groups. My colleagues and I have projected how these fertility differences will change the global religious landscape. As shown in Fig. 18.2, we have projected that the number of Muslims globally will nearly equal the number of Christians by 2050. The global proportion of atheists, agnostics, and other people who do not affiliate with a religion—although rising in countries such as the United States and France—will decline. The global Buddhist population will be about the same size it was in 2010, while the Hindu and Jewish populations will be larger than they are today. In Europe, Muslims will make up 10% of the overall population. India will retain a Hindu majority but also will have the largest Muslim population of any country in the world, surpassing Indonesia. In the United States, Christians will decline from more than three-quarters of the population in 2010 to two-thirds in

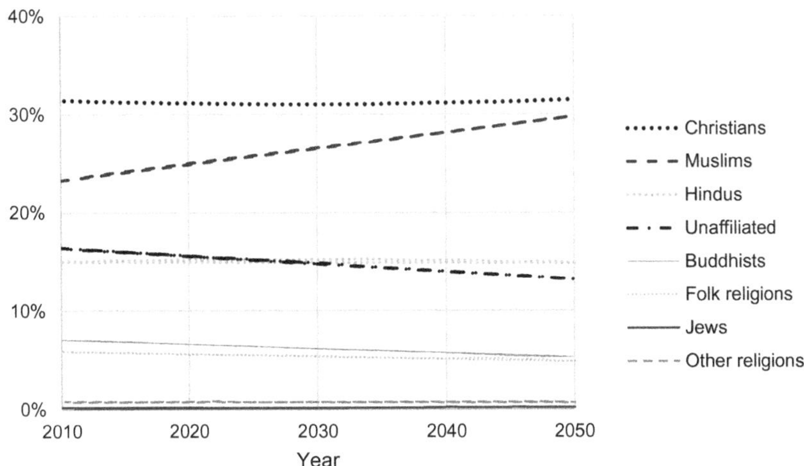

Fig. 18.2 Projected changes in the global religious landscape, 2010 to 2050. Based on [94]

2050, and Muslims will overtake Jews as the largest non-Christian religion [93, 94]. Shifts in the religious landscape may imply that fertility eventually increases unless Muslim childbearing patterns fully converge to the global average.

Fertility and Population Aging

Lower fertility is also causing shifts in the age structure of the global and also many regional populations: Namely, the relative share of young people is decreasing [31]. Following fertility declines, the world is now approaching a situation in which the proportion of dependent children is decreasing relative to the proportion of adults in prime working ages. In 1950, there were 1.8 people aged 15 to 64 years for each child younger than 15. Today, there are 2.5, and by the end of the century, there will be 3.4 working age adults for each child [32]. Experts often discuss how fertility decline can create a temporary *demographic dividend* when the working-age population becomes proportionately larger than the non-working-age share of the population (i.e., dependent children and older, non-working people). With fewer people to support and more people working, resources are freed up which can be invested in accelerating a country's economic development and well-being (e.g., investments in infrastructure, more educational spending per capita, more opportunities for women to engage in paid work, more household savings for old age).

Lower fertility and fewer dependent children on their own are no guarantee that there will be a demographic dividend, however. Asia experienced a demographic dividend in the late twentieth century and the gross domestic product increased sevenfold. Despite similar decreases in fertility, economic growth in Latin America was only about twofold around the same time, reflecting Latin America's lower investment in education among other factors [95]. Recent analyses have suggested that the demographic dividend is, to a significant extent, in fact an *education* dividend; that is, improvements in education appear to be much more important for stimulating economic growth than changes in the age structure alone [96, 97, 98].

Along with decreases in late-life mortality, lower fertility and further fertility decline will contribute to an increase in the proportion of older people in the global population. Although population aging is inevitable due to lower mortality, fertility determines how fast population aging takes place. The share of the global population aged 65 + years increased from 6% in 1990 to 9% in 2019, and it is projected to increase to 16% by 2050 [99]. In virtually every country in the world, older people (65 + years) comprise a growing share of the population, though differences in the speed of fertility and mortality declines imply that there are and will continue to be great differences in the speed and extent of population aging across nations.

Figure 18.3 shows how the *median age* (i.e., the age that divides the population into two equally-sized groups, such that 50% of the population is younger, and 50% is older) of each world region has changed and is projected to change between 1950 and 2100 [31]. As seen in the figure, the population of all world regions with the exception of Africa got older between 1950 and 2020, and all world regions are projected to get older in the future. So far, the oldest populations have been in Europe and North America, but by 2100 it is projected that the populations of Latin America and the Caribbean and Asia will be as old or

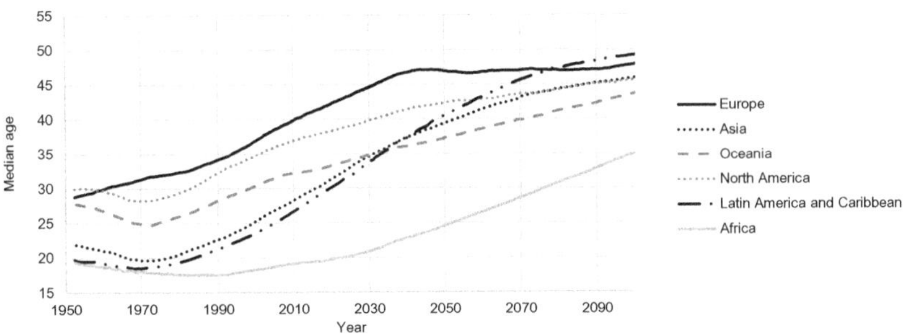

Fig. 18.3 Median age by world region, 1950 to 2100. Based on [31]

older. Between 2019 and 2050, the fastest population aging will occur in the least developed countries: By 2050, the share of older persons is projected at least to double in Northern Africa and Western Asia, Central and Southern Asia, Latin America and the Caribbean, and Eastern and South-Eastern Asia [99]. In many countries, there is fear the population will *grow old before growing rich*, such that countries will have limited capacity to implement social security systems that will ensure a high quality of life at older ages.

The aging of the global population will challenge governments around the world in many ways, not least with respect to economic growth, social security, and healthcare service provision [100, 101, 102, 103]. There are several ways that governments can ameliorate the challenges of an aging population. One way is to accumulate capital so that it is possible to live off the dividends even if large proportions of the populations are no longer working [104, 105, 106, 107]. Other strategies include increasing workers' productivity through skill improvements and developing new technologies, extending the length of working life, and increasing female participation in the labor market. It is also important to note that, contrary to common stereotypes, older populations do not necessarily have worse health or cognitive status [58, 108, 109, 110]. In fact, the same chronological age can mean very different things in different countries. My colleagues and I have shown, for instance, that a 77-year-old in Japan is as healthy as a 60-year-old in India [109]. Countries that are demographically older may in fact have more cognitively and physically healthy people than countries that are demographically younger [109, 110, 111]. Evidence from low fertility countries tends to suggest that old age health and functional level is improving. New generations of older individuals have better cognitive functioning [112, 113, 114] and are physically stronger [115] than previous generations of older people, and there is large potential for individuals to work to advanced ages [116]. Lower poverty [117], high vaccine coverage [118], and compulsory schooling [119] may have contributed to a delay in or less age-related cognitive decline.

In sum, population aging is not nearly as disastrous as many people assume. There may also be particular benefits to having an older population, including reduced risk of violent conflicts, wars, and disputes [120, 121, 122]. Criminal activity is concentrated among younger age groups; violence is committed mainly by men from the early teens to the early thirties [123, 124, 125]. Changing age structures are a key reason why projections suggest that there will be a sustained decline in the proportion of the world's countries troubled by internal conflicts, from about 15% in 2009 to 7% in 2050 [126]. The relatively high fertility and large adolescent populations in sub-Saharan Africa as well as some nations in East and South Asia may imply that these regions will continue to be at risk for internal conflicts.

Fertility Shapes Our Shared Future

Fertility is more important for shaping future population developments now than at any earlier point in history. In just two centuries—a blink of the eye in evolutionary terms—the human population has increased exponentially. The pace of increase has been much higher in Africa and Asia than elsewhere. Due to declining fertility, the rate of global population growth is slowing, and the populations in many countries will in fact decline. The world's population is likely to grow more African, older, more religious and specifically more Muslim. Countries with higher fertility will end up with a larger share of the world's population, but it is uncertain whether having more people will translate into more economic, military, or political influence in the world.

The extent to which population growth is "good" or "bad" depends on the context as well as the outcome considered. Many people—and even more scientists—believe that a reduction in population growth is good for people and especially beneficial for the planet, easing pressure on scarce resources, reducing congestion, and increasing ecological sustainability. At the same time, however, people tend to dislike the idea that their *own* national, ethnic, cultural, or ideological group may dwindle in size. High population growth and population decline each come along with their own set of challenges, and their consequences depend on the populations' level of education and technological level [54, 127], as well as government response. Countries with high fertility are challenged to avoid getting stuck in the "poverty trap" as well as address the consequences of high population density which include infectious disease, higher housing prices, unemployment, and less space for wildlife and nature. Countries with low fertility face a different set of challenges, such as low economic growth, maintaining fiscal sustainability, and providing adequate health care and social services to older populations.

Is stagnant or declining population a big economic problem? It doesn't have to be. In fact, in a world of limited resources and major environmental problems there's something to be said for a reduction in population pressure. But we need to think about policy differently in a flat-population economy than we did in the days when maturing baby boomers were rapidly swelling the potential work force.

—Paul Krugman, influential American economist, in an opinion piece for written for The New York Times *in 2021 [10]*

Education is key to optimizing human welfare. Increasing education in (sub)populations where it is low would effectively reduce fertility, increase productivity, and increase the potential for innovations that reduce the human impact on the environment. Countries that have invested more in health and education also tend to experience less "functional aging" at the population level in spite of having older age structures. A smaller population of highly educated people may also wield more influence than bigger but less-skilled populations, particularly in an age of rapid automation. More education is thus more likely to improve a country's economic and cultural might than more babies.

References

1. Estrada, A., Garber, P. A., Rylands, A. B., Roos, C., Fernandez-Duque, E., Di Fiore, A., et al. (2017). Impending extinction crisis of the world's primates: Why primates matter. *Science Advances*, 3(1), e1600946. https://doi.org/10.1126/sciadv.1600946.
2. Robock, A., Ammann, C. M., Oman, L., Shindell, D., Levis, S., & Stenchikov, G. (2009). Did the Toba volcanic eruption of ~74 ka BP produce widespread glaciation? *Journal of Geophysical Research: Atmospheres*, 114(D10). https://doi.org/10.1029/2008JD011652.
3. Ambrose, S. H. (1998). Late Pleistocene human population bottlenecks, volcanic winter, and differentiation of modern humans. *Journal of Human Evolution*, 34(6), 623–651. https://doi.org/10.1006/jhev.1998.0219.
4. Huff, C. D., Xing, J., Rogers, A. R., Witherspoon, D., & Jorde, L. B. (2010). Mobile elements reveal small population size in the ancient ancestors of Homo sapiens. *Proceedings of the National Academy of Sciences*, 107(5), 2147–2152. https://doi.org/10.1073/pnas.0909000107.
5. Weisman, A. (2005, February 6). Earth without people. *Discover*, pp. 60–65. Retrieved from https://www.discovermagazine.com/planet-earth/earth-without-people.
6. YouGov. (2019). Survey: Prince Harry and has said he will only have at most two children, saying any more would be irresponsible for the planet. Do you think limiting the number of children you have for the sake of the planet is or is not necessary? https://yougov.co.uk/topics/education/survey-results/daily/2019/07/31/b6541/1. Accessed October 2 2020.
7. Kivisild, T. (2014). Genetic bottlenecks in archaeology. In C. Smith (Ed.), *Encyclopedia of global archaeology* (pp. 2997–3000). New York: Springer. https://doi.org/10.1007/978-1-4419-0465-2_677.
8. Manning, S. (2008). Year-by-year world population estimates: 10,000 BC to 2007 AD. https://scottmanning.com/content/year-by-year-world-population-estimates/. Accessed 26 May 2021.

9. Pala, M., Olivieri, A., Achilli, A., Accetturo, M., Metspalu, E., Reidla, M., et al. (2012). Mitochondrial DNA signals of late glacial recolonization of Europe from near eastern refugia. *The American Journal of Human Genetics*, 90(5), 915–924. https://doi.org/10.1016/j.ajhg.2012.04.003.
10. Krugman, P. (2021, May 17). Learning to live with low fertility, Opinion. *The New York Times*. Retrieved from https://www.nytimes.com/2021/05/17/opinion/low-population-growth-economy-inflation.html.
11. McEvedy, C. (1978). *Atlas of world population history*. Harmondsworth: Penguin Books.
12. Roser, M., Ritchie, H., & Ortiz-Ospina, E. (2019). World population growth. https://ourworldindata.org/world-population-growth. Accessed 26 May 2021.
13. Klein Goldewijk, K., Beusen, A., & Janssen, P. (2010). Long-term dynamic modeling of global population and built-up area in a spatially explicit way: HYDE 3.1. *The Holocene*, 20(4), 565–573. https://doi.org/10.1177/0959683609356587.
14. Cohen, J. E. (1995). *How many people can the Earth support?* New York: Rockefeller University.
15. Durand, J. D. (1977). Historical estimates of world population: An evaluation. *Population and Development Review*, 253–296. https://doi.org/10.2307/1971891
16. Li, H., & Durbin, R. (2011). Inference of human population history from individual whole-genome sequences. *Nature*, 475(7357), 493–496. https://doi.org/10.1038/nature10231.
17. Haub, C. (1995). How many people have ever lived on earth. *Population Today*, 23(2), 4–5.
18. Caldwell, J. C. (2006). Back to the future: The great mortality crises. *Demographic transition theory* (pp. 387–396). Dordrecht: Springer. https://doi.org/10.1007/978-1-4020-4498-4_16.
19. Hays, J. N. (2005). *Epidemics and pandemics: Their impacts on human history*. Santa Barbara: ABC-CLIO.
20. Morse, S. S. (2007). Pandemic influenza: studying the lessons of history. *Proceedings of the National Academy of Sciences*, 104(18), 7313–7314. https://doi.org/10.1073/pnas.0702659104.
21. Alfani, G. (2013). Plague in seventeenth-century Europe and the decline of Italy: An epidemiological hypothesis. *European Review of Economic History*, 17(4), 408–430. https://doi.org/10.1093/ereh/het013.
22. Maddison, A. (2010) Statistics on world population, GDP, and per capita GDP 1–2008 AD. Groningen: Groningen Growth and Development

Centre, University of Groningen. http://ghdx.healthdata.org/record/statistics-world-population-gdp-and-capita-gdp-1-2008-ad. Accessed 26 May 2021.

23. Wolleswinkel-Van den Bosch, J. H., van Poppel, F. W., Tabeau, E., & Mackenbach, J. P. (1998). Mortality decline in The Netherlands in the period 1850–1992: A turning point analysis. *Social Science & Medicine*, 47(4), 429–443. https://doi.org/10.1016/s0277-9536(98)00060-4.
24. Murray, C. J., Barber, R. M., Foreman, K. J., Ozgoren, A. A., Abd-Allah, F., Abera, S. F., et al. (2015). Global, regional, and national disability-adjusted life years (DALYs) for 306 diseases and injuries and healthy life expectancy (HALE) for 188 countries, 1990–2013: Quantifying the epidemiological transition. *The Lancet*, 386(10009), 2145–2191. https://doi.org/10.1016/S0140-6736(15)61340-X.
25. McKeown, R. E. (2009). The epidemiologic transition: Changing patterns of mortality and population dynamics. *American Journal of Lifestyle Medicine*, 3(1_suppl), 19S-26S. https://doi.org/10.1177/1559827609335350.
26. Dye, C., & Williams, B. G. (2010). The population dynamics and control of tuberculosis. *Science*, 328(5980), 856–861. https://doi.org/10.1126/science.1185449.
27. Huynen, M. M., Vollebregt, L., Martens, P., & Benavides, B. M. (2005). The epidemiologic transition in Peru. *Revista Panamericana de Salud Pública*, 17(1), 51–59. https://doi.org/10.1590/s1020-49892005000100010.
28. Mathers, C. D., Stevens, G. A., Boerma, T., White, R. A., & Tobias, M. I. (2015). Causes of international increases in older age life expectancy. *The Lancet*, 385(9967), 540–548. https://doi.org/10.1016/S0140-6736(14)60569-9.
29. United Nations (1973). The determinants and consequences of population trends: new summary of findings on interaction of demographic, economic and social factors. Population studies no. 50. New York: United Nations.
30. Diers, C. J. (1974). Historical trends in the age at menarche and menopause. *Psychological Reports*, 34(3), 931–937. https://doi.org/10.2466/pr0.1974.34.3.931.
31. United Nations. (2019). World Population Prospects 2019. https://population.un.org/wpp/. Accessed 25 May 2021.
32. Roser, M. (2019). Future population growth. https://ourworldindata.org/future-population-growth. Accessed 26 May 2021.

33. Garenne, M. (2017). Record high fertility in sub-Saharan Africa in a comparative perspective. *African Population Studies*, 31(2). https://doi.org/10.11564/31-2-1043.
34. Roth, G. A., Abate, D., Abate, K. H., Abay, S. M., Abbafati, C., Abbasi, N., et al. (2018). Global, regional, and national age-sex-specific mortality for 282 causes of death in 195 countries and territories, 1980–2017: A systematic analysis for the Global Burden of Disease Study 2017. *The Lancet*, 392(10159), 1736–1788. https://doi.org/10.1016/S0140-6736(18)32203-7.
35. Moreland, S. (2006). Egypt's population program: Assessing 25 years of family planning. [Brief prepared for the US Agency for International Development]. http://www.policyproject.com/pubs/countryreports/Egypt%2025%20yr%20retro%20Final.pdf. Accessed 26 May 2021.
36. Khadr, Z. (2012). Changes in the demographic profile of the Egyptian population: Prospects and implications. In H. Groth, & A. Sousa-Poza (Eds.), *Population dynamics in Muslim countries* (pp. 131–146). Berlin, Heidelberg: Springer.
37. German Statistical Office. (2020). Population projection. https://www.destatis.de/EN/Themes/Society-Environment/Population/Population-Projection/_node.html.
38. Dyson, T., & Murphy, M. (1985). The onset of fertility transition. *Population and Development Review*, 11(3), 399–440. https://doi.org/10.2307/1973246.
39. Malthus, T. R. (1798). *An essay on the principle of population as it affects the future improvement of society, with remarks on the speculations of Mr Godwin, M Condorcet, and other writers.* London: J. Johnson. https://archive.org/details/essayonprinciple00malt_1. Accessed 26 May 2021.
40. Hollander, S. (2017). Thomas Robert Malthus (1766–1834). *The Palgrave Companion to Cambridge Economics* (pp. 233–256). Springer.
41. Levin, S. M. (1966). Malthus and the idea of progress. *Journal of the History of Ideas*, 92–108. https://doi.org/10.2307/2708310.
42. Pew Research Center. (2015). Public and scientists' views on science and society. https://www.pewresearch.org/science/2015/01/29/chapter-3-attitudes-and-beliefs-on-science-and-technology-topics/#population-growth-and-natural-resources-23-point-gap. Accessed 26 May 2021.
43. Boretti, A., & Rosa, L. (2019). Reassessing the projections of the World Water Development Report. *npj Clean Water*, 2(1), 1–6. https://doi.org/10.1038/s41545-019-0039-9.

44. Rohr, J. R., Barrett, C. B., Civitello, D. J., Craft, M. E., Delius, B., DeLeo, G. A., et al. (2019). Emerging human infectious diseases and the links to global food production. *Nature Sustainability*, 2(6), 445–456. https://doi.org/10.1038/s41893-019-0293-3.
45. Traverso, S. (2016). How to escape from a poverty trap: The case of Bangladesh. *World Development Perspectives*, 4, 48–59. https://doi.org/10.1016/j.wdp.2016.12.005.
46. Tabata, K. (2003). Inverted U-shaped fertility dynamics, the poverty trap and growth. *Economics letters*, 81(2), 241–248. https://doi.org/10.1016/S0165-1765(03)00188-5.
47. Troen, I., & Troen, C. (2017). Has Israel reached the limits of growth? The economic and ecological absorptive capacity of Israel/Palestine. *The Journal of the Middle East and Africa*, 8(4), 309–323. https://doi.org/10.1080/21520844.2017.1403234.
48. Lee, J., & Wang, F. (2001). *One quarter of humanity: Malthusian mythology and Chinese realities, 1700–2000*. Cambridge, MA: Harvard University Press.
49. Nicolini, E. A. (2007). Was Malthus right? A VAR analysis of economic and demographic interactions in pre-industrial England. *European Review of Economic History*, 11(1), 99–121. https://doi.org/10.1017/S1361491606001894.
50. Winch, D. (2013). *Malthus: A very short introduction*. Oxford: Oxford University Press.
51. Asadullah, M. N., & Savoia, A. (2018). Poverty reduction during 1990–2013: Did millennium development goals adoption and state capacity matter? *World Development*, 105, 70–82. https://doi.org/10.1016/j.worlddev.2017.12.010.
52. Oeppen, J., & Vaupel, J. (2002). Broken limits to life expectancy. *Science*, 296(5570), 1029–1031. https://doi.org/10.1126/science.1069675.
53. Piketty, T. (2014). *Capital in the twenty-first century*. Cambridge, MA: Harvard University Press.
54. Boserup, E. (2017). *The conditions of agricultural growth: The economics of agrarian change under population pressure*. New York: Routledge.
55. Togman, R. (2019). Populate or perish (Europe 1870–1945). *Nationalizing Sex: Fertility, Fear, and Power* (pp. 50–80). New York: Oxford University Press. https://doi.org/10.1093/oso/9780190871840.003.0004.
56. Bowles, N. (2019, March 18). 'Replacement theory,' a racist, sexist doctrine, spreads in far-right circles. *The New York Times*. Retrieved

from https://www.nytimes.com/2019/03/18/technology/replacement-theory.html.
57. King, L. (2002). Demographic trends, pronatalism, and nationalist ideologies in the late twentieth century. *Ethnic and Racial Studies*, 25(3), 367–389. https://doi.org/10.1080/01419870020036701d.
58. Bricker, D., & Ibbitson, J. (2019). *Empty planet: The shock of global population decline*. London: Hachette UK.
59. Van Dalen, H. P., & Henkens, K. (2011). Who fears and who welcomes population decline? *Demographic Research*, 25, 437–464. https://doi.org/10.4054/DemRes.2011.25.13.
60. Kerr, J. T., & Currie, D. J. (1995). Effects of human activity on global extinction risk. *Conservation Biology*, 9(6), 1528–1538. https://doi.org/10.1046/j.1523-1739.1995.09061528.x.
61. Sui, X., Mao, L., Liu, Y., & He, F. (2018). Mapping relative extinction risk for biodiversity conservation. *Biological Conservation*, 226, 168–176. https://doi.org/10.1016/j.biocon.2018.07.01.
62. Crist, E., Mora, C., & Engelman, R. (2017). The interaction of human population, food production, and biodiversity protection. *Science*, 356(6335), 260–264. https://doi.org/10.1126/science.aal2011.
63. Bowen, W. M., & Gleeson, R. E. (2018). The evolution of human settlements: From Pleistocene origins to Anthropocene prospects.
64. Dirzo, R., Young, H. S., Galetti, M., Ceballos, G., Isaac, N. J., & Collen, B. (2014). Defaunation in the Anthropocene. *Science*, 345(6195), 401–406. https://doi.org/10.1126/science.1251817.
65. Crutzen, P. J. (2006). The "Anthropocene". *Earth system science in the Anthropocene* (pp. 13–18). Berlin, Heidelberg: Springer.
66. Bar-On, Y. M., Phillips, R., & Milo, R. (2018). The biomass distribution on Earth. *Proceedings of the National Academy of Sciences*, 115(25), 6506–6511. https://doi.org/10.1073/pnas.1711842115.
67. Fears, D. (2019, May 6). One million species face extinction, UN report says. And humans will suffer as a result. *Washington Post*. Retrieved from https://www.washingtonpost.com/climate-environment/2019/05/06/one-million-species-face-extinction-un-panel-says-humans-will-suffer-result.
68. Hayes, A. C., & Adamo, S. B. (2014). Introduction: Understanding the links between population dynamics and climate change. *Population and Environment*, 35(3), 225–230. https://doi.org/10.1007/s11111-014-0208-1.
69. Bergstrom, R., Caddell, R. A., Chynoweth, M. W., Ellsworth, L. M., Henly-Shepard, S., Iwashita, D. K., et al. (2013). A review

of solutions and challenges to addressing human population growth and global climate change. *International Journal of Climate Change: Impacts & Responses*, 4(3). https://doi.org/10.18848/1835-7156/CGP/v04i03/37178.
70. The World Bank. (2021). CO2 emissions (metric tons per capita). https://data.worldbank.org/indicator/EN.ATM.CO2E.PC?end=2014&start=1960&view=chart. Accessed 26 May 2021.
71. Ma, Y. (2010, June 1). China's view of climate change. *Policy Review*. Retrieved from https://www.hoover.org/research/chinas-view-climate-change.
72. Guan, D., Hubacek, K., Weber, C. L., Peters, G. P., & Reiner, D. M. (2008). The drivers of Chinese CO2 emissions from 1980 to 2030. *Global Environmental Change*, 18(4), 626–634. https://doi.org/10.1016/j.gloenvcha.2008.08.001.
73. Cafaro, P., & Crist, E. (Eds.) (2012). *Life on the brink: Environmentalists confront overpopulation*. Athens, GA: University of Georgia Press.
74. Bongaarts, J., & O'Neill, B. C. (2018). Global warming policy: Is population left out in the cold. *Science*, 361(6403), 650–652. https://doi.org/10.1126/science.aat8680.
75. Jyoti, K. P., & Painuly, J. P. (1994). Population, consumption patterns and climate change: A socioeconomic perspective from the South. *Ambio*, 23(7), 434–437. www.jstor.org/stable/4314249.
76. Toth, G., & Szigeti, C. (2016). The historical ecological footprint: From over-population to over-consumption. *Ecological Indicators*, 60, 283–291. https://doi.org/10.1016/j.ecolind.2015.06.040.
77. Bradshaw, C. J., & Brook, B. W. (2014). Human population reduction is not a quick fix for environmental problems. *Proceedings of the National Academy of Sciences*, 111(46), 16610–16615. https://doi.org/10.1073/pnas.1410465111.
78. Monforti-Ferrario, F. O., G., Schaaf, E., Guizzardi, D., Olivier, J.G..J., Solazzo, E., Lo Vullo, E., Crippa, M., Muntean, M., Vignati, E. (2019). *Fossil CO2 and GHG emissions of all world countries*. Luxembourg: P. O. o. t. E. Union. https://op.europa.eu/en/publication-detail/-/publication/9d09ccd1-e0dd-11e9-9c4e-01aa75ed71a1/language-en. Accessed 26 May 2021.
79. Satterthwaite, D. (2009). The implications of population growth and urbanization for climate change. *Environment and Urbanization*, 21(2), 545–567. https://doi.org/10.1177/0956247809344361.

80. Ritchie, H., & Roser, M. Greenhouse gas emissions. https://ourworldindata.org/greenhouse-gas-emissions. Accessed 26 May 2021.
81. Acar, S., Söderholm, P., & Brännlund, R. (2018). Convergence of per capita carbon dioxide emissions: Implications and meta-analysis. *Climate Policy*, 18(4), 512–525. https://doi.org/10.1080/14693062.2017.1314244.
82. Jackson, N. (2004). When the population clock stops ticking. In R. White (Ed.), *Controversies in environmental sociology* (pp. 92–112). Melbourne: Cambridge University Press.
83. McCollum, D. L., Zhou, W., Bertram, C., De Boer, H.-S., Bosetti, V., Busch, S., et al. (2018). Energy investment needs for fulfilling the Paris Agreement and achieving the Sustainable Development Goals. *Nature Energy*, 3(7), 589–599. https://doi.org/10.1038/s41560-018-0179-z.
84. Gonella, F., Almeida, C., Fiorentino, G., Handayani, K., Spanò, F., Testoni, R., et al. (2019). Is technology optimism justified? A discussion towards a comprehensive narrative. *Journal of Cleaner Production*, 223, 456–465. https://doi.org/10.1016/j.jclepro.2019.03.126.
85. Crutzen, P., & Ramathan, V. (2000). The ascent of atmospheric sciences. *Science*, 290(5490), 299–304. https://doi.org/10.1126/science.290.5494.1098b.
86. Büttner, T., & Grübler, A. (1995). The birth of a "Green" generation?: Generational dynamics of resource consumption patterns. *Technological Forecasting and Social Change*, 50(2), 113–134. https://doi.org/10.1016/0040-1625(95)00052-C.
87. Smith, T. (2012). Public attitudes towards climate change and other global environmental issues across time and countries, 1993–2010. Policy workshop: Public attitudes and environmental policy in Canada and Europe, Canada-European Transatlantic Dialogue, Carleton University in Ottawa, Canada.
88. Fagan, M., & Huang, C. (2019, April 18). A look at how people around the world view climate change. Retrieved from https://www.pewresearch.org/fact-tank/2019/04/18/a-look-at-how-people-around-the-world-view-climate-change/. Accessed 28 May 2021.
89. Campbell, M., Cleland, J., Ezeh, A., & Prata, N. (2007). Return of the population growth factor. *Science*, 315(5818), 1501–1502. https://doi.org/10.1126/science.1140057.
90. Menz, T., & Welsch, H. (2012). Population aging and carbon emissions in OECD countries: Accounting for life-cycle and cohort effects.

Energy Economics, 34(3), 842–849. https://doi.org/10.1016/j.eneco.2011.07.016.

91. Wynes, S., & Nicholas, K. A. (2017). The climate mitigation gap: Education and government recommendations miss the most effective individual actions. *Environmental Research Letters*, 12(7). https://doi.org/10.1088/1748-9326/aa7541.
92. United Nations. (2019). *World Population Prospects 2019: Highlights*. New York: U. Nations. https://www.un-ilibrary.org/content/publication/13bf5476-en. Accessed 26 May 2021.
93. Pew Research Center. (2015). *The future of world religions: Population growth projections, 2010–2050*. Washington, D.C.: P. R. Center. https://www.pewforum.org/2015/04/02/religious-projections-2010-2050/. Accessed 26 May 2021.
94. Stonawski, M., Skirbekk, V., Hackett, C., Potančoková, M., Connor, P., & Grim, B. (2015). Global population projections by religion: 2010–2050. In B. J. Grim, T. M. Johnson, V. Skirbekk, & G. A. Zurlo (Eds.), *Yearbook of International Religious Demography 2015* (pp. 99–116). Leiden: Brill. https://doi.org/10.1163/9789004297395_004.
95. United Nations Population Fund. (2016). Demographic dividend. https://www.unfpa.org/demographic-dividend. Accessed 26 May 2021.
96. Lutz, W., Crespo Cuaresma, J., Kebede, E., Prskawetz, A., Sanderson, W. C., & Striessnig, E. (2019). Education rather than age structure brings demographic dividend. *Proceedings of the National Academy of Sciences*, 116(26), 12798–12803. https://doi.org/10.1073/pnas.1820362116.
97. Lutz, W., Cuaresma, J. C., & Sanderson, W. (2008). The demography of educational attainment and economic growth. *Science*, 319(5866), 1047–1048. https://doi.org/10.1126/science.1151753.
98. Cuaresma, J. C., Lutz, W., & Sanderson, W. (2014). Is the demographic dividend an education dividend? *Demography*, 51(1), 299–315.
99. United Nations. (2019). World Population Ageing 2019: Highlights. New York: United Nations. https://www.un.org/en/development/desa/population/publications/pdf/ageing/WorldPopulationAgeing2019-Highlights.pdf. Accessed 26 May 2021.
100. Rudolph, A. (2016). Pension programs around the world: Determinants of social pension. Courant Research Centre Discussion Papers No. 212.Georg-August-Universität Göttingen. https://www.die-gdi.de/uploads/media/CRC-PEG_DP_212_social_pension.pdf. Accessed 26 May 2021.

101. OECD. (2021). Ageing and employment policies - statistics on average effective age of retirement. https://www.oecd.org/els/emp/average-effective-age-of-retirement.htm. Accessed 26 May 2021.
102. Apt, W. (2014). A demographic view on security. *Germany's new security demographics* (pp. 31–53). Dordrecht: Springer. https://doi.org/10.1007/978-94-007-6964-9_5.
103. Tyrowicz, J., & Van der Velde, L. (2018). Labor reallocation and demographics. *Journal of Comparative Economics*, 46(1), 381–412. https://doi.org/10.1016/j.jce.2017.12.003.
104. Carone, G., Costello, D., Guardia, D., Nuria, Mourre, G., Przywara, B., et al. (2005). The economic impact of ageing populations in the EU25 member states. Directorate General for Economic and Financial Affairs European Economy Economic Working Paper No. 236. Rochester, NY. Accessed 26 May 2021.
105. Rosado, J. A., & Sánchez, M. I. A. (2017). From population age structure and savings rate to economic growth: Evidence from Ecuador. *International Journal of Economics and Financial Issues*, 7(3), 352–361. https://dergipark.org.tr/tr/pub/ijefi/issue/32021/354258?publisher=http-www-cag-edu-tr-ilhan-ozturk.
106. Yakita, A. (2017). *Population aging, fertility and social security*. Cham: Springer.
107. Cuevas, A., Karpowicz, I., Mulas-Granados, C., & Soto, M. (2017). Fiscal challenges of population aging in Brazil. IMF Working Paper No. 17/99. https://www.imf.org/en/Publications/WP/Issues/2017/04/26/Fiscal-Challenges-of-Population-Aging-in-Brazil-44850. Accessed 26 May 2021.
108. Skirbekk, V. F., Staudinger, U. M., & Cohen, J. E. (2018). How to measure population aging? The answer Is less than obvious: A review. *Gerontology*, 1–9. https://doi.org/10.1159/000494025.
109. Chang, A. Y., Skirbekk, V. F., Tyrovolas, S., Kassebaum, N. J., & Dieleman, J. L. (2019). Measuring population ageing: an analysis of the Global Burden of Disease Study 2017. *The Lancet Public Health*, 4(3), e159–e167. https://doi.org/10.1016/S2468-2667(19)30019-2.
110. Skirbekk, V., Loichinger, E., & Weber, D. (2012). Variation in cognitive functioning as a refined approach to comparing aging across countries. *Proceedings of the National Academy of Sciences*, 109(3), 770–774. https://doi.org/10.1073/pnas.1112173109.

111. Kämpfen, F., Kohler, I. V., Bountogo, M., Mwera, J., Kohler, H.-P., & Maurer, J. (2020). Using grip strength to compute physical health-adjusted old age dependency ratios. *SSM-Population Health*, 11. https://doi.org/10.1016/j.ssmph.2020.100579.
112. Thorvaldsson, V., Karlsson, P., Skoog, J., Skoog, I., & Johansson, B. (2017). Better cognition in new birth cohorts of 70 year olds, but greater decline thereafter. *The Journals of Gerontology: Series B*, 72(1), 16–24. https://doi.org/10.1093/geronb/gbw125.
113. Skirbekk, V., Stonawski, M., Bonsang, E., & Staudinger, U. M. (2013). The Flynn effect and population aging. *Intelligence*, 41(3), 169–177. https://doi.org/10.1016/j.intell.2013.02.001.
114. Hülür, G., Ram, N., Willis, S. L., Schaie, K. W., & Gerstorf, D. (2019). Cohort differences in cognitive aging: The role of perceived work environment. *Psychology and Aging*, 34(8), 1040. https://doi.org/10.1037/pag0000355.
115. Strand, B. H., Bergland, A., Jørgensen, L., Schirmer, H., Emaus, N., & Cooper, R. (2019). Do more recent born generations of older adults have stronger grip? A comparison of three cohorts of 66-to 84-year-olds in the Tromsø study. *The Journals of Gerontology: Series A*, 74(4), 528–533.
116. Vandenberghe, V. (2019). Health, cognition and work capacity beyond the age of 50: International evidence on the extensive and intensive margin of work. *International Labour Review*. https://doi.org/10.1111/ilr.12174.
117. Mani, A., Mullainathan, S., Shafir, E., & Zhao, J. (2013). Poverty impedes cognitive function. *Science*, 341(6149), 976–980. https://doi.org/10.1126/science.1238041.
118. Gale, S. D., Erickson, L. D., Berrett, A., Brown, B. L., & Hedges, D. W. (2016). Infectious disease burden and cognitive function in young to middle-aged adults. *Brain, Behavior, and Immunity*, 52, 161–168. https://doi.org/10.1016/j.bbi.2015.10.014.
119. Schneeweis, N., Skirbekk, V., & Winter-Ebmer, R. (2014). Does education improve cognitive performance four decades after school completion? *Demography*, 51(2), 619–643. https://doi.org/10.1007/s13524-014-0281-1.
120. Hegre, H., Karlsen, J., Nygård, H. M., Strand, H., & Urdal, H. (2013). Predicting armed conflict, 2010–2050. *International Studies Quarterly*, 57(2), 250–270. https://doi.org/10.1111/isqu.12007.

121. Nordås, R., & Davenport, C. (2013). Fight the youth: Youth bulges and state repression. *American Journal of Political Science*, 57(4), 926–940. https://doi.org/10.1111/ajps.12025.
122. Urdal, H. (2006). A clash of generations? Youth bulges and political violence. *International Studies Quarterly*, 50(3), 607–629. https://doi.org/10.1111/j.1468-2478.2006.00416.x.
123. Björkenstam, E., Björkenstam, C., Vinnerljung, B., Hallqvist, J., & Ljung, R. (2011). Juvenile delinquency, social background and suicide—a Swedish national cohort study of 992 881 young adults. *International Journal of Epidemiology*, 40(6), 1585–1592. https://doi.org/10.1093/ije/dyr127.
124. Sailas, E. S., Feodoroff, B., Lindberg, N. C., Virkkunen, M. E., Sund, R., & Wahlbeck, K. (2006). The mortality of young offenders sentenced to prison and its association with psychiatric disorders: A register study. *The European Journal of Public Health*, 16(2), 193–197. https://doi.org/10.1093/eurpub/cki169.
125. Quetelet, A. (1842). *A treatise on man* (trans: R. Knox). Edinburgh: Chambers.
126. Dupuy, K., Gates, S., Nygård, H. M., Strand, H., & Urdal, H. (2016). Trends in armed conflict, 1946–2014. Conflict Trends 2–2017.Oslo: P. R. I. Oslo. https://www.prio.org/Publications/Publication/?x=8937. Accessed 26 May 2021.
127. Peterson, E. W. F. (2017). The role of population in economic growth. *SAGE Open*, 7(4). https://doi.org/10.1177/2158244017736094.

19

Fertility Policies: Past, Present, and Future Directions

Most national governments around the world have tried and continue to try to influence fertility in some way. Just about every country in the world has policies aimed at reducing unintended pregnancies and adolescent fertility. Historically, most fertility policies have aimed to *reduce* fertility as a means of slowing population growth. More recently, governments in low fertility countries are explicitly trying to boost fertility or relieve some of the challenges of parenting. In this chapter, I review what countries around the world have done in the recent past and what they are doing in the present to influence fertility, as well as evidence about the effectiveness of different measures.

V. Skirbekk, *Decline and Prosper!*,
https://doi.org/10.1007/978-3-030-91611-4_19

What Constitutes a Fertility Policy?

> *A woman who rejects motherhood, who refrains from being around the house, however successful her working life is, is deficient, is incomplete.*
>
> *—Recep Tayyip Erdogan, President of Turkey, in 2016 [1]*

Any government policy that explicitly aims to reduce or increase fertility, or which aims to alter the costs and benefits of childbearing, can be described as a fertility policy. Most countries have policies explicitly aimed at reducing adolescent pregnancy and policies that directly affect access to contraception, abortion, and reproductive health care and education. Fertility policies are sometimes explicitly *anti-natalist* (i.e., designed to reduce fertility) or *pro-natalist* (i.e., designed to increase fertility). Common anti-natalist measures include raising (and enforcing) the legal minimum age for sexual consent and marriage. Anti-natalist policies can also take the form of information campaigns that highlight the challenges of having "too many" children and/or the benefits of smaller families. Common pro-natalist measures include providing new parents with financial support (e.g., a lump sum of money awarded when a baby is born; family allowances; paid parental leave; and tax breaks for families). It could also take the form of subsidized housing, free schooling, the right to flexible work schedules, affordable family healthcare services, as well as information campaigns on the benefits of having a family and the risk of involuntarily childless.

In this chapter, I mainly focus on policies that explicitly aim to alter fertility or the costs and benefits of having children. It is important to realize, however, that many policies affect fertility as a "side effect" of reaching some other objective. Every country has, for instance, policies that affect the length of education, the cost and availability of housing, women's empowerment, how well work can be combined with childbearing, and child labor laws. Policies that mitigate economic risk (e.g., pensions, unemployment benefits) and affect the affordability and quality of health care can affect fertility, too, as they determine the extent to which children are needed to provide economic security [2–4]. Even monetary policies that affect interest rates and the availability of loans can be relevant for fertility, as such policies affect income and the likelihood that people can afford to buy a house or apartment. In practice, policies that *indirectly* affect fertility often affect fertility just as much if not more than policies that target fertility directly.

Fertility Policies of the Past

In the aftermath of World War II, rapid population growth prompted many national governments and international organizations to try to reduce fertility in poorer, high fertility countries. At the time, there was a general consensus that reducing fertility was necessary in order to reduce poverty, support development, and reduce the risk of conflict and resource depletion [5–7]. Historians have noted, however, that the world's richer countries were also motivated to reduce fertility in poor countries for less altruistic reasons. By reducing population growth in poorer countries, richer countries may have sought to limit poor countries' political and military power, build political alliances, and secure access to poorer countries' natural resources by lowering domestic demand [8–10].

The first anti-natalist policies generally aimed to reduce unintended fertility by increasing the use of contraception, sterilization, and abortion; raise the age of marriage; as well as shift preferences from larger to smaller families. Some of the earliest national family planning programs were launched in South and East Asia. In 1952, India officially adopted a national population policy and launched the National Family Planning Programme. The program had the explicit objective of "reducing the birth rate to the extent necessary to stabilize the population at a level consistent with the requirement of the national economy." The Indian government aimed to meet the objective by implementing a government-run family planning program, which began by advocating the rhythm method of birth control [11]. Pakistan and Sri Lanka were the next to implement family planning programs in South Asia, while Hong Kong, South Korea, Singapore, and Taiwan led the way in East Asia [6]. Policies in South Korea, for example, improved access to family planning information and modern contraception, extended female and male education, and improved women's labor market opportunities; as a result, childbearing was drastically postponed [12] and fell from more than six children per woman in 1960 to fewer than two children per woman in 1984 [13–15]. At the same time, South Korea transitioned from being one of the poorest countries in the world to one of the richest [16].

Family planning poster from Hong Kong, 1952. Image: Public domain, https://commons.wikimedia.org/w/index.php?curid=956180.

The remarkable success of the family planning programs in East Asia in the 1960s prompted the spread of similar policy attempts through much of the developing world during the 1970s and 1980s. In Bangladesh, where family planning policies had failed in the 1960s, a door-to-door outreach family planning program conducted in rural villages had stimulated a 15% decrease in fertility in the program villages by 1982 [17]. During the 1970s, Indonesia introduced the National Population and Family Planning Board to establish a "small, prosperous family" as the Indonesian norm and to reduce unintended fertility by promoting the use of contraceptives. At the time, just 5% of the Indonesian population used contraception and the TFR was 5.6 children per woman. In 2019, the TFR in Indonesia was 2.3 [18].

In the late 1960s, 1970s, and 1980s, population control policies in some countries took a more aggressive turn. Considerable pressure was put on local authorities to reach quantified targets, such as the 1978-quota of 50,000 sterilizations per month in Bangladesh [19]. In turn, couples—and women in particular—were often coerced into having fewer children. India offered land, money, loans, clothes, housing, radios, subsidies, and/or loans for men and women who were sterilized. Mass sterilizations were carried out, particularly among poorer social groups, and often without informed consent. The policy was highly controversial and unpopular among many of those affected—and eventually created a backlash against political leadership and a change in government [20–22]. China adopted the One Child Policy in 1979, probably the largest and most stringent fertility policy ever implemented. The One Child Policy intended to reduce fertility by promoting IUDs after one child and sterilization after a second child. People who had more children had to pay fines and lost opportunities for government employment, and their children could lose access to education or health services. The One Child Policy was not revoked until the end of 2015 [23–25]. At the same time that several countries enacted aggressive anti-natalist policies, Romania enacted aggressive pro-natalist policies under dictator Nicolae Ceauşescu. Believing that a larger population would restore the country's economic might, Ceauşescu issued Decree 770 in 1966, which completely banned all contraceptives and nearly all abortion, and increased taxes for childless adults. The decree was not overturned until the year of Ceauşescu's death in 1989 [26].

By the 1990s, the tide had turned against population policies that explicitly aimed to reduce fertility. Feminist groups, who had previously championed fertility reduction [27, 28], began to argue that policies should focus on improving women's reproductive autonomy and maternal and child health as opposed to reducing fertility per se [29, 30]. Private donors and non-governmental organizations interested in promoting development likewise shifted their focus away from trying to reduce fertility toward helping women realize their own fertility preferences and improve reproductive, maternal, and infant health [30]. The 1994 Cairo Conference on Population and Development represented a watershed in terms of ending quantified fertility goals [10]. Policies designed to limit fertility to one or two children were thereafter increasingly seen as interfering with women's right to control their own reproduction [31, 32]. Around the same time, high consumption in the world's richer countries as opposed to high fertility in the world's poorer countries became to be seen as the major driver of human's environmental impact [9, 33]. Some say that it has now become taboo to even discuss the idea of "overpopulation" or the possibility of reducing fertility for environmental reasons [34].

Contemporary Fertility Policies

Today, intergovernmental organizations such as the United Nations and the World Bank agree that addressing fertility is an integral part of addressing broader developmental and environmental issues [35, 36]. Fertility has also increasingly become a part of national political agendas of governments around the world [37]. The percentage of countries with an explicit fertility policy increased from just 14% in the 1970s to 70% in 2015 [38]. In 2015, 42% of national governments had policies designed to *lower* their fertility, while 28% of governments had policies designed to *raise* their fertility [37].

They [Europeans] want as many migrants to enter as there are missing kids, so that the numbers will add up. We Hungarians have a different way of thinking. Instead of just numbers, we want Hungarian children.

-Viktor Orbán, Prime Minister of Hungary in 2019. Orbán has pledged that women with more than four children will never pay income tax [39].

Countries with above-replacement fertility tend to have more anti-natal policies, while countries with below replacement fertility tend to have more pro-natal policies. There are, however, some exceptions. After the TFR fell below four children per woman in the early 2000s, Saudi Arabia shifted its aim from maintaining to raising fertility. Nevertheless, Saudi Arabian fertility has continued to fall; in 2019, the TFR was around 2.3 children per woman [37, 40]. The only high fertility country in Africa that explicitly aims to raise fertility is Gabon, which had a TFR around 3.5 children per woman in 2018 [38]. Gabon has a fairly small population (around 2 million in 2020) and large oil reserves which may imply that the country believes it can afford a larger population [41].

Figure 19.1 shows the percentage of countries that have had policies to raise, maintain, or lower their fertility over the past decades. Notably, many more countries are trying to raise their fertility than in the past. In low fertility countries, pro-natal policies are often designed to address the gap between people's desired and actual fertility [42, 43], and many governments worry about the negative consequences of involuntarily childlessness [44, 45]. Several formerly high-fertility countries saw their fertility unexpectedly fall below the replacement level [46, 47], causing some governments—particularly in East Asia—to reverse their anti-natal policies. After decades of anti-natal policies, Singapore now has strong pro-natal policies [48, 49]. The policies have been, however, largely ineffective; Singaporean fertility remains one of the lowest in the world [50, 51]. After the One Child Policy was phased out, fears of rapid population aging and declining economic progress led China to enact pro-natal policies in the 2010s [52]. Chinese policies now incentivize the two-child family, though Chinese fertility has remained low [53, 54]. In

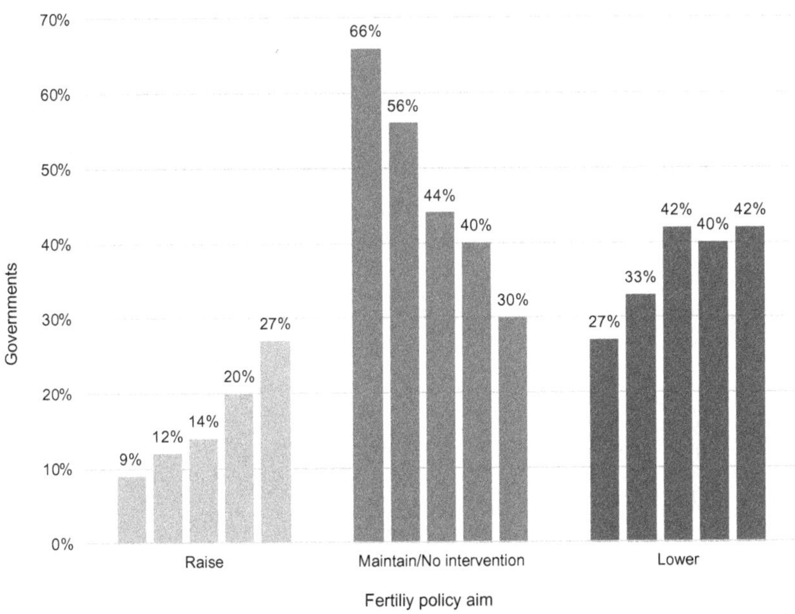

Fig. 19.1 Percent of global governments with fertility policies to raise, maintain, or lower fertility, 1976–2015. Based on [38]

South Korea, fertility fell below 1 child per woman in the 2010s [55, 56]. In the third quarter of 2019, fertility was just 0.69 children per woman in the capital Seoul, one of the lowest levels of fertility observed in modern times [57]. The government reacted by subsidizing childcare leave and providing free nurseries, cash subsidies, and other incentives [56, 58, 59].

Contemporary fertility polices in countries with above replacement fertility tend to focus on strengthening women's reproductive autonomy, particularly the right to avoid unintended pregnancies [60, 61]. There is widespread support to provide especially adolescent women with access to the information, services, and support that they need to avoid pregnancy [62]. Globally, in 2015, an overwhelming majority of governments (84%) provided direct support for family planning, and nearly every country in the world (91%) had at least one policy specifically aimed at improving the reproductive and sexual health of adolescents [37]. In

2015, the most common fertility policy measure was the provision of school-based sexual and reproductive education to adolescents (76%), followed by expanding the enrolment and retention of girls in secondary school (57%) [37]. India, for instance, aims to reduce the TFR from 2.3 children per woman in 2019 to 2.1 children per woman by 2025 [63]. Current Indian policies are designed to boost reproductive education and health care, increase access to affordable contraception, and promote women's rights. Some Indian states also restrict people with more than two children from running in local elections or having a government job [64].

The United States is the only OECD country without statutory paid parental leave. All other OECD countries provide at least 12 weeks of paid maternal leave [65].

By now, most countries worldwide also have policies to ease the financial situation of families and reduce work/family conflict. Globally, nearly all (99%) governments provide paid or unpaid maternity leave with job security, and over half (54%) provide paternity leave with job security [37]. Another 31% allow flexible or part-time work for working parents [37]. Many governments provide some sort of financial support for families, either through child or family allowances (67%), subsidizing childcare (63%), paying a "baby bonus" (54%), or providing a tax credit for dependent children (31%) [37]. Figure 19.2 provides an overview of global policies. More developed regions tend to have more generous policies than less developed regions, with the exception of maternity leave which is slightly more common in less developed regions.

Fertility policies are sometimes eugenic in nature, with the goal of either reducing the fertility of people seen as having "undesirable" traits, or increasing the fertility of people with "desirable" traits. The most well-known examples of eugenic fertility policies are probably those from Nazi Germany, but in fact many countries around the world have had some form eugenic policy at one time or another. Policies have commonly coercively restricted the fertility of people who were poor, disabled, mentally ill, criminals, or from particular racial and ethnic groups. Until

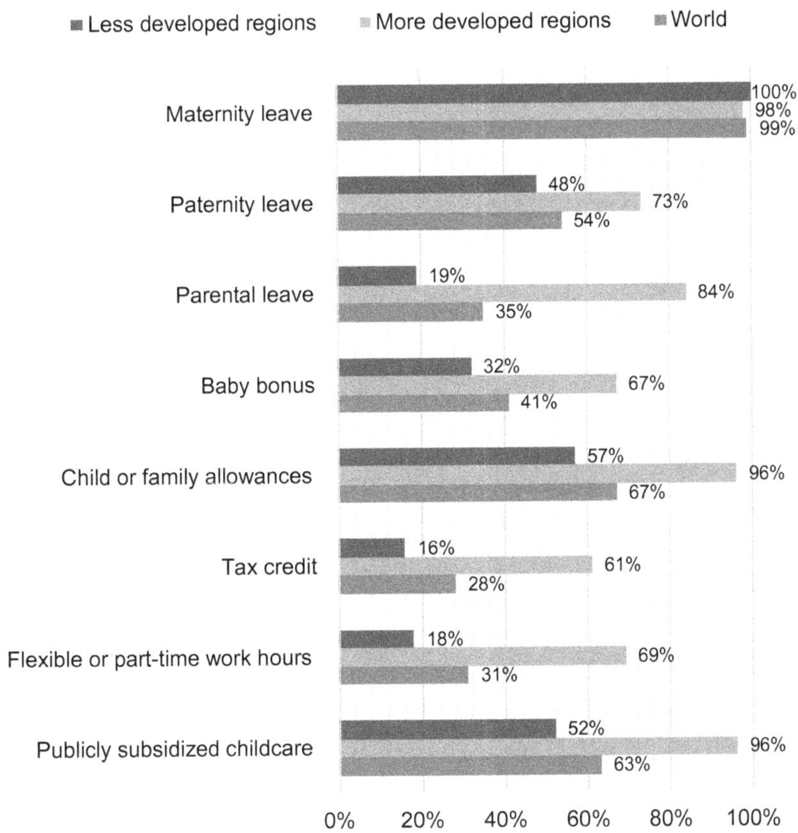

Fig. 19.2 Fertility policies around the world. Based on [37]

it was revoked in 1979, legislation in the state of California in the United States sanctioned the non-consensual sterilization of over 20,000 patients in state-run homes and hospitals [66]. The two-child policy in some Indian states has been criticized as a way of limiting the growth of India's Muslim population—as Indian Muslims tend to have more children than Indian Hindus (albeit less so in recent decades) [67]. Singapore provides incentives for highly-educated women to have more children, and incentives for low-educated and poor women to get sterilized [68]. Many countries continue to discourage people with cognitive challenges and severe health problems to have children [69–71].

Do Fertility Policies Make a Difference?

It is often difficult to determine the extent to which a fertility policy has been effective for several reasons. First, it is difficult to isolate the effect of a policy from all of the other broader societal changes that may be taking place at the same time. There is rarely data about what would have happened had the policy not been in place. The population control policies of the past were often implemented in developing countries at the same time that education was expanding, and economic conditions along with family and gender norms were changing. It is also difficult to isolate the effect of a specific fertility policy because countries tend to more or less simultaneously implement multiple measures. Baby bonuses, childcare benefits, and parental employment security are often introduced at the same time, which makes it difficult to determine which measures are most effective. Finally, most analyses of the effects of a particular fertility policy are limited to data from just one or possibly a few countries during a specific period (e.g., pro-natal policies tend to be implemented when there has been substantial decline in births). It is therefore hard to say whether the same fertility policy would have the same effect in a different country or time period. Policies that may have been effective in one period and one country for one social group may be wholly ineffective or have other effects in a different setting [72, 73].

Successful Family Planning Policy in Iran...Reversed

Between 1990 and 2003, Iran's total fertility rate fell from well above five children per woman to below two children per women, one of the fastest fertility declines ever observed in a major population [40]. The decline was largely due to a national campaign encouraging small families, improvements in women's status, free contraception, provision of family planning services also to rural and low-income populations, rural development and literacy programs, and—very importantly—support from the country's Islamic leadership [74–76]. Concerns about an aging and shrinking population led the Iranian government to reverse its stance in the mid-2010s; access to free contraception has been reduced and the motto of the Ministry of Health and Medical Education has been changed from "two children is ideal" to "*at least* [emphasis added] two children is ideal" [77].

There are some unique situations in which it is possible to identify the causal effects of a fertility policy. One example is from Bangladesh, where the fertility rate and many other outcomes were followed closely in a sample of 141 villages from 1974 to 1996 [17]. Between 1977 and 1996, half of the villages in the observation sample received a door-to-door outreach family planning and maternal-child health program. By 1982, fertility in the program villages had declined 15% more in the program than in the control villages. Moreover, fertility remained at the reduced level throughout the observation period. The program also had a number of positive effects on women's health, earnings and household assets, and children's health and education. The Bangladeshi study therefore suggests that family planning programs can not only effectively reduce fertility, but also contribute to the empowerment of women—which in turn can affect reproduction in the next generation. Other quasi-experimental studies in Malaysia [78], Northern Ghana [79], and Columbia [80] similarly suggest that family planning programs resulted in a 10–15% decline in national fertility. Many other studies likewise suggest that anti-natal policies accelerated the process of fertility decline in developing countries [6, 81–84]. The coercive policies of the past were with little doubt effective—India's sterilization programs (particularly during Indira Gandhi's regime) or China's One Child Policy (particularly during the first years of the program) averted millions of births [21, 85, 86]—but were certainly a disaster from a human rights perspective.

Policies designed to decrease fertility generally appear to be much more effective than policies aimed at stabilizing or raising fertility in low fertility countries [41, 87, 88]. Based on data from 133 countries, one study concluded that anti-natalistic policy explained about one-third of the decline in fertility over and above other potentially confounding factors (e.g., gross domestic product, share of urban population). In contrast, many pro-natalistic policies appear to be unrelated to fertility change [41]. In the mid-2000s, for instance, Australia began offering mothers a baby bonus at birth and expanded access to affordable childcare. The policy changes coincided with an increase in the TFR from 1.73 to 1.96 children per woman. Although it appeared that the pronatal fertility policies had caused something of a baby boom, closer analysis revealed that changes in the distribution of education, income, occupation, and parity during this pattern mattered more than the new policies [89]. In Poland, the implementation of a more generous baby bonus (Polish parents received approximately 1600 USD yearly per child for 2019) failed to increase the Polish TFR, which remains low at around 1.4 children per woman [90]. Pro-natal policies can also sometimes backfire or have unintended consequences. Providing financial support to parents can sometimes decrease female labor force participation and thereby worsen economic dependency ratios (i.e., the ratio of working to non-working people) in the shorter term [91, 92]. In Israel, state-sponsored assisted reproductive technologies (ART) has led to greater female economic participation, as more women postpone births [93].

While many studies have investigated whether pro-natal fertility policies are related to childbearing [94–97], just a handful provide more conclusive evidence of causality. According to data from natural experiments, the length and generosity of parental leave tend to have no or only moderately positive effects on fertility [98–100]. Increasing access to childcare was found to slightly raise fertility in natural experiments in Belgium [101], Sweden [102], and Germany (among those with lower income) [103], while a cash benefit paid to the mother immediately after birth slightly increased fertility in Spain [104] and Australia [89] in the short, but not always in the long term. A natural experiment in Quebec found that the introduction of more beneficial tax incentives for families with children increased short-term period fertility (timing of childbearing) but did not affect cohort fertility (i.e., family size) [105]. Natural experiments have also found that better health insurance—in particular providing access to ART at the end of the reproductive window—has had very slight [106] or no effect [107] on fertility. In sum, the effects of pro-natal policies appear to be modest at best. It may be, however, that many pro-natalistic policies are just too new for any effect to show up in the data. The true consequences of a policy can often only be observed decades after its implementation, when data on cohort fertility becomes available.

Challenges to Government Intervention

Many of the most important drivers of fertility can be extremely difficult and expensive to change. In order to be effective, policies in the lowest-fertility Asian countries would probably have to simultaneously tackle the very high costs of raising children and housing, low governmental support for families, and the persistence of traditional ideas about gender and family [108]. By now, many East Asians have internalized a low fertility norm [81, 109], and policies that only moderately alter the costs of childbearing are unlikely to be effective. In Southern and Western Europe, economic uncertainty and weak financial institutions appear to be a major barrier to childbearing [72, 108]. Increasing fertility would therefore probably necessitate lowering the costs of housing and restructuring the financial sector.

Concerned about its declining population, the Ulyanovsk region of Russia established the "Day of Conception." People have the day off and are encouraged to celebrate by procreating. Couples who have a baby nine months later are awarded various prizes including money, cars, and refrigerators [110].

Another challenge to implementing fertility policies is that they are sometimes unpopular. Many people see reproduction as a strictly personal choice and feel that the government should not interfere in such an intimate and private matter. Many people associate fertility policies with eugenics or with the coercive policies of the past. Fertility policies may also be perceived as selectively promoting the growth or decline of specific ethnic groups or national populations [111]. Some groups in Iran, for instance, see family planning as a United States-driven attempt to limit the number of Muslims, or a Saudi-driven attempt to limit Iranian or Shia influence [112, 113]. While there is often no clear political "left–right" division with regard to population issues [114, 115], conservative and religious groups may oppose certain anti-natalist measures such as increasing the availability of contraception and abortion, or providing sexual and reproductive education in schools

[116–118]. Pressure from conservative groups in the United States led former President Ronald Reagan to adopt the so-called gag rule in 1984. The gag rule (which was still in effect at the time of writing in 2021) bars any healthcare organization from receiving funding from the United States if they perform or support abortions [119]. Anti-natalist policies may also be at odds with the pro-natalistic beliefs of most world religions.

It may also take many years for fertility policies to have the desired effect. "Rewards" from fertility changes (e.g., changes in the proportion of employed versus financially-dependent people, less pressure on the environment due to population growth) are often only reaped many years later. Politicians may therefore have little incentive for fighting for unpopular or controversial policies involving sensitive issues such as abortion, gender relations, social security, or fiscal sustainability [120–122].

What Countries Should Be Doing

In my opinion, fertility policies have generally moved in the right direction. Today, most fertility policies primarily focus on improving reproductive autonomy and reducing unintended births, as opposed to reaching some specific, quantifiable target. But much more needs to be done. Even in the world's most developed countries, many people lack the tools needed to control their own reproduction and understand the consequences of their reproductive behavior.

In the high fertility countries, extending female and male education, creating new work opportunities for women, and improving social security systems may effectively reduce fertility while also benefitting individuals and society in a number of other ways. In high fertility countries, information campaigns often fail to reach the people most in need; for instance, mass media campaigns to limit fertility in West Africa often fail to reach adolescents and poorer rural women [123]. In some contexts, the misconception that population size determines population influence needs to be addressed. Given the importance of religion as a determinant of fertility, empowering more people to take control of their own reproduction may hinge on the involvement of religious leaders.

In the low fertility countries, men and women often have more freedom to choose whether to partner, marry, and have children (and if yes, when and with whom). This, in my opinion, is a good thing. But freedom can also be challenging, and there appears to be a growing number of people who are unable to have as many children as they would like. New structures to help adults in their 20s and 30s make informed fertility choices are needed. Young adults not only need to be informed about how to avoid pregnancy, but also need to be better informed about their own fertility, the limits of ART, and how they can realize their fertility intentions and overcome potential hurdles.

So far, few policies have effectively addressed some of the main barriers to fertility, including the economic position of the young—which has worsened over recent decades in many countries [124]. Policies which address younger peoples' opportunities on the housing and the labor market may be much more important for increasing fertility than, for instance, a one-time cash incentive. The traditional life path of first completing education, then establishing a career, and finally forming a family may not be viable as education lengthens and finding a well-paid, stable job takes much longer. Policies that increase the compatibility of higher education and childbearing (e.g., through part-time study programs) and provide financial assistance for parents unrelated to salaries may help more people realize their own fertility ideals.

Policies also need to focus on improving work-life balance, and not just once people have become parents. One of the main reasons that people unintentionally end up childless in the low fertility countries is because they have problems establishing a stable partnership. Establishing and maintaining a partnership take time and energy, and may be incompatible with the demands of a job or career that requires long hours or frequently moving to a new city or even country. Many professional couples find that they are unable to pursue their careers in the same city. Even in the world's most gender egalitarian countries, professional women are often forced to choose between having a career and having a family. Governments could consider providing incentives for organizations to allow distance work. The opportunity to work from home may help more professional couples to have children without sacrificing their careers.

Policies also need to keep up with the times. To be effective, fertility policies need to account for changes in romantic partnerships. In many countries, fewer people marry; there are also more same-sex couples, and growing shares of same-sex couples want children [125]. Policies thus need to ensure that unmarried and same-sex parents receive the same benefits as married heterosexual parents. Policies must also take into account that the reasons why people over- or undershoot their own fertility ideals may systematically differ across social groups, and there may not be a "one size fits all" solution. By sponsoring fertility research, governments can accelerate the accumulation of knowledge of the determinants of fertility and what works for whom.

So far, policies to raise fertility in the low fertility countries have been modestly effective at best. It is time for governments in the low fertility countries to accept and adapt to a future with fewer children, moderate population decline, and population aging. Instead of asking themselves "How can we get people to have more children?", governments should start asking themselves, "How can we best adapt to a society with fewer children?" and "How can we fairly construct a society to support a diversity of life styles?" Helping people to lead fulfilling lives—with many, just one or two, or without children—should be the goal. Governments need to pay attention to the growing risk group of low-educated and childless men and create new structures for the second half of life more generally. Many people will not be grandparents; they will need other opportunities to create a sense of legacy and non-kin sources of support. Societies need to consider how one best can support meaningful intergenerational interaction outside of the family and the formation of "families of choice," which may include adjusting the legal rights of people who are neither married nor related but are nevertheless committed to each other.

References

1. Turkey's Erdogan says childless women are 'incomplete' (2016, June 6). *Al Jazeera*. Retrieved from https://www.aljazeera.com/news/2016/06/06/turkeys-erdogan-says-childless-women-are-incomplete/.

2. Nugent, J. B. (1985). The old-age security motive for fertility. *Population and Development Review*, 75–97. https://doi.org/10.2307/1973379.
3. Cain, M. (2018). Fertility as an adjustment to risk. In A. S. Rossi (Ed.), *Gender and the life course* (pp. 167–182). London and New York: Routledge.
4. Cain, M. (1981). Risk and insurance: Perspectives on fertility and agrarian change in India and Bangladesh. *Population and Development Review*, 7(3), 435–474. https://doi.org/10.2307/1972559.
5. Robinson, W. C., & Ross, J. A. (2007). *The global family planning revolution: Three decades of population policies and programs*. Washington, DC: The World Bank.
6. de Silva, T., & Tenreyro, S. (2017). Population control policies and fertility convergence. *Journal of Economic Perspectives*, 31(4), 205–228. https://doi.org/10.1257/jep.31.4.205.
7. The World Watch Institute (2012). *State of the world 2012: Moving toward sustainable prosperity*. Washington, Covelo, London: Island Press.
8. Thoradeniya, D. (2016). Altruism, welfare, or development aid? Swedish aid for family planning in Ceylon, 1958 to 1983. *East Asian Science, Technology and Society: An International Journal*, 10(4), 423–444. https://doi.org/10.1215/18752160-3684005.
9. Hartmann, B. (2010). Rethinking the role of population in human security. In R. A. Matthew, J. Barnett, B. McDonald, & K. L. O'Brien (Eds.), *Global environmental change and human security* (pp. 193–215). Cambridge, MA and London: The MIT Press.
10. May, J. F. (2012). *World population policies: Their origin, evolution, and impact*. Dordrecht, Heidelberg, New York, London: Springer Science & Business Media.
11. Maharatna, A. (2002). India's family planning programme: An unpleasant essay. *Economic and Political Weekly*, 37(10), 971–981. Retrieved from www.jstor.org/stable/4411847.
12. Yoo, S. H., & Sobotka, T. (2018). Ultra-low fertility in South Korea: The role of the tempo effect. *Demographic Research*, 38, 549–576. https://doi.org/10.4054/DemRes.2018.38.22.
13. Anderson, T., & Kohler, H.-P. (2013). Education fever and the East Asian fertility puzzle: A case study of low fertility in South Korea. *Asian Population Studies*, 9(2), 196–215. https://doi.org/10.1080/17441730.2013.797293.
14. Choe, M. K., & Park, K. T. (2018). How is the decline of fertility related to fertility preference in South Korea? In S. Gietel-Basten, J. Casterline, &

M. K. Choe (Eds.), *Family demography in Asia* (pp. 305–322). Cheltenham and Northhampton: Edward Elgar Publishing. https://doi.org/10.4337/9781785363559.00025.

15. Foreit, J. R. (1982). The transition in Korean family planning behavior, 1935–1976: A retrospective cohort analysis. *Studies in Family Planning*, 13(8–9), 227–236.
16. The World Bank (2020). World Bank open data. https://data.worldbank.org/. Accessed 25 May 2021.
17. Joshi, S., & Schultz, T. P. (2007). Family planning as an investment in development: Evaluation of a program's consequences in Matlab, Bangladesh. Yale University Economic Growth Center Discussion Paper No. 951, IZA Discussion Paper No. 2639, iHEA 2007 6th World Congress: Explorations in health economics paper. https://papers.ssrn.com/sol3/papers.cfm?abstract_id=962938.
18. Hasnan, L. (2019, August 24). Indonesia plans for less babies. *The Asean Post*. Retrieved from https://theaseanpost.com/article/indonesia-plans-less-babies.
19. Khan, A. R., & Swenson, I. (1978). Acceptability of male sterilization in Bangladesh: Its problems and perspectives. *Bangladesh Development Studies*, 6(2), 201–212.
20. Mohanty, S. K., Mishra, S., Chatterjee, S., & Saggurti, N. (2020). Pattern and correlates of out-of-pocket payment (OOP) on female sterilization in India, 1990–2014. *BMC Women's Health*, 20(1), 13. https://doi.org/10.1186/s12905-020-0884-1.
21. Gupte, P. R. (2017). India: "The emergency" and the politics of mass sterilization. *Education About Asia*, 22(3), 40–44. Retrieved from https://www.asianstudies.org/publications/eaa/archives/india-the-emergency-and-the-politics-of-mass-sterilization/.
22. Henry, M. (1976). Compulsory sterilization in India: Is coercion the only alternative to chaos? *The Hastings Center Report*, 6(3), 14–15. https://doi.org/10.2307/3561648.
23. Feng, X.-T., Poston Jr., D. L., & Wang, X.-T. (2014). China's one-child policy and the changing family. *Journal of Comparative Family Studies*, 45(1), 17–29. https://doi.org/10.3138/jcfs.45.1.17.
24. 400 million births prevented by one-child policy (2011, October 28). *People's daily*. Retrieved from http://en.people.cn/90882/7629166.html.
25. Hesketh, T., Lu, L., & Xing, Z. W. (2005). The effect of China's one-child family policy after 25 years. *New England Journal of Medicine*, 353(11), 1171–1176. https://doi.org/10.1056/NEJMhpr051833.

26. Leidig, M. (2005). Romania still faces high abortion rate 16 years after fall of Ceauşescu. *BMJ (Clinical research ed.)*, 331(7524), 1043. https://doi.org/10.1136/bmj.331.7524.1043-a.
27. Staggenborg, S. (1991). *The pro-choice movement: Organization and activism in the abortion conflict*. New York and Oxford: Oxford University Press.
28. Hodgson, D., & Watkins, S. C. (1997). Feminists and neo-Malthusians: Past and present alliances. *Population and Development Review*, 23(3), 469–523. https://doi.org/10.2307/2137570.
29. Coole, D. (2016). Population, environmental discourse, and sustainability. In T. Gabrielson, C. Hall, J. M. Meyer, & D. Schlosberg (Eds.), *The oxford handbook of environmental political theory* (pp. 274–288). Oxford and New York: Oxford University Press. https://doi.org/10.1093/oxfordhb/9780199685271.013.35.
30. Eager, P. W. (2017). *Global population policy: From population control to reproductive rights*. London: Routledge.
31. Gudorf, C. E. (2014). After Cairo: New complexities in fertility and development. *The Heythrop Journal*, 55(6), 1091–1101. https://doi.org/10.1111/heyj.12206.
32. DeJong, J. (2000). The role and limitations of the Cairo international conference on population and development. *Social Science & Medicine*, 51(6), 941–953. https://doi.org/10.1016/S0277-9536(00)00073-3.
33. Fletcher, R., Breitling, J., & Puleo, V. (2014). Barbarian hordes: The overpopulation scapegoat in international development discourse. *Third World Quarterly*, 35(7), 1195–1215. https://doi.org/10.1080/01436597.2014.926110.
34. Washington, H. (2019). The tragedy of overpopulation denial. *What can I do to help heal the environmental crisis?* (pp. 68–86). London: Routledge. https://doi.org/10.4324/9780429324666-5.
35. Steiner, A. (2017). Administrator statement to the 2nd regular sessions of the UNDP executive board. September 6, 2017. Retrieved from https://www.adaptation-undp.org/achim-steiner-undp-administrator-statement-2nd-regular-session-undp-executive-board.
36. The World Bank & the International Monetary Fund (2016). Global monitoring report 2015/2016: Development goals in an era of demographic change. Washington, DC: The World Bank. https://openknowledge.worldbank.org/handle/10986/22547. Accessed 26 May 2021.

37. United Nations (2018). World Population Policies 2015: Highlights. New York: United Nations. Retrieved from https://www.un.org/en/development/desa/population/publications/pdf/policy/WPP2015/WPP2015_Highlights.pdf.
38. United Nations (2016). World Population Policies Database. https://esa.un.org/PopPolicy/about_database.aspx. Accessed 25 May 2021.
39. Walker, S. (2019, February 10). Viktor Orbán: No tax for Hungarian women with four or more children *The Guardian*. Retrieved from https://www.theguardian.com/world/2019/feb/10/viktor-orban-no-tax-for-hungarian-women-with-four-or-more-children.
40. United Nations (2019). World Population Prospects 2019. https://population.un.org/wpp/. Accessed 25 May 2021.
41. Ouedraogo, A., Tosun, M. S., & Yang, J. (2018). Fertility and population policy. *Public Sector Economics*, 42(1), 21–43. https://doi.org/10.3326/pse.42.1.2.
42. Nishimura, T. (2012). What are the factors of the gap between desired and actual fertility?: A comparative study of four developed countries. Discussion paper No. 81, School of Economics, Kwansei Gakuin University. Retrieved from https://www.researchgate.net/publication/254426501_What_are_the_factors_of_the_gap_between_desired_and_actual_fertility_-_A_comparative_study_of_four_developed_countries.
43. Beaujouan, E., & Berghammer, C. (2019). The gap between lifetime fertility intentions and completed fertility in Europe and the United States: A cohort approach. *Population Research and Policy Review*, 38, 1–29. https://doi.org/10.1007/s11113-019-09516-3.
44. Freedman, L. P., & Isaacs, S. L. (1993). Human rights and reproductive choice. *Studies in Family Planning*, 24(1), 18–30. https://doi.org/10.2307/2939211.
45. Kuang, B., & Brodsky, I. (2016). Global trends in family planning programs, 1999–2014. *International Perspectives on Sexual and Reproductive Health*, 42(1), 33–44. https://doi.org/10.1363/42e0316.
46. Keilman, N. (1998). How accurate are the United Nations world population projections? *Population and Development Review*, 24, 15–41. Retrieved from http://www.jstor.org/stable/2808049.
47. Wilson, C. (2004). Fertility below replacement level. *Science*, 304(5668), 207–209. https://doi.org/10.1126/science.304.5668.207c.
48. Sun, S. H.-L. (2012). *Population policy and reproduction in Singapore: Making future citizens*. London and New York: Routledge.

49. Yap, M. T., & Gee, C. (2018). Fertility preferences in Singapore. In S. Gietel-Basten, J. Casterline, & M. K. Choe (Eds.), *Family demography in Asia* (pp. 291–304). Cheltenham and Northhampton: Edward Elgar Publishing. https://doi.org/10.4337/9781785363559.
50. Swee-Hock, S. (2016). *Population policies and programmes in Singapore.* Singapore: ISEAS-Yusof Ishak Institute.
51. Chen, M., Yip, P. S., & Yap, M. T. (2018). Identifying the most influential groups in determining Singapore's fertility. *Journal of Social Policy*, 47(1), 139–160. https://doi.org/10.1017/S0047279417000241.
52. Zeng, Y., & Hesketh, T. (2016). The effects of China's universal two-child policy. *The Lancet*, 388(10054), 1930–1938.
53. Mo, L., & Wei, Y. (2020). The urgent need for changes to current fertility policies. In L. Mo, & Y. Wei (Eds.), *China's demographic dilemma and potential solutions* (pp. 129–136). Singapore: Springer. https://doi.org/10.1007/978-981-10-1491-8.
54. Zeng, Y., Zhang, X., & Liu, L. (2017). From "selective two-child policy" to universal two-child policy: Will the payment crisis of China's pension system be solved? *China Finance and Economic Review*, 5(1), 14. https://doi.org/10.1186/s40589-017-0053-3.
55. Park, E. H. (2020). Ultra-low fertility and policy response in South Korea: Lessons from the case of Japan. *Ageing International*, 45, 1–15. https://doi.org/10.1007/s12126-020-09365-y.
56. Bak, H. (2019). Low fertility in South Korea: Causes, consequences, and policy responses. In A. Farazmand (Ed.), *Global encyclopedia of public administration, public policy, and governance* (pp. 1–11). Cham: Springer. https://doi.org/10.1007/978-3-319-31816-5.
57. Kim, S. (2019, November 27). South Korea set to break own record on worlds lowest birth rate. *Bloomberg*. Retrieved from https://www.bloomberg.com/news/articles/2019-11-27/south-korea-set-to-break-own-record-on-world-s-lowest-birth-rate.
58. Yang, J.-j. (2020). Korean social welfare policies. In C.-i. Moon, & M. J. Moon (Eds.), *Routledge handbook of Korean politics and public administration* (pp. 420–434). London: Routledge. https://doi.org/10.4324/9781315660516.
59. Kim, E. J., & Parish, S. L. (2020). Family-supportive workplace policies and South Korean mothers' perceived work-family conflict: Accessibility matters. *Asian Population Studies*, 16(2), 1–16. https://doi.org/10.1080/17441730.2020.1721837.

60. Bellizzi, S., Mannava, P., Nagai, M., & Sobel, H. L. (2020). Reasons for discontinuation of contraception among women with a current unintended pregnancy in 36 low and middle-income countries. *Contraception*, 101(1), 26–33. https://doi.org/10.1016/j.contraception.2019.09.006.
61. Guttmacher Institute (2014, September 17). New study finds that 40% of pregnancies worldwide are unintended. Retrieved from https://www.guttmacher.org/news-release/2014/new-study-finds-40-pregnancies-worldwide-are-unintended. Accessed 25 May 2021.
62. United Nations, Department of Economic and Social Affairs, & Population Division (2020). World Fertility 2019—Early and later childbearing among adolescent women. New York: United Nations. https://www.un.org/en/development/desa/population/publications/pdf/fertility/World_Fertility_2019.pdf.
63. Health Ministry launches two new contraceptives (2017, September 5). *United News of India.* Retrieved from http://www.uniindia.com/health-ministry-launches-two-new-contraceptives/india/news/980681.html?fromNewsdog=1&utm_source=NewsDog&utm_medium=referral.
64. Page, V. (2017). Child policy in India. Investopedia. https://www.investopedia.com/articles/personal-finance/051415/indias-twochild-policy.asp. Accessed 25 May 2021.
65. OECD (2019). PF2.1. Parental leave systems. OECD. https://www.oecd.org/els/soc/PF2_1_Parental_leave_systems.pdf. Accessed 19 May 2021.
66. Stern, A. M. (2005). Sterilized in the name of public health: Race, immigration, and reproductive control in modern California. *American Journal of Public Health*, 95(7), 1128–1138. https://doi.org/10.2105/AJPH.2004.041608.
67. Basu, A. M. (2020). Make no mistake, a population control policy will target the marginalised. The Wire. https://thewire.in/rights/india-population-control-policy. Accessed 25 May 2021.
68. Yap, M. T. (2003). Fertility and population policy: The Singapore experience. *Journal of Population and Social Security (Population)*, 1(Suppl.), 643–658. Retrieved from http://203.181.211.2/webj-ad/WebJournal.files/Population/2003_6/24.Yap.pdf.
69. Gyngell, C., & Selgelid, M. (2016). Twenty-first century eugenics. In L. Francis (Ed.), *The Oxford handbook of reproductive ethics* (pp. 141–158). New York: Oxford University Press. https://doi.org/10.1093/oxfordhb/9780199981878.013.7.
70. Turda, M., & Gillette, A. (2016). *Latin eugenics in comparative perspective*. London and New York: Bloomsbury Publishing.

71. Efron, Y., & Lifshitz Aviram, P. (2019). Conditional parentage is the new eugenics. *Child and Family Law Review*, 8(1), 19–49. Retrieved from https://lawpublications.barry.edu/cflj/vol8/iss1/2.
72. Thévenon, O. (2016). Decreasing fertility in Europe: Is it a policy issue? In M. Koenraad, K. Neels, C. Timmerman, J. Haers, & S. Mels (Eds.), *Population change in Europe, the Middle-East and North Africa* (pp. 101–136). London and New York: Routledge.
73. Matysiak, A., & Węziak-Białowolska, D. (2016). Country-specific conditions for work and family reconciliation: An attempt at quantification. *European Journal of Population*, 32(4), 475–510. https://doi.org/10.1007/s10680-015-9366-9.
74. Erfani, A., & McQuillan, K. (2008). Rapid fertility decline in Iran: Analysis of intermediate variables. *Journal of Biosocial Science*, 40(3), 459–478. https://doi.org/10.1017/S002193200700243X.
75. Taghizadeh, Z., Behmanesh, F., & Ebadi, A. (2016). Marriage patterns and childbearing: Results from a quantitative study in north of Iran. *Global Journal of Health Science*, 8(3), 1–9. https://doi.org/10.5539/gjhs.v8n3p1.
76. Vahidnia, F. (2007). Case study: Fertility decline in Iran. *Population and Environment*, 28(4–5), 259–266. https://doi.org/10.1007/s11111-007-0050-9.
77. Karamouzian, M., Sharifi, H., & Haghdoost, A. (2014). Iran's shift in family planning policies: Concerns and challenges. *International Journal of Health Policy and Management*, 3(5), 231–233. https://doi.org/10.15171/ijhpm.2014.81.
78. Babiarz, K. S., Miller, G., Valente, C., Lee, J., & Tey, N. P. (2017). Family planning and fertility behavior: Evidence from twentieth century Malaysia. Center for global development working paper 470. Washington, DC: Center for Global Development. Retrieved from https://www.cgdev.org/sites/default/files/family-planning-and-fertility-behavior-evidence-malaysia.pdf.
79. Debpuur, C., Phillips, J. F., Jackson, E. F., Nazzar, A., Ngom, P., & Binka, F. N. (2002). The impact of the Navrongo Project on contraceptive knowledge and use, reproductive preferences, and fertility. *Studies in Family Planning*, 33(2), 141–164. https://doi.org/10.1111/j.1728-4465.2002.00141.x.
80. Miller, G. (2010). Contraception as development? New evidence from family planning in Colombia. *The Economic Journal*, 120(545), 709–736. https://doi.org/10.1111/j.1468-0297.2009.02306.x.

81. Hancock, T. (2018, January 18). China births fall despite relaxation of one-child policy. *Financial Times*. Retrieved from https://www.ft.com/content/835c057e-fc5c-11e7-9b32-d7d59aace167.
82. Hvistendahl, M. (2017). Analysis of China's one-child policy sparks uproar. *Science*. October 18. American Association for the Advancement of Science. https://www.sciencemag.org/news/2017/10/analysis-china-s-one-child-policy-sparks-uproar. Accessed 25 May 2021.
83. Feng, W., Gu, B., & Cai, Y. (2016). The end of China's One-Child Policy. *Studies in Family Planning*, 47(1), 83–86. https://doi.org/10.1111/j.1728-4465.2016.00052.x.
84. Hesketh, T., Zhou, X., & Wang, Y. (2015). The end of the one-child policy: Lasting implications for China. *JAMA*, 314(24), 2619–2620. https://doi.org/10.1001/jama.2015.16279.
85. Hartmann, B., & Standing, H. (2016). Coercive sterilization. *International Perspectives on Sexual and Reproductive Health*, 42(1), 50. https://doi.org/10.1363/intsexrephea.42.1.050.
86. Wang, C. (2012). History of the Chinese family planning program: 1970–2010. *Contraception*, 85(6), 563–569. https://doi.org/10.1016/j.contraception.2011.10.013.
87. Lopoo, L. M., & Raissian, K. M. (2018). Fertility policy in developed countries. In S. L. Averett, L. M. Argys, & S. D. Hoffman (Eds.), *The Oxford handbook of women and the economy* (pp. 173–193). New York: Oxford University Press. https://doi.org/10.1093/oxfordhb/9780190628963.013.20.
88. Thévenon, O. (2016). The influence of family policies on fertility in France: Lessons from the past and prospects for the future. In R. Rindfuss, & M. Choe (Eds.), *Low fertility, institutions, and their policies* (pp. 49–76). Cham: Springer. https://doi.org/10.1007/978-3-319-32997-0_3.
89. Parr, N., & Guest, R. (2011). The contribution of increases in family benefits to Australia's early 21st-century fertility increase: An empirical analysis. *Demographic Research*, 25, 215–244. doi:https://doi.org/10.4054/DemRes.2011.25.6.
90. Kotowska, I. E. (2019). Uwagi o urodzeniach i niskiej dzietności w Polsce oraz polityce rodzinnej wspierającej prokreację [On births and low fertility in Poland and family policy supportive for childbearing]. *Studia Demograficzne*, 2(176), 11–29. https://doi.org/10.33119/SD.2019.2.1.

91. Matysiak, A., & Vignoli, D. (2008). Fertility and women's employment: A meta-analysis. *European Journal of Population*, 24(4), 363–384. https://doi.org/10.1007/s10680-007-9146-2.
92. Loichinger, E., & Skirbekk, V. (2016). International variation in ageing and economic dependency: A cohort perspective. *Comparative Population Studies*, 40(5). https://doi.org/10.12765/CPoS-2016-04.
93. Gershoni, N., & Low, C. (2017). The impact of extended reproductive time horizons: Evidence from Israel's expansion of access to IVF. University of Pennsylvania Population Center Working Paper (PSC/PARC). Retrieved from https://repository.upenn.edu/psc_publications/15/.
94. Gauthier, A. H. (2007). The impact of family policies on fertility in industrialized countries: A review of the literature. *Population Research and Policy Review*, 26(3), 323–346. https://doi.org/10.1007/s11113-007-9033-x.
95. Sobotka, T., Matysiak, A., & Brzozowska, Z. (2019). Policy responses to low fertility: How effective are they? Technical division working paper, population & development branch. United Nations Population Fund. https://www.unfpa.org/publications/policy-responses-low-fertility-how-effective-are-they. Accessed 25 May 2021.
96. Shen, K., Wang, F., & Cai, Y. (2020). Government policy and global fertility change: A reappraisal. *Asian Population Studies*, 16(2), 1–22. https://doi.org/10.1080/17441730.2020.1757850.
97. Bergsvik, J., Fauske, A., & Hart, R. K. (2020). Effects of policy on fertility: A systematic review of (quasi) experiments. Discussion Papers. Statistics Norway. https://www.ssb.no/en/forskning/discussion-papers/effects-of-policy-on-fertility-a-systematic-review-of-quasiexperiments. Accessed 25 May 2021.
98. Lalive, R., & Zweimüller, J. (2009). How does parental leave affect fertility and return to work? Evidence from two natural experiments. *The Quarterly Journal of Economics*, 124(3), 1363–1402. https://doi.org/10.1162/qjec.2009.124.3.1363.
99. Cygan-Rehm, K. (2016). Parental leave benefit and differential fertility responses: Evidence from a German reform. *Journal of Population Economics*, 29(1), 73–103. https://doi.org/10.1007/s00148-015-0562-z.
100. Dahl, G. B., Løken, K. V., Mogstad, M., & Salvanes, K. V. (2016). What is the case for paid maternity leave? *Review of Economics and Statistics*, 98(4), 655–670. https://doi.org/10.3386/w19595.
101. Wood, J., & Neels, K. (2019). Local childcare availability and dual-earner fertility: Variation in childcare coverage and birth hazards over place and

time. *European Journal of Population*, 35(5), 913–937. https://doi.org/10.1007/s10680-018-9510-4.

102. Mörk, E., Sjögren, A., & Svaleryd, H. (2013). Childcare costs and the demand for children—Evidence from a nationwide reform. *Journal of Population Economics*, 26(1), 33–65. https://doi.org/10.1007/s00148-011-0399-z.
103. Gathmann, C., & Sass, B. (2018). Taxing childcare: Effects on childcare choices, family labor supply, and children. *Journal of Labor Economics*, 36(3), 665–709. https://doi.org/10.1086/696143.
104. González, L. (2013). The effect of a universal child benefit on conceptions, abortions, and early maternal labor supply. *American Economic Journal: Economic Policy*, 5(3), 160–188. https://doi.org/10.1257/pol.5.3.160.
105. Parent, D., & Wang, L. (2007). Tax incentives and fertility in Canada: Quantum vs tempo effects. *Canadian Journal of Economics/Revue canadienne d'économique*, 40(2), 371–400. https://doi.org/10.1111/j.1365-2966.2007.00413.x.
106. Schmidt, L. (2007). Effects of infertility insurance mandates on fertility. *Journal of Health Economics*, 26(3), 431–446. https://doi.org/10.1016/j.jhealeco.2006.10.012.
107. Machado, M. P., & Sanz-de-Galdeano, A. (2015). Coverage of infertility treatment and fertility outcomes. *SERIEs*, 6(4), 407–439. https://doi.org/10.1007/s13209-015-0135-0.
108. Gauthier, A. H. (2015). Social norms, institutions, and policies in low-fertility countries. In N. Ogawa, & I. Shah (Eds.), *Low fertility and reproductive health in East Asia* (pp. 11–30). Dordrecht: Springer. https://doi.org/10.1007/978-94-017-9226-4_2.
109. Adams, J. (2016). Why do women want children? The case of Hong Kong, China: A lowest-low fertility context. *Marriage & Family Review*, 52(7), 632–653. https://doi.org/10.1080/01494929.2016.1140106.
110. Procreation day delivers results (2007, August 15). *Washington Post*. Retrieved from https://www.washingtontimes.com/news/2007/aug/15/procreation-day-delivers-results/.
111. Roberts, D. (2017). I'm an environmental journalist, but I never write about overpopulation. Here's why. Vox. https://www.vox.com/energy-and-environment/2017/9/26/16356524/the-population-question. Accessed 25 May 2021.
112. Roudi-Fahimi, F. (2004). Islam and family planning. PRB MENA Policy Brief. Washington, DC: Population Reference Bureau.

113. Pipes, D. (1996). *The hidden hand: Middle East fears of conspiracy*. New York: St. Martin's Griffin.
114. May, J. F. (2017). The politics of family planning policies and programs in sub-Saharan Africa. *Population and Development Review*, 43(S1), 308–329. https://doi.org/10.1111/j.1728-4457.2016.00165.x.
115. Goldstone, J. A., Kaufmann, E. P., & Toft, M. D. (Eds.) (2012). *Political demography: How population changes are reshaping international security and national politics*. Boulder: Paradigm.
116. Jeffery, R., & Jeffery, P. (1997). *Population, gender and politics: Demographic change in rural North India*. Cambridge: Cambridge University Press.
117. Schellekens, J., & Anson, J. (2011). *Israel's destiny: Fertility and mortality in a divided society*. New Brunswick, NJ: Transaction Publishers.
118. Heaton, T. B. (2011). Does religion influence fertility in developing countries. *Population Research and Policy Review*, 30(3), 449–465. https://doi.org/10.1007/s11113-010-9196-8.
119. van der Meulen Rodgers, Y. (2018). *The global Gag Rule and women's reproductive health: Rhetoric versus reality*. New York: Oxford University Press.
120. Thévenon, O. (2011). Family policies in OECD countries: A comparative analysis. *Population and Development Review*, 37(1), 57–87. https://doi.org/10.1111/j.1728-4457.2011.00390.x.
121. Lavy, V., & Zablotsky, A. (2011). Mother's schooling and fertility under low female labor force participation: Evidence from a natural experiment. NBER working paper series 16856. Cambridge, MA. http://www.nber.org/papers/w16856. Accessed 25 May 2021.
122. Tan, P. L. (2017). The impact of school entry laws on female education and teenage fertility. *Journal of Population Economics*, 30(2), 503–536. https://doi.org/10.1007/s00148-016-0609-9.
123. Jacobs, J., Marino, M., Edelman, A., Jensen, J., & Darney, B. (2017). Mass media exposure and modern contraceptive use among married West African adolescents. *The European Journal of Contraception & Reproductive Health Care*, 22(6), 439–449. https://doi.org/10.1080/13625187.2017.1409889.
124. Sanderson, W. C., Skirbekk, V., & Stonawski, M. (2014). Young adults failure to thrive syndrome. *Finnish Yearbook of Population Research*, 48, 169–187. https://doi.org/10.23979/fypr.40934.

125. Kolk, M., & Andersson, G. (2018). Two decades of same-sex marriage in Sweden. A demographic account of developments in marriage, childbearing and divorce. *Demography*, 57(1), 147–169. https://doi.org/10.1007/s13524-019-00847-6.

20

Low—But Not Too Low—Fertility Is a Good Thing

Humans were relatively rare for more than a hundred thousand years, but then came to dominate the entire planet within a brief period of time. Most of the population growth of our species has occurred only within the last 200 years or so. The most intense period was from 1950 to 2020, during which the global population more than tripled from 2.5 to 7.8 billion people. The reason that humans are now so numerous is because we continued to have relatively high fertility—in line with the evolutionary drive to procreate—at the same time that mortality radically decreased. In most Western countries, mortality declined gradually and fertility was already lower than in other world regions when the pace of mortality decline started to pick up. In other world regions, fertility was much higher before the onset of mortality decline *and* mortality declined much faster. As a consequence, population growth has been comparatively low in Europe and its cultural offshoots. This is why the West's share of the world population has dramatically dropped over the course of the last century. It seems likely that the European marriage pattern and early spread of education and literacy were key drivers of the diminishing share of Westerners, as well as the West's historically high living standards.

V. Skirbekk, *Decline and Prosper!*,
https://doi.org/10.1007/978-3-030-91611-4_20

Global fertility has been cut in half in just the last 50 years, from about five children per woman in the late 1960s to about just two and a half children per woman in 2019 [1]. Better access to effective and safe contraception, educational expansion and, somewhat ironically, both religion and secularization have all been important drivers of fertility decline. Education and religion affect fertility via multiple pathways, including when and whether if people marry, contraceptive use, fertility ideals, and ideas about appropriate gender roles. Lower infant and child mortality, changes in partnerships, increased costs of childbearing, changes in the labor market and skill biased technological change, the changing role of women, along with more alternative, competing ways to spend one's time during the reproductive years (e.g., travel, establishing a career) have also contributed to changes in reproductive behavior. Today, fewer people marry and, when they do marry, they tend to marry later. People are also having children later and tend to prefer smaller families than in the past. Higher socioeconomic status now tends to be related to having fewer children.

It seems likely that global fertility will continue to decline in the decades to come, though we still don't know enough about how fertility works in order to make accurate predictions. Unforeseen economic booms and recessions along with catastrophic events—which are expected to increase due to global warming—might bring about some surprises. Even minor fertility reductions especially in large, high-fertility populations have the potential to fundamentally alter the future of global fertility (e.g., Pakistan, Nigeria, Ethiopia, Egypt, and DR Congo are all among the world's 20 largest populations, with fertility above three children per woman at the time of writing).

In many ways, fertility decline has been a success story. Especially women now have more opportunities to exploit their potential in education and in the labor market. A majority of births worldwide today are planned, though clearly there is still a lot of room for improvement—even in the world's most developed countries. The number and proportion of adolescent births have dropped dramatically. Research suggests that most people prefer to have smaller families with no more than three children, and that a small, but perhaps growing minority would rather not have any children at all. Low fertility (albeit not to too low) and low population growth have gone hand-in-hand with improved economic conditions and better health [2, 3]. In families with many children, each person has to make due with fewer resources, which can negatively affect the health of both parents and children [4, 5]. Fewer children means that more can be invested in the education of each child, which can have many positive effects for individuals, families, and society. Lower fertility has meant that particularly women have had more resources to participate in other spheres of life beside reproduction. All else held equal, lower fertility has also reduced humans' negative impact on the environment. These are all very good things.

Our changed reproductive behavior has, however, also resulted in a number of new challenges. One challenge is the polarity between and within countries. More and more countries have fertility below the replacement level, while fertility remains above 3.5 children per woman in about a third of the world's countries. Within many high fertility countries, fertility in rural areas far exceeds that in urban centers. There are also often large differences between people with more and less education, and between people who are religiously unaffiliated and those who are highly religious. How can the global community and national governments adequately and fairly address the divergent needs of populations with high and very low fertility? How can societies be constructed so that people with many, few, or no children can all live happy, productive, and meaningful lives? These are questions with no easy answer.

In the low fertility countries, there is also the challenge of increasing, coincidental childlessness—especially among men. It appears that many young people need additional support establishing a stable partnership, a steady job, and adequate housing. People also need to be better informed about their own fertility and the limits of assisted reproductive technologies (ART). So far, policies designed to make it easier or create incentives to have children have not been hugely successful. New approaches are needed to help more people to realize their own fertility preferences. Due to population aging, new structures are needed for the second half of life. Fewer older people are likely to be grandparents and fewer will be able to rely on kin for assistance.

There is no question that our fertility today will dramatically affect our collective future. Even minor changes now will have a major impact later.

It is my view that countries should accept—if not embrace—low fertility, and focus on how to make the most of a world with fewer children. Previous books about fertility have taken an alarmist tone about either population decline (e.g., *Empty Planet: The Shock of Global Population Decline* by John Ibbitson and Darrell Brick [6]) or overpopulation (e.g., Stephen Emmot's *10 billion* [7]). I am more optimistic about the human ability to adapt. I also think that there is much to be gained from more conscious consideration of how our own fertility choices impact not only our own lives, but also other people, other species, and the environment. We should all be invested in ensuring that every person on the planet has access to quality education, safe and effective contraception, reproductive autonomy, the opportunity to become a parent if one so chooses, and the opportunity to leave a legacy and be closely connected with other people even without biological children.

References

1. Roser, M. Fertility rate. https://ourworldindata.org/fertility-rate. Accessed 26 May 2021.
2. Oneill, B. C., Dalton, M., Fuchs, R., Jiang, L., Pachauri, S., & Zigova, K. (2010). Global demographic trends and future carbon emissions. *Proceedings of the National Academy of Sciences*, 107(41), 17521–17526. https://doi.org/10.1073/pnas.1004581107.
3. O'Neill, B. C., Liddle, B., Jiang, L., Smith, K. R., Pachauri, S., Dalton, M., et al. (2012). Demographic change and carbon dioxide emissions. *The Lancet*, 380(9837), 157–164. https://doi.org/10.1016/S0140-6736(12)60958-1.
4. Phua, K. H., Yap, M.-T., Khilji, S. S., & Lee, H.-P. (2015). Development of public health in economic transition: The middle-income countries. In R. Detels, M. Gulliford, Q. A. Karim, & C. C. Tan (Eds.), *Oxford textbook of global public health* (pp. 48–61). Oxford: Oxford University Press. https://doi.org/10.1093/med/9780199661756.003.0004.
5. Akokuwebe, M. E., & Okunola, R. A. (2015). Demographic transition and rural development in Nigeria. *Developing Country Studies*, 5(6), 90–102. https://www.iiste.org/Journals/index.php/DCS/article/view/20925.

6. Bricker, D., & Ibbitson, J. (2019). *Empty planet: The shock of global population decline*. London: Hachette UK.
7. Emmott, S. *10 Billion*. New York: Penguin Random House.

Glossary

Age-specific fertility rate The average number of live births had by women of a given age in a year. The sum of age-specific fertility rates (typically for women aged 15–49) in a given year equals the total fertility rate.

Age-specific mortality rate The number of deaths in a specific age group divided by the number of persons in that age group in a population. Age-specific mortality rates are often expressed as the number of deaths per 1000 or 100,000 people.

Anti-natalist policies Policies which explicitly aim to reduce fertility. This can include encouraging fewer children through campaigns stressing the burden of having large families, sterilization campaigns, or policies that create disincentives for people with larger families (e.g., fewer rights, greater tax burdens, less financial support, or opportunities).

Celibacy Remaining unmarried *or* not having sexual relations. In some cultures and periods, remaining unmarried implied that one did not have sexual relations. Today, celibacy is commonly used to refer to people who do not have sexual relations.

Child mortality rate Typically defined as the number of reported deaths among children under 5 years of age in a given time period expressed as deaths per 1,000 individuals in this age group.

Cohabitation Living together with a romantic partner without being married.

V. Skirbekk, *Decline and Prosper!*,
https://doi.org/10.1007/978-3-030-91611-4

Cohort fertility How many children people born in a particular year (or other time interval) have actually had when they have reached the end of their reproductive window, generally defined as a particular age between 40 and 50 years of age.

Coitus interruptus A method of birth control in which a man withdraws his penis from a woman's vagina prior to ejaculation in order to avoid insemination. Also known as withdrawal or pulling out.

Crude birth rate The number of births per 1000 individuals in a population.

Crude death rate The total number of deaths in a population within a given time period, typically a year. The crude death rate is often expressed as the number of deaths per 1000 or 100,000 individuals in the population.

Demographic transition multiplier (DTM) The relative change in population size between the initial and late stages of the demographic transition. If a country's population grew from one to five million over the course of the demographic transition, the DTM would equal five.

Demographic transition The societal shift from high mortality, high fertility to low mortality, low fertility.

Epidemiological transition The shift from communicable to non-communicable diseases as the leading causes of death over time.

Ethno-political conflicts Ongoing hostility and opposition between two or more ethnic, national, or ideological groups of people.

Eugenics The desire and intention to alter fertility patterns in order to decrease the occurrence of characteristics regarded as inheritable and undesirable in the population.

Family planning The provision of resources that help individuals attain their desired number of children. Family planning programs may include education about reproduction, birth control, and options for dealing with an unintended pregnancy; the provision of contraception; reproductive health care and treatment of involuntary infertility.

Fecundity The biological capacity to have a child. Fecundity can refer to either an individual or to a couple.

Fertility ideals The number of children a person perceives as optimal, either for themselves (personal fertility ideal) or for people in general (general fertility ideal).

Fertility intentions How many children a person actually plans to have, taking into account one's own, perhaps less-than-ideal life circumstances.

Gametes Sex cells, specifically ova (egg cells) for women and sperm for men.

Gross reproduction rate The average number of daughters a woman would give birth to, assuming that she survives her reproductive years and the age-specific fertility rates and sex ratio at birth observed in the current period remain constant over her reproductive life.

Infant mortality rate The number of reported deaths among children younger than 1 year old divided by the number of live births in the same year. Often expressed as the number of deaths per 1000 live births.

Kin marriage (or consanguineous marriage) Marriage between genetic relatives.

Life cycle surplus The ages at which an average person is a net financial contributor, specifically when average income exceeds average consumption. Unpaid labor (e.g., in the home) can be considered in the calculation of income.

Life expectancy (at birth) How long an average person born in a given year would live if exposed to age-specific death rates observed in from age 0 to highest ages for which there are data. Life expectancy is the most common measure of longevity. It can be calculated from at any age, but is most commonly calculated from birth. It is typically calculated (typically because of data availability) as a period measure, based on observations in a given year.

Longevity The length of life. Commonly used as a synonym to life expectancy at birth or how long one would live under a given set of circumstances.

Malthusianism The belief that, if left unchecked, population growth will ultimately result in human misery, poverty, starvation, and greater mortality.

Marital fertility rate The average number of children had by married couples.

Median age The age that divides a population into two equally-sized groups, such that 50% of the population is younger, and 50% is older.

Natural fertility The number of children an average woman would have if she were to have regular, unprotected sex across her entire reproductive life span.

Natural population growth Population growth driven by mortality and fertility change, excluding any migration.

Net reproduction rate The average number of daughters a woman would have if she were subject to the age-specific fertility and mortality rates of a given year for her entire reproductive window. The NRR takes into account that some women will die before the end of their reproductive window.

Opportunity costs The potential benefits foregone when one alternative is chosen over another. The opportunity costs of having and raising children include income lost due to parental leave, reduced working hours, decreased career opportunities due to labor market interruptions, or foregone education/training.

Period fertility The number of births within a particular time interval, usually one year. Period fertility is much more variable than cohort fertility. The total fertility rate is an example of a period fertility measure.

Primary infertility When an individual or a couple has not become pregnant after at least one year of unprotected sex.

Pro-natalist policies Policies designed to increase fertility, such as providing financial benefits to new parents and/or families, subsidizing or providing housing for people with children, or subsidizing daycare and schools.

Religiosity The extent to which individuals are devoted to a religious faith. Measures of religiosity include how often people attend religious services, the strength of their beliefs, or how religious they say they are.

Replacement level The number of children per woman needed to maintain the current population size. Higher mortality rates (particularly at younger ages) imply higher replacement levels.

Secondary infertility The inability to have an additional child.

Secularization The gradual distancing of a society or individual from religious values and institutions.

Skill-biased technological change The hypothesis that technological advances increase the labor market demand for people with higher skills and more education and decrease the demand for those who have few formal skills or lack education.

Social status An individual's or group's access to important cultural, material, or social resources relative to other individuals or groups; his or her place in the social hierarchy. A person's or group's position in the social hierarchy may be defined by, for instance, wealth, income, education, caste, occupational, or tribal rank.

Total fertility rate (TFR) The TFR is the most widely-used measure of fertility. It is the number of children an average woman would have if she were subject to the age-specific fertility rates observed in a given year throughout her reproductive lifetime. TFR is a period measure of fertility.

Two sex net reproduction (2SNRR) The mean number of offspring surviving to mid-reproductive age per person. Unlike the NRR, the 2SNRR considers both women and men and their number of surviving sons and daughters.

CPSIA information can be obtained
at www.ICGtesting.com
Printed in the USA
LVHW080538090123
736726LV00003B/131

9 783030 916107